D1474183

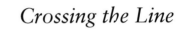

Crossing the Line

Crossing the

LINE

Nonviolent Resisters Speak Out for Peace

ROSALIE G. RIEGLE

CASCADE *Books* • Eugene, Oregon

CROSSING THE LINE
Nonviolent Resisters Speak Out for Peace

Parts of chapter 2 were included in *Voices from the Catholic Worker*, ed. Rosalie Riegle Troester (Temple University Press, 1993) and Rosalie G. Riegle, *Dorothy Day: Portraits by Those Who Knew Her* (Orbis Books, 1993).

Roy Bourgeois interview © Nicole Sault
Narration by Barry Roth © Barry Roth
Narration by Doris Sage © Doris Sage
Narration by Meredith Dallas © Anthony Dallas and C. Arthur Bradley
Three paragraphs from Dyllan Taxman interview of Jim Forest © Jim Forest

Scripture text in this work is taken from the *New American Bible*, revised edition © 1970 Confraternity of Christian Doctrine, Washington, DC is are used by permission of the copyright owner. All Rights Reserved.

Cascade Books
An Imprint of Wipf and Stock Publishers
199 W. 8th Ave., Suite 3
Eugene, OR 97401

www.wipfandstock.com

ISBN 13: 978-1-61097-683-1

Cataloging-in-Publication data:

Riegle, Rosalie G.

Crossing the line : nonviolent resisters speak out for peace / Rosalie G. Riegle.

xxiv + 378 p.; 23 cm—Includes bibliographical references and index.

ISBN 13: 978-1-61097-683-1

1. Pacifists—United States—Case studies. 2. Pacifism—United States—Case studies. I. Title.

JZ5584 U6 R54 2013

Manufactured in the USA.

To Mary Moylan (1936–1995)

*Unremembered participant in the Catonsville Nine
draft board raid,*

*in hopes that she will someday be written into history
with a book of her own*

Mary Moylan, 1970. © Bob Fitch.

Contents

List of Photographs | xi

Acknowledgments | xiii

Abbreviations | xvi

Introductory Notes | xix

Prologue: Jailbird Stories—a Roundtable Discussion | 1

1   **World War II—Lonely Pacifists** | 29
    Ralph DiGia; William Lovell; Meredith Dallas;
    Don Benedict

2   **America, the Beautiful—Protest in the Fifties** | 50
    Tom Cornell; Karl Meyer; Judith Malina;
    David McReynolds

    AN INTERLUDE: WAR AND PRISONS | 60

3   **Vietnam—The Burning Times** | 61

    Refusing the Draft | 63
       Marty Harris; Randy Kehler

    Catholic Workers Destroy Draft Cards | 73
       David Miller; Jim Wilson; Tom Cornell

Contents

Destroying Draft Files—The Milwaukee Fourteen | 85
Doug Marvy; Jim Forest; Father Lorenzo Rosebaugh, OMI

Destroying Draft Files—Women Against Daddy
Warbucks | 100
Maggie Geddes

4 Beating Swords Into Plowshares—
United States | 108
Jerry Ebner; Art Laffin; Sue and Bill Frankel-Streit;
Barry Roth; Susan Crane

AN INTERLUDE: SLEEPING BEAUTY | 134

5 Beating Swords Into Plowshares—Europe | 135
Ireland | 135
Ciaron O'Reilly; Deirdre Clancy

Scotland | 144
Brian Quail; Jane Tallents; Ellen Moxley

The Netherlands | 162
Frits ter Kuile

Germany | 168
Hanna Jaskolski; Wolfgang Sternstein with
Gisela Sternstein

6 School of the Americas | 187
Roy Bourgeois; Father Lorenzo Rosebaugh, OMI;
Rebecca Kanner; Kathleen Rumpf; Steve Jacobs;
Lisa Hughes; Tina Busch-Nema; Anonymous Couple

7 Behind the Bars | 228
Jeff Dietrich; Renaye Fewless; David Gardner; Doris Sage;
Father Steve Kelly, SJ; Bill Frankel-Streit; John Heid

AN INTERLUDE: LET'S FILL THE JAILS | 256

8   **Challenge and Change** | 258
     Liza and Bryan Apper; Marian Mollin; Father Larry
     Morlan; Frank Cordaro; Scott Albrecht; Mike Sprong;
     Stephen Kobasa

9   **The Prophet Priests** | 299
     Father "Bix" Bichsel, SJ; Father Peter Dougherty;
     Father Bob Bossie, SCJ; Father Jerry Zawada, OFM;
     Father Lou Vitale, OFM

10 **War Tax Resistance** | 325
     Juanita Nelson; Susan Crane; Karl Meyer; Randy Kehler

     Epilogue: Endings and Beginnings—Grace Paley | 341
     Appendix: Suggestions for Further Reading | 347
     Index | 351

Photographs

Mary Moylan, 1970 | v
Ralph DiGia, 1992 | 29
Union 8 seminarians get prison terms, New York, 1940 | 36
Meredith Dallas, 2009 | 38
Civil defense drill protest, New York, 1956 | 51
Judith Malina in DOPS prison in Brazil, 1971 | 55
Marty Harris, 2004 | 62
David Miller, 2004 | 76
Draft card burning, New York, 1965 | 78
Tom Cornell and Catholic Worker cat, 2005 | 82
Bob Graf and Gerry Gardner burn draft files, Milwaukee, 1968 | 87
Jim Forest, 2007 | 90
Father Lorenzo Rosebaugh, OMI, 2006 | 98
Linda Forest Orell tossing up shredded draft files, New York,
    1969 | 102
Plowshares hammers, 2003 | 110
Deadly Force sign | 125
Aegis Plowshares: Phil Berrigan, Daniel Sicken, Barry Roth,
    Tom Lewis, Kathy Boylan, 1991 | 126
Disarm Now Plowshares at day four of trial, 2011 | 133
Frank Cordaro, Steve Jacobs, Ciarron O'Reilly blockade the gates at
    10 Downing Street, 2011 | 136
Pitstop Plowshares pray with symbols of their action, Glenstal
    Abbey, 2003 | 140
Ellen Moxley carrying dismantling tools, 1999 | 156
Trident Three banner, 2012 | 157

Victory at court: Ulla Roder, Angie Zelter, Ellen Moxley, 1999 | 159

Frits ter Kuile, 2008 | 168

Hanna Jaskolski, 2007 | 173

Pershing to Plowshares: Susanne Mauch-Friz, Heiki Huschauer, 1986 | 181

Wolfgang and Gisela Sternstein, Stuttgart, 2007 | 186

Martin Sheen speaking at the School of the Americas Watch vigil, 2004 | 189

Rosalie Riegle at SOA gate, beginning of vigil, 2004 | 190

Puppets at SOA vigil, 2011 | 190

Roy Bourgeois dancing at the end of the SOAW vigil, 2004 | 194

SOAW procession, 2011 | 197

Altered School of the Americas sign, 1997 | 202

SOAW Catholic Worker House of Hospitality, Columbus, Georgia, 2004 | 205

Steve Jacobs at Catholic Worker SOAW house, 2004 | 207

SOA fence with memorials, conclusion of vigil, 2004 | 210

Jeff Dietrich, 2004 | 228

David Gardner, 2004 | 232

Renaye Fewless, 2007 | 235

Lisa Hughes, 2004 | 238

Dan and Doris Sage, 2005 | 241

Father Steve Kelly, SJ, and Father John Savard, SJ, San Francisco, 1989 | 245

Bill Frankel-Streit's sketch from prison bunk, 1991 | 251

John Heid, 2005 | 252

Liza and Bryan Apper, 2004 | 258

Feast of the Holy Innocents Pentagon action, 1983 | 267

Gods of Metal Plowshares, Andrews Air Force Base, 1998 | 270

Frank Cordaro arrested at an anti-NATO protest at Obama campaign headquarters, 2012 | 271

Defaced billboard at Offutt Air Force Base, 1980 | 275

Gods of Metal Plowshares: Kathy Boylan, Frank Cordaro, and a B-52, 1988 | 279

Lynsters Farm Catholic Worker Community, England, 2012 | 285

Photographs

Bonnie Urfer and Mike Sprong silence Trident, Wisconsin, 2000 | 286

Mike Sprong, 2005 | 290

Anne Somsel and Stephen Vincent Kobasa, 2005 | 297

Father Peter Dougherty, 2010 | 304

Father Jerry Zawada, OFM, 2004 | 314

Duane Bean and Father Jerry Zawada, OFM, Missouri Peace Planting, 1988 | 318

Father Lou Vitale, OFM, and Father Jerry Zawada, OFM, 2005 | 320

Juanita Nelson, 2005 | 326

Susan Crane, 2005 | 329

Karl Meyer, 2004 | 331

Randy Kehler, 2005 | 334

Betsy Corner speaking at a 1991 war tax rally, Greenfield, MA | 338

Grace Paley, 1984 | 342

Women's Action at the Pentagon, 1980 | 344

Acknowledgments

Thanks first to my family, especially for the blessing of my seven grandchildren. They are the wellspring of my hope. My daughter Meg Murphy has been a perceptive reader at all stages of this book, and I can't thank her enough for her good advice. Friends in the Catholic Worker (CW) and throughout the peace movement have been patient with my fact-checking and other emergency requests, as well as their usual generous selves in offering spectacular photos, leads to great resisters, endless encouragement, and warm hospitality—often at the last moment—during my travels to collect the interviews. Special thanks to Harry Browne of Dublin, for interesting insights during his interview and lively hospitality afterwards. I really enjoyed my stay with him, his wife the poet Catherine Ann Cullen, and their nimble daughter, Stella. Another narrator, oral history colleague Marian Mollin, was especially helpful as she urged me to examine my motives for writing the books.

I acknowledge and give thanks for the many resisters who, like Phil Berrigan, joined the "the cloud of witnesses" before I was able to interview them. Thirteen of the peace people whom I interviewed have joined that blessed band since I started the project. May they rest in peace.

All the narrators in this oral history project fit time with me into their busy lives, often on scant notice, and were generous with their honesty and their memories. It truly is their book, not mine. I thank especially the many I interviewed whose voices I couldn't fit into these pages or in the companion volume, *Doing Time for Peace*: the late Sr. Dorothy Marie Hennessey, Bill Griffen, John Hogan, and Tom MacLean; Sue Ablao, Gary Ashbeck, Amy Baranski-Jewett, Johnnie Baranski, Sanderson Beck, Monica Benderman, Jerome Berrigan, Pam Beziat, Brian Buckley, Thom Clark, William Cuddy, Matt Dalosio, Elton Davis, Felton Davis, Sam Diener, Aine Donovan, Mary Driscoll, Rick Gaumer, Bob Gilliam, Clare Grady, Teresa Grady, Jennifer Haines, Joe Maizlish,

Acknowledgments

Jasiu Malinowski, Martina Linnehan, Fr. Joe Mulligan, SJ, Sr. Dorothy Pagosa, SSJ-TOSF, Robert Reiss, Dan Sage, Valerie Sklarevsky, Sr. Miriam Spencer, CSJP, Starhawk, Susan van der Hijden, Brian Watson, and Helen Woodson. They were generous with their time and their memories, and I regret deeply that there just wasn't room for their memories to appear in either book. All the interviews are available in audio and in both verbatim and edited transcripts in the Catholic Worker Archives at Marquette University's Raynor Library in Milwaukee. As always, I made it through the project only because of a whole lot of help from Phillip M. Runkel, the curator of those archives. His unfailing courtesy, patience, and promptness is a gift to the entire faith-based peace movement.

The transcribers: it's no exaggeration to say that I couldn't have completed this project without them, either. First, there's Johannah Hughes Turner, who transcribed the majority of the interviews. Hillel Arnold, Maura Conway, Fran Fuller, and Kate Hennessey also gave prompt and professional service. Ariane Dettloff of Cologne, Germany not only served as interpretor for Hanna Jaskolski but carefully transcribed Hannah's interview into English.

Johannah Turner is more than a transcriber, more than a friend; perhaps I could call her a compatriot, a fellow citizen of the community of resisters which has consumed my life for the last eight years. As a birthright Catholic Worker whose mother Marge Hughes was the warm heart of hospitality at Tivoli on the Hudson, Johannah grew up close to Dorothy Day and to many at the Worker. So Johannah knew the history and was often extremely helpful in my research. She was also a careful editor of the manuscript at a crucial point in its preparation. But over and above all that, she—and she alone—got me through learning a new program and decoding the formatting procedures that are now so much a part of all publishing ventures. I still often tore my hair out, but Johannah kept me sane through the final stages, and I couldn't have finished without her superb problem-solving talents.

I took all the photos not otherwise credited, and I thank the many other photographers for their artistry and permissions to reprint. For help in finding the photographs, in addition to the photographers and all the narrators who shared and answered questions, I thank Betsy Arsenault, Garrison Beck, Kathy Boylan, Bob Graf, Martin Hall, Marcia Kelly, Chrissy Nesbitt, the Open Door Community, Nora Paley, and Angie Zelter. I especially thank photographer Rachel Walsh, who was able to get all the photos into fine shape. Also helpful were Tracy Ablen and

Denis Coday of the *National Catholic Reporter*, Rob Cox of the University of Massachusetts Archives, Wendy Chmielewski and Mary Beth Sigado of Swarthmore College Peace Collection, Morgen MacIntosh Hodgetts of DePaul University Special Collections and Archives, Sky Hall of War Resisters League, the Oblates of Mary Provincial House, and the Fifteenth Street Friends Meeting.

For sending me material that I was able to use, appreciation goes to Attorney Marianne Dugan and to her mother, attorney Sheila Dugan, to Father Thomas Hereford, and to Suzanne Belote Shanley of the Agape Community. Several years ago my undergrad roommate Adele Schepp Young alerted me to the quotation on hope by Victor Havel, written while he was in prison. It has become a touchstone for me. Thanks, Adele!

Special thanks go to Jerry Ebner, whose stories of prison life first aroused my curiosity, to Father John Dear, SJ, for suggesting the subtitle, and to my friend Karen Skalitsky for her provocative editing suggestions. Carl Bunin's weekly e-mail, "This Week in History," sustained me in my goal of bringing a personal voice to our country's rich peace and justice history. Felice and Jack Cohen-Joppa, publishers of the *Nuclear Resister,* were unfailingly helpful in finding people with whom I'd lost contact.

I couldn't have kept going without the support and encouragement of my extended family and friends, both in Saginaw, Michigan, and in my new home of Evanston, Illinois. Creating this book has greatly expanded my community, and so a final gift of gratitude goes to those I have forgotten to thank. You are all a part of who I am. Mistakes and misjudgments are mine, and mine only.

Abbreviations

ACLU	American Civil Liberties Union
BOP	Bureau of Prisons
CCC	Civilian Conservation Corps
CCNV	Community for Creative Nonviolence
CD	civil disobedience
CND	Campaign for Nuclear Disarmament
CO	conscientious objector
CORE	Congress of Racial Equality
CPF	Catholic Peace Fellowship
CW	Catholic Worker
DSEI	Defense Systems and Equipment International
EUCOM	United States European Command
FCI	Federal Correctional Facility
FOR	Fellowship of Reconciliation
ICPJ	Interfaith Council for Peace and Justice
INF Treaty	Intermediate Range Nuclear Forces Treaty
MoD	Ministry of Defense
MP	Member of Parliament
NATO	North Atlantic Treaty Organization
NWTRCC	National War Tax Resistance Coordinating Committee
ROTC	Reserve Officers' Training Corps
SCND	Scottish Campaign for Nuclear Disarmament
SOA	School of the Americas (see WHINSEC)
SOAW	School of the Americas Watch
UAW	United Auto Workers
WHINSEC	Western Hemisphere Institute for Security Cooperation (formerly School of the Americas)
WRL	War Resisters League
WTR	War Tax Resistance

Introductory Notes

It seems we almost have a national policy of violence. It feeds down from the top, into the drugs and the gang warfare. Our terrifying foreign policy and atomic arsenal is all part of it, and I think it gives people a sense of helplessness.

—MEREDITH DALLAS

I listen to learn. In this, my third oral history project, I listened to learn from people who have refused to be helpless in the face of a violent world, people who say with their bodies that they do not accept the status quo of permanent war and preparation for war and in doing so, risk going to jail or prison. I wanted to find out what moves people like me—white and middle-class and educated—out of their comfort zone into the unknown of a prison term. How and why do they change from peace activists who to go meetings to war resisters who go to jail? What happens to them when they get there? Importantly, why do they continue to resist in the light of seeming failure, when no matter what they do, the war-making goes on?

To answer these questions, I interviewed 173 people from the United States and Europe, listening from 2004 to 2008 and then spending several years shaping and editing two collections of oral history, this book and a companion volume, *Doing Time for Peace: Resistance, Family, and Community*, published by Vanderbilt University Press. Each book has a different focus and can be appreciated separately, but they fit together well. *Doing Time* has a family focus; *Crossing the Line* has a historical focus and ranges from World War II draft resisters to contemporary Catholic Workers protesting NATO's world-wide reach.

Howard Zinn said, "Our problem is civil obedience."[1] The people I interviewed don't obey, they make trouble. Making trouble in order to achieve social change is deep in the fabric of our country. In a decision against the police in a recent wrongful arrest suit, Federal Judge Jed S. Rakoff wrote:

> What a huge debt this nation owes to its "troublemakers." From Thomas Paine to Martin Luther King, Jr., they have forced us to focus on problems we would prefer to downplay or ignore. Yet it is often only with hindsight that we can distinguish those troublemakers who brought us to our senses from those who were simply . . . troublemakers. Prudence, and respect for the constitutional rights to free speech and free association, therefore dictate that the legal system cut all non-violent protesters a fair amount of slack. Let us hope that other judges hear this decision and that nonviolent civil disobedience can continue to hold its rightful place as a cornerstone of our liberty.[2]

The resisters I interviewed are nonconfrontational in their resistance and try to practice personal nonviolence, especially in their contacts with arresting police, so they rarely receive media coverage, unlike protests that become violent and unlike the Vietnam era with its screaming headlines about priests who burned draft files. Starhawk, a nonviolent Wiccan peace activist from California, told me, "When we were in Palestine, doing demonstrations [against the Wall], the media would say, 'Call us if there's blood!' Literally."

After listening to the stories, I recognized that nonviolent resistance to war has a strength, a longevity, and a unity that has rarely been recognized. I also found that my fear of prison had disappeared. Losing one's freedom by being incarcerated is never pleasant, never comfortable. But it is indeed do-able. In fact, many more of us may have to go to prison in order to preserve the free speech freedoms which provide our "cornerstone."

1. Howard Zinn, *The Zinn Reader: Writings on Disobedience and Democracy* (New York: Seven Stories, 1997), 436.

2. Judge Jed S. Rakoff, United States District Judge, Southern District of New York, June 7, 2012, Garcia v. Bloomberg, 2012 WL 2045756, attached to www.cityroom .blogs.nytimes.com/2012/06/08/judge-rules-against-police-in-brooklyn-bridge-arrests/.

Many of the narrators in this volume are Catholic Workers, living either in community as I did for ten years at the Mustard Seed and Jeannine Coallier Catholic Workers in Saginaw, Michigan, or in friendship with a house, as I do now, living alone in Evanston but closely connected to the White Rose Catholic Worker in nearby Chicago. The Catholic Worker movement, founded by Dorothy Day and Peter Maurin in 1933, has remained personalist, organic, and nonhierarchical, and seems to be thriving as never before, with new communities coming too fast to count. (See www.catholicworker.org for a constantly updated list of communities and an excellent search engine for all of Dorothy Day's writing.) In ways that vary from community to community, Catholic Workers try to live radically the Sermon on the Mount, practicing the voluntary poverty, prayer, hospitality, resistance to war and injustice, and intellectual and spiritual formation espoused by the founders.

Catholic Workers and the other faith-based resisters whose narrative I collected are not super-heroes and certainly not without flaws, as you will see. They're regular folks, living alone, with families, or in community with others: teachers and produce managers and social workers and nurses, nuns and priests, students and retirees. They may have faith, but they're not without questions; and their thoughts about the role of Christians in the world offer a strong challenge to the fundamentalism of the religious right.

They form a loosely connected but cohesive group of progressive faith-based activists with a unity which transcends sectarianism. Sometimes they even call themselves the "peace people." "Did you meet some new peace people?" my friend Joni would ask me when I returned from an interview trip. These peace people are Roman Catholic and Quaker and members of other Christian denominations. They're also Buddhists and Jews and those who profess no formal faith but are inspired and activated by those who do.

They are united by a plethora of internet sites and community newsletters and by national gatherings such as those held yearly to protest the School of the Americas at Ft. Benning, Georgia. They have similar goals but live them out in diverse ways, with some attending vigils or becoming part of large national protests, some lobbying Congress or planning campaigns against specific abuses, and some providing the necessary support for those arrested for saying the strongest no to the abuses. Except for two of the Vietnam resisters, most of the people in this book would say they're part of the peace movement, not the anti-war movement.

> It hardly has membership criteria and there are no by-laws, but a . . . a kinship spirit sort of evolves. You realize that there are sympathies of purpose, similarities in perception about the world . . . I learned that there was a place within that community for a variety of voices and that the callings were varied and manifold. People worked to recognize that the people who did support were all part of the resistance and part of the community, too, and the actions would be impossible without what they provided. (Stephen Kobasa)

When I started the project, I took as my guiding definition the words of Jim Wallis of *Sojourners* magazine: "Protest is speaking; resistance is acting. To protest is to say that something is wrong, resistance means trying to stop it."[3] In fact, some don't even agree with the Wallis definition.

> I wouldn't want to draw too fine a line between resisters and activists, because it tends to set up a hierarchy and I don't believe in that. Some people would say resistance means some form of civil disobedience. I prefer to see it as any form of noncooperation with that which supports and perpetuates war and injustice. So in that sense, writing a letter, speaking out publicly, standing in a vigil—whether or not it's civil disobedience—all of that is a kind of resistance. Not paying your war taxes certainly is a form of resistance. There are times when to put your name out there publicly can be an enormous act of resistance, depending on where you live, where you work, what kind of position you have in society. Very risky and very scary. And very life-changing, with sometimes incredible consequences.[4]

The narrators in the collection practice the honored way to make change that we traditionally call civil disobedience, mostly by crossing the property borders that protect weapons and their delivery systems. They can't physically stand in the way of a bomb but they *can* sound their "no" by trespassing at the Pentagon, at military bases and the museums that glorify war, at recruiting stations and federal buildings and presidential campaign headquarters and companies that profit from making military hardware. Mostly they're arrested for trespass, with sentences ranging from a few days to months and months in our post

3. Jim Wallis, "From Protest to Resistance," *Sojourners* 13/2 (1984) 4.
4. Randy Kehler interview, Marquette Archives.

9/11 world, especially if they are "repeat offenders." Sometimes they symbolically damage the property by pouring their own blood or pounding with hammers and their resistance is called a Plowshares action after the Isaiahan injunction to "beat swords into plowshares." These actions bring even longer sentences but the resisters consider the trial and the resulting prison as part of their witness, a redemptive sacrifice for peace in the world. Plowshares resisters don't pay fines and rarely use legalities to reduce their prison time.

Another difference between the faith-based resisters and others who are arrested for protesting war is that now, instead of using the negative "disobedience," some call it "moral obedience" or "Gospel obedience" or even "divine obedience."

Recoding and Shaping the Narratives

Instead of coming to the interviews as a social scientist, collecting data and making my own conclusions, I came with a mission—that by listening to people and then bringing their words to print, I might be able to nudge readers to question, as I did, their own attitudes and actions. And who knows? Perhaps to cross lines of their own.

I'm what's called a participant observer, I guess, as I've been working for peace since the Vietnam War, although the penalties for my several arrests have been minimal. I knew some of those I interviewed, sometimes well, especially if I had interviewed them for my first two oral histories or met them through my life as a Catholic Worker.[5] And for every interview, I could have done hundreds of others. Many of the recordings were done at the Faith and Resistance gatherings explained in Chapter 4, using small MP3 recorders and lavalier microphones. I gave narrators the opportunity to turn off the recorder if they wanted to speak privately, and sometimes I'd turn it off myself to talk off-the-cuff about an issue.

I think my candor encouraged theirs and often our interviews were like conversations, although I'd encourage them to talk about themselves and we tried not to gossip. I do worry that some readers may have been present at events described in the interviews and recall them

5. *Voices from the Catholic Worker* (Philadelphia: Temple University Press, 1993) published under the name of Rosalie Riegle Troester and hereafter cited as *Voices*; Riegle, *Dorothy Day: Portraits by Those Who Knew Her* (Maryknoll, NY: Orbis, 2003).

differently. Remember that memory is always interpretive and inescapably colored by where we're standing when events happen, both literally and figuratively. Readers who are peace people themselves will know the vocabulary; others may find the words unfamiliar, perhaps hinting at a jargon. I've tried to define as I go along, but please be patient with this unfamiliarity, knowing that your understanding will grow as you read.

I'd come to the appointments with printed questions but rarely used them. Instead, I'd try to take on the narrator's emotional state and let my questions come in response to what they were saying. Early on in my work as an oral historian, I learned the blunt honesty of Robert Coles, to "take people at their word."[6] I wasn't afraid to challenge, but I'm not a reporter, setting up straw situations to get a hot story. Instead I wanted to explore motivations as well as the how of it all—how one prepares for an action, deals with arrest and incarceration, plans for the trial, and goes to prison.

After the interviews were professionally transcribed, I edited them and sent them to each narrator for their approval, giving them time to suggest corrections and clarifications. I then edited and arranged again, eliminating the embolalia—the wordiness we all take on when talking—and removing my questions and chatty asides when I could. In compiling the books, I also tried to eliminate repeated ideas among the interviews. Hardest of all has been omitting so many fantastic stories in order to make the resulting collections affordable. Thankfully, all 173 interviews are available to anyone who visits the Catholic Worker Archives at Marquette University in Milwaukee, hereafter cited as Marquette Archives.

I have loved becoming an oral historian because it fits so well with the theories of literature I had read as a graduate student. In good literature, the reader sees the complexity of truths. In oral history, there are also many descriptions and many truths, not *the* truth. Just as when one reads literature, what individual readers see, react to, and remember will depend on what they bring to the reading. I hope the truths in these stories will bump up against the truths readers hold—challenge them, inspire them, worry them, and move them to action. For as Randy Kehler told me, "It's the silence that allows it to happen."

6. Robert Coles, *The Call of Stories: Teaching and the Moral Imagination* (Boston: Houghton Mifflin, 1989), xi.

A Note on Sources

At the end of the book, you'll find "Suggestions for Further Reading." Within those suggestions, several sources have been particularly helpful to me. For the first three chapters, I relied on *The Power of the People: Active Nonviolence in the United States*, (hereafter cited as Cooney and Michalowski).[7] For Chapters 4 and 5, the preeminent resource was Art Laffin's *Swords Into Plowshares* (hereafter cited as Laffin).[8] I have occasionally used portions of my own earlier oral histories, especially in Chapter 2. Websites to which I often referred were that of the School of the Americas Watch for Chapter 6,[9] and that of the Nuclear Resister.[10] Interesting Plowshares photos to complement Chapters 4 and 5 are available online.[11]

A recent book with exciting conclusions is *Why Civil Resistance Works* by Erica Chenoweth and Maria J. Stephan.[12] In it, the authors analyze 323 major social struggles between 1900 and 2006 and quantify that since 1900, nonviolent campaigns around the world have been twice as successful as violent ones.

Three archives with abundant resources for studies of this nature are the Catholic Worker Archives, which contain all my recordings and supplementary material as well as the verbatim and edited manuscripts from all three of my oral history projects; the Swarthmore College Peace Collection; and the Berrigan Collection in the Special Collections and Archive Department of DePaul University in Chicago.

7. Robert Cooney and Helen Michalowski, eds., *The Power of the People: Active Nonviolence in the United States* (Philadelphia: New Society Publishers, 1987). This is from a manuscript by Marty Jezur.

8. Art Laffin, *Swords Into Plowshares: A Chronology of Plowshares Disarmament Actions, 1980–2003* (Washington, DC: Rosehill, 2003).

9. Online: www.soaw.org.

10. Online: www.nukeresister.org.

11. Online: www.flickr.com/photos/frank_cordaro_and_the_dm_catholic_worker/sets/72157624586733305/show/.

12. Erica Chenoweth and Maria J. Stephan, *Why Civil Resistance Works: The Strategic Logic of Nonviolent Conflict* (New York: Columbia University Press, 2011).

Hope

> Hope is a state of mind, not of the world. Either we have hope or we don't; it is a dimension of the soul, and it's not essentially dependent on some particular observation of the world or estimate of the situation. Hope is not prognostication. It is an orientation of the spirit, and orientation of the heart; it transcends the world that is immediately experienced, and is anchored somewhere beyond its horizons . . . Hope, in this deep and powerful sense, is not the same as joy that things are going well, or willingness to invest in enterprises that are obviously heading for success, but rather an ability to work for something because it is good, not just because it stands a chance to succeed. The more propitious the situation in which we demonstrate hope, the deeper the hope is. Hope is definitely not the same thing as optimism. It is not the conviction that something will turn out well, but the certainty that something makes sense, regardless of how it turns out.[13]

Despite it all, despite the continuing wars and environmental depredation and racism and the frightening loss of our constitutional freedoms since 9/11, I believe that God has good planned for the universe and its peoples. My prayer is that reading *Crossing the Line* sustains your hope, as writing it did mine.

---

13. Victor Havel, *Disturbing the Peace* (New York: Vintage, 1991), 181.

Prologue

Jailbird Stories

Jailbird stories were the genesis of this book. In the spring of 2004, I was sitting with other Catholic Workers in an Omaha church basement, trying to decide if I would "cross the line" at Offut Air Force Base and risk six months in federal prison to live out my deep desire for peace in this world. Jerry Ebner and others started telling prison stories, some about themselves, some about the men and women with whom they were incarcerated. This sharing seemed both delightful and painful for those doing the remembering, and it was really helpful on all accounts for us as potential law-breakers.

It was then that I realized I knew very little about what went on when people like me—mostly white, mostly educated, mostly middle-class—purposefully did something that put them into jail or prison. I wanted to find out and realized other people did, too. So my latest oral history project was born, with 173 interviews in the US and Europe between 2004 and 2008.

Of course, I became intensely interested not only in what happened after people went to jail but in why they made the decision to be arrested as war resisters in the first place and what they did about that decision. Later chapters tell these stories—stories of motivations, the actions themselves, and the resulting trials and also relate many individual prison experiences. This prologue gives a first taste of what it was like to be behind bars.

I've constructed it as a free-wheeling discussion, as if we were all sitting in one room, with some people taking the floor for extended periods, in ways similar to what happens whenever people share experiences.

As in all group discussions, people sometimes interrupt each other or change the topic. They may say something you don't understand at first, or make statements you question or disagree with. I hope you will feel yourself a part of the dialogue, and that you carry the ideas to friends and colleagues.

I take as my model the Catholic Worker tradition of roundtable discussions for the "clarification of thought." This phrase was CW co-founder Peter Maurin's phrase for the intellectual work that was so much a part of his vision. So, although the words are as those I interviewed spoke them, the organization of this chapter is constructed. In real time, the participants talked to me, not to each other, and the interviews happened at different times and different places.[1] Some of these prisoners of conscience know each other in real time, but some don't. I participate in the discussion as a moderator, and I sometimes provide a fictional bridge in the individual narrations. I invite you to believe that this discussion *could* have happened. In fact, it sounds a lot like the one I heard in that Omaha basement eight years ago when I first learned that "jail is a door to another place in this country."[2]

We start with Dr. Wolfgang Sternstein of Stuttgart, Germany. He was jailed nine times for resisting nuclear missiles and has been called the "grandfather of the German peace movement."

Ro: Dr. Sternstein, much of what you told me I also heard from other people. One of the differences, though, is that many Germans approved of your campaign, while we don't generally feel that approval in the US, especially of campaigns which involve nonviolent direct action. So maybe your prison experience was perhaps easier than some.

Wolfgang: Even so, I had great anxieties before my first prison stay. It was for a blockade at EUCOM in '82. I was really intimidated by the walls, and all the barbed wire and then the huge door. So I thought, "Is it really necessary that I go into this?"

You see, it was not absolutely necessary. I had only a fine, and I had decided not to pay, but my supporter friends would have paid it if I'd asked them to. So I had a choice that time. But I realized that if I went on with nonviolent actions, it would be good to have a little

---

1. For the most part, speakers are identified by where they lived when I interviewed them. Prisons mentioned are all federal facilities unless stated otherwise.

2. Brian Kavanagh interview, Marquette Archives.

taste of what to expect. The first sentence was reduced to four days only, so it was really only a little time.

Many things you experience are intimidating and cause troubles, perhaps. For instance, having to undress when you come in for the first time is very uncomfortable. Most importantly, to know you can't get out. But I had some friends who gave me good advice. Especially [Fr.] Carl Kabat. He told me not to oppose or resist in prison. Gandhi said the same thing. Going to prison is in itself a witness, and that's the main thing: to show it doesn't endanger you and that you can overcome the problems and the fear of being incarcerated.

It became easy for me and I had the best times of life in prison—the most intense, most creative, most worthwhile times. I discovered that prison can be a challenge for you to really become aware of your real task in life. You are really alone with yourself, and what I experienced is that . . . [long pause] it's difficult to describe. You get a new feeling. That you are concentrated, in a way you never experience outside. You realize what really matters, and you are forced to rest on yourself, and your belief, your faith. Therefore I would recommend it for everybody.

Well . . . not everybody. I don't dare to talk about the usual prisoners. If you go into a prison because you've done something wrong, not you alone but the whole family is punished and often your future is destroyed. It was different with my situation. I got such a lot of letters and supporting actions by family and by friends, but it's a very individual decision, even for people in the peace movement. But for me, I couldn't get enough of it. [Chuckles.]

I had a lot of privileges. I was able to get books in Rottenburg, what I call my "home prison." In fact, I wrote most of two of my books in prison. I had to write in longhand, but that's easy because you have a lot of time, and the state is taking care of you. You usually have to work in German prisons, but because I had a book deadline, the director allowed me to work for only five hours instead of the usual seven. The afternoon and the evening were free. It was wonderful because the cell was locked up and no one disturbed me.

Now I wasn't always that lucky. In the first times, I had to go to a four-person cell—very noisy—but the comrades, the coprisoners, were so eager to take care of me and yes, so respectful. We had two tables in the cell. The larger of the two was to eat, and they gave the small one to me. "For your books and your writing." Even in prison you find some fine characters, and they did all they could to not be noisy.

My longest prison term was six months. After six months you are really worn out, even though your family can visit three times a month. My sons were very proud of their father who was in jail, but for my wife it was not easy, because everything fell on her shoulders. I would say she took on the harder part. We got a lot of support, but she was very alone. My wife and I, we have a very intense connection, so when I'm away for such a long time, that is very hard for her.

Ro: Yes, most peace prisoners say the ones on the ouside do the hardest time. But let's hear from some who've had tough times inside. Greg, you've had some dangerous times, haven't you, in your several years as a peace prisoner?

Greg Boertje-Obed, Duluth Catholic Worker: The hardest experiences have been when fights break out. It's not natural for me to intervene but an inner voice frequently says that I have to, and I find that difficult. The most traumatic was in the DC jail. I was in there for quite a while and we had a Bible study and a prayer group and you get to know people.

The jail was very repressive. Food was scarce and people were on edge. One day these two guys had a stand-off. I knew both of them. One was a strong Muslim and one was a Christian who'd attended our prayer group. They'd had an altercation previously and weren't supposed to have any contact. Well, the guards made a mistake and let them both out [together] to get their lunch. The one who was a Christian had a shank. (That's a long metal rod sharpened on the cement so it works like a knife.) A couple of us jumped in between them and raised our hands into the air. He didn't stab, but he was brandishing his weapon wildly. It seemed to go on for a long time, with the guard no help at all, just standing there, waiting for backup. Eventually other guards did come. That was probably the most traumatic time.

Ro: This question is a little sensitive, Greg, but you're a small man, and I think every man's fear is that he'll be raped in prison. Did you ever feel sexually threatened?

Greg: Well, I had to learn to deal with my fears over possible homosexual advances. One time there were suggestions made by an inmate I regarded as a friend. I reflected on it, and what came was that I ought to resist advances and trust God. A thought came that I might die and I accepted that. A short time later, I spoke with the friend and all the fears and potential trouble just vanished. It was very freeing to face that fear and then to trust.

Marty Harris of Lomita, California: I got lucky when I went to federal prison for resisting the draft in '68. Didn't get sent to Lompoc. You know what they call Lompoc? "Gladiator School." Because the guys there are rape artists, and when you walk in, they see new meat! With my blond hair . . . Unless you're willing to fight right away, somebody would make you their punk, as they call it. But we didn't have that situation at Stafford, where I went.

Ro: Richa, you resisted the draft, too. Are you able to talk about your prison experience?

Richa [Chandler] of Grand Rapids: Yes. Yes, I will. It was in 1968; I had just turned twenty-one. First they took me to Baltimore City Jail, just a terrible, terrible jail. My very first night there, I was raped by my cellmate. And then again the second night. Rape does something psychologically. I just wanted to die, and I just kind of lay on the cell floor for a couple of days. Finally they took me to the hospital and then put me in another jail, and finally I went into the federal system for two years.

First I was in the Federal Youth Prison, and that didn't work out at all. Then I was transferred to the hole in Lewisburg Penitentiary. The solitary confinement was terrible. I needed the support of people and I was just alone, all alone. Finally I was just losing it. Wanted to obliterate consciousness and started banging my head against the wall. Literally.

But something stopped me; I'm not sure what because it wasn't the pain. My sense of survival, I guess. One day I determined that whatever it took, I was going to deal with being raped, and the way I was going to deal with it was to talk about it, to freely express what had happened and to learn to overcome the fear.

See, part of the devastation of the rape was that I had given in to my own fear. Looking back on it, I couldn't have done anything else, I guess. I had no experience, no knowledge of dealing with any such thing.

Ro: Does the fear of rape keep some male resisters from risking arrest?

Richa: I've heard that from a lot of people. That's one of the reasons I raise the issue, both in prison and out.

Ro: Is there any way men can keep this from happening?

Richa: I think there is. I've since talked with quite a few folks who have dealt with it in different ways. Some [like Greg] have been able to prevent it, basically by having a clear sense of themselves and being respectful to the other but also being clear and just saying an absolute "No!" Also, you have to realize that you may well be hurt or die and be prepared for that to happen.

Approaching it nonviolently *can* work. Today, I work with both men and women rape victims, and I've put out a pamphlet about people who, in most cases, have successfully dealt with those situations by having that . . . that presence of mind. Of course, it's pretty obvious that the people who are most together—most trained, older, more mature—are better able to deal with those things. There will always be some who are vulnerable.

I fought a lot of guilt. I felt I should have done things differently and in talking with others, I find that's almost universal. Anyone who is raped is a victim, but we all seem to blame ourselves at first, and it's work to get past that.

Ro: Yes, I imagine that's true for every rape, no matter who or where. Now many of you are Catholic Workers. How does that life fit with life in jail?

Ciaron O'Reilly of the London CW: Hey! Prison is a great place to be as Catholic Workers, because it's the most intimate place to be with the poor. It's not your soup kitchen or your CW house, where you can ask people to leave. You're at their place and undergoing the same indignities. When I was in prison in Brisbane, we'd meet a lot of the young aboriginal men who had lived with us [at the Catholic Worker there]. That was always interesting, being their guests in prison. They'd help us out by smuggling up vegetarian food or telling us what to be careful of. So it was a wonderful mutuality in terms of hospitality.

Karl Meyer of Greenlands CW in Nashville: You soon find out that people in prison are just as decent as other people. Like most everyone, they were out there hustling, trying to make a living. But they were doing capitalism in an unapproved way. Instead of selling cigarettes or alcohol, most of them are in for selling crack cocaine or marijuana or things which are illegal but no more harmful than the stuff that it's legal to sell. They weren't making weapons, they weren't selling missiles or machine guns to a dictatorship. If they had been, they'd be in the White House. But if they sell a handgun to another street hustler, they're in the big house.

Ciaron: In most of my jail experiences I've been an ethnic minority—whether it was the nine months where I was the only white guy in a Texas jail or the five months in Darwin, which is 95 percent indigenous. So that has been very educational for me in terms of my own prejudices and in terms of my own privileges as a white male.

Ro: What does the general prison population think of your being in jail for resisting war?

Frank Cordaro of the Des Moines Catholic Worker: Well, one of the common denominators is no one likes the government at that point. So they're pretty much unanimous in understanding that you've got a beef with the government, even if it's not their particular beef.

Father Steve Kelly, SJ, of the Pacific Life Community: I've found that the better off the inmate, the greater the objection [to our way of protesting]. The poor guys get it.

Ellen Grady DeMott of the Ithaca Catholic Worker: You know, there were so many things I had to learn, things the other prisoners seemed to know. Often they were cultural things. For instance, one day when I was sweeping, I accidentally swept over a woman's foot.

She looked at me like I had stabbed her or something, and I said, "Oh, Diane, I'm sorry, I'm really sorry." She just growled at me and didn't say anything, and wouldn't you know? I ended up sweeping her foot again!

At that point, she picked up the broom and she spat on it. I was like, "What did I do? What did I do?" Finally, somebody explained to me that it's bad luck to get your feet swept if you're in jail. Diane was getting out in two days, and she did *not* want to come back. I had just jinxed her, but she broke the jinx by spitting on the broom. Now everybody in the room knew about this superstition except me. So I tell women resisters to maybe just be humbler and willing to learn from the women. They have a lot to share with you. And have something simple you can bring to share with them, like folding peace cranes or teaching them to knit.

Frank: For most of them, doing time is just a part of their lives, and they know how to do it because they've done it or known people who have. So they can give us all sorts of tricks to make the time easier.

Brian Terrell of Strangers and Guests Catholic Worker in Iowa: You know, I'd always felt brave and strong in prison, doing something noble and in solidarity with the poor, and feeling I was just like them. Once I spent a couple weeks in the Scott County Jail in Davenport. Now this is an old-style jail and you couldn't not listen to other people's telephone conversations. I call home, and hear how our supporters wanted to put up the bail money for me, and I'm saying, "No, I'm okay. It's just a couple of weeks."

But then the phone went to somebody else, and I heard, "I don't care what you have to do! Get that money and get me the fuck outta here!" My response to my family made me a Martian to them, showed me that no matter how much prison solidarity I practice, I'm irrevocably different, and they know it.

Jerry Ebner of the Omaha Catholic Worker: Prison really isn't that much different than the rest of the world, as far as injustice goes. It's just more in-your-face. Now there *is* a kind of informal and unspoken hierarchy between long-timers and short-timers. Long-timers know pretty much everything about the power structure—who's strict [among the guards], who's loose, who benefits, who loses when you interact in that power structure. That sort of thing. If you're a short-timer, long-timers generally won't bother to get to know you. The questions rarely get to innocence or guilt. I guess for the most part, though, people looked at me as "You're a good guy; you really don't belong here." So you know that they are somehow saying that some people are guilty and some are innocent.

Another thing: prison is a ready-made environment for works of mercy. If you just blend in with everybody else, and stop talking and start listening to other inmates, you can figure out an awful lot of what's hurting people. Among men it may not be so evident right away, but once you get to know them, you find a lot of people who desire mercy and forgiveness but don't know how to go about it.

Frank: You know, when I was in Polk County Jail in 2004 for an action at Offut Strategic Air Command, I spent the first two weeks in a medical ward. Not an easy place to do time. But it was a grace time, because I met some very needy, hurting people. I was doubled up in a single cell with Shawn. He's in his twenties and he's got mental issues. He's really childlike, and he's got two kids himself. I remember one day I was hiding in my cell. He came in and he asked what I was doing.

I said, "God! I've got to get away from these people; they're just all over me all the time."

He says, "Well, you're a pastor.[3] You're a man of God. They really need to talk to you." I was humbled, right to the heart. Because he was right. "You're the pastor and they need you." The kid sobered me up, and I stopped being so self-consumed and just let the time go and spent a lot of time listening to the same stories, over and over again, trying to give a little balance, a little continuity, a little affirmation to people.

John LaForge of Nukewatch: The hardest thing is not being able to help another inmate, because their need is so immediate and in-your-face. [Pause.] And most of the time, in my experience, you can't do a thing.

Jerry: There are possibilities for peer counseling, stuff the chaplains should be doing. Some of the chaplains are good, some not so good. They're BOP (Bureau of Prison) employees and trained with a gun, so they're not trusted. But you're one among equals and that gives you the availability to enter into people's lives, once you get to know them.

The fundamentalist chaplains, though—they're tough to deal with. A lot of that theology really condemns people. Some people even think God brought them to prison to save their souls. I have a hard time with that. God doesn't build prisons to convert people. God doesn't build these prisons at all! But there are ways of comforting the afflicted. Sometimes it's just bringing a little joy and happiness, in spite of all of the oppression.

Fr. Lou Vitale, OFM, of Pace Bene: In the long run, the chaplains are cops with collars. Like military chaplains. Yeah, they may be there for the guys but they're both employed by the system. The ones that don't fit that, of course, are the volunteers who come into the prison from outside. Some of them are good. The Franciscans have thought of doing that kind of thing in the military.

Fr. Steve: Sometimes the chaplains became better jailers than the guards, because they'd initially be perceived by the guards as soft on inmates, so they work hard to dispel that notion. Fundamentalist Protestants fit really well, because their lines of authority are very clear. For them, God has ordained any authority you come across. From the president

3. Frank Cordaro was still an ordained priest in 2004.

of the country to the warden of the prison, all authority comes directly from God. So prisons love the fundamentalist clergy.

Now, the Catholic ones that I've come across for the most part have been . . . They'll listen to me. But who pays their salary? In some cases, especially for jails, the local bishop may provide a budget for staffing jails with chaplains or church workers. These are to some degree less compromised, but subject to removal if they don't play ball. If there's a conflict between what the Church is asking and what the prison is asking, the policies of the prison will win out. No matter who is it—priest or sister or layperson.

For instance, it's the policy of the prison that a priest who is locked up cannot be a leader of any set of prisoners. Now, de facto, a priest is a leader of the praying community of Catholics. So we'd end up having communion services instead of Mass, because the priest that's locked up can't lead the Eucharist. You can imagine how I feel about this. Of course, we've had a lot of underground Masses.

Sr. Carol Gilbert, OP, of Jonah House: The prison chaplain [at Alderson] was a woman, an Episcopalian priest. She was wonderful! The Catholic priest was older and just *so* conservative. Just no life in his Masses. For awhile I was going to both Catholic and Episcopalian services, and then I decided that was dumb. "Why am I putting myself through this, just so people won't wonder about the nun who's not going to her church." So I started going to Chaplain Walker's Masses.

Joni McCoy of Saginaw, Michigan: In Lexington, I remember an ecumenical service at Thanksgiving. With everyone—Catholic, Protestant, Native American, Jewish, Muslim. It was a wonderful, wonderful service. Only in a small area like this where everyone is together could you do this. Outside, we're so separated.

Brian: You know, I had a good chaplain once, at the prison camp at Marion. When I got there and introduced myself, he said, "I was hoping they'd send you here so I could meet you! I read about you in *The Catholic Worker*.

Father John. He was an oddity in the prison system, that's for sure. A Trinitarian priest, and a Vietnam veteran with a prosthetic leg. They kicked him out, though, I guess because he wanted to bring some prisoners to the local parish for Easter Vigil. The prison said he couldn't, but he did it anyway. Just drove in with a van and picked people up, which was pretty easy to do 'cause it was a camp. Anyway, a few weeks after I left there, they got rid of him.

Steve Jacobs of the Columbus, Missouri Catholic Worker: I was lucky in that respect, too. When I was at Leavenworth for my year-long School of the Americas sentence, I had a warm relationship with the Catholic chaplain, Father Greg Steckle. He let us have programs with the SOA Watch videos and the film *Romero,* so I was able to educate people in the camp about the whole issue. None of the guards ever came, though.

You know, a lot of people are afraid of jail. I haven't had really bad experiences, for the most part. Maybe it's because I'm kind of easygoing and I don't take offense at a lot of the ridiculousness and bureaucratic stupidity. And sometimes there would be some kinda sweet things. Like at Christmas, when I was in Leavenworth, we all got extra chocolate milk, and the guards gave us these little presents, like packets of microwave popcorn and candy bars. And everyone got a plastic drinking mug that said "Leavenworth Prison USP." Like a souvenir mug. I still have mine, as a kind of trophy, I guess.

Jerry: A lot of the guards come out of the army and go to the BOP so they can get another pension. You're right; there are some good guards. And some are just trapped in a job and they don't like it. My own father was a part-time prison guard at one time. Never ever talked about it at home. None of them talk about it. You get to know some of the guards and you understand why. If you ask them direct questions . . . you know, they're not the enemy.

Deirdre (Dee) Clancy of Dublin, Ireland: Well, I saw . . . For instance, there was a mentally ill woman in our prison who shouldn't have been there. She had flashes of violence, and her cell was always . . . Her food would be strewn all over the cell, so she had a cell of her own. But one way [the guards] had of bullying inmates was to put them in her cell.

Now one or two of the guards were very nice, but some of them were . . . I think they had problems themselves. And, in fact, I know a woman who was involved in a research project on all the prisons in Ireland. She said that at Limerick Prison, where I was, the levels of alcoholism and drug use were actually the highest among the guards themselves. Particularly the alcoholism.

Ro: I wonder if that's true in the States, too. Someone—I think it was Rae Kramer of Syracuse—made the point that the guards are prisoners, too.

Art Laffin of Dorothy Day CW in Washington, DC: I remember when I was in prison for the Trident Nein plowshares action, some guards would come by late at night and want to talk. They knew why we were there and that we were not typical prisoners, so we had engaging conversations. Even with the warden and with chaplains. You ask them, "Why are you participating in the system of oppression? Why not be about the work of restorative justice?" So you get into some very good discussions.

Karl: A lot of these guards used to be farmers. They want to have these new prisons built in their depressed farm communities so they can have jobs, and they work in them to earn enough to save their farms. The farmer—the person who does the most essential work of society— is not compensated adequately, so they take a job in which they're rightfully despised as human zoo-keepers and lose their dignity.

Jackie Allen-Doucot of the Hartford, Connecticut CW: I had one really horrible jail experience with a guard in the Niantic jail in Connecticut. They always do a speculum exam at that jail, right after you come in, even if you're there for just one night. We know people who've gotten diseases from bad speculum exams there and during the 80s there was a campaign of resisters challenging that kind of intrusive search. Are they searching for weapons or just trying to intimidate us? No one has ever documented that urban legend that someone smuggled in a pocket knife inside her vagina.

Every time I'd ever been in Niantic for some little demonstration, I've always refused the speculum exam. Sometimes I'll be put in isolation [for refusing], but the nurses there have been pretty good, actually, and they fudge the reports or something. In fact, they seem to support us, which shows you don't always know who you're reaching.

But this time when I refused, a really horrible lieutenant hauled me into his office. I was, unfortunately, wearing some big handcuff earrings, and I think they set him off. He started screaming at me: "Who do you think you are? You think this is all a joke, don't you?"

Then another officer, a young guy, said, "What would you think if I told you I could have four men hold you down and they could do that to you?"

"I would think that would make you a rapist."

Well! He freaked out and started going for me. Thankfully, the other officer stepped in between us, and I was able to refuse. So nothing bad ever came of it, except that I was pretty scared.

Ellen: But I want to tell you about my experience with one of the guards. My first encounter with him was pretrial and he was an angry bear. Nasty! Always yelling at people. So I just tried to steer clear of him, you know. Then when I ended up in isolation—this is still presentence—he'd have to bring me food. He'd want to talk about nuclear weapons, and I realized he was trying to figure stuff out.

Later, after sentencing, I had a job mowing the lawn, a great job. One day he pulled up in his car and told me that he was quitting his job. He said he'd been really moved by what Greenpeace was doing and that he was going to become a member of Greenpeace. I realized the guy had been struggling! And that's probably what this "bear" quality was about.

Ro: A happy ending. Can we talk medical care? I've heard some horror stories.

Rae Kramer of Syracuse Peace Council: Well, I'll tell you! [I'm a doctor's wife,] and you cannot rely on them to have the normal kind of responses to illness or injury. I tell everyone who's contemplating an action that will take them to prison: "Go in as healthy as you possibly can and do everything you can to *stay* healthy."

Fr. Steve: Well, I don't know. I've seen people in all kinds of degrees of health, you know, who live with it for a time, in a very patient way. If at the right time you can call for outside support and all that . . . I wouldn't say you have to be vigorously in good health to do resistance. But of course, we have those supports we can call on.

Like when I had a cataract: The optometrist kept saying, "It's just a little piece of skin floating in front of [your pupil]." It took Ramsey Clark and two congresspersons and a senator to even get the warden to ask the doctor who was in charge of the medical department. Finally, I was taken out to the ophthalmologist. He looked at my eyes for ten seconds and said, "This man has a cataract."

Kathleen Rumpf of Syracuse Jail Ministry: Yeah, just the simplest kind of diagnosis. And the "crazy meds" are peddled like candy. So many of the psychotropic drugs they use in prison—the old, cheaper generics, especially—cause diabetes and other serious and life-threatening illnesses. And if you get diabetes in prison . . . I mean you just *can't*!

You can't get treatment. You can't get what you need in terms of diet, in terms of foot care. There's no podiatrist. What they were doing [at Carswell] was amputating instead of being proactive and getting women's feet taken care of. It was cheaper for them to amputate than to treat.

Sister Jackie Hudson of Ground Zero Center for Nonviolent Action: The prisons in Victorville were on a former Air Force base, so the water was contaminated. In fact, the doctor told a woman who came back from surgery not to shower. "If you want to bathe, do it in bottled water."

Paul Magno of Washington, DC: There's sure a big difference in facilities, so maybe we should define terms.[4] After our Plowshares action in Florida in 1983, we spent several months in local jails, but most of the time in federal prison camp. And it *is* a camp. A jail has bars. Prison has high concrete walls and guard towers. A camp doesn't have any fences, only lines that you're not permitted to cross. So you police yourself rather than all the responsibility for supervision being on the institution. In one respect, it's less dehumanizing; having some responsibility over your own life leaves you a more functional human being. If you go into the dungeon for three years, you become dysfunctional in terms of responsibility for yourself. Prisons can really lobotomize prisoners.

Ro: But by your voluntary obedience, by choosing to cooperate, you're buying into what they want you to be.

Kathy Kelly of Voices for Creative Nonviolence: When you're in a maximum security prison, as I was at Lexington, there's no question about cooperation. It's that or the SHU. We used to joke that the guards had only ten words in their vocabulary: "No talking in the hallways, count, chow, and where's your pass?"

You could only move ten minutes out of the hour and you'd better have a pass signed by a guard to go from Point A to Point B. It was difficult to go to the library, for example, because there were only ten minutes when you could make a move, and if you couldn't find a guard to sign your pass and hope the library was open, forget it.

Even-numbered prisoners could make phone calls on three days a week and odd-numbered prisoners on three other days. You had

4. The segment by Paul Magno appears in a slightly different form in *Voices*, 207.

to wait in line, a long time—an hour or more—just to sign up for a phone call.

I didn't like waiting in line at all. You wait in line to turn in your laundry, and you wait in line to collect the laundry, and you wait in line to buy stamps, and wait in line to get anything from the medical people. You wait in line for mail call. Wait in line to eat. Wait in line to be searched. Imagine your worst experience of waiting in a long line at the post office and then put that in every day, five or six times. In Lexington, you couldn't even read while you were waiting.

Also, you could never touch another prisoner. I remember my friend. Her mother had been a Polish prisoner in a concentration camp in Germany. Both mother and daughter got involved in a credit fraud. Barbara's mother arrived in a wheelchair, crippled with rheumatoid arthritis. When she came out of the admission place, standing unsteadily, Barbara went up to hug her. A guard immediately said, "You know it's not allowed to touch any other prisoner. I'm going to give you a shot." (A shot is a demerit; a certain number of them put you in solitary confinement.) Any level of common sense is subordinated to this preoccupation with doing things according to the rules. Just like the army, the rules rule.

But I actually found it easier in Lexington to get a night's sleep than I did when I was at Pekin, which is minimum security. In Lexington, I had a real room with a locked door and four women; in Pekin, there was a dorm called an alley, with thirty women. Isn't it interesting that they call it an alley? Who lives in an alley? Animals and . . . Anyway, in the alley, the guards did a count four times during the night, shining a flashlight in your face each time. So sleeping was easier in maximum security.

Kathleen: Yeah, they count you all the time. But the "big count" is at 4:30 every day, in every federal prison. And the numbers have to clear, have to match, before you go to dinner and get your mail and all of that. It's called the stand-up count and there's no joking around. When someone dies, they write on the stand up count, "Escape by death."

Frank: Jails sure are different than prisons. In 2006, I spent some time in a county jail in Kansas. It was only ten years old but was built so cheaply it was already falling apart. The county built it to make money and the fed would pay to put people there while they were in transit.

The dishtowels at the Des Moines CW were larger than the towels we got, and hygiene was a real problem. They'd bring in cleaning materials three times a day, around meal times. A mop and a bucket with mostly dirty soap water, a small white plastic container with bleach water, a tiny rag, a dirty broom and filthy dustpan.

Toilet paper was the most valued commodity, something to die for! Each inmate is issued two rolls of toilet paper a week plus each cell gets one extra roll a week. It's all we had to clean the sinks, the table tops, and our eating utensils. If you dropped something on the floor, you cleaned it up with toilet paper. If you want a napkin at your meal, toilet paper is your only option.

Art: One of the sustaining things for me in jail has been prayer and reading the Scriptures. You read the Scriptures differently in prison. When you're reading in the Acts of the Apostles where the Christian community was locked up, for example—you feel really feel connected. There's one passage from Paul's Letter to the Romans which was a great inspiration to me in a low moment. In Romans 8, he writes that nothing can separate us from the love of Christ. Neither hardship, persecution, nor famine, on and on. Nothing! In the hardest and the loneliest moments in jail or prison, I've been strengthened by that.

When I'm in prison, I also think about what other prisoners have experienced and realize that what I'm experiencing is nothing compared to theirs. For instance, I visited a prison in El Salvador where prisoners had been tortured. Now I think psychological torture goes on in the prisons in this country, and physical torture to some extent; but I saw prisoners at the Mariona Prison in San Salvador who had burn marks and knife marks on their chests and their backs.

In 1988 I was in prison for three days in Honduras with twelve other US peacemakers calling for an end to US military intervention in Central America. We acted at the US Military Base in Palmerola, which was the main US military command center for operations in Nicaragua, El Salvador, and Guatemala at that time. Anyway, we were held incommunicado for three days.[5] Thirteen of us in a cell that was only five by thirteen. Dirt floor, and the back of the cell used for a toilet. Men and women together. No meals served and no access to clean water. This is the way people are treated elsewhere around

5. See also Judith Williams's story of this prison time in Chapter 4 of *Doing Time for Peace*.

the world. So that puts my jail experiences here in a very different perspective.

Kathleen: Hey, can we lighten up a bit? This is just getting too heavy, and it wasn't *all* like Frank describes, or like Central America. Let me tell the story I call "missing a bird." It was in the Syracuse jail after the Griffiss Plowshares. One thing I'd done before doing the action was to put a needle into my shoe. I was savvy enough to know that you try to take in what you could get away with, and a needle is good to have. We're in the jail and it's getting close to Christmas. We're building relationships with the women on the cell block and we'd talk through the days, and we'd sing and we'd do all kinds of things.

One day, there was a shakedown. Suddenly you hear the dogs barking and toilets flushing. See, the women realize a shakedown has started, and they're flushing down anything they think might be contraband. Now we'd been folding peace cranes in the cell block, and with my smuggled needle, I'd string them up with blanket threads. The peace cranes put some beauty into a really cold place.

Then the deputies came onto our cell block, loud and disruptive. In a shakedown, they pull you out of your cell and take you into another room and strip search you to make sure you don't have contraband on your body. Then they search your cells. Back in our block, they took our peace cranes, took down all that lovely color and hope. These huge guys with these huge biceps and huge arms and huge necks are grabbing these peace cranes and yelling out, "We got more! Here's some more!" Finally they finished. It was exhausting, just an awful thing and there was a heaviness in the air.

A little while later, a captain comes up. Clare [Grady] starts in with him about the peace cranes. Now she'd never been in a prison before and she was such an innocent. "Why did you take the peace cranes?" He's telling her it could be contraband, it could be this and that. Totally ridiculous conversation. Suddenly, I couldn't help it. I interrupted and I said, "You know, captain, there's one bird you didn't get." He turned to look at me and I gave him the finger. [Hearty laughter.]

At first, he was almost in shock. But he couldn't escape the irony; he just couldn't. So he began to laugh and we became fast friends, this captain and I. He was a prisoner, too. He could not escape. That bird I gave him set a tone in the cell block.

Neil Golder of Ithaca, New York: I could see some humorous things, too. Like when the guys would play chess. They'd smash the chessman down on the table. [Assumes loud, deep, rasping voice.] "Okay, motherfucker, you're *gone!*"

But there's such an armoring that people maintain when they're in those situations and it's very hard. People, or at least men, aren't going to be vulnerable to each other in jail; it's just too dangerous.

Sr. Carol: I'm not sure it's the same with women. At Alderson—and Sister Ardeth had this at Danbury, too—we lived so closely with one another and shared at such a great depth, you know, personal tragic stories. It was really a privilege to be allowed to learn so much because the sharing is so deep. Both from those who have grown up abused and have absolutely nothing and from women who are very wealthy, highly educated, very together, like Martha Stewart.

Ro: Oh, that's right. She was there when you were.

Sr. Carol: Yes, but I won't talk for the book about our relationship. To be part of that the circle of all the women's lives, it's really humbling.

Martha Hennessey of Maryhouse in New York: I remember when I was in prison. A woman was sent to us from the Concord State Hospital, a New Hampshire mental facility. She was actively psychotic, and I don't know why she was sent to the Women's House of Correction. I remember bringing her some food at one point. I touched her hand and she said to me, "I'm not the witch they make you think I am." She obviously needed care and she wasn't getting it.

Rae: Nobody hears these stories because people in prison are just invisible. That was the dominant impression I had from the women in Danbury. Let me tell you about the interviews I did, to help people see them. I wanted to take a kind of snapshot, to help make them visible, so I designed a survey and interviewed people. Vetted the questions with some of the women I knew and they probably weren't great questions, but I had enough of a social-science background that they weren't terrible. It was qualitative rather than quantitative, and I think the women wanted to talk, wanted the opportunity to tell their stories.

I asked each of the women to sign an authorization: "I understand that I do this survey voluntarily, and it's not part of the prison." I told them what the purpose was and guaranteed it'd be totally,

totally anonymous. I ended up doing about seventy-five interviews and a friend did about another thirty in Spanish.

Ro: Did you ask permission?

Rae: I didn't ask, but I did it under their noses, and I'm sure they knew I was doing *something*. I had been told that the big thing was not to ask people why they're there, but I acknowledged that at the beginning of the interviews, and did it anyway and it worked. I wanted to uncover the impact of their being in prison, especially on their kids. And I wanted to learn about the judicial process. "Did they feel coerced to plea bargain?"

I heard stories like, "Well, this guy was my guy and he was dealing dope and he pleaded the guy on top of him, but the only guy I had to plead for was him, and they already had him, and I had nothing to offer." So the woman's in prison for forty-eight months, and the guy's out in sixteen. She has no chips, no bargaining chips. And charged with conspiracy.

I heard one story about a grandmother. The grandmother's at home and the feds are in the house with her, and the grandson, in his early twenties, calls her. Grandma says, "Don't come home; the feds are here." And *Grandma's* gone for five years!

Every woman but one was amazingly forthcoming about telling me why they were in Danbury, so I don't know whether the mythology needs changing, or whether it was the survey itself [that made it easier for women to talk about it]. The sad ending to this story is that I haven't done anything with the survey. I've still got it, though.

Kathy: Yes, we need to get the stories out. Especially to the people who might have power to change things. I used to see this assistant warden bring students to Pekin and kind of take them around as though it were a trip to the zoo. No interaction to speak of between the students and the prisoners. I wish very much that these law students or university students would have stayed in with us overnight. Or for a week. They'd learn a lot about the courage of these women who are facing eight- or nine-year sentences. They have just such tremendous character to get up in the morning. Removed from families and friends, often feeling terrific guilt for children left behind. Amazing, interesting women! Kindly women!

I remember when I spent the year in Lexington—at a maximum security prison—for the Missouri Peace Planting.[6] So many rules! It was especially hard on the mothers. Like Gloria . . . Every Friday night she'd wait in line to sign up for an early morning call. I'd be the only one in the day room so early, grabbing the quiet time to read, so I couldn't help but overhear her call. Someone would pick up the phone at the other end and presumably put the telephone receiver to the ear of an infant.

Then Gloria would croon, "Momma's gonna tickle your feet. Oh, yes! You're momma's baby and momma's gonna tickle your feet. Momma loves you. Oh, yes! Momma loves you so, so much!" At the end, Gloria would hang up the phone. She'd rise and leave the room, walking like a queen, with tears streaming down her face.

Sr. Carol: Oh! It just makes your heart sick! And so many of these women have such struggles when they get out, with no work, and no programs. And maybe physically they *can't* work. Many of the women I spent time with in Alderson—some with white-collar occupations and with drug charges, many in their late fifties—are going to be in their sixties or seventies when they get out. Many haven't paid into Social Security. They're ex-felons, so they can't get work. They've never had the connections with a community of women like they made in the prison. That's all gone for them when they get out. The government is fostering a lot of people who just won't make it. They have so many people on probation to supervise that nobody gets anything. They never look at people as individuals.

Ro: Now Carol, you won the right to go to your home for probation—to Jonah House, even though other "felons" were living there. Do you think that your refusal to be cowed by the system might have helped other women to fight for what they need?

Sr. Carol: Yes, it did—in some ways, anyway. The women loved that I won, that I was able to come home. But I'm not sure other women would've won. We have privileges of race and education and contacts that most of the women will never have.

Caitlin Harwood, Creighton University: Because of that privilege, I don't think I got as much out of the prison experience as I could have. I was at Alderson, too, but with SOA prisoners of conscience [POC]

6. See Father Bob Bossie's and Father Jerry Zawada's narration in Chapter 9 for some details of that action.

the whole time I was in. Because I had that community, I was isolated within it. People would point us out when we walked around the compound, and it was just sort of a weird thing. So I didn't become as close to the other women as I could have. It also stuck out that I had privilege because I was there by choice.

Ro: Did the guards privilege you?

Caitlin: Some did and some didn't. My boss at the landscape shop had a lot of respect for the prisoners of conscience, though. Initially we were—this is another privilege thing—they put all the POC women on a squad together to do weeding. One of the other women said it was a racist thing and a privilege thing when everybody else had to mow. Vera Brown and I told her we didn't choose it and then we talked to the boss and said we wanted to mow. I think it probably redeemed us a little bit in the eyes of the other women.

Oh, I've got a neat story about a guard. We used do POC solidarity once a week, meeting in the music room in the rec center. One night we were sitting there and talking when this corrections officer walks in. Well, he grabs a guitar, closes the door, and starts playing and singing for us. He played Bob Marley's "Redemption," which is an amazingly powerful song and has so much meaning, especially when one is in prison. It was incredible! He made me realize our common humanity—everyone who was there, guards and woman, and . . . all of it.

Ro: William, you were arrested with Caitlin. What did you learn from your prison experience?

William Slatterly, Creighton University: Gosh, a lot, starting with actually crossing the line, which was probably one of the better moments of my young life at the time. I was incredibly at peace with myself because it was one of those rare times when I was living out my ideals in a fundamental and tangible way. I could feel a confidence that from then on I could try to find the best response—the nonviolent response—to whatever situations I'd be in.

Ro: What about your parents?

William: For them, it was a big wake-up call. "Uh, oh! He actually believes all this stuff we taught him." My mother was my support person at the trial. I went right in after sentencing. Got the full tour. From Muskogee to the Crisp County Jail to Atlanta to . . . ah, the transfer center in Oklahoma City and then to Terre Haute, Indiana, and then finally after two months to Oxford, Wisconsin, which is about two and a half hours from my parents' house. I say it was my Rhodes scholarship—I went to Oxford and I toured the country.

Tom Cordaro of Naperville, Illinois: Oh, I remember when that happened to me. We used to call it the merry-go-round.[7] It has the effect of making you disappear. When you get to the new place, you may not have the ability or the right to make a phone call, to contact your support people on the outside. And before you finally get a stamp to mail a letter, you may be moved again. It's a way of keeping prisoners in this kind of no-man's land.

The last time I was in the federal system, I started in Omaha, Nebraska. My destination was Sandstone, Minnesota. I was first sent down to Leavenworth, Kansas. From Leavenworth to Terre Haute, Indiana. From Indiana I was to go up to Michigan and then down to Chicago and from Chicago finally to Sandstone. Now these movements aren't quick. You could be in transit for months and months.

In my case, though, the merry-go-round turned out much for the better for me and for the movement. The one letter I was able to get out was to my mother, Angela Cordaro, God bless her! She got that letter to Tom Fox at the *National Catholic Reporter*. He organized the whole damn country! They were just overwhelmed by all the letters, and got so frightened that when I got to Terre Haute, they decided to put me in a camp. Because of mom's initiative. A lot of the public would never have known about this floating Siberia except for her.

William: Yeah. I was lonely during those two months [on the road], but it was a strange loneliness because there are people everywhere, especially in county jails. And always the noise. The TV is always blasting, and everybody's always shouting. But when finally you're in a place for awhile, you definitely create some beautiful strong friendships.

I was eighteen when I went in, just old enough to be with adults. Some understood and some didn't. They were all my uncles. They'd say, "Oh, you damn kid! Why aren't you in school?" Actually, when I left, a couple of guys said to my sister, who picked me up, "Don't ever let him do this again."

One thing I never figured out, though, was how to talk to them about the blatant sexism. It's rampant in prison. Every woman is

---

7. Tom Cordaro's memories appear in a different form in *Voices*, 389–90.

purely objectified in the way [the men] talk about them—both the women they know and ones they don't. I could never find a good way to say anything about it, other than just, "Dude, that's not cool." Eventually, they decided not to talk like that around me, but that didn't really change anything.

Ro: How did you get away from the noise?

William: Go inside myself, I guess, and just shut it off. I used to close my eyes and just sit quietly and think or meditate and then try to bring that calm out to other people. After I learned the prison culture and the pecking order, I at least tried to provide a nonviolent presence.

You know, in prison, you're forced to confront yourself. You can finally be the subject matter of your own mind and because there are few distractions, you might be able to see an accurate photo, warts and all. So prison can be the forging area for the way you want to live.

John LaForge of Nukewatch: Yes, it can be, but I've got a story I want to tell from my first time in jail, a cautionary tale if you will. The first time I was in court, I got slammed with a six-month jail term, right out of the gate. Went right from the courtroom to Beltrami County Jail in northern Minnesota and was in with the poorest of the poor.

The jailers offered me a job as a trusty. Now I don't know why you're called a trusty because it makes you not trusted, either by the other inmates or the jailers. But it means you get privileges in exchange for doing work. And one of the privileges—the reason I took the job—was that you get a day off your sentence for every week that you're a trusty.

Well, I'd never do that again! Here I am, a white, college-educated, middle-class kid who gets this choice job. I didn't know. I didn't realize that even my being in that jail was having a big impact. Because all the time, supporters picketed outside the jail, drawing attention to the case. So it was in the guards' best interests to get me out as soon as possible, and here I was cooperating with them in that.

Being a trusty is terrible. The jailers lean on you because they have the power to withdraw the status and throw you back into general population. All the other inmates think you're ripping them off, because you get these perks, like a manual typewriter. Now it was good in one way because I was able to type letters for inmates, but it was hard to make up for being separated and mistrusted. As I said, I learned. Never again will I be a trusty.

Ro: Can we talk about other kinds of working in prison? I know when you're in federal institutions you have to work. No one I interviewed would take a job with UNICOR, the government owned and run work program, even though it "pays" better than other work in the prisons. But what kinds of work did you do?

Susan Crane of Jonah House: Oh, I'd like to speak to that 'cause I've done different things. For a while, when I was in prison in California, I was teaching, because that's my trade. I tried to teach at the student's point of interest. People in prison are used to writing letters and they're interested in what affects them most, so I'd remember that in my work.

The story I want to tell is about the time when Pope John Paul was visiting Cuba in 1998. Assata Shakur, a member of the Black Panthers, had escaped from prison and received asylum in Cuba. She's become something of a folk hero to young African-Americans but is a continuing problem for the FBI, of course. When the pope was coming to Cuba, Assata wrote him a letter explaining what happened and why she was there. It was a very beautiful letter, only about a page and a half long, and I had a copy.

The students would read books on their own and do a book report to the class, either write it or speak it. One of the women had read *Assata: An Autobiography*, and she was presenting her book report. So I distributed Assata's letter. In it she talks about what it was like for her in prison and how she got closer to God. She talked also about how the prison system is racist and the court system is unjust.

The letter just pulls at your heart, and the students were very touched. And the discussion afterwards . . . it was a real discussion, it was good. But that was the end of my teaching career in the prison because my new boss had been sitting in on the class. He said I was teaching opinions as if they were facts.

I said, "What opinions?

"Well, that the justice system is racist."

From there I began gardening for the Rec Department, maintained this beautiful garden in the Rec Field. The women liked the gardens and I was happy there. But one morning, I went out to check to see what grew overnight, and saw all these women, digging up the garden.

It was no longer the Rec Department's Garden. General maintenance had taken it over and they were digging it all up. That just crushed me! I had grown these six-foot tall sunflowers from seed, and they brought so much color. You know, in the prison, you're color deprived, and those flowers brought happiness, and now they were gone.

Then I got another job collecting garbage. You go around the whole compound in the evening with a big, big cart and throw all the bags of garbage in it and then take 'em out to the trash compactors. That was a lot of fun, but I guess you could call it downward mobility, as far as prison status goes. [Laughs.]

When I'm in a jail, I try to take a job, even if you don't have to. I usually try to mop the floors because it gives me the freedom to move around. I can help other women, especially the ones who come in with addiction difficulties and are withdrawing. If you're mopping, you can clean up after them, and bring a word of encouragement.

Sr. Carol: I cleaned bathrooms at Alderson, and this might sound kinda odd, but I think what was personally best for me in prison was learning how to really make sacred the cleaning of those godawful bathrooms. I don't do well with bugs and dirt and smells and . . . And I could actually go in every day and clean all those toilets and showers. There were some very sick people at Alderson, and you can't believe the condition some of the toilets would be in, so that was one thing I was proud of, that I was able to make that into sacred work. And the other good thing, as I said before, was to just be allowed to witness the deep sharing about women's lives. So many of them would get hooked into UNICOR because it paid a few cents more an hour.

Kathy: In the dish room at Pekin, I earned eleven cents an hour, something like five dollars a week. If you worked at UNICOR, I think you could start at eighty cents an hour and maybe even get as high as $1.25 or more. UNICOR at Pekin manufactures these small cages to pick up undocumented immigrant children at the border and deport them. They make the little ones.

Items on commissary were overpriced, so there's a big temptation to work for the higher wages at UNICOR. A pair of gym shoes would be sixty or seventy dollars. Walkman radio sets were probably sixty dollars. A box of Fig Newtons or a big bag of M&Ms would be a big treat, and they would probably be three dollars and seventy-five cents.

Sr. Carol: UNICOR was getting ready to be a phone center at Alderson when I was there. They tell the women they're preparing them for work in the world. And I say, "Not unless you want to move to India or Pakistan or Thailand, because the reason you have that job here in the prison is because [companies] aren't willing to pay what they would have to pay workers on the outside." It's all connected. On the international level, we have militarism, we have the arms dealers, we have all these folks who are making the profits from Halliburton on down. On the domestic level, it's the prison scene and it's the prison industry. There's a deep connection between the two.

Ro: Karl you've been at this longer than anyone else in this discussion. Why do you keep on getting arrested?

Karl: Yes, I guess I have. Uh . . . For a couple of years in the late '50s and early '60s I was probably the most vigorous practitioner of civil disobedience and going to jail in the American peace movement. I keep a tally of arrests for people who ask. It's up to fifty-eight now, with twenty-four convictions and twenty-eight different jails. Federal correctional institutions, federal penitentiaries, a jail in Le Havre, France [during the Los Angeles to Moscow Peace Walk] and a detention at Saigon International Airport.[8]

When I first got started in the '50s, it was very rare to go to jail. So you got a lot of attention and a lot of respect in the movement. It gave us a voice and we got a lot of press. Then, in the '60s, with the civil rights movement and the Vietnam War and the protests against nuclear power plants, large numbers of people began to [be arrested] for nonviolent civil disobedience. More people were doing it, so there was less fear but also less respect.

Now we don't go to jail for the sake of going to jail. We go to jail for two reasons. One is because in our perverted society it's a way to get attention for ideas and issues. The other thing is simply the moral imperative, over and above what one's religion would say about it, which to you folks is a lot. When someone says to you, "Either you will go over to a foreign country and you will kill whoever happens to be in the way, or we will put you in jail," it's a moral imperative to say no.

Also, we have these unalienable rights of free speech. To me, it's a moral imperative to defend them, not to surrender them because some Secret Service agent comes and tells you where to stand. They

8. In 1966, Meyer went to Saigon with Brad Lyttle, Barbara Deming, and four others. They unfurled a peace banner in front of the US Embassy and were immediately arrested and expelled from the country.

have a "designated protest zone" at the Liberty Bell in Philadelphia, for crying out loud!

We have to defend these rights which were in the Constitution. In the '40s and the '50s, when I got started, they were in the Constitution, but they didn't exist in the peace movement and the civil rights movement. We won recognition of the rights that were already there. Now, we need to defend those rights from being taken away from us. That's all there is to it.

I

World War II—Lonely Pacifists

American pacifists have always refused to fight, with most of them coming at first from the traditional peace churches—Quakers, Amish, Church of the Brethren, and Mennonites. The draft was reinstated in 1917 and opposition to World War I came mostly from these churches and from the Left. Eugene Debs ran for president under the American Socialist Party ticket while he was in prison for resisting the war.[1]

Four thousand men were granted CO status during this draft, and twenty thousand worked in noncombatant occupations but under military authority. Men who wouldn't serve and who couldn't claim a religious CO received long prison sentences; seventeen were even sentenced to death. All were eventually commuted and most were released after three years. These early CO prisoners were treated poorly, often sent to the hole, and sometimes tortured. The War Resisters League (WRL) was founded in 1923, in part to support secular COs.[2]

Along with the Fellowship of Reconciliation (FOR) and the Women's Peace Society, WRL made the '30s a decade where peace seemed a possibility. Dramatic protests and solemn prayer services helped a nation to remember the horrors of World War I. But when the drums of war began to beat for World War II, the only peace groups not to abandon their absolute pacifism were the WRL and the Catholic Worker movement. Dorothy Day successfully campaigned for Roman Catholics to become

1. Cooney and Michalowski, 50.

2. Ibid., 45. WRL's current work against the US militarism includes war tax resistance, counter-recruitment, and cooperation with other groups on rallies, vigils, and direct action to end wars in the Middle East.

religious COs, but the movement she cofounded lost much of its following and episcopal support for affirming their anti-war activities. In all, fifty-two thousand men were classified as COs during World War II and 6,086 refused to cooperate with the draft, choosing instead to go to prison.[3]

Like many, I saw World War II as the "good war." The late Howard Zinn, a bombardier in Europe during the waning months of that conflagration, originally thought so, too. In 2004, he was asked by the Smithsonian Institution to speak at a World War II memorial celebration. Instead of praising the war, as sponsors expected, he talked about how the so-called "good war" wasn't, how it "was accompanied by too many atrocities on our side—too many bombings of civilian populations . . . too many betrayals of the principles for which the war was supposed to have been fought."[4]

The men in this chapter, pacifists all, knew all along that war wasn't the answer. The narrators are WRL's Ralph DiGia and three other lonely pacifists—Bill Lovell, Meredith "Dal" Dallas, and Donald Benedict—Union Theological Seminary students who went to prison to protest the draft law, even though they would have been exempt as seminary students.

Ralph DiGia (1914–2008)

Ralph DiGia "wore his radicalism in his life, not on his sleeve," wrote David McReynolds.[5] Born of Italian anarchist immigrants, Ralph told the US Attorney's office he was a conscientious objector as soon as he received his induction notice. They sent him to a War Resisters League (WRL) lawyer for advice. At that time, conscientious objection that was not religiously based wasn't legally recognized, and Ralph spent over two years in federal prison, heading straight to WRL when he got out.

Ralph DiGia, 1992.
© Ed Hedemann.

3. Ibid., 95.

4. Howard Zinn, "Dissent at the War Memorial," *The Progressive* (August, 2004); online: www.progressive.org/august04/zinn0804.html.

5. David McReynolds, "Ralph DiGia, 1914–2008," *The Catholic Worker* (March–April, 2008) 6.

In 1955 he became Office Manager and served until 1994, doing the thankless work of worrying about finances and stuffing envelopes as well as going through many arrests for nonviolent civil disobedience. Although he was officially retired when we met, he still volunteered every day with WRL. When he died, a Muslim friend of his, with whom he had worked in Bosnia, called him a "hidden saint."

Ralph: The '30s was sort of an anti-war decade; people still remembered World War I, and they didn't want to go back to war. My father was a Socialist and connected with a group of Italian socialist immigrants—barbers, tailors, laborers—and he used to take me to some of the meetings. There, of course, I began to learn about the poor, and the economic system here, and I began to get an antigovernment outlook. I remember when I was about thirteen, going to a protest about the Sacco and Vanzetti execution. So I had that kind of background. No religion at all, although my mother was very religious.

Then I went to the City College of New York with a lot of other working class people, because it was a free college then. They had what they called Military Science—we call it ROTC now—and there were little demonstrations against that.

Then came the draft in ['40.] The draft, as I remember, passed by just one vote in Congress. That shows you the atmosphere of the country at that time—just one vote! I had gotten acquainted with Gandhi's theories, and I decided I was a conscientious objector. (I wasn't religious then, although that changed in the Vietnam War.)

I didn't know the War Resistance League. In fact, I wasn't involved with any organization, but I had decided to refuse induction. My father approved of what I believe in, but the night before, he was very distressed. "Ralph, you're going to ruin your whole life." (See, going to jail in the '40s wasn't like going to jail during the civil rights movement when you were proud.) The next morning, though, my mother said, "Ralph, your father said you should do what you have to do." She didn't want me to go into the army, but she didn't want me to go to jail, either, so she just felt awful.

You know, it was the US Attorney's office that sent me to the War Resisters League. So see, I do owe the government something! [Laughs.] I guess the WRL and the Attorney General's office would kind of cooperate with each other in cases like mine. Now no one can believe that today, but that's my wonderful story.

Ro: Isn't that amazing? They sent you to your life, actually.

Ralph: Yes. This was in '41 and I didn't get to jail until early '43. The first prison after West Street was Danbury.[6] I met other people there who were conscientious objectors, and that was reassuring. In a sense, Danbury would be considered an easy jail. (Now this was the old Danbury, of course.) Most of the people were in for fraud and faking ration stamps for gasoline, and this and that, so their sentences were low, like six months or a year. But the conscientious objectors had two or three years. So that was the beginning of the rest of my life, the beginning of my life.

Ro: Did you spend your whole two years at Danbury?

Ralph: No, no, no. Just one year. Because I was a troublemaker. See, in Danbury, the dining halls were segregated. Blacks—Negroes, they were called then—sat at separate tables. You could make up your own courses and teach them at night, so we made one. Called it Sociology or something, and the warden approved it because he thought it was good public relations. And in the class we discussed the problem of segregation and decided we had to do something about it.

So we started a strike. We had talked with the warden, and he said, "Sorry. My hands are tied. Washington has to make this decision." The thing about it . . . you're not giving up anything in a way if you go on strike in prison, because you still get fed and your freedom has already been taken away. On the outside you'd have a job, and you can't quit it because you need income. At a certain point, a group of us—probably about eighteen—refused to work. Right away they separated us from the rest of the prison because we were troublemakers.

We kept the strike for four months. Through the WRL, people got in touch with Washington, and with ministers. Congressman Adam Clayton Powell was very active, and he and others put the pressure on Washington.

You know, even though my mother was religious, my father wasn't. I had grown up thinking that being Christian didn't mean a thing, that Christians didn't share my political views and didn't seem to care about anything important. But during the strike in Danbury, there were some young seminarians. Really, really religious. Then

6. West Street is the street name for a federal Metropolitan Correctional Institution which serves as an entry and transfer point for federal prisoners in New York City.

there was a group of us who were confirmed atheists. My experience had been that religious people didn't care, and they were amazed that there were anarchists or socialists who were *also* antiwar! So we got together on this, and we learned to respect each other, and we worked together on the strike.

On February 1 the seating was changed. We did it! They integrated. Just at Danbury, though, not at all the federal prisons. Later on, we went on strike again. See, everyone but the COs could get parole, so we took that on as an issue. More or less the same group, but other people joined us. Every Wednesday another one of us would refuse to work. This went on for many weeks, until finally they separated us. I went to Lewisburg, Pennsylvania, with three other people.

Lewisburg was different from Danbury. Some heavy stuff, and no chance of changing the segregation there. No matter where you are, though, the worst thing about prison is the lack of freedom and following petty little rules. But like everything else, you get accustomed to it. It becomes your home—your community—and you begin to live into the moment.

Another thing you have to remember is that, for me, it wasn't a matter of being free, it was a matter of being either in the army or being in jail. Army or jail? That's a different choice than between freedom and jail. The army was something I couldn't agree with. Not that I agree with prison, but at least it was my choice. And it was an easy choice.

But I remember about two weeks before I was to be released. It was summertime, and I was working outside on a labor gang and just wearing my undershirt.

A guard came over and said, "Hey, put on your shirt!" I tried to explain, but he said it again.

I tried again to explain, and he said, "Are you disobeying an order?"

"Yes." And he immediately called the captain. They right away took me downstairs to the hole. I was just in there overnight, and the reason I mention it is that I had only two weeks to go, and when I said that "yes," I endangered my release.

I had a three-year sentence, and I think I did about twenty-eight months, the same as most people with three-year sentences. All the so-called bad things I did didn't make any difference, but with disobeying an order, they could've taken away my good time and made me stay longer. But I just *had* to say yes to the guard. I was sure glad it worked out, but that shows you the kind of pressure you're under, and sometimes you just can't take it anymore, with just yes or no propositions.

When I went to Lewisburg, we came in as bad guys because of the strike, and they put us in a special section with some of the tough ones, the people who are always in trouble. After a couple of days, one of the other prisoners threatened us: "You're making trouble for us. Because you're here, the guards come around all the time, and we don't like that. So get out!" That was scary!

The next morning, though, somebody else in the section asked me if I knew Dave Dellinger, who was also at Lewisburg. I hadn't met him yet, but this guy knew we [thought alike], I guess, because then he said, "Any friend of Dave Dellinger is a friend of mine. If anything happens here, just let me know, and we'll take care of it." So he protected me because of Dave.

Not that this guy was nonviolent! [Laughs.] Later I found out it was because Dave Dellinger had a very good reputation among all the prisoners. See, if someone on his work gang got punishment, he'd support him, so they all liked him, not just the COs.

I got out in June and the war ended in [August], and right away people wanted to forget that it ever happened. I didn't feel any animosity, even in getting a job. I started working for an accountant and volunteering at War Resisters League. Went to the meetings and eventually they offered me a job. I was Office Manager, and I got arrested [with them] many, many times.

Ro: When young people come to talk to you about resistance, what do you tell them?

Ralph: Well, during the Vietnam War I did a lot of counseling, and I'd explain what choices they had—either refusing to go, or going to Canada, or going underground, or becoming a CO. I also tell them that going to prison isn't the end of life. It's a different experience, but it isn't really the end if you believe in what you're doing. During the civil rights movement, when everybody was arrested, it got easy to say that going to jail was okay.

It used to be that if you went to Canada, you could come back, but now they've changed that whole thing, and if you go, you won't be accepted for asylum. Or you may not be able to come back.

When I speak to people, I don't try to convince them, even about nonviolent resistance. I just tell them their choices and show them they're do-able. Once in a while a young person today will ask me if they should register. I tell them it's up to them. There are so many people who haven't registered that the government can't rule against them. Except, of course, to deny financial aid.

There's no draft now, but there's the late entry program. They get kids in school to sign up and then when they get out of school, they have to go. But what they don't know is that it's very easy to get out of it because you haven't signed a contract. When the time comes, you say you've changed your mind and there's no penalty.

Ro: Ralph, how do you put your prison experiences in the context of your whole life?

Ralph: You know, everything that happened to me is my life, including the prisons. It's what I wanted, and I feel satisfied with it, that I was able to carry out what I believed in. I tell people to just go as far as you can. Push your own limits and keep going and continue to stand up for nonviolence. Anybody can do what I did, going step by step as far as they can, to make this a better world and make nonviolence a way of life. If something is important to you, take the chance and stand up for it.

On October 16, 1940, the first day of registration under a new draft law, eight young men announced that they would refuse to register. They were William N. Lovell, Richard J. Wichlei, Meredith Dallas, David Dellinger, Joseph Bevilacqua, George M. Houser, Donald Benedict, and Howard E. Spragg.[7] All were students at Union Theological Seminary in Manhattan and they would have received a ministerial exemption. But as pacifists, they refused anyway, and served a year in Danbury for their stand. I was able to interview Bill Lovell and Don Benedict. Meredith Dallas is represented here by an interview with his son which I combined with an older interview by C. Arthur Bradley.

All three made different life choices: Meredith and Don refused a second time and were sent back to prison, but finally Don decided "Hitler had to go" and joined the war effort. Bill completed seminary

7. Left to right in photo on p. 36.

in Chicago after serving his prison term. Meredith left the ministry and went into theater in Yellow Springs, Ohio; Bill and Don worked together for the church for their entire long lives.

Bill Lovell (1915–2008)

Bill Lovell was born in China of missionary parents, graduated from Yale in 1936, and began seminary at Union Theological School in 1938 after working at a small machine shop and becoming interested in trade unions.

Bill: I'd like to start by paraphrasing something I wrote recently. I have come to realize that my Christian pacifism has different roots than those we expressed in 1940. Then we seemed to believe that if [enough] people committed themselves to nonviolence, the country would not go to war.

We didn't have an answer to Hitler. Even though we disagreed with Hitler and with the persecution of the Jews, we didn't have an answer to that crisis. You see, every crisis has some kind of a beginning. For instance what happened in Germany was built up after the First World War, when Germany was so persecuted by the economic settlements. Today's crisis in the Middle East goes back to Britain's empire-building of years ago. Since [my World War II days], I've come to see that one who calls himself a Christian pacifist realizes that he or she cannot be responsible for an adequate solution to every crisis and must finally agree—or decide—that he or she has failed. But you still go on and witness to love as the final purpose of God, over and against any evils of the time.

Love is the purpose of God in the final analysis. You fail in any particular moment in witness to that purpose, but you just keep on going. Why? In recognition that it was that kind of love for which Jesus died. And that kind of love for which all of us ought to be willing to die if the time comes. As a socialist and a pacifist, I will continue to be active politically; as a Christian pacifist, if it comes to "up against the wall," then I'll have to go to jail again.

[Long pause.] Back then, at Union Seminary in Manhattan, there was a group of us. George Houser and Dave Dellinger and I were the only ones at first. We were in a Socialist-Pacifist cell at the school and we prayed and talked together, and it was from that group that we decided—some of us decided—not to register. When my mother was asked why I made this decision, she said, "Well, that's what he's been taught all his life." My father was a member of the FOR from way back before I was born.

Ro: Why do people like your parents hear the pacifist message of Jesus and not everyone?

Bill: That's a good question. Even today, I don't know the answer. So many people don't have the same conception of Jesus's ministry as I have. Ministers and chaplains . . . some of them I don't agree with at all, don't agree with what they think is important. Back then we differed a lot, too. After our time in Danbury, for instance, some of us transferred to Chicago Theological Seminary where the president himself was a pacifist. Albert Palmer. Three of the group didn't go back to seminary at that time but did a community ministry in Newark, New Jersey. Meredith Dallas, Don Benedict, and Dave Dellinger, and they all served second terms in prison for refusing to carry registration cards. We didn't carry them either, but they didn't arrest the ones [at the seminary in Chicago].

[Before the war], the antiwar movement was very strong. Norman Thomas was held in high regard, and the United States didn't get into the war until a couple of [months] after our arrest. (In fact, we were out of jail before Pearl Harbor occurred.) People forget that the country was divided at the beginning, with many opposing the war. Of course, President Franklin Delano Roosevelt called the country to war with a very strong voice.

Union 8 Get Prison Terms, 1940. © Bettmann/Corbis via AP Images.

Ro: "Everyone is a pacifist in peacetime," as they say. So you wrote your statement and distributed it to the newspapers as well as to other schools. And then what happened?

Bill: Well, we got a great deal of mail, some supporting us and some disagreeing with us. I think we were among the first COs, so we got quite a deal of publicity, and we weren't prepared for that. The trustees of the seminary didn't like it at all.

We expected to be arrested and we were. They picked us up in the administration hall where all the seminarians were supposed to register. Our attorney, Michael Walser, wanted us to plead not guilty, but we refused and the judge sentenced us to a year and a day, although we only served about eleven months.

We were friends with most of the inmates [at Danbury], but after awhile some of the newer inmates turned against us, because the country was getting caught up in war fever. The long-termers protected us, though, and they knew that we were Socialists and in favor of working people. Once in awhile we'd protest something and be put in solitary, but it wasn't really that difficult. We sang a great deal and I remember we fasted for a few days until they gave us Bibles.

Ro: Now, you've kept in touch with your coresisters, but did you keep in touch with any of the other prisoners after you were released?

Bill: No, I didn't. I happened to see one of them in later years, though. He was a busboy on one of the trains coming from Chicago to New York. I recognized him, he recognized me, and we didn't say anything. But he never brought me a bill. [Laughs.] Now the guys who went to Newark, in the ashram there, they *did* stay in touch, and some of the inmates would stay with them when they came out.

After Bill finished seminary in Chicago, he worked with Don Benedict in Detroit, organizing a community ministry as well as serving as secretary for the FOR in Michigan. Then he joined Howard Spragg as co-pastor of South Congregational Church, which was among the first interracial churches in the country. Other ministries included campus work at the University of Chicago and nineteen years at the National Council of Churches. When the family moved back to Chicago in 1981, he helped to found the North Suburban Peace Initiative. When we met, he was living in a retirement community but still preaching occasionally and excited about his work with Don Benedict in beginning Protestants for the Common Good. The two old friends founded this organization to counter the increasing right-wing fundamentalism of the mainline churches; it continues under new leadership.

Meredith Dallas (1916–2010)

Meredith Dallas, or "Dal," was born in Detroit and graduated from Albion College before entering Union Seminary in New York. During the

summer before his imprisonment, he joined fellow resisters David Dellinger and Donald Benedict in an intentional community in Newark, New Jersey. After his first term, he returned to this ashram, as they called it, but was rearrested and sent to prisons in the South. After he was released for good in 1945, he and his wife Willa moved to the college town of Yellow Springs where he made theater his life work. As his 2010 obituary said, Dal "found his church in the Antioch Area Theater."[8]

Meredith Dallas, 2009.
© Tony Dallas.

Dal: I was shaping up to be the fair-haired boy, the minister-to-be, but I didn't have the money for college, so I worked for a year before getting a scholarship to Albion. Worked with the Michigan Youth Congress, which I later realized was a Communist front kind of affair. The Communist Party was coming in fairly strong at that time in America. Organized labor. The Scottsboro trial. I had gotten involved in this kind of thing mainly through the Church, and I was serious about it. There was hopefulness for a new society and I liked partaking of that, but I felt a great discomfort with these Communists. They

8. About two-thirds of this narrative is from an interview recorded by Dallas's son Tony and transcribed by the author in 2007. The remaining third is used by permission from a 1988 interview by C. Arthur Bradley titled, "Meredith and Willa Dallas Memoir." Archives/Special Collections, Norris L. Brookens Library, University of Illinois at Springfield, IL. Some of the same words occur in both interviews.

just didn't . . . I didn't believe them, you know. [They] also worked for peace and antiracial stuff. I remember chanting "Black and white, unite and fight" around a hotel.

Then I started at Albion. I liked college a lot, liked studying. And I began doing some acting and discovered I liked that, too, and was pretty good at it. I was making orations—orations on peace—and I remember I won some money at a state contest because I could really ring a bell. I was a serious young man, though, and in the plays I took the parts of serious young men. But at that time, I didn't have any idea of going into theater; I was in philosophy and speech, in preparation for preaching as a minister. I used to go out on Sundays and preach at some of the rural churches. It seemed all external, kind of putting on a show.

Tony: Did you feel you had an appetite for glory, maybe more than other people?

Dal: Um . . . I was aware of a kind of showiness, a phoniness . . . Looking back on that . . . that young man, his pretense was maybe stimulated by a good voice and a good mind and a great talent for speaking. [Long silence.]

Then I went to Union Seminary. I think I got a scholarship or something. It was stimulating to be in Manhattan, but I didn't really enjoy the seminary. You know, I was from a working background, and I didn't feel easy with that total intellectual aristocracy. But I met Dave Dellinger and Donald Benedict there and soon the three of us moved to Harlem. David was kind of the prime mover with us, and we found we were of similar minds. What we were seeking, or what we felt, was a more primitive Christianity. Something beyond the ideas, the intellectual thing. We were not terribly enamored of the Church.

We'd take people into the house from the "jungle." We didn't call it a Catholic Worker house but it had that quality. We moved to Newark that summer, and other people joined us, including Willa [Winter, who became my wife]. Then in the fall we commuted back to Union, but by that time we were into the whole draft thing. Classwork . . . it just went by the board and our main focus was responding to the draft.

In terms of Christian ministry, it was important to be a conscientious objector, and I'd been saying that, you know, all through college. At that time it was in terms of beliefs; I'm aware now that [we] were human beings struggling with all [these issues] at the time.

And still are in many ways. I'm also aware that more often I put my power in terms of *not* doing things, into objecting or stopping. Later on, after being imprisoned, I got really tired of that conscientious objector stance and wanted to get rid of it and join the world.

We didn't register and we were arrested and arraigned, and I think there was a grand jury hearing. It was all done politely, in a way. It was terribly . . . uh, proper. Moral and upright and proper. The seminary was totally negative to it, though. When we took our stand, we became kind of outlaws.

It was a nationwide case—these bright Union ministerial students. I didn't like to have people [following] us in the street when we were going up to the trial. Didn't like the cameras and the pictures in the newspapers and all that jazz. My parents were nonplussed. It was hard, I think, for them to reach out to understand it and there wasn't a great deal of communication. But when the time came, they did support me.

People were very helpful. A. J. Muste, for instance, was with us all the way.[9] He was very perceptive and gentle. Always I remember his warmth and understanding and wisdom. He was used to conflict and that was helpful to us. We had planning sessions about the trial. A lot of rhubarb in it. Anything against the right establishment, we had a little piece of that.

We were making a stand only, because as ministerial students, we wouldn't have been drafted anyway. I'm not sure I would have done that on my own. I never felt that I was personally terribly brave or courageous, so I doubt whether on my own I'd have gotten into any of [it.] I'm not sure.

We talked at churches and organizations. I remember preaching at Abyssinan Baptist Church, where Adam Clayton Powell was. Well, I didn't really preach; I just kind of said some things in the service. I was up there in the pulpit and I got that wave of energy from the congregation, [the energy] that happens in a Black church. It was really something. But [the trial] was really quite simple.

Tony: So do you think you won in a sense?

Dal: A moral victory! [Chuckles wryly.] I'm sure we must have said that.

9. A. J. Muste graduated from Union and was a lifelong leader in the nonviolent movement for social change. Over the years, he worked with a wide array of organizations, including the FOR, the Congress of Racial Equality (CORE), and the WRL. See online: www.ajmuste.org/ajmbio.htm.

Tony: How did you feel then?

Dal: Uh . . . Kind of a whole combination of things. Felt terribly righteous but also afraid and wondering, along with being brave just at that moment. There was kind of a solid resistant core to me, resistant rather than active. I'm pretty sure I would not have recanted, even if we were to be shot, which was one of the options at one point. They actually thought that we'd be charged with treason, which was a capital offense. You see, ours was the first opposition to conscription, so there wasn't any precedent, and the government and the militarists were really after us.

The trial and sentencing were kind of all arranged. When they read the sentence, they said if we agreed to register, they'd reduce our sentence. The judge was very courteous and sympathetic, and, I think, very moved by the whole thing, and he gave us the lightest sentence [he could.]

Willa and I were married right before I went to prison. [We were] all under a lot of pressure. I think the whole world was under a lot of pressure then, because of the war. At the time, I felt that the persecution of the Jews and Hitler's extraordinary nature grew out of the reprisals by the Allies after the first World War. I feel mixed about that now; if I hadn't had the Union connection, I think I might have gone into the ambulance service or something like that. Where I would have been helping but not part of the killing. I couldn't have done that.

After we were sentenced, we were taken to West Street and there were all sorts of rumors that we'd be sent to Leavenworth, or to a federal mental hospital prison. But then the warden came [to get us] from Danbury, Connecticut. He wanted us to be on "his side," in the prison, but when it became clear to him that we were throwing in our lot with the rest of the prisoners and not becoming his henchmen, he turned on us. He was a dangerous man in the sense of being vain and . . . at times he acted swishy. Some of the men called him "La Paloma," the little pigeon.

[When I got to Danbury], I had a sense of the newness of the building, the smell of new plaster and cement. My prison number was 298, which shows you how new it was. On the ride up, [the warden] was talking about how innovative it was, that it would be different [from other prisons]—with no walls and so on. Well, there wasn't any wall because we lived *in* the wall! The prison was four sides around an open yard with no access to the outside except a front and back gate. So there was that kind of double talk.

To give you another example, there'd be a shakedown every couple of weeks. The guard would come in and turn everything upside down, mattress and all. They'd confiscate stuff that you weren't supposed to have. Like, the guys would steal pieces of wood and make boxes. Crosses were popular, too. They'd burn matches and use the burnt ends to make designs on the wood. These items were confiscated in the shakedown, and then one day when I was up front, I found that they were up on exhibit as inmates' handiwork.

The food was always good and there was plenty of it. Eggs or cereal or pancakes for breakfast. A lot of pork steak [at dinner.] It didn't matter how good the food was or how many movies you saw or how many entertainments we could do, we were still not free.

I even did a show. "FCI Utopia."[10] I think I played the warden. A guy named Butcher wrote the play, and he was into Gilbert and Sullivan. [Sings a brief Gilbert and Sullivan take-off.] I guess the warden thought at first it was some kind of occupational therapy, but the show had a short run because they found out what we were satirizing.

Oh, our best story! Don Benedict was a real good softball pitcher. When we were at the seminary, I'd go to Central Park with him and play first base. And oh, my God! He was a fantastic pitcher! Really! The prison had a baseball team and of course he pitched. There was a big game coming up, and we'd been put in solitary for something or other, and the warden wanted to let him out so he could pitch. Benedict said, "Oh, no." Not until they let us all out. So they did!

We were marched into the mess hall after everybody was seated. And all the fellows started cheering and banging their cups on the table. You should have heard it! The warden got real red in the face and phst . . . he left!

But anyway, we got out after awhile. There was "good time," so we didn't have to be there for the whole year and a day. It was great to get out, just wonderful! I remember we went up to the farm then. Willa and the other women were already there. The FBI was always floating around. It got so we could spot them anywhere, with their gabardine suits. Finally they raided the farm early one morning, before anyone was awake. I don't know why [they did it that way] because we were always open and sending them everything.

10. FCI stands for Federal Correctional Institution, one of several acronyms in use by the Bureau of Prisons (BOP) for the various kinds of prisons in the system.

See, somehow they'd registered for us when we left [prison] and when David and my names came up to be drafted, about a year and a half later, we refused and were sentenced a second time.

The second sentence was three years, but I only served two or something like that. On my way to prison in Ashland, Kentucky, I'd stay overnight at county jails. I remember one somewhere in West Virginia. A fierce place! The women prisoners were upstairs and the men were downstairs. They had dry toilets—no running water, just pipes. And the toilets were their intercom system. Picture these guys with their heads in the toilet on the first floor, hollering obscenities to the women upstairs. And the women also had their heads in the toilet and would holler obscenities back down. Unbelievable!

Dellinger was already at Lewisburg this second time and they had all started a hunger protest against censorship of the mail [in prison.] So I joined that hunger strike and stayed on it until my bellybutton began to stick out. I was on kitchen detail and after awhile I just got hungry and began tasting things and . . . and I got an . . . uh, an overwhelming feeling that I wanted to quit objecting. Wanted to join the human race. The hunger strike didn't end censorship, by the way. The system was pretty entrenched.

From then on, I kind of earned my way out. I began studying medicine very seriously. Got books and worked in the hospital as an outpatient nurse. It was a busy place and the doctor there was a good person. I worked in the pharmacy and learned all about X-ray and thought I'd do medicine when I got out.

Then I was asked if I wanted to be in charge of a clinic in a new federal prison camp for juvenile prisoners. It was housed in an old CCC camp in Natural Bridge, Virginia. I was treated like a member of the staff and that surprised me. I had a whole lab, with a microscope for slides, plus a full clinic. I was there about six months, and they gave me everything I asked for. I learned a helleva lot. It was a wonderful and rewarding experience. I diagnosed an appendix and got the kid in time. Treated lots of stuff for these young boys. Had my own room right there at the back of the clinic. Willa and I could make out when she came down to visit.

But it was wonderful to get out. So marvelous! I went in the first time in 1941 and got out for good in '45. But even then I was on parole so I was restricted as to how much money I could make—only $1200 a year or something like that. But anyway, I gave up the idea of medicine and decided to go into the theater. I was tired of service-oriented stuff and the ministry had long since paled, and I was enjoying the theater.

Got a scholarship to Case Western and moved to Cleveland. Finally convinced Willa to move up there with me for support because I really . . . I had begun to feel unhinged. Like I was going to fall apart. I was just terribly anxious. I'd left that whole ministerial set and the prison thing and then coming out and wanting to fit in and making the move to doing something that I wanted to do. I . . . I guess it was the classic confrontation between theater and church. I'd become unmoored from a whole bunch of things that had given me some purpose or centering in my life. So it was kind of a harrowing time for awhile. Willa being there gave me support so I could eventually work it out.

In 1949, Meredith was appointed to the faculty of Antioch College in Ohio and became the central figure for theater and drama in Yellow Springs for many years. Before retiring, he had played many of the greatest Shakespearean roles: King Henry, Hamlet, Marc Antony, and others. He passed away in the fall of 2010, and I am saddened that I never met him, particularly as his sister Mickey Dallas Kammer was one of my best friends during the time my children were growing up.

In 2007, when he sent me the tapes of his interview with his father, Tony Dallas wrote: "Dad's time in prison and the magnitude of horrors perpetuated by the Germans in World War II have not made the decision sit easy on his conscience. He is at his core a principled man, guided by his own moral compass. [In 2005] he told me that he was pleased with the major decisions he had made in his life—which specifically included going to prison—for he realized these decisions were made from a clear sense of moral purpose, not in capitulation to a bandwagon movement, but on his own."

Don Benedict (1917–2008)

I interviewed Don Benedict, the pitcher Meredith Dallas talks about, in August of 2007. He also grew up near Detroit, graduated from Albion College, and went to Union Seminary.

Don: When we seminarians moved to Harlem, some people thought we were trying to make a big splash. We were afraid that the seminary was going to kick us out, but they didn't, and we kept our scholarships, too. We even got a group of professors to come down for a meeting, which was quite a feat. We were down on Eighth Avenue and it was a pretty rough place. We had trouble getting an apartment because [the landlord] thought we were setting up a whorehouse. [Laughs lightly.] But we finally got it, and we kept picking up people off the street. Took 'em home and cleaned them up and so forth. A couple of guys took all our typewriters one day.

Ro: So you had a kind of hospitality house and even more chance to talk about your pacifism. When did you decide you weren't going to register?

Don: When the draft law came along. We had a lot of meetings in the seminary before we decided not to go. Twenty-two guys signed the original document because we felt we shouldn't be privileged because of our occupation. But then all but eight of us pulled out when they saw that it was going to mean breaking a federal law.

So we were arrested and tried and sentenced, and then we went first to West Street, in New York City. Actually, we had a great time at West Street, when we could get together. But I and another guy were tapped by the prison officials to clean out the drug chamber. A whole lot of Chinese guys had been picked up on drug charges and, you know, they crapped all over the place. Our first job was to clean that up. We later learned they were trying to fix it so we'd say we wanted out.

I remember the dining area at West Street was segregated, and Dave Dellinger broke the line and walked right into the Black chamber, so he got put away in solitary. Later on we protested the same thing in Danbury.

Ro: Don, I've heard you were a pretty good softball pitcher.

Don: Well, I'd pitched a lot in college and I had gotten pretty good at it. And that's a story! At Danbury, on the second Saturday we were there, a team from Danbury came in to play the prison team. That day I struck out nineteen out of twenty-one or something like that.

The warden, of course, was pushing the softball and everyone was excited about a second game scheduled a week later. Well, in the meantime, we'd gone on strike. Refused to work on International Student Peace Day. They put us all up in a separate building but

45

before that, the warden got the whole prison out to the courtyard and made a speech about how we were really striking against our beloved president, Franklin Delano Roosevelt.

He said, "I want you men to know this, and you take care of it." In other words, he was asking them to give us the business in the yard. But one of the prisoners yelled out: "Warden, we've heard your side of the story. Let's hear theirs."

The warden said, "Into the mess hall!" Broke it up. [Laughs.]

So we're in solitary and the ball game is the next day, and of course I wasn't there. Now this warden was very unhappy because the prisoners kept yelling for me. Finally he gave in, and came to get me out to come and pitch. But I said to the other guys, "I'm not going to go out and have you still in here." So I didn't go, and I guess they lost the game.

The next week, when game time came, the guys started to yell again for me to come out and pitch. The warden came to get me and I told him the same thing again. Well! About five minutes later, all the doors opened and the guards yelled "Ball game!" So we all got out and I went out and pitched.

After I got out, I was arrested a second time. Dave Dellinger and Meredith and I hadn't gone back to seminary but were living together in a kind of ashram in Newark. See, I was really taken by people like Gandhi and Nehru. What I had in mind, I guess, at least in those early days, was a lay movement among the workers. Without the benefits of church buildings and so forth. We shared all our money and took a dollar a day or something. I was married by then and we all lived together and worked. (When I got out of jail the second time, she'd made another choice, so I got a divorce, and that was the end of that.)

Ro: Where were you when you were arrested the second time?

Don: I had moved out to Detroit with my wife, and we had started another ashram there with Bill Lovell. I worked as a Youth Minister in a big Methodist church and we had this house on Alexander Street. It was a stopping off place for all the radicals from around the country. We had eight or ten people living in this place and we had a storefront and had dances.

During the race riots . . . I'll never forget this! Whites were running around carrying big table legs and trying to kill any Blacks they saw. And people were hiding Blacks in the streetcars to keep them from being killed. It was rough! Finally, the National Guard came right up our street with their machine guns.

After the second arrest, I got three years and was sent back to Danbury. There was a great hurrah there, knowing that I was coming back to pitch. But I finally decided Hitler had to go. I'd been put in solitary because I'd gone on strike [in support of] the United Mine Workers, and it was while I was in solitary that I finally decided. They let me out and I enlisted and went to Texas for basic training and got into the Air Corps. I was on my way to Iwo Jima, when the bomb was dropped on Japan.

Ro: What did your fellow resisters think about your changing your mind after being arrested twice for draft resistance?

Don: The other guys were really very good about it, and that always impressed me. We've all remained good friends. I used to visit Dave Dellinger every summer in Vermont, and I always had very good relations with all of them, even though I'm not a pacifist like they are. I've come to feel that there are times when men kind of force things to happen. Even if it's wrong. Because I . . . well, that's the best way I can explain it.

I think Christian pacifism is right for those who feel that it's right. On the other hand, I think that it's possible that you have to make judgments sometimes within political reality, and there are times when force has to be used. I sympathize with pacifists, certainly, and understand them, but I am too much a person that has to be involved politically, I guess.

Despite these theological differences with Bill Lovell, Don worked closely with him and other members of the Union Eight for his entire life. After he left the service, he returned to seminary and graduated. Then he and others started storefront churches, first in Harlem and then in Cleveland, before moving to Chicago where he directed the City Missionary Society for twenty-two years. Even after retirement he continued to work to eliminate racism and counter the drumbeat of violence, especially with the founding of Protestants for the Common Good.

These four World War II resisters continued, each in their own way, to urge their country toward the ideals they stood up for as lonely pacifists in the '40s. All four have died since I interviewed them, so I am grateful their brave stories have been recorded. In June of 2012, George Houser of Santa Rosa, California, was the only living member of the Union Eight.

2

The Fifties—America the Beautiful

After World War II ended, people wanted to forget about war and its causes, reap the fruits of prosperity, and tend to their individual lives. So we have the decade of the '50s, remembered as quiet and peaceful, despite the increasing chill of the Cold War. Most people wanted to believe in the goodness of America and the rightness of our government's actions. But the testing of the hydrogen bomb began to awaken the peace movement, and when New York State made it a misdemeanor to fail to take cover during the nationwide civil defense drills, some people said "No!" and stayed in the sunlight. Tom Cornell, Karl Meyer, Judith Malina, and David McReynolds tell the story.[1]

Tom Cornell

Tom: It all started then, all the direct action that has made so much difference. The Eisenhower administration had sent all the homeowners in the United States a little yellow pamphlet saying, "Build a fallout shelter. In the unexpected event that our government's efforts to prevent nuclear attack prove unsuccessful and there is a war, if you don't have a shelter, rip your front door off and put it on the side of your house, heap up some earth and get under it and stay there for two weeks." It was ludicrous beyond belief.

---

1. All four stories in this chapter are from interviews recorded for my first two oral histories and available in the Marquette Archives. Meyer's and Malina's are printed in a longer form in Chapter 2 of *Dorothy Day: Portraits by Those Who Knew Her*, 51–57. The first paragraph of Cornell's appears on page 33 of *Voices* and a longer version of Malina's on pages 81–86.

I was still in college when the first civil defense protest happened, driving some kids down to the Catholic Worker on Chrystie Street. We heard on the car radio that some Catholic Workers and others had been arrested in City Hall Park. When we got down to the Worker, people were calling from all over the place. "Yes, Bishop, Dorothy [Day] is in jail."

It was Ammon [Hennacy's] idea, and Dorothy said, "Sounds good. We'll all sit in the park when the rest of New York goes underground." It happened with just that kind of casualness. It turned out to be a big deal. Really mushroomed after a few years, mostly due to Dave McReynolds' efforts.

Karl Meyer

Karl Meyer was also one of those arrested in these protests. He was nineteen and already a pacifist. Had dropped out of the University of Chicago and was working at Barnes and Noble in New York.

Karl: I had read in *The Catholic Worker* where Dorothy and Ammon Hennacy and a few others had refused to take shelter during the compulsory air raid drills, and I decided at the last minute to join them. I was afraid I'd be late, so I hailed a cab. "Step on it, buddy!"

Got down to Chrystie Street and walked upstairs at the Catholic Worker. Dorothy and Ammon were there, and some others, including Judith Malina and Julian Beck, the anarchists of the Living Theater. About a dozen people. Everybody was just sitting around talking, preparing to go out at the appointed time and sit on the park benches. As I recall, Dorothy was even knitting. It was that kind of a gathering. Both Dorothy and Ammon were tremendous warm conversationalists. I introduced myself and said I'd like to join them.

Dorothy said to me, "Well, that's fine. But there's a couple things you should know. One is we plead guilty and two, we don't take bail." (They didn't want to get involved in the legal process, just wanted to do civil disobedience.) "Now, you don't have to do it that way. But if you go with our group, we prefer that you do."

Right then, I would say, I crossed over from being a careful moderate to becoming a radical. I said I'd go along with it. Dorothy didn't ask me my age or anything. There was just that acceptance: you were a responsible person and you had made your choice.

Civil Defense Drill Protest, 1956. © Robert Lax.

So I went out and sat with them on the bench, and we were arrested. That night I slept on the floor of the cell with Ammon and Julian Beck. All night long I was being prepared for jail by Ammon, whose prison record went way back to being a nonregistrant in World War I. He was very relaxed, not afraid at all, so that certainly gave me confidence. I can't remember the details of the conversation, but I know he talked about realities, talked about relationships with people. He touched on the subject of homosexuality and threats of rape and so on, which are the things that maybe scare men most about going into prison.

Ro: So he communicated fearlessness to your nineteen-year-old self.

Karl: Yeah. But I wasn't a fearful person to begin with. I grew up in the country and in a family that wasn't fearful, so we weren't always being cautioned about everything. When we went to court, we pleaded guilty, and got thirty days in jail. I was the only juvenile in the group, so I was sent to Rikers Island, away from the rest, and I guess Dorothy and Ammon worried about me that whole thirty days. She knew that jails can be very rough places for people who aren't equipped to deal with them.

Ro: Can you remember anything specific about this first time in jail?

Karl: Well, I do remember one incident. In jails, the common bathroom is open, so the guards can monitor what's going on. I was sitting on the toilet one day, and two or three young men came into the bathroom. They sat on the other toilets around me, and they began to fence around about my sexuality and the possibility that I might be a homosexual. What sticks in my mind is that at one point a guy said to me, "At Green Haven, it would be shit on your dick or blood on my razor."[2]

I just sort of said, "Well, it's good that I'm not at Green Haven, isn't it?" I wasn't afraid, but there I was, sitting on the toilet with three or four guys around me. Nothing happened that time or later, and I was fine in prison. When I got out, I immediately went down to the Catholic Worker, and from that time on, I was in with Dorothy and Ammon.

Actress Judith Malina was imprisoned with Dorothy Day for her participation in the protests. Her memories were given to me in 1987. In 2012 she was still proclaiming pacifist ideals in her play "History of the World," performed by the Living Theatre she and Julian Beck cofounded.

Judith Malina

Judith: The air raid drills were setting up a kind of warlike, fearful ambience. Creating an attitude of fear and preparedness for the worst. I think we were right to protest it. I was a little worried when I got to City Hall Park because a CBS camera was there, and here I was handing out *Catholic Workers*, and I thought my good Jewish mother might be a little shocked. Not at seeing her daughter protest against the war mentality, because she knew my pacifism, but wondering about my religious affiliation in associating myself with the Catholic Workers.

I have since had reason to be very proud to associate myself with them. I certainly feel a very deep affinity to Christianity on the level on which they practice it, even a religious and theological affinity as it seems very close to what I believe in as a Jew. At that [civil defense protest], I remember Bayard Rustin taking us up to the War Resisters League and explaining that we had to hold placards because otherwise the newspapers could write anything at all underneath our

2. Green Haven was a state detention center for young men.

picture. He told us where to sit when the sirens went off and gave us some ground rules about what to do, which was good as this was my first arrest.

It was a long trial, and I don't remember the various permutations of pleading guilty or pleading not guilty. And in what sense of the word "guilt" is one guilty? The Twentieth Century Fund wanted to extend the power of their vast resources, so lawyers insisted that we plead not guilty.

Dorothy said "No! We did exactly that which was against the law." And of course we were not guilty in the deeper sense of guilt, but we broke the law when we didn't take shelter. Only Dorothy's strength against all these lawyers held us firm in our guilty plea.

Ro: I remember hearing about a scene in the courtroom when you and the judge were not . . . Uh, you didn't see eye-to-eye, perhaps.

Judith: It wasn't that, certainly. Judges don't have to see eye-to-eye with defendants. In a courtroom, people are trapped into a very humiliating form of behavior. Always. Anyone. In any court. Because you can't even speak unless a certain person says you can. A certain type of order is kept, and it's very destructive to the psyche and to the dignity of the human being. And I think you trivialize it by telling it as a funny story.

What happened is that the judge said Ammon's name wrong, said "Ammon Henakky" instead of "Ammon Hennacy" and some of our people laughed at his mispronunciation.

He said, "What are the people laughing at?"

And I piped up, without permission to speak. I said, "Well, you see, we haven't eaten all day because you're holding us here. And that makes people giddy."

The judge said, "Miss Malina, have you ever been in a mental institution?"

I said, "No. Have you?"

"Thirty days in Bellevue for psychiatric observation!" [Judith bangs once on a nearby table, as if a gavel is coming down.] Because of my impertinent question, he immediately questioned my sanity. I had done nothing outside of being a little bold, you know. A little disrespectful, maybe.

Then all hell broke loose. Absolute hell! The Catholic Worker people were there in the courtroom, and the War Resisters League, and people from the Ford Foundation, and a lot of people from different newspapers. There was a huge uproar, and I was carried out. But the point of that story has to be the humiliation, not the humor.

After the sentencing, when we got to the House of Detention, we were strip searched like everyone else. It was extremely humiliating, but I have a tough skin. But Dorothy . . . Dorothy had been chaste for many, many years. When a chaste woman is poked like that and subjected to really thoughtless handling in which someone searches the inside of her body, without any consideration for the dignity of the person they're searching . . . When it happened, I was standing in the outer part of the office and I heard her cry out in pain.

Dorothy and I shared a cell. She was reading Tolstoy at the time, reading a story called "God Sees the Truth but Waits." In political activism, there's a seeming contradiction between the activists who take the step, make the decision, and those who possess a certain quietism of allowing God to do the work. Of stepping aside and looking at the suffering and saying, "Where I can, I will prevent it. On the other hand, this is the way of the world."

Here we come to the contradiction between activism and holiness and activism and anarchism. Anarchism is activist. Dorothy walked out on the street to make that protest in order to make what anyone would call trouble. That is, she wanted people to notice the contradiction, so she sat out in the street in the sunlight, saying, "I'm not going to fall into a hole because I'm afraid my fellow man is going to kill me. I'm not going to support that structure."

This is an active decision, challenging the whole society. And also a tension-building decision. Everyone went underground, but Dorothy said, "I will not go." A very strong act of will, an act of will in which she contradicts what everybody wants her to do, including the Church. All the Church people went underground, and she wasn't doing what the Church was suggesting in this instance. On the other hand, she wasn't doing what the Church was not suggesting. She wanted to inspire the Church to take a more strongly pacifist position and worked very hard to do that, all the time managing very skillfully to stay out of direct conflict with it.

It was a great privilege and marvel to be secluded with a woman like that, to come close to such a soul. A beautiful experience. But a contradiction, too, because the jail was also the most horrible place I'd ever been in. Surrounded with . . . with ugliness. Architectural ugliness and more. Whole layers of suffering and misery. So it was incredible to be exposed, at the same time, to both the highest that the human spirit is capable of and the most incredible expressions of suffering.

Judith Malina imprisoned in Brazil, 1971.
© Collection of Judith Malina.

Dorothy became very quickly a legend in the prison. There was a lot of press and a picket line outside. Most of the guards were Catholic, and they'd come to her to have their Bibles blessed and their rosaries kissed. Priests came on pilgrimage. And the wealthy. She was always sort of annoyed about this, at how people were outwardly . . . but then I'm sure she was absolutely heavenly when she confronted them, because she responded to any human being. She responded the same way to these terrified, struggling, suffering women in jail, these women who couldn't speak without uttering the Oedipal adjective.

There was such fear there. Most of the women were in that wheel of repeated suffering. Like their mothers and their grandmothers and their great grandmothers, all without really steady men in the family, a succession of women falling back into prostitution or drugs, going through the same suffering and misery. And feeling really indicted by fate. Angry and victimized. Angry and struggling. Somehow Dorothy managed to bring a certain light.

My relationship with Dorothy for those thirty days was very girlish. We talked a lot about sexuality and woman's life. We talked about children, all those things. Very deeply . . . very deeply. But we were also determined to have fun. In spite of the tragedy around us. In spite of the seriousness of our cause. Certainly, either of us was willing to break into highly serious rhetoric at any moment. But Dorothy had a certain spirit of joyousness. After lights out, she would first read me something from the *Lives of the Saints*, and I would read something from our [Jewish] liturgy, and we'd talk about holy things. Then after awhile, we'd start telling funny stories and laughing a lot, too. It was wonderful that we had both.

As Tom Cornell said, it was David McReynolds who took the civil defense witness from a protest to a successful campaign.

David McReynolds

David McReynolds: Dorothy Day's impact, her existential/religious position, was what moved a "political" person like me to turn a witness into a mass protest. Every year from 1955 to 1959, Dorothy was jailed for her refusal to take shelter. She would just sit at her ease on a park bench near City Hall and wait for the State to arrive.

I was in Los Angeles in 1955 when we got the news. My response at that time was that it was crazy, typical of the "marginal edge" of the pacifist movement, et cetera. I felt that the ordinary guy in the street would never understand people getting arrested for refusing to take shelter.

A year later, I arrived in New York for my life as a professional radical bureaucrat and joined the straggly line that walked up and down outside the Women's House of Detention where Dorothy and Judith Malina and the other women protesters were imprisoned.

I remember how once a priest came, chatted with the two cops on duty, joined the line itself for a couple of turns, and then went inside to visit Dorothy. It was funny how the police changed their attitude, once the priest had given our line a kind of "blessing from Rome." But those were not popular years for the peace movement.

At first, it didn't occur to me to join Dorothy. Yet each year I grew more disturbed that a good woman whose work was not insurrection, but simply the feeding of the hungry and the housing of the homeless, was inside this huge concrete structure (now long since torn down) in the center of Greenwich Village, prevented from practicing her most innocent of vocations.

Finally, in 1959, I asked Ammon Hennacy if he felt the Catholic Workers would mind if a Socialist joined their protest. He said,

"The more the merrier." So in 1959 I joined Dorothy, Ammon, and the handful of others and was arrested. I only stayed one night in jail, since I had no record in New York. Dorothy, as I recall, got ten days. The climate seemed to be changing, with new people joining the protest. So in 1960, with the advice of Bayard Rustin, I formulated a strategy and wrote leaflets that said something along these lines:

> If you think the Civil Defense program is crazy, but do not believe in breaking the law, come to City Hall Park when this year's Civil Defense drill is held, and when the sirens sound, leave the Park. You will not have broken any law, but by being there will have shown your opposition to this program of alleged "Civil Defense." If you do believe in civil disobedience, but can't afford to be arrested for whatever reason—a sick child at home, a job you can't afford to lose, cowardice, a wife who would be worried to death if you got arrested—stay in the park after the sirens have sounded and leave when the police arrive and give the order to leave. We will not feel you have abandoned us; we will feel supported because you stayed as long as you could. And if you feel that this is your year, that you are prepared for arrest and a jail term that might be as long as one year, then stay with us and join us in arrest.

Three levels and no moral judgments. On the appointed day, close to a thousand gathered in City Hall Park. When the sirens sounded, no one moved. Those who had planned to leave when the sirens went off just looked around, saw how many were there, and decided to stay, too.

When the police arrived and warned people to disperse, some did retreat, but not to shelters, just to the corners of the Park. There were still 500 people in the Park when the police warned that they would be arrested. The response—totally unrehearsed—was a wave of applause.

The police moved back and forth through the crowd, warning and threatening, and then the crowd began to sing "America the Beautiful" and "God Bless America." Again, totally without any plan. The police finally arrested something like twenty-six people, maybe including Dorothy, but I'm not sure. Then they left. I climbed a park bench and said, "We've won!"

Not quite. The next year, in 1961, the political organizers had taken over. Finally! We used the same strategy. Two thousand people turned up, and only those of us who organized it were arrested, I think a total of about fifty-two. We served twenty-five days in jail. That was the last year of the drills. With Dorothy's inspiration, and the political tactics of the radical organizers, the drills were beaten and the government defeated.

An Interlude

"War and Prisons: A Time for Abolition"

John Schuchardt

From my experience as a veteran, then as a criminal defense attorney, and then for two years as a prisoner, I have come to conclude that prisons are a Weapon of Mass Destruction, destroying literally millions of lives in prison and damaging millions more of family members . . . The connections between war and prisons need to be ever more deeply explored and exposed. Why for decades have 25% of prisoners been veterans of war? I know where there are thousands of prisoners of war and missing in action: in the jails and prisons of America. It's long past the hour to bring them home. Bring them home from war. Bring them home from prison. War and prison go together. In fact, war and prisons are two faces of the same reality. Both are entirely dependent upon fear and the creation of enemies.[1]

John Schuchardt participated in two Plowshares actions, the first one in 1980 and a second in 1983. In 1990, he and his wife Carrie founded the House of Peace in Ipswich, Massachusetts. The House of Peace is a physical and spiritual refuge for victims of war, in community with adults with special needs.

---

1. Excerpted from "War and Prisons: A Time for Abolition," *The Servant Song* 8/4 (2000) 6.

3

Vietnam—The Burning Time

After Lyndon Johnson's election in 1964, the peace movement began to shift from generalized protests against hydrogen bombs to specific protests against the growing battle for the hearts and minds of peasants in Vietnam. College-age men faced a revitalized draft and Pope Paul VI pleaded to the United Nations in 1965, "No more war, war never again!" But war came, with yearly escalations, more and more men drafted—or refusing to be drafted—and a country increasingly divided, with large portions of the young soured and angry at a government no longer seen as benevolent.

Those tumultuous years seem long ago, even to those of us who lived through them. To most of the world now, they're history, tinged with nostalgia and much misinformation. Alongside tales of flower children and hippies stand stories of principled peace activists who sacrificed years of their lives to end the war that divided the country and drained its resources. This chapter contains the recollections of nine people who were there—draft resisters, draft card burners, and those who followed the lead of the Berrigan brothers and others and destroyed the "improper" property of draft file records.[1] According to Sister Anne Montgomery, RSCJ, Fr. Dan Berrigan, SJ, was the first one to talk about property that is so improper it has no right to exist. "Property is what enhances human life. If it kills human life, it's not true property, because it's not what's proper to human life."[2]

1. For the story of the first two draft board raids, see *Doing Time for Peace*, chap. 1.

2. Sr. Anne Montgomery interview, Marquette Archives.

Protests during the Vietnam era—roughly from 1964 to 1972—took many forms and were colored by abrupt cultural changes in those tumultuous times. Thousands of young men fled to Canada, tried to escape the draft by various other methods, or sought legal conscientious objector status. A site sponsored by the Swarthmore Peace Collection reports that a total of 170,000 men received CO deferments with perhaps 300,000 more denied deferment. Nearly 600,000 illegally evaded the draft with about 200,000 formally accused of draft offenses. Between 30,000 and 50,000 fled to Canada; another 20,000 fled to other countries or lived underground in America.[3]

Counseling men in danger of the draft became one of the main occupations of local peace groups, with the American Friends Service Commission, FOR, WRL, the Catholic Peace Fellowship, and other groups supplying national leadership and sending trained counselors to communities across the country. This chapter begins with two very different experiences of refusing the draft—Marty Harris from Lomita, a working-class part of Los Angeles, and Randy Kehler from Scarsdale, an upscale suburb of New York City. Unlike most of the resisters in this oral history, these men *didn't* cross a line; they simply refused to step across the induction line when asked to do so by the armed forces. The rest of the chapter presents narratives from the Catholic Left, particularly those influenced by Dorothy Day, co-founder of the Catholic Worker. Three Catholic Workers—Jim Wilson, David Miller, and Tom Cornell—talk about their public acts of burning draft cards and the ensuing prison time. Finally, we hear from participants in two of the dramatic draft file actions which followed the original Baltimore Four and Catonsville Nine events, where draft files were defaced with blood or burned. Three of the Milwaukee Fourteen talk about their parts in the 1968 action and the prison that followed and Maggie Geddes, now an attorney in Sacramento, describes a large women-only action called "Women Against Daddy Warbucks," which happened in New York City the following summer. I also interviewed participants in the Chicago Fifteen action who is still a resister—Fr. Joe Mulligan, SJ—and two of "the Four of Us," young Loyola University graduates who were acquitted in a draft board action in Evanston, Illinois.[4]

3. Anne M. Yoder online: www.swarthmore.edu/library/peace/conscientious objection/co%20website/pages/PrimaryResourcesNew.htm.

4. Oral histories of the two Chicago actions are compiled in a booklet, available by contacting the author at riegle@svsu.edu.

Refusing the Draft

MARTY HARRIS

Marty: I don't consider myself a CO, a conscientious objector. I'm a PO, a political objector. I just didn't want to see Vietnamese people being killed. I'd been interested in politics since I was a kid, and always reading the newspaper. A Poli Sci major at El Camino Junior College, right close by here in LA. I felt we were making a political mistake as soon as we got involved in the Vietnam War, and of course the more I studied it, the more I became sure of my point of view.

Marty Harris, 2004.

No religion involved in this at all! In fact, I would say that I am a confirmed agnostic. Now my tendency is to be somewhat religious. My *tendency*. If it wasn't for those darn religious people, I might be religious. [Laughs.]

Ro: How did you feel about the practice of nonviolence?

Marty: Well, we read [Thoreau's] *Walden* in the history class. And the lit class. And in the philosophy class. Then in "The Intellectual History of the US," they talked about Martin Luther King and Gandhi. So lots of talk. I didn't have a real total understanding, but I'd read about the Mexican War of 1845 and how Thoreau wouldn't pay his taxes and Emerson came over to the jail and said, "What are you doing in there, David?" And [Henry David] Thoreau said, "Well, what are you doing out there?"

Between 1965 and 1968 I got more radical, and I thought— I *thought!*—that I was a revolutionary. In fact, I thought I was a revolutionary when I went to jail. Now I don't regret going to jail and actually standing up to the government, but as far as it being a political movement . . . I had a . . . what do you call it? An epiphany.

Now it *did* change things. We stopped the draft. But . . . was that all good? I don't know! Now we've got this other foolishness. Paid mercenaries, basically. There's no "will of the people." But I guess a lot of it is that I'm more conservative now than I was then. We thought the "revolution" was going to free our minds, but instead, Hollywood put it in a box and sold it. "Sex, drugs, and rock 'n roll" was a failure! A failure.

Ro: But draft resistance?

Marty: It was all part of the same movement. I was a revolutionary. We were going to change everything. Start on page one, and tear out the pages and create a whole new society. Then I guess maybe I lost the faith. David Harris was in prison when I was, and I didn't see him or any other leaders who could get above the personal. Didn't meet any Alexander Hamiltons or George Washingtons.

But going to jail was the right thing to do. See, I was working class, so I knew guys in Vietnam. I was getting a student deferment and they were getting Vietnam. Why was my life any more valuable than theirs? So I wrote out a thing and sent it with the [draft] card. I remember giving a speech at the Unitarian Church. I think there were three or four others [speaking], but I was the only one of the resistance group. The others were philosophy majors or something, talking about Camus, but we never saw those guys ever again.

Anyway, I turned in my card and got reclassified pronto. Got married on a Friday, three days before my induction date. Went right through the whole induction until the end, but when they told me to take the step forward, I didn't. Everybody else in the line went into the army. I walked out the door and didn't get indicted until the next December.

Ro: Was your wife pregnant by then?

Marty: Oh, no! I wasn't going to be *that* foolish. [Laughs.] I wasn't going to go to jail and leave my wife pregnant. Which is another thing David Harris did. Of course, his wife was a millionaire, so that's the difference. I have a wonderful wife, and we've been married all these years and she supported me one hundred percent in my resistance.

I went to Stafford, which was, at the time, about half COs and Jehovah Witnesses and half Mexicans and short-timers. Working class guys like me, we mixed with the other guys. But that was a tough deal. I befriended a couple of them when they came out, and then you could see them go in a certain direction, and it was sort of painful. One was a very good friend, and I don't see him much anymore. There were some agents in there, too, but we didn't know quite exactly who they were. They wanted to find out what was going on in "the movement."

I served nineteen months out of a forty-two-month sentence. Went to jail in March of 1969 and my brother, who was five years younger, joined the Air Force in February of 1969. So my parents had to deal with these two different things. It was tough. My dad said, "I understand what you're doing, Marty, but boy! You'll have a record for the rest of your life, and people will call you a coward." My parents stood by me, though, through thick and thin.

We're working-class people. That's another thing I found out—most of the other draft resisters were middle-class, and I'm just a working-class stiff. I lived working-class, and when I came back, I put my nose to the grindstone and gained respect through how I supported my family. One thing: I never, ever, used the fact that I was a felon as an excuse for not providing for my family. In fact, that's what made me a workaholic, in a sense. I didn't want anybody to say they weren't going to hire me, so I went in business for myself. I started out with a vegetable and egg route, and then I bought a store [and now I'm doing wholesale].

Oh, and another thing: I have three children, and when they grew up, I never preached to them that I went to jail. Although they knew. I didn't want them to feel they had to be lefties or anything. They are this precious thing—your children—and I didn't want to preach to them about how I did the moral thing. In fact, I still try to look at this not as a moral thing, but as a political act.

If you go back to the Greeks, you know, the word "polis" means society. People all the time say, "Oh, that's just political!" Hey! Your whole life is political! Who you work with and how you relate to each other and how you get along—it's all political! You know, your life . . . it's like you go from one movie set to another.

When you're in jail, it's another movie set. But I was bored to death there. It was a study in boredom. I read a lot of books, I had wonderful friends, and we talked about heavy things, but I was bored even though we had a lot of fun. [The resisters in prison] were trying to find—or to make up—something that we could resist because that's what we were—resisters. But really, there wasn't that much to resist.

What can I say? You get what you want to get out of life. I was a political objector, and I wanted to make my point. I knew, when I went in there, that we couldn't win Vietnam. The Vietnamese had the right of self-determination, and if they want to be Communists, well, I don't necessarily think that's good, but . . . If we'd had a different government, we could have met Ho Chi Minh halfway. He thought the US Declaration of Independence was the greatest document ever written.

Ro: What "famous last words" do you have?

Marty: I just think this is a great country. That's my famous last word. When I went to jail, my picture, and the whole story, was on the front page of the local newspaper. When I got out, I came back to my neighborhood, and they all accepted me. I stood up for what I believed in and they respected that. We have a great tradition in this country. The only problem is that there's not enough people willing to do what I did.

That's the other thing I still believe: If you really feel strongly about your rights, then you should protest. At the beginning of the Iraq War, I'd see these people out protesting, and I'd talk to them and say I thought we needed to go into Iraq. *Now*, of course, I don't think that, but at the time, I did. But I also said to them, "I'm sure glad you guys are out here! Our government is talking about killing people and changing the direction of our country. And if anybody thinks that we shouldn't talk about it, they're a fool. Protesting is what keeps our country vibrant and keeps hope alive."

RANDY KEHLER

Randy Kehler signed a draft refusal statement while at Harvard and worked in the anti-Vietnam war movement in San Francisco after graduation, deciding to resist the draft completely instead of applying for CO status.

Randy: I grew up in an upper middle-class family. Went to supposedly really good schools: Scarsdale High, two years at Phillips Exeter Academy, then to Harvard College. The words "nonviolent" or "pacifist" or "war resistance" didn't mean a thing to me, though, until the summer of 1963. I went into New York City one night for a jazz festival. Got off at 125th Street, smack in the middle of Harlem, and walked into a huge street rally. It was totally all Black folk, with a fiery orator. I was completely spellbound—me, a white kid from the suburbs. Pretty soon these young Black guys came up behind me, laid their hands gently but firmly on my shoulders, and said, "You'd better come with us; you could get hurt here."

They led me into this little storefront and then up these stairs. It turned out to be the Harlem office of CORE (Congress of Racial Equality). They were organizing for the march on Washington later that summer, the one that became the "I have a dream" march. Well! I stayed with them until late that night, helping with their mailing, learning about what they were doing. And then, for the rest of the summer, I raised money in Scarsdale for buses to Washington and went down on one myself. So that was my political awakening.

Oh! One other thing! One day on the bus leaving Harlem, I sat next to this little old guy. He didn't even say "Hello," just handed me a WRL calendar from the early '60s. The page he showed me had the life of a guy named Max Sandine. Sandine had been born in Russia. He refused to fight in the Czar's armies and fled to the States. Was drafted by the US for World War I but refused to go along with that, too, so he was imprisoned and actually sentenced to be executed. This Max Sandine went on [resisting] and refused to pay his war taxes, and was conscripted again for World War II, even though he was an older man.

After I read this calendar page, the guy said to me very simply, "I am Max Sandine." So, in one short summer, I had my eyes opened both to the civil rights movement and to pacifism and war resistance. I was nineteen years old.

My own first act of resistance was when I was a senior at Harvard—and I did it with great fear and trembling. I signed a public statement that was printed in the student newspaper, saying that the undersigned refused to cooperate with the draft. If called, we would not go, and we would publicly encourage other young men not to go. A couple months later, I sent my draft card back. I went to grad school at Sanford, but dropped out after two weeks and wandered into the Mid-Peninsula Free University, south of San Francisco.

They were offering a million free courses and this one was on the history, philosophy, and practice of nonviolence, taught by Roy Kepler, Ira Sandperl, and Joan Baez. When they said the practice of nonviolence, they meant the *practice*! Soon the whole seminar group was sitting in at the Oakland Induction Center, and I went to jail for ten days. While I was in jail, I was recruited to join the War Resisters League. Worked full-time for them until 1970 when I was sentenced to two years in federal prison [for refusing the draft].

My parents testified as character witnesses at the trial. My father gets up on the stand, with his silver hair and conservative blue suit, looking like a very dignified businessman, which he was. [Voice fills with emotion.] He said to the judge, "Your Honor, if you want to put somebody in prison, put me in prison. Randy's just doing what we taught him: 'Love your enemy' and 'Thou shalt not kill.'"

They visited me once, and in fact I had a lot of visitors at Stafford that first year; but after awhile I didn't want any more to come. After you've adjusted to life inside, to go out into a closely guarded prison yard, where you aren't allowed to touch anyone and to have to talk about what's going on in the world, it was just . . . It played with my soul too much to keep making that transition. Prison became my life. It was too painful to go in and out of it.

I was recruited by the prison staff to teach a GED course, but I kept having run-ins with the guards. One time they wrote me up for asking too many questions. Another time they wrote me up for having "a bad attitude toward this prison and prisons in general." (I wanted to frame that one, you know!) Finally I said I couldn't work with them anymore. I thought I'd be sent out immediately, because as soon as you don't cooperate in minimum custody you're —boom!— back to maximum custody, the big house.

They didn't send me out for weeks, though, and nobody could figure out why. Later I found out that some lifer types—tough characters, who'd done years in places like Alcatraz—had floated an anonymous rumor that if I was moved, they'd burn down the dining hall.

Ro: So these tough guys defended you, even though it might jeopardize their release. How did you make these connections?

Randy: Well, I enjoy people and I don't lecture. I listen and want to hear their stories. Before you go to jail, the government types tell you that the other prisoners will "hate guys like you, and tear you limb from limb. 'You commie bastard traitor, you won't fight for your country.'" That sort of thing. We found just the opposite. The great majority thought, "Good for you! You told the government to go fuck themselves!" And they'd say exactly that. Even though they didn't necessarily share the same sentiments, they saw it as an act of resistance. They understood standing up to "the Man." And in fact, many of them *were* against the war.

Anyway, after I refused work, I sat around all day. Played handball and wrote in my diary and played my guitar. Then we heard that prisoners at Leavenworth had gone on strike, demanding minimum wage. They were making furniture for like fifteen cents an hour. I was pretty much an organizer. (I guess you could say organizing is in my blood.) So we organized a sympathy strike. Boycotted our dining hall and tried to smuggle out press releases saying that it was a solidarity strike. After that, I was outta there!

I was sent to La Tuna, in El Paso, where there were eight hundred prisoners and only a half dozen draft resisters. It was a regular prison with huge thick concrete walls and barbed wire fences and gun towers and electric sliding metal gates everywhere. Big dormitories where you'd live in double bunks like hamsters.

So it was harsher, in a way. But in another way, I was more comfortable. In Stafford, I had been my own guard. Because it was close to the highway, with no gun towers and no fences, I could have walked out at night, stuck out my thumb or arranged to get picked up, which a lot of people did, especially the Mexicans. Most of them didn't get very far, but . . . at La Tuna, it was real clear.

It took a lot of adjustment, though. Learning all the new unwritten rules. I cooperated for the first six months or so because I wanted to know these guys and wanted them to know me. That way, I'd have some support if I decided not to cooperate or to organize.

I was assigned to a carpentry shop and had a wonderful boss, one of the warmest, most kind-hearted human beings I've ever met in my whole life. I had just started to learn to love [working with] the lathe, when he asked me to make a gavel for the federal judge in El Paso.

A lot of the people in that prison had been sentenced by that judge, including one of my best friends, a sweet young kid from Santa Clara County, who had gotten five years for coming across the border with a few ounces of marijuana. So I said to Mr. Brawley, the carpentry boss, I said, "I can't do this. I just can't do it!" And he was so good! He put his hand on my shoulder and he said, "You know, if a man can't take pride in his work, he shouldn't have to do it."

After six months, I became involved in a number of organizing projects, sort of like at Stafford. We did a study of how bad the health conditions were—got affidavits and all this stuff—and sent up letters and petitions to the warden. He'd promised to take action and never did, so finally I wrote him a letter listing a hundred and one things I opposed about the way the prison was run and said I couldn't cooperate and quit the carpentry shop.

Of course, I was instantly sent to the hole, which is sort of a cellar beneath the lowest level, a little dank, dark cell with one light bulb out in the hall for twelve cells. That's where they try to break you. A metal rack to sleep on and one blanket, no mattress. Freezing cold. There's nothing to do. Locked down twenty-four hours a day. I was there for three weeks.

With one exception, I didn't have such a bad time at all. See, some of the guys down there were Mexicans who were turned in for coming across the border illegally. Usually *after* they harvested the crop, of course. (It'd be a great deal for the employer. They've done the job and you don't have to pay them.) Some of these guys had severe mental illness and were literally going nuts, and they'd be sent to the hole. They'd bust the toilet, just kick it until it broke, to try to flood the cells. They'd issue these blood-curdling cries and bang their heads on the wall, and it was agony to hear them because you couldn't do a thing about it. So that was the horrible part.

In other ways, I survived fine, though. Mostly I meditated or did yoga. Recited anything that I had memorized: songs, poems, and what-not. I sang and sang and sang. From folks songs to Christmas carols to church hymns. Anything, just to sing . After three weeks, they put me into a semi-solitary cell, one floor above. I think they really sent me up there to get hurt, because they put me in with an outwardly homosexual man.

In prison, homosexuality—at least in the prisons I was in—isn't like homosexuality on the outside, for the most part. It's a huge power thing. There's a population of people in prison who pretend they're women. They take on women's names, they tailor their uniforms to be tight, wear whatever they can get to approximate lipstick. Talk in high squeaky voices, and make themselves completely subservient to their "old man," who is the dominant member of this couple.

The "old men" were these super-macho guys who didn't think of themselves as homosexuals at all! Even though they were sexually involved with other men who were obviously men, in prison they weren't men. You had to pinch yourself and say, "Is this real?"

Ro: Would the men fight other men and the women-men fight other women-men?

Randy: Oh, yes. The "women" would not seriously fight, just scratch each other or what-not; but the men could get into serious fighting over a "woman." So anyway, I'm put in a cell with one of these "women," and this poor fellow said to me [Feigning a high-pitched voice.]: "Oh, oh, oh! If my old man finds out you're in here, he'll kill me! He'll kill you, too!" The poor guy was scared to death.

So I found out who his "old man" was and talked to him when they let me out for a break. He was a tough character, all right, but he laughed and he said, "Aw, I wouldn't hurt him. And besides, I know you're not there to take him away from me."

Eventually they sent me up another floor and put me in with Tod Friend, who was both a draft resister and a draft file burner. Tod was great! We were together twenty-three hours a day in a nine by six cell for the last nine months of both of our imprisonments. I got into this wonderful rhythm of reading, writing, playing the guitar. Taught myself macramé. (They'd let us order crafts. We couldn't go to a craft room but they'd bring the stuff to the cell.)

You know, through most of my twenty-two months in prison, I would say I was quite enjoying myself. I realized that I had as many happy moments in prison as out of prison. Also difficult and sad and confused and all the other moments. But in terms of how I felt, it was no different

Now when I was in security, I couldn't organize. But the irony was that while I was in lock-up, the prisoners mounted the first strike in La Tuna's forty-year history. The old Anglo cons would say, "You're wasting your time organizing here. Too many Mexicans. Three squares a day here, a bunk to sleep on, what else could they want?" Also, many of the guys were doing long time and were at the end of their term and didn't want to blow it. But suddenly there was a strike, and the prison was shut down for three days. And you know who led the strike? The Mexicans! Because they were being treated horrendously. Lots and lots of discrimination.

And the funny thing: I got blamed for the strike, even though I was locked up, because I knew all the Mexican heavies. You see, the Mexican community had their own Spanish-language newspaper, and I was the translator and really the only Anglo involved in the newspaper. Of course the guards know who knows who, as they've got snitches everywhere. So they just *assumed* that I was behind the strike, and they stopped my meals and exercise and just slipped food under the cell door. I hadn't organized the strike, but I guess I was flattered that they *thought* I'd done it.

Ro: How did it feel when you got out?

Randy: I had a much more difficult transition than I ever would have imagined. For instance, I was scared to death of riding in cars. These little metal boxes with rubber wheels that go speeding down narrow highways, passing within a couple of feet of metal boxes speeding ninety miles an hour in the other direction. It's crazy!

I also felt intensely lonely. Nobody understood. It's not their fault, but nobody could possibly understand unless they've been there. Even though I'd tell them and I'm telling you now, there's still no way anyone can ever really know what it's like. I was thrilled to see the people I loved again, but felt like I'd just come from Mars and couldn't tell them about it. So when Tod [Friend] got out, two weeks later, I was so . . . God, I was . . . lighter! Oh, jeez! I'm sure it's like people who come back from war. They know that nobody back home will ever, ever understand what they've been through.

Before I got back into the anti-war movement, I went to Mexico and tried to write a book about my experience. One of the senior editors at E. P. Dutton asked to see my manuscript, and then he called me into New York.

"It's a very interesting story. But tell me, didn't you ever see any race riots?"

"No."

"What about guards beating up prisoners?"

"Well, I'm pretty sure there was [some], but I didn't see it."

"Were you ever raped?"

"No." I said. "There were rapes, but I wasn't involved."

He shook his head and said—and these were his exact words: "In today's shouting book world, a gentle story like this will never sell." Then his postscript really added insult to injury. "Besides which," he said, "the Berrigans have already told this story.[5]" So I never submitted it anywhere else. [Long pause.]

I guess the other thing I want to say . . . I went to a demonstration right [after I was released], at the Oakland Naval Base. Lots of CD (civil disobedience) and cops on the loose, banging people over the head and swinging people around and making arrests. When I saw a cop drag a friend of mine to the ground—just really being unnecessarily brutal—I came within an inch of jumping on the cop. Then I stopped and realized, "Oh, my God! My nerves are really frayed." I had to leave the demonstration.

Ro: So maybe the lock-up was a little more damaging than you'd thought it was?

---

5. Fr. Dan Berrigan, SJ, published *The Trial of the Catonsville Nine* as a play in 1970, with Beacon Press. The Phoenix Theater presented it at Good Shepherd-Faith Church in New York in February, 1971.

Randy: I think so. At least temporarily. I don't think there was any lasting damage. And I've never, ever regretted for a moment that I went to prison. I'd do it again, without hesitation, under similar circumstances.

Randy did, in fact, spend more time in lock-up. See Chapter 10 for the campaign to save his family's house from seizure for war tax resistance.

Catholic Workers Destroy Draft Cards

Catholic Workers were among the first to speak out against the growing US involvement in Vietnam. The New York CW community became a mecca for young people dissatisfied with their country's troop involvement in Southeast Asia. There they joined with War Resisters League and other peace groups in mounting protests and making connections with other antiwar initiatives. Their primary focus, however, was responding personally and individually to the war. This response often included facing persecution by publicly destroying draft cards.

DAVID MILLER

David Miller was the first person to burn his draft card publicly after Congress specifically prohibited it. He later became a social worker and then a lawyer; today he's a writer and a musician and is married to the nonviolent Wicca leader Starhawk. I interviewed him in San Francisco on the anniversary of his draft card burning.

David: I'd already refused induction once; they just sent me a new draft card. Then Al Urie asked me to represent the draft noncooperator position at a big protest in Manhattan. There'd be fifteen or twenty speakers, so I'd only have about five minutes. I was very shy at the time, so I decided to burn my card instead. "Surely that will take the five minutes." Now I was pretty sure I'd go to jail at some point for draft resistance, so the draft card burning was only one part of the whole strategy. I didn't have any idea how this would catch on or how much publicity we'd get.

The night before I did it, Tom Cornell tried to talk me into waiting for more people to burn them together. I decided not to wait, though, because if I did, I'd be back to having to give a speech. I didn't announce it beforehand, but maybe Al let the press know, because it went around.

The draft card burning was on a Friday and the next day there was a big demonstration in Central Park and a march down Fifth Avenue. On Monday, several of us from the Catholic Worker traveled up to New Hampshire, to St. Anselm's College. We were going to put out a table with peace literature, maybe talk to a few classes, let the right-wing Catholics at the college accost us, that kind of thing. But the FBI swooped in and picked me up, very early in the morning, when I was standing outside the motel. I made bail the next day. The trial wasn't until spring.

Ro: What did your folks think about this?

David: My mother was always on my side, even though she wasn't very political. My father was very much on my side. He even wrote a letter about it to the local paper. (I carried that letter in my wallet for many years.) He basically said he was proud of his son. He was always staunch working class and a pro-union Democrat. I remember when his sister said she was going to vote for Ike. My father exploded: "You like to eat, dontcha? Well, then, vote Democrat!"

Ro: During Vietnam, a lot of working-class people thought of draft resisters as the "other class," the college kids. How did that work with you?

David: Well, I was working class, no question about that. When we played the game at the Catholic Worker of "more working class than thou," as you do from time to time on the Left, I always did very well because I grew up in public housing. My mother was a seamstress and my father was a machinist, so I was really solid there. [Laughs.]

But then I went to college, to LeMoyne in Syracuse, so I was college-educated. Truthfully, that was where I found the ideas that propelled me towards the Catholic Worker and towards resistance, but the ideas were always in the background of my family, too. I got involved in the civil rights movement and that led to the peace movement, which was a short step if you were practicing and believing in nonviolence and social justice.

The other part of it was the people at Le Moyne. Dan Berrigan and a number of others were really involved in social justice. It was a great time for Catholics with John XXIII as the pope. *Pacem in Terris* and *Mater et Magistra*—those documents were very, very powerful for folks in the social justice movement, and I was really immersed in them as a college student.

Ro: Oh, yes! What about your trial?

David: Well, I was represented by ACLU cooperating attorneys—you know, guys in private practice. I remember doing well on the stand, because I was direct and straightforward. Because I'd admitted everything, there was really no way of attacking me. It was a question of whether the law was constitutional or not. The lawyers said that they expected the judge to rule in favor of the constitutionality of the law, which he did, and the original sentence was thirty months probation. The provision, though, was that I would have to obtain and carry a new draft card, and I certainly wasn't going to do that.

The sentence was put off because the case was appealed. I lost the appeal—my appeal, my particular one—because the Supreme Court declined to review it. I had violated the probation by refusing to carry the card, so I was sentenced to two and a half years for that. A week into the sentence, there was another draft card burning case from the Boston area, and the First Circuit ruled differently. Said the law *was* unconstitutional. So the government automatically appealed it to the Supreme Court, and I was released until that appeal was heard [and the Court decided it was constitutional]. I was out for a whole year, and that's when Catherine [Swann] and I had a Catholic Worker house in DC and also a baby daughter.

I didn't go back to jail until June of 1968. Went first to Lewisburg in Pennsylvania and then to the farm camp at Allenwood for about a year. I finally began to not cooperate, after about ten months or so, so I was sent back to the penitentiary, to the wall. Maximum security.

Doing time was hard for the first months. I was really psychologically and emotionally fighting it. After a couple of weeks in the main population of the penitentiary and then a month in segregation because I refused to work, I decided not to hit my head against the wall anymore and to just do the time.

Ro: Yeah. This is maybe a goofy question, but is there anything you can remember as being kind of memorable in a positive sense?

David: Ah . . . that's hard. I survived it. [Weak laughter and long pause.] I don't . . . It's not a positive experience. It's debilitating. Any institutional, essentially fascist situation like that, of military might corralling people—it's not good. You *do* make some friendships, you learn some things, learn about yourself and about other people. Remember that old saying that the army makes a man out of you? You *do* come to grips with some things, but it's not right. The military is really very, very bad training. Same with prison. [Pause.] Six months after I got out of prison, Kate took the kids and went back to England, where she was from.

Ro: David—and you don't have to answer this if you don't want—do think the prison experience put a strain on the marriage and maybe eventually did it in? Is that a fair . . .

David: Oh, yeah. No question about it. And also we were very young. It was a Catholic Worker romance, and we were very young Catholic Workers. Dorothy always said the young people find one another at the Catholic Worker. Because it's very idealistic, with a lot of intensity around the work itself. The sixties were a particularly intense time. Very volatile. Even in the best of circumstances, it would be hard. But with us and a lot of other couples, the specter of resistance and prison was always there. We had an "action romance." You meet in the intensity of a demonstration. Over a period of time, an action generates lots of sexual energy as well as political energy. The attractions are immediate and intense and then they wane.

Ro: Now the draft card burning was thirty-nine years ago today. Would you do it again?

David: Yes, absolutely. I'm not sorry that I did it then; I'm very, very glad. It was a difficult experience, hard for me and hard for my family, but I had a lot of support and I'd still do it again.

Now I hope not to be in a situation where I go to prison again. I'm more mature and I read the energy better. If it has to happen, then it has to happen, but I'll do what I can to avoid it. I won't court it in the way I did as a young man, when it seemed inevitable. I'm not saying that was wrong—I think it was good—but I've got a different viewpoint now.

I've always, always owned the draft card burning. I was always David Miller, the draft card burner, but my e-mail—draftcardburner@yahoo.com—is relatively recent. The book is relatively recent.[6]

Ro: How do you see the young David Miller connecting with this David Miller?

David: Well, that's interesting. I think in terms of thirty, thirty, thirty. For the first thirty years of my life, generally speaking, I was young, idealistic, radical, Catholic, going to prison, starting a family. The next thirty years were sort of in between, but extremely important to that time was raising two families. Being available to my kids, even though I was divorced from both partners. Those thirty years were family time and work time.

And then the last thirty years—writing the book and now starting to write songs and poetry and do Wicca workshops and music. I think it's going to be even more creative, sexier, more political than the other two.

David Miller, 2004.

JIM WILSON

In another early resistance action, Jim Wilson, Roy Lisker, Marc Edelman, David McReynolds, Gordon Christiansen, and Tom Cornell burned their draft cards together in Union Square a month after David, on November 6, 1965. Jim was twenty-one and the only one of the group living at the Catholic Worker. He had attended St. Anselm's College in New Hampshire but left school to march for civil rights in Selma. When he came back from the South, he went to "Catholic Worker school" with Dorothy Day in New York.

Ro: Jim, why didn't you just go for the CO instead of burning your draft card?

Jim: Well, I thought about it when I was at St. Anselm's. As I became more involved with people at the Worker and saw the folks who were

6. David Miller, *God Made Honky Tonk Communists: A Memoir about Draft Card Burning, Witchcraft, and the Sexual Meaning of Ballgames* (Oakland, CA: Regent, 2002).

coming to the conclusion of total noncooperation with the draft, I realized that was a truer position to take. And a stronger one.

If you look back at the headlines of that whole period, the numbers of young Catholics in the movement were pretty awesome. Dorothy Day knew that this was creating confusion within the Catholic Church, and she understood the paradox: she'd been preaching nonviolence for a long time, and now it was getting to a much larger audience.

The young people at the Catholic Worker all became very close very quickly because we were all clearly involved in and affected by the draft. The women, too. The draft was a very male issue, but young women had the same religious and philosophical beliefs, and they were very supportive. I think they were also able to see a real role model in Dorothy in terms of strength and position-taking and that type of thing. As a matter of fact, my wife Raona did an action with some other women shortly after I went to prison. They sat down in front of military vehicles at a Memorial Day parade. (We had gotten married during this period of my draft refusal.)

Now there were people who were looking at protests from a political perspective and public relations perspective and then people like me who were involved because of a specific kind of belief. Lots of discussions. And you know? Years later, I asked for my FBI file as part of the Freedom of Information Act, and it clearly indicates that there was someone who was participating in this whole thing, and . . . and reporting it to the FBI.

I myself had no sense of what our action meant on a larger level, how the newspapers or the TV or the country in general would view these things. I was just trying to identify the right thing to do. I finally told them I'd be a part of that public protest. Because of Dorothy Day's influence, really. See, from her I learned that anger can be appropriate, and that it's not necessarily bad. Dorothy could be angry, but the key, I believe, was that she was angry about the right things. We did our action at Union Square and Dorothy and A. J. Muste were both on the platform.

Ro: Hecklers were calling her "Moscow Mary," weren't they?

Jim: And yelling at us, "Burn yourselves, not your cards!" Then, as we were lighting the cards, someone shot a fire extinguisher out of the crowd. The first thought I had—and I think others thought the same thing—was that it was gasoline and we were all going to blow up.

After we burned our cards, the whole process seemed to move slowly. FBI agents interviewed me at the Catholic Worker and I said that yes, I'd done it. It turned out that of the people up there with me [on the stage at Union Square], I was the only one with an active draft card, the only one who was in imminent danger of being drafted. That came as kind of a surprise to me, and I felt a little bit left out there to hang, you know.

Draft card burning at Union Square, New York, 1965. Tom Cornell, Marc Edelman, Roy Lisker, David McReynolds, James Wilson, Gordon Christiansen (head behind Wilson), A. J. Muste. © Neil Haworth.

Also, the political piece of the movement was saying that everybody was going to stand together and plead not guilty, so it would work its way through the courts where they would challenge the law. Well, "Sorry folks! That wasn't my intention." So I went my separate way.

In my trial, I took the absolute Catholic Worker position . . . or what was viewed as that, with no attorney involvement. Basically I pled guilty and that was it. No arguing the case one way or the other. The judge was very much affected by what I said and what other people said, though, and he didn't sentence me to prison but instead gave me probation. I was absolutely amazed! They printed the statement I wrote in *The Catholic Worker*. Here it is. [Hands it to Rosalie.]

Ro: Oh! Can you read the end of it into the tape?

Jim: Sure! [Reading.] "My freedom is very important to me. Freedom to walk through the streets of every city and catch the wind on my face. Freedom to gather with friends and drink ale and sing songs. Freedom to love people of every shape, color, and size. Freedom to bring joy to those who are sad. Sometimes the freedom to cry with those who are crying. These are the things that are important to me and in order to keep them for myself and others, I will gladly go to jail. And others will follow me and still others will follow them. For the free man and the Christian will soon realize that he will have to go to jail. So build more prisons and make them large and we will all be together. The freedom that is tingling in my bones and in my soul cannot be held in by iron bars."

Ro: Oh, Jim! It was such a Technicolor time. Do you miss that aliveness?

Jim: I do, Rosalie. I'm involved in my work now, in things that keep me excited and passionate, but I miss the music and the camaraderie. And we *did* make a difference! I've thought about this a lot. Those actions made a tremendous difference in the sense that there isn't a draft right now. That was the major accomplishment and that was our focus—that conscription was wrong and that people shouldn't cooperate with it. Now I'm not sure that the alternative has ended up being much better, but . . .

Anyway, after the trial, I went back to the Worker and started to do the soup line again. Within probably ten days, I received a notice from the Selective Service Office in New Jersey to report for induction. (Now we know that the timing on all these things was done purposely; they'd read the newspaper and knew I'd received probation.) I didn't show up for induction and very quickly I was indicted for refusing to report. The judge gave me three years. It was not a pleasant thing.

Ro: And your parents?

Jim: Oh, my parents . . . I was not good to my parents. They heard about the draft card [burning] and about all of this stuff on national news. Now I understand that we should have talked. I came from a very patriotic and middle-class family. Rotary and so forth. So needless to say, they were embarrassed. I was basically in the leaving-the-nest years, on my own for the first time. I was doing my thing and I did it, but wasn't communicating very clearly with them. At first, it was very difficult, but over a period of time, they became tremendously supportive.

I was in the House of Detention in Manhattan for like three months, even though everybody else was getting shipped out to prisons. Dorothy would visit me, and my wife, who was pregnant, and I remember Dan and Phil Berrigan both came. Phil in his memoir said that it was the Dave Millers and the Jim Wilsons who influenced him and Dan early on. They were close to the Worker, through liturgies and that type of thing. Really a very close sense of community.

One day the guards took me to court to hear new charge—violating the probation that the judge had given me for the draft card burning. Peter Fleming was the prosecutor.[7] He argued that every day that I refused to report for induction was a separate violation and that there should be a three-year sentence for each one of those days. I just stood there in shock!

Judge Weinfeld said to me, "This is a very complex case, Mr. Wilson. I know your position about noncooperation with the system, and that you don't want an attorney and so forth, but I really recommend that you have an attorney."

Well, I gotta tell ya', Rosalie, he convinced me! I knew Bill Kunstler, the famous civil rights attorney, and he came in, and we basically beat that charge.

So then I was sent to Lewisburg. Lewisburg is an old, old, old traditional federal penitentiary with high stone walls and high ceilings. Everything is concrete and very restrictive. That was a bad time, a difficult time. Lewisburg was not a pleasant place at all.

When you first go through the whole humiliation of the strip searches and so forth, and uh . . . the nakedness in front of guards, it's all . . . you get used to it, but that initial humiliation is pretty difficult. Later I was sent to Allenwood, which is a camp and not so restrictive. Other prisoners: I have some kind of street-sense, I guess, and I was also able to make friends. If you have the right friends in prison, you don't need to worry about anything else. Actually, even before the draft card burning, I had a breakfast meeting with Dave Dellinger, to

---

7. Just for historical information, Peter Fleming was an attorney for Richard Nixon during Watergate. A very conservative prosecutor. At the time, he was very pro-government, pro-war, pro-everything. (*Aside by Jim.*)

talk about consequences and those types of things. People wanted to make sure I understood what I was letting myself in for.

Ro: What about noncooperation in prison?

Jim: Well, I remember being in the hole for something, probably a work refusal. For me, it was a gut thing. You knew the point when you really just had to say no. Some people did a very clear black and white thing–total noncooperation. They were viewed, frankly, as pretty crazy. And probably in the process went a little bit crazy themselves. I remember an individual who had to be physically moved from place to place. They chose not to move him, so he went into solitary confinement, and that's where he stayed. I have a great deal of respect for somebody who's able to pull that off. I'm not sure about effectiveness, but that's for the person to judge.

For me, if you pick and choose, and you're able to say sometimes, "This is really wrong and I'm not going to cooperate," it becomes more meaningful. On the other hand, if you're trying to change the prison environment, sometimes that *does* call for banding together in total noncooperation. It's just a . . . it can be a very lousy system. Any level of protection is gone; if [the guards] get mad enough at you, they can do anything they want.

Ro: Now as I'm remembering, your baby was born while you were in Allenwood.

Jim: Yes. Nathan, my oldest son. There were supposedly arrangements made so I'd know when my wife went into labor and again when the baby was born. But I didn't find out for twenty-four hours because the guard who was in charge didn't follow through.

I came out of prison with a whole different attitude. For starters, I saw a lot of people who were sitting around talking the talk but not walking it. After being in prison, it wasn't real easy for me to sit in on all these philosophical discussions.

It was also extremely difficult going into the outside world, period. Just simple things like talking on the phone. I couldn't cope with all the people and all the activity. And the violence. If violence breaks out in prison, somebody intervenes. Prison is a controlled environment, and the streets in New York weren't controlled.

So we knew we needed to get out of the city. What finally convinced us . . . We lived on the fifth floor of a walk-up and a cat-burglar type person came in through the window one evening. With my son right in the front room! This person just came in and took things and went out the window and up over the roof and that just . . . If I hadn't just gotten out of jail, I guess, I could've dealt with it because that's the way it was in New York, but that seemed so very scary to me at the time.

Moving upstate helped. But I lost a period of time and my family lost a period of time and . . . I think of the relationship issues and so forth.[8] I know I changed. I think some of the ways I react to things, even now, relate back to the prison experience.

Ro: Jim, would you go to prison again, given the same circumstances?

Jim: Oh, definitely! Given the same circumstances, definitely. Things just had to change. And they did for awhile, but now we're back. We had strong beliefs and community and . . . there was hope.

Tom Cornell

Catholic Worker Tom Cornell has been living the CW life in one way or another ever since he graduated from Fairfield University. We met for our latest interview in the room at Maryhouse CW in New York, where vol-

unteers mail out *The Catholic Worker.* Tom "burned nine consecutive draft cards" before finally being imprisoned for this 1965 action.[9] His first burning, in a story which bridges the fifties and the sixties, seems almost flippant.

Tom Cornell and Catholic Worker Cat, 2005.

Tom: The only use I ever found for a draft card was to show I could legally drink a beer. Which, as a matter of fact, was the occasion of the first time I burned mine. It was 1960. Summertime. A Polaris submarine protest with the Committee for Nonviolent Action in New London, Connecticut.

8. Jim and Raona's marriage was a casualty of the Vietnam resistance.

9. Francine du Plessix Gray, "The Ultra-Resistance: On the Trial of the Milwaukee Fourteen," *New York Review of Books* 13/5 (September 25, 1969). Also available online: www.jimandnancyforest.com.

The Selective Service System had finally given me a classification I'd asked for, the 1–O, meaning that I would only be subject to the draft into alternative civilian service. During the four years the government was deciding whether or not I was a conscientious objector, I was trying to decide whether or not I was a noncooperator. I came to the conclusion that I was.

The demonstration: I was out on the water in this little rowboat. I weighed about 120 pounds at that time, not terribly strong, and was rowing with all my might toward the George Washington, the first missile-bearing nuclear submarine, still in dry dock. The idea was to unfurl banners and hold up placards asking the civilians to quit their jobs. "Refuse to work on the ship of death."

We didn't intend to get within the legal limits of the thing, but I lost control of the rowboat and headed right into the George Washington. I actually touched it—had to put my hand out to push us away from the hull. It was a very unsettling feeling, touching a machine that could incinerate all of Europe in a flash, bearing sixteen missiles, each of them to be armed with a nuclear weapon.

Anyway, I pushed away and was able to get back to the opposite shore and discharge the passengers. Then a friend and I went to a bar and the bartender asked if I was legal. I showed him my card, and when he handed it back to me, I said, "I don't want it" and burned it then and there in the ashtray. It was symbolic to me, my sacramental act of severing myself from the Selective Service System and becoming a noncooperator.

Now, the fact of the card's existence in no way facilitated the drafting of a person, and Selective Service even admitted this on the stand during my trial for publicly burning it later, in 1965, in the action with Jimmy Wilson. So why make the burning of the draft card illegal? Technically it was called "interference with the administration of the United States government," but in fact it was to squelch dissent.

Ro: But why did you burn your draft card in 1965 if you were already a CO and wouldn't go into the army anyway?

Tom: Because I had to. Because television cameras were aiming at me and I know what a good picture is. I may not have been draft eligible, but I was responsible legally for that God-damn card. I was publicly urging young men to acts of resistance, so I had some kind of moral obligation to share that vulnerability, and I shared it by burning the card. And well you remember what a tremendous impact those draft card burnings made. It was the biggest thing in the resistance movement up to that point.

We'd been having a very hard time breaking through to the press. I knew that the men and women actually writing the news stories had a great deal of skepticism about the war and a great deal of sympathy for us white, mannerly, well-spoken resisters. They also like to talk to people who can talk 'cause they make their living by copying it down. I had met all the *Times* correspondents for Southeast Asia, and I knew they were seeing through the tissue of lies the government was putting out. When the draft card burning took place, the *Times* helped to choreograph it, told us when to have it and where, so we would hit the Sunday papers. God! We're on every front page of every paper! Television interviews and radio interviews and Merv Griffin . . . all that stuff.

One day I asked Marvin [Karpatkin], my lawyer—bless his memory—why we got so much publicity. He had a psychological take on it. Said the burning of the cards was a castration symbol, as he put it, as if we were cutting off our fathers' gonads.

I was lucky to get only six months. The judge took into consideration that we were no longer draft eligible, but we were found guilty anyway. We appealed, but it took three years before the Supreme Court refused to hear us. So we went to prison in 1968.

I had written a statement upon burning the draft card, describing in some depth precisely how I felt about it at the time. (And since then, I haven't changed in the slightest, not in that regard.) *Commonweal* published my statement in a box opposite an editorial in which, for the first time, they took a position against the bombing of North Vietnam.

Destroying Draft Files

While individuals and groups refused induction and burned their draft cards in great numbers, others moved to destroying the draft records themselves. Inspired by the two Maryland draft board raids of 1968, others in the Catholic Left moved away from strict Gandhian nonviolence to clandestine actions. The Wisconsin action known as the Milwaukee Fourteen happened a few months after the Baltimore and Catonsville actions, when a shocked citizenry first saw priests and others setting fire to government records; the women-only action in New York was one of many surprises the next summer.

THE MILWAUKEE FOURTEEN

On September 24, 1968, fourteen men broke into the offices of nine Milwaukee draft boards, loaded over 10,000 draft files into burlap bags, and carried them to a nearby square. Using the same symbol as their predecessor action in Maryland—the Catonsville Nine—the men doused the files with homemade napalm and burned them, standing in prayer around the pyre and waiting for the police to arrive. The men were Don Cotton; Michael Cullen; Father Robert Cunnane, CSS; James Forest; Jerry Gardner; Bob Graf; Reverend Jon Higgenbotham; Father James Harney; Father Alfred Janicke; Doug Marvy; Fred Ogile; Father Anthony Mullaney, OSB; Brother Basil O' Leary, CFC; and Father Larry Rosebaugh, OMI, later known as Father Lorenzo because of his work in Central America. I interviewed four of the group, all playing different roles in the action, all sharing different stories.[10]

Doug Marvy

Doug Marvy had been teaching math at the University of Minnesota and volunteering at the Twin City Draft Information Center when someone from the Catonsville Nine came through, and he was hooked. He attended a retreat in New Jersey, along with several hundred others.

Doug: I guess it fit my sense of outrage. At the retreat, I right away joined a couple dozen people to talk about a civil disobedience action. It soon boiled down to fourteen, but we got right to work and did the action a little over three weeks later. I was the only one who wasn't Catholic and was the nuts and bolts of the operation, with another man helping me in scouting the building and so forth. I'll let him remain unnamed, as he wasn't part of the group who actually acted.[11]

In those days, we could get the press involved before the action, so we had live coverage. In fact, that video clip of us burning the files is still all over the internet.[12] The press at the time were loose enough

10. See *Doing Time for Peace* for narratives by Michael and Annette Cullen.

11. Milwaukee Fourteen participant Bob Graf identified John Hagedorn as this collaborator in an e-mail of November 3, 2010, and I contacted Hagedorn who confirmed on November 4, 2010 that he was tried, convicted on two counts of conspiracy, and received three years' probation. His laconic conclusion: "I didn't do much."

12. See www.nonviolentworm.org/Milwaukee14Today/HomePage for this video and other memories, compiled by Bob Graf.

to accept a phone call saying, "Meet me on the corner of X and Y because something's gonna happen, and I'll take you there." They all showed up and were herded into a van and dropped off right in front of the action.

The press were all indicted and nothing happened to them, but the word was posted: "Don't do this again." In fact, not too much later an action in Washington DC made the same attempt to inform the media but that time the FBI—or maybe it was the police—showed up instead. It became much more dangerous for folks to get involved who didn't plan on getting arrested.

On the day of the action, we met in a nearby warehouse at about 5:00 in the afternoon. Jim Harney said something like, "If anybody has any doubts about their inability to be nonviolent, I'm out." That was really the only time I can remember that we talked about nonviolence.

The building was still open for cleaning when we went in. I wore a janitor's outfit so I'd look like I belonged there. The keys were handed to me after [Fr. Larry Rosebaugh] took them from the cleaning lady, and I opened all the doors [to the nine draft board offices.] There was a van waiting outside with the napalm. Don Cotton, I think, brought that up. I remember emerging from the building and giving the sign to Don.

It happened at sundown, around 6:00, and as the files burned, we gathered around the fire, arms linked. While we were saying a prayer and reading our statement, the police came. As I recall, they almost casually took our arms and walked us to the paddy wagon. We had our hearing about two o'clock in the morning and the next night were transferred to the county jail. Bail was some outrageous amount, a quarter of a million dollars, or something like that.[13]

A day or so later, the defense committees went into operation. We had a lot of support, with lawyers trying to get our bail reduced and all that stuff. As bail money was raised, people started getting out. The folks who had more exposure got out first because they could speak and raise money for the defense. I was there to the end, like five or six weeks, and I remember some folks being angry because they'd raised money specifically for me, and I didn't take advantage of it. I finally got out on bail in October, and the trial wasn't until May, so we had plenty of time to prepare. We all went

13. Duke CIT Presentation, "Archive for the 'Milwaukee 14' Category," cites the figure as $415,000 (*duke.umwblogs.org/category/milwaukee-14/*).

to the Catonsville Nine trial, so that gave us an idea of what it might be like, and we were also finally able to spend time together.

Bob Graf and Jerry Gardner as the draft file fire
was starting. Milwaukee, 1968. © Gary Ballsieper.

I became one of the recruiters for other draft board actions.[14] Spent most of my time on the road, and became a kind of national consultant on locks and break-ins. I remember casing a draft board building for some people in Cleveland, Ohio. Had this whole disguise—a wig and a suit and tie—and walked around inside and took notes and then went into the bathroom and made sketches and detailed this great plan to give to the group.

Then as I was walking out of the building, I looked up, and there was a gun turret pointing right at me! The Cleveland draft board was across the street from a garage to the Federal Reserve Bank. I'd planned the exit for the burglary to be right in front of this gun turret. "Cancel this plan, dude!" [Laughter.]

Our trial: There was a key group of heavy lawyers—Kunstler and that guy from Detroit—a tall, skinny guy, as I recall. And then a

14. Paul G. Pierpaoli, Jr. writes that there were over one hundred similar actions across the country between 1968 and 1972. "Baltimore Four," in Spencer C. Tucker, ed., *The Encyclopedia of the Vietnam War: A Political, Social, and Military History* (New York: Oxford University Press, 2001), 92.

local Wisconsin lawyer. We had a big line-up of famous folks—Howard Zinn and all these historians and . . . I mean, once Kunstler was involved, it just swung into gear.

We were supposed to have two trials, both a federal and a state. I was cited for contempt in both of them, for not standing up for the judges and once for talking after he told me to stop. The state trial went fine, but of course we were convicted: burglary, arson, and theft. Big block headlines: "Milwaukee 14 Guilty." And then the federal trial was supposed to start.

See, the feds were angry at the state because they wanted to try us first, so we'd get more prison time on charges of conspiracy and all that. But after our state trial, they couldn't get a federal jury. The judge said that out of 127 potential jurors, or something like that, he'd only found one person who didn't know we were guilty. That person was a recluse and the judge said he could keep going until we found twelve recluses but that was hardly a jury of our peers. [Chuckles.]

So there was just the state trial. We got a two-year sentence. I was sent to Waupun, a maximum security prison, for the whole fourteen months [I served]. I stayed in a few months longer than most of the others because I was refused parole at my first hearing, probably because I participated in a prisoners' strike.

I made some decent friends among the inmates. There were two people that I spent quite a bit of time with, insofar as you could in a maximum security penitentiary. The only real time together was at an exercise yard for a couple of hours three evenings a week, with a bit more on the weekends. At night, locked up alone, I could have one book at a time. I was able to enroll in courses at the University of Wisconsin, and they'd send me one book. When I'd send it back, I'd get the next one. I took Minnesota History and Conversational Russian and several other courses, just for something to do. When I was in solitary confinement, there was only a Bible and a dictionary.

Ro: Now you don't come to nonviolence from a Bible tradition. What do you think gave you your beliefs?

Doug: I don't know as I can answer that. I wouldn't associate nonviolence as being a belief of mine. I came to the antiwar movement and to this action in particular from the point of view of efficiency and rationality. The draft files for me were purely symbolic. I didn't think the impact of denying the army the 10,000 folks from the files we burned was worth thinking about. Now that might have happened, but it was secondary. It was more the efficiency of showing that the resistance was rising and that there'd be more of it. I wasn't wedded to the submission to arrest; it was fine with me if people wanted to hit and run, but submitting would make the action more known, and increase the possibility of other people doing something to resist as well. Nonviolence for me at that time was a tactic. It was not a principle.

Ro: What about now?

Doug: The same. I haven't seen anything that would particularly turn me on to getting involved that wasn't nonviolent, but it's still not a principle, in that sense, for me.

Ro: What did you do when you left prison?

Doug: I worked in what we called the movement for about six years. Mostly local stuff. I had a probation officer who was sympathetic and in fact, he'd tell me when the FBI asked about me, and he wouldn't give them any information. [Long pause.]

Ro: Uh . . . what made you stop after six years?

Doug: The short answer is that I didn't know what to do. What I had been doing no longer made sense. The entire Left-wing movement I had associated with, and as I understood it, self-destructed—or historically destructed, or whatever—and I no longer understood it well enough to know where or how to remain a part of it. Or even if there was an "it."

In a larger framework, one of the big differences between the Vietnam era and this era is the kind of underlying optimism we had back then, not only in the Catholic Left but in the other bigger Left of which the Catholic Left was a part: the international Left—people in the anti-imperialist movement all over, from Algeria and Vietnam to South African and China.

I think the whole thing imploded in the middle '70s because some sense of realism came to people about what was really going on in the "revolutionary movement." I identified with the Vietnamese. I thought of myself as fighting for the National Liberation Front, and that made sense for me, made it even okay to go to prison.

Today there's not that kind of motivation. It's hard to get excited about fighting for the Iraqi resistance, for instance. I go to demonstrations and I talk to people and I . . . But I don't have an ongoing activity and I sure don't feel a part of a growing movement.

Ro: Would you still call yourself an activist?

Doug: Sheesh! I feel like an unemployed activist. Isolated and unemployed.

Jim Forest

Writer Jim Forest has been part of the faith-based peace and justice movement since coming to the Catholic Worker as a young man. He's lived in Holland for many years but travels to the states each year to lecture on Dorothy Day, Thomas Merton, Russian iconography, and the Orthodox Peace Fellowship, which he founded. Jim's narrative is composed of two interviews in addition to the one I recorded in 2007—one when we met in Holland in 1989 and a 2004 interview by Dyllan Taxman.[15]

Jim Forest, 2007.

Jim: I don't know if I've ever been much of a radical. My concern has always been more, uh . . . sacramentally-based, I would say. If you believe, as I do, that every person is made in the image of God, it's a responsibility, not just an idea. How you relate to the other person, even your enemy, has to witness the awareness that the person bears the image of God, is known to God, is dear to God, and is as capable of conversion as anybody. If God can convert me—which is a major miracle, God knows!—He certainly can convert others.

Ro: But you sure were radical during the Vietnam era—the Baltimore Four and the Catonsville Nine and the Milwaukee Fourteen . . .

Jim: Yeah, these were radical, I'd have to admit. I still think about them and struggle with some of the questions. I was in the Catholic Worker, and the Catholic Worker's radical approach was centered on care for people. All people. The Catholic Worker has probably been saved

15. The Taxman interview is copyright Jim Forest and is available online at www .jimandnancyforest.com/2006/03/03/looking-back-on-the-milwaukee-fourteen/.

by that centering. And all of us who are part of the Catholic Worker probably are saved by that.

Ro: Dorothy Day had trouble with the Milwaukee Fourteen, didn't she?

Jim: She did. Oh yes! But she never said, "To hell with you!" She had second . . . her first thoughts were quite different from her second thoughts. I heard Dorothy praise the Catonsville Nine in a talk she gave at the National Liturgical Conference, and her opinion meant a great deal to me.[16] I wish she had the second thoughts sooner than she did, because then it would have been the Milwaukee Thirteen.

I approved of the Baltimore Four. These were our friends, and I knew something was brewing with Catonsville Nine before it happened, but I didn't know exactly what. Right afterwards, I became the more or less press secretary of their Defense Committee. Designed a brochure, did press releases, arranged presentations.

When George Mische asked me if I'd be interested in taking part in a similar action, largely because of Dorothy's praise for them, I felt obliged to say yes. We had a wonderful group. Several Catholic priests and one was a Benedictine monk, Tony Mullaney. Another was [Basil O'Leary], a Christian Brother who had a Ph.D. from Notre Dame University and was Chair of the Economics Department at St. Mary's College in Minnesota. A very sober person—not your typical activist, not by any stretch. Indeed, I don't think any of us were typical activists. There was a very deep spiritual life carried on by most members of this group, and it was very strongly Catholic, although not entirely.

We met together maybe a half dozen times before the action. Part of it was just practical stuff, of course. We were lucky that one of the people in the group, Doug Marvy, had been in the Navy like me. He'd been in the construction battalions. "Opening a door? No problem!" [Laughs.]

Ro: What was your job?

Jim: I was more or less the press secretary. I wrote the statement. We all tinkered with it, but I was the principal author. I probably did as much traveling and speaking as anybody in the group.

Ro: Were you scared when you were doing the action?

16. In a letter to Fathers Dan and Phil Berrigan on May 1, 1968, Day wrote, "I could only think that it was a very strong and imaginative witness against conscription." Robert Ellsberg, *All the Way to Heaven: The Selected Letters of Dorothy Day* (Milwaukee: Marquette University Press, 2007), 343.

Jim: Terrified! I can remember my knees shaking like leaves in the wind.

Ro: Most of you wore suits, according to the newspaper pictures.

Jim: Oh, sure. We weren't . . . if you're going to try to communicate with people, you've got to dress for it. To show your respect for the people you hope will be interested in what you've done and why.

The only thing I've always regretted about the whole thing—well, maybe not the only thing, but one of the things—is that we hadn't reckoned on the cleaning woman being there. And I thank God to this day that this poor, very upset, older woman whose English was not fluent . . . Thank God she didn't have a heart attack! She was absolutely terrified. We did our best to reassure her, but at the same time we didn't want her racing out of the building to stop what we were doing. It must have been like a nightmare for her.

Other than that, the whole thing was ideal. There was a tiny triangular-shaped park in front of the building, dedicated to the memory of those who died in the First World War. We brought the nine bags down, and had this so-called homemade napalm, a mixture of detergent and gasoline. For us, it was a symbolic way of connecting our action with the napalm that was being used against human beings in Vietnam.

We stood around, we read from the Gospel, we prayed a few prayers, we waited for the Fire Department and the police to arrive. We were in the county jail for a month, with a ridiculously high bail.

I was amazed at the impact in the media—more than I would have expected: a two-page photo in *Life*, front page coverage in newspapers across the country, reports on TV news programs nationwide, national press attention while the trial was going on, respected poets and scholars coming to Milwaukee to support us, lots and lots of mail.[17] One of the "epistles" in Leonard Bernstein's "Mass" was a letter about visiting me in prison. Now, thirty-eight years later, it's just one item on a long list of protest actions during the Vietnam War.

Dyllan: Do you think that your actions that day had an effect on the draft?

Jim: Sure. For starters it closed down conscription [in Milwaukee] for a time. For several months, the only people who were sent to the war from there were volunteers. Judging from the mail we received, I think we helped more draft-eligible people decide that they wouldn't take part in the war. The fact that about half our groups were Catholic

17. The next three paragraphs are from Dyllan Taxman's interview.

priests meant that our action had particular impact on the Catholic Church. It probably was a factor in the opposition to the war that was increasingly voiced by the Catholic hierarchy.

Dyllan: Do you think that your motives for this protest were understood by the public?

Jim: There were a great many who understood. It was, after all, a very simple deed. The religious basis was clearly expressed. A major goal was to encourage more draft resistance and indeed there *was* more. But of course many people were astonished or even scandalized to see Catholic priests and committed lay people putting their freedom on the line by an act of civil disobedience. I think the trial was at least as important as the action. We hoped to put an immoral and illegal war on trial, and that's pretty much what happened.

We had a tremendous defense committee! Marc Stickgold volunteered his services. He was a brilliant lawyer who had been federal attorney for the State of Michigan. I have enduring respect for him. And William Kunstler, about whom I'm much less enthusiastic, but nonetheless he was a very interesting guy. (Eventually we fired him and defended ourselves.) I also liked the prosecution lawyers. They were good and honest people, and I respected them. When the trial was over and when they won, the head of the team of prosecution lawyers volunteered his services to take care of our appeal.

Because we defended ourselves, we didn't have a lawyer with us at the defendants' table. But Stickgold was in the courtroom, and at night we'd evaluate the case with him. We spent a great deal of time—each of us, to the extent that we were able to—doing our legal homework, reading law and case histories and so forth.

I also loved the judge. He was a . . . I mean, we argued with him, and we were no doubt very unpleasant to him in some ways, but we tried our best to reach him as a fellow human being, and I think to a considerable extent we did. It was a trial in which moral issues entered the courtroom.

That's one of the problems now. Today it's practically impossible for the courtroom to be a place of real moral drama. Today it's just, "Did you or did not dent this or burn that or pour blood on this silo." . . . No question of the morality or the legality of the weapons. We were able to use the justification defense and to talk about the New Testament.

We were found guilty, of course. I was sentenced to two years and I actually served thirteen months, [getting out] on good behavior. Before the trials, we had negotiated with the courts that if we were convicted both in federal and state court, the federal time would be served concurrently but in the state prison system. This was all Marc Stickgold's doing. Most of the time I was in Waupun, which is a maximum security prison in central Wisconsin, but for a little while—maybe two months or so—I was in a low security forestry camp. That didn't work. I didn't mind being in a wall-less prison. I loved working on streams in the state park system and all, but I didn't like the dormitory, and I really didn't like the guards. And they hated me and blocked a lot of my mail, for instance. I couldn't even receive the *National Geographic*. Finally I told them they could either send me back to maximum security or I'd start breaking regulations so that they'd *have* to send me there.

The prison system really wanted to keep the group separate, and they were nervous about me because of being a writer. (I found that out, because somebody I knew was working in the warden's office, and he saw a telegram between some of the administrators. "Watch out for Forest. You know, he's a writer.")

One thing: For me, it was a wonderful thing to be stopped dead in my tracks, not to be rushing around the country and speaking all the time. There's always a danger in being in front of an audience too much. It's hard to cultivate humility. You can get into a kind of . . . I wouldn't say rock star mentality, because God knows you're nothing like that, but still, comparatively speaking, people are more impressed with you than they should be. And you get more impressed with yourself than you should be. It was very nice to be taken off that conveyor belt and to be put in a situation of more or less monastic enclosure, and to try to recover a more serious and a more disciplined spiritual life. I would spend part of each day reading the New Testament, and I had certain prayers I would follow. I went to Masses at every possible opportunity, and then there was time to read. I could use the State University library system, so I was able to read Russian literature. All the books Dorothy [Day] said I should read. Tolstoy! In most state prisons, you'd be lucky to get Zane Grey. [Laughs.]

Ro: How did it feel when you got out?

Jim: Well, the best thing about it was I was able to see my son Ben for the first time in well over a year. He was eight. The worst thing about that whole Milwaukee Fourteen period was how little contact I had as a father with my son. My wife and I were separated, and I was busy "saving the world" so he was living with my mother.

Ro: What did your mother think of your action?

Jim: My mother was always very supportive. I think if I robbed banks she would've been supportive. Her sons could do no wrong.

Ro: What did you do when you got out?

Jim: I worked for *Commonweal* [magazine] for a little while. Lived in the Emmaus House community and was still somewhat involved in resistance activities. Nearby lived some nuns who had done some draft board actions or something and were under intense FBI surveillance, as were we. They had a car with two FBI agents, twenty-four hours a day, in front of their house.

Can you imagine what that cost? Not to mention the agents across the street in the rented apartment with all the cameras and so forth. It was surveillance meant to terrify. We discovered listening bugs in our telephones and stuff like that. It was somewhat funny, in a way, and it just became part of our lives, but it was also a nuisance.

And then there came the Harrisburg case; I was involved very much as press secretary for the trial.[18] But that was the end of the line for me. That's when I finally decided I couldn't be part of it anymore. One of the major problems of this type of action is its reliance on secrecy, and the secrecy breeds suspicion. Also, the move from what came to be called stand-around actions like ours to hit-and-run actions was part of that continuum, getting further and further away from what I would call true nonviolence.

In the end, it's the power of truth. To the extent that you bear witness to the truth, that can be a significant witness indeed. But if it becomes a witness to paranoia or to contempt or to anger, then it doesn't contribute very substantially to anybody's conversion. Because, nonviolence essentially aims for conversion: my conversion

---

18. The Harrisburg seven was another group involved in what came to be called the ultra-resistance. It included Phil Berrigan and Elizabeth McAlister, who later married. They were accused of conspiring to kidnap Henry Kissinger and blow up steam tunnels in DC, with evidence supplied by an FBI informer who smuggled letters between the two while Phil was in prison for draft file destruction. A dramatic trial resulted in only minor convictions, all of which were overturned on appeal.

and your conversion. We both need . . . We both have not yet become the person that God calls us to be.

Father Lorenzo Rosebaugh, OMI (1937–2009)

Fr. Lorenzo: When I was young, I wanted to be a baseball player. I even tried out for the Cardinals, along with about a thousand other kids. I made it to the last cut but then only two people got signed. Now I'm a priest in the Oblates of Mary Immaculate, and of course that's a long story, but . . . We're basically a missionary order with the idea to serve the poorest, most marginalized people.

After novitiate I went to one of our seminaries down in Mississippi. This was in the early sixties. Met Phil Berrigan there, and we used to sneak over to New Orleans and visit him. Then one or two of the guys thought it would be a great idea to invite Dorothy [Day] down. Well, the superiors didn't think it was so good, but somehow she came, anyway! We weren't supposed to talk to her personally, though, and it was the same thing when Phil would come.

When I got out of the seminary, the war in Vietnam was really heating up. They didn't think our class was mature enough for the missions, so they sent me to a parish in St. Paul, Minnesota, with a very strict Polish priest. I didn't last very long with him. [Laughs.] Then I taught school in Duluth and then got to Chicago where I worked in the inner city, which was great. I met Mike and Nettie Cullen [of Casa Maria in Milwaukee] and went on the retreat where we decided on the Milwaukee Fourteen action. I remember grabbing Dan Berrigan: "I don't think I know enough about the war situation. I'm against it and everything, but I don't know if I could get up and explain it. "

He says, "I've got only one question for you: Is killing right or wrong? That's all you have to know."

So it all worked out. We all came from different backgrounds but we came together in Milwaukee and had a little Mass and then we walked down to the city. Some were dressed as janitors. I and Brother O'Leary were dressed as clergy. We told the cleaning woman that we were coming for a meeting and she couldn't understand that, but we got the keys from her.

Ro: Did you have to take the keys by force?

Fr. Lorenzo: She didn't even know what happened. I just picked them out of her apron and handed them to [Doug Marvy who unlocked the doors.] Then we closed the door and started talking to her, and that's when she got kind of excited. Thought I was Father Groppi and started accusing me of all this horrible stuff. [19]

Then the other woman came down from upstairs, and we let her in and then closed the door again. We were trying to explain what we were doing and at the same time put all the draft files into these big bags. There was nothing physical about it, but the women *did* get kind of scared and upset. Basil O'Leary was the most gentle soul, so we didn't have any trouble, and the whole thing took only about twenty minutes. No violence at all.

We stayed inside with the women and watched out the window while the others set fire to the files outside in the plaza. A police car was passing by and I guess he called headquarters. Somebody heard him say, "You'd better send somebody. A bunch of hippies are having a bonfire in the plaza." That's as much as they knew. But once the police came, they saw what was going on, and we were arrested.

We were thirty days in the Milwaukee Jail, and then we were let out for nine whole months before the trial. So we got the word out—spoke at colleges and on the radio. In Milwaukee there was a debate in the newspapers every day. "Were those guys crazy or did they have a message?"

When we first walked into the jail, and the police saw the Roman collars, they started making fun of us. "I wouldn't want any of my sons and daughters going to confession to those bastards," and things like that. But those were a good thirty days. I think we fasted, and we were in this big room by ourselves. We were getting notes under our door from the inmates, saying, "Nice to have you" and all that. Fr. Groppi had pickets outside. It was good.

The trial was good, too, and we all had our say. Right after the trial, we were shipped off to Waupun State Prison. Our sentence was a year and a day. After three months or so in maximum security, they sent Jim Forest and myself and Jim Harney out to a minimum security place.

I was milking cows, and that was a great job! The farmer was great, too! But the cows! It was supposedly the best herd in all Wisconsin but

---

19. Father James Groppi (1930–1985) was a civil rights activist in Milwaukee, noted for controversial but ultimately successful tactics.

in a very short time these cows were giving no milk at all. The prisoners came from the city, see, and they were cussing and yelling and even hitting the cows, trying to get the milk to come out. [Laughs.] I'd bring my books out and read and the farmer didn't have any trouble with me, no sir. But then one of the guards said, "No books!"

So I said, "Well, no books, no work." I refused. It was so ridiculous! They put me in the hole, and my social worker came and tried to talk me out of it. I didn't change my mind, so they shipped me back to the big prison, to maximum security. I didn't work very long there, either, because of some trouble with a big guy who was trying to have me do his work. The long and short of it, I spent an extra ten months in solitary and didn't get out for good behavior like the rest of the guys. But I'm glad that I made those decisions. My sense is that it's all the same system, so refusing to work is continuing the action while I'm in prison.

After he was released, Father Lorenzo continued to preach with his body, working first with Casa Maria in Milwaukee and then hitchhiking down to Brazil. Dom Helder Camera, bishop of Recife, asked him to do street work in the slums after a man died on the bishop's doorstep from eating dirt. From that street experience, Fr. Lorenzo was arrested a second time and jailed in a stark cell where some of the prisoners were made to dance in the nude.

He also spent another year in prison for an action against nuclear weapons manufacture in Amarillo. His last arrest was in the original action at the School of the Americas with then-Maryknoll priest Roy Bourgeois. (See Chapter 6.) Padre Lorenzo was killed in a car-jacking in Guatemala on May 18, 2009. At his funeral Mass, the Mexican provincial of his order called him a "mix of Saint John the Baptist and Saint Francis of Assisi."

Father Lorenzo Rosebaugh, OMI, Guatemala, 2006. © Bob Graf.

Women Against Daddy Warbucks—Maggie Geddes

The next summer after the Milwaukee Fourteen action—on July 1, 1969—seven women broke into Selective Service headquarters in Manhattan after the building had closed for the day. They worked for hours, shredding over 6,000 A-1 draft files from five draft boards in Manhattan and the Bronx, tearing out telephone lines, and removing the "A" and the "1" from typewriters. Then they left, taking several pouches of the draft files with them. Two days later, as announced, they surfaced at a large demonstration at Rockefeller Center, throwing the shredded files like confetti before some of them were arrested. The name of the group: "Women Against Daddy Warbucks." I interviewed Maggie Geddes, one of the leaders of the group. She's now an attorney in Sacramento.

Maggie: How did we decide to do a women's only action? Long story. Remember the poster with Joan Baez that said, "Girls say yes to men who say no." People didn't use the word "women" in those days. [Laughs wryly.] It was supposed to turn the militarism thing on its head, to say in a tongue-in-cheek way that it was manly to resist the draft. Some of us thought there must be a way to make a statement *as women* about women's opposition to war that was more substantive than the classic support role reflected by that poster. Yes, there were long-standing women's organizations like Women Strike for Peace and Women's International League for Peace and Freedom, but we were young, we were active, and we wanted to be *more* active, and as women.

    I was working as the office manager for the Catholic Peace Fellowship (CPF) in New York. Jill Boskey, one of the other women in the Daddy Warbucks action, was a staff person with New York Resistance, right across the hall. The spring before, five or six women had burned draft cards in Central Park, in order to represent their willingness to also take risks, and Jill had been one of those women.

    At the same time as this anti-war work, we were forming our identities as women, collectively and individually. The second wave of the feminist movement was a major influence. Prior draft board actions, like Catonsville and Baltimore and Milwaukee Fourteen, had been mostly men. Before our action, only Mary Moylan and Marjorie Melville had done this kind of action.[20] CPF had been very

20. Two women had participated in the hastily-planned Chicago Fifteen action in May, 1969. (Gray, "Ultra-Resistance.") The Catonsville Nine women were Mary

involved in organizing support for the Catonsville actions these women took part in.

Now some of what I'm going to say will be said with a cautionary note. For one thing, caution becomes ingrained if you spend a long time in political action that requires secrecy and planning. Also, I've lost track of most of the other people in the action, and I don't want to talk about them without their permission.

Ro: Marian Mollin's article in *Oral History Review* identifies five of you, so you, Jill Boskey, Kathy [Czarnik], Valentine [Green], and Pat [Kennedy] are on record as being involved.[21] If you'd rather not mention any other names, that's okay. I want to hear *your* story.

Maggie: Well, there's no reason not to say that Linda [Forest Orell] and Barbara [Webster] were arrested. They were. That's a different issue than whether or not they were involved in the action, but yes, I'll just stick to my own involvement.

Within the Catholic Left, there was *enormous* opposition to us doing an action that united feminism and the anti-war movement. We had opposition from the start, more from people in the "Catholic Left" than the Left as a whole, because the so-called Catholic Left was involved with all the post-Catonsville developments.

Phil Berrigan was very opposed. Had . . . Uh . . . Let me think of how to say this. It's hard to imagine now that this historical period—the late sixties—was a time when almost anything women did in order to try to find their identity and assert themselves as separate people distinct from men was derided and ridiculed. In the worst terms imaginable. There was something fundamentally threatening to men—and to many women—when we tried to do that. When we talked about the idea with some of the men in the Catholic Left, a number of them thought it was terrible! They used the word "divisive"

Moylan (1936–1995) and Marjorie Melville. Marjorie joined her husband Tom in the action after returning from Guatemala where they had been Maryknoll missionaries. They served two years in prison. Mary Moylan went underground, like the Berrigan brothers, but was mostly ignored by the media and those on the Catholic Left. Even the FBI paid only sporadic attention to her case, and she evaded arrest for eight years. Eventually she turned herself in and served three years in Alderson. Shawn Francis Peters includes a chapter on Moylan in *The Catonsville Nine: A Story of Faith and Resistance in the Vietnam Era* (New York: Oxford University Press, 2012), 281–92.

21. See Marian Mollin, "Communities of Resistance: Women and the Catholic Left of the Late 1960s," *Oral History Review* 31/2 (2004) 35.

and other similar words about it—and about us, seemingly—for even coming up with the idea.

Now I want to add that although we did it as women, there were individual men in the movement who supported us and thought it was a good idea. But the hierarchy, if you will, of the draft board destruction community, including Phil Berrigan and John Grady and other people, were extremely opposed to it and saw us in hostile terms.

There was a point at which there was no communication between our [planning] group and the larger group that was involved with organization events, because they were so totally hostile to women doing this and to our doing it on our own terms. I . . . I just can't tell you how difficult it was to be treated as if we were bubbly little misguided know-nothings!

I remember, for example, a demonstration in DC, in maybe 1968, where a woman from SDS stood up to say something, and she was actually hooted down. And at an early gathering of the Catholic Left draft board people, a woman was laughed at for just trying to get a word in. It happened all the time. And it took . . . resolve, I guess, is one word for it, to keep trying to be heard.

Because there was so little outside support, we started to draw in more, both individually and as a group. We'd talk about it with some of the men but not all of them. So there were two kinds of secrecy going on, one of them being that you just had to be secret to be able to plan a draft board action that was obviously illegal. Then there was also this other level of sorting through who would support you and who wouldn't, from within the group that supposedly were your allies.

Perhaps because we had to function on our own, we developed a different mode than the sort of martyr-like "standing by" that had preceded us. We had to come into ourselves with supportive groups of individual women and men who weren't directly involved in the action but who wanted to help us in any way they could. The isolation enabled us to think outside the box and come up with different ways of doing things—the confetti, going in overnight, not staying around to be arrested.

There had been a ritualistic aspect to the Catonsville and Baltimore and Milwaukee actions, with priests and others who were extremely credible adults. That intentionality was wonderful and had a terrific historical impact. But I think that if we'd used those same symbols, for whatever reason, maybe because we were women and didn't have those particular credentials, and didn't even have a common Catholic background . . . well, we *couldn't* do it the same way. I don't want to inflate it by saying we did it on our own terms, but it just became this other thing. We weren't trying to set up a model or anything; we just had other ideas as to how we'd do it.

It turned out to be really great. We were able to destroy the files of seven or eight Manhattan draft boards, including the South Bronx and parts of Brooklyn. A lot of men who weren't able to avoid being drafted were from Harlem and South Bronx and parts of New York that had large minority populations. So for me, the best part was being successful at disrupting all of that. A great impact! And when we showed up at Rockefeller Center, there was a real celebration and a huge, huge demonstration.

The Selective Service office was one floor in an eighty-story commercial building, and the people who did the action and the people who were helping us spent a lot of time casing it, figuring things out. Eventually a plan developed: how to stay in the building overnight after it closed and how to get into the Selective Service office and all of that. We were there for an entire night, so we didn't take the files out but shredded them by hand, for hours and hours. We brought these big shoulder bags in with us to bring out some of the shredded files for the demonstration.

Linda Forest Orell at Times Square, 1969. © John Goodwin.

Ro: How did you feel when you were inside the building doing the actual action?

Maggie: I remember two feelings: One was terror, one was excitement. We waited in a janitor's closet for the building to close. It had to be late enough so the security people had gone, so we were hours and hours smashed together inside a closet. It was pitch dark, and that's when I was scared.

Once we got inside the Selective Service office, I was still scared, but I was also excited that we'd be able to do what we'd come for. There was a conference room with a big table, and people brought the contents of the file cabinets in to us, and I remember sitting there with others for an awfully long time—tearing and tearing and tearing [draft files] into narrow strips.

Getting into the building was the most dangerous part. My memory is that [three people] came down from a floor above us and in through a window [to unlock the door from the inside]. Jill [Boskey] got rope burns on her hands when she was practicing. I and other people had been inside the office when it was open, so we had a general sense of where things were. Once we were inside, it just happened organically in terms of who was doing what. It wasn't organized; everybody just worked together. I remember shredding mostly, but I think we all did various things during the night, to get everything done that we'd planned.

Ro: After you finished, was it difficult to get out of the building? I presume there were guards someplace.

Maggie: My memory is that there weren't. From having looked at the building for months beforehand, we learned that the security people were there in the late evening and then again in the early morning. We worked around their schedules, and just walked out the front door after we'd finished.

Ro: That's amazing! How far along were you on the planning when you came up with the idea of surfacing with the confetti?

Maggie: We already had the name and a written statement when we worked that part out. The most important thing, absolutely, was that we were doing it as women. We tried to make connections between the war and corporate involvement by our name and by having the demonstration at Rockefeller Center, where Dow Chemical and other war-related companies had headquarters.

The demonstration was set for July 3 and we were in the building the night of July 1. We were in hiding for July 2, in an apartment on the Lower East Side, and while we were there, we made posters for the demonstration. They had a black background, with the strips of paper on it, all jumbled together. The strips were about an inch wide, and so you could identify words like "Selective" or "1A" and we'd taken those keys off all the typewriters when we were in the office.

We also spent some of that day mailing letters to people whose names we took from the phone book, putting pieces of the draft files in them with a letter we'd written and had copied ahead of time. Also we sent letters and pieces of the files to different corporations located around Rockefeller Center, explaining what we'd done and asking people to oppose the war.

Ro: How did you decide who was going to publicly surface?

Maggie: There were always just five of us who were willing to identify ourselves and to speak publicly about the action and go to jail for it. Seven of us went into the building, but only five of us signed our names to the flier we'd prepared to hand out at the demonstration. Six women were arrested. I was not, but the other four Daddy Warbucks women were, along with Linda Forest and Barbara Webster.

We went up and down in terms of our numbers [in the group], for many reasons, the opposition I referred to earlier being one of them. Towards the end, we also had to make sure we had enough participants to make it happen. We knew that to be effective we needed to have more than the five, so we decided it would be okay to have other people help us who weren't willing to take the consequences. Those two people included one man.[22] He'd been a strong supporter of the idea of a women's action all along, and in the end was a vital part of pulling it off, along with Pat Kennedy and Jill, who had a major role in the logistics.

Of course we struggled over whether it would still be a "women's action" if it included a man. The planning had gone on with fits and starts for a long time, dealing with the hostility, then trying to separate from that, and trying to get more women committed to the action. We ended up just wanting to make it happen and decided not to keep looking for some magic larger number of women. So we asked him and [another woman] to make sure we'd have enough people to pull it all off.

I think the reasons the FBI grabbed Barbara Webster and Linda Forest at the demonstration was . . . well, both Barbara and Linda were very active in the anti-war movement in New York, and no doubt known to the FBI. But also at the beginning of the demonstration, they each asked if they could throw some of the confetti around. Maybe some combination of those two things was why they were arrested.

22. This man was Charlie Dobbins (Maggie Geddes, e-mail to author, March 6, 2012).

Before the demonstration, the feds didn't know which women had been in the Selective Service offices, except for Pat Kennedy. We'd all worn rubber gloves when we were in the building, in order to be able to control our own appearances afterwards at the demonstration, but Pat's gloves broke during the night. She was a long-time activist whose fingerprints the FBI would have had for sure, so there was no question that she was going to be arrested, and she was. As soon as they saw her, six or eight of the FBI grabbed her, hoisted her above the shoulders of the crowd, and horizontally took her out to waiting police cars. Carried her right through the department store across the street.

The morning after the action, when we got to the safe house, we'd called the local New York anti-war organizations to tell them about the action and ask them to tell the media that there'd be a demonstration at which we'd surface and take responsibility. When we got to Rockefeller Center, it was crawling with plainclothes guys and as soon as we began to toss the shredded files, they started grabbing the women tossing them. But not me! Other than Pat, they didn't know who else had participated. There weren't any "plants" in our group because we'd been successful in maintaining our own security.

The articles in the media were amazing! Front-page coverage, but oh my goodness! They were so sexist, so reflective of the times. I can't remember if they even interviewed any of us. That immediate impact—both in terms of being a women's action and being a successful anti-war action—was really wonderful.

The follow-up impact was diluted by all sorts of complications, though. First, we didn't go to trial. So the impact was diluted because we didn't have the support of the people who usually organize around a trial. We kept trying to extend the impact, but it was hard. Other developments were occurring on almost a daily basis, like a major police action against the Black Panthers. Without the organizing focus of a prosecution and trial, public attention moved on pretty quickly.

When we got our FBI files years later, it seemed that the decision not to prosecute us had been made at the New York US Attorney's Office. That office decided it wouldn't be a good idea to have another political trial because trials became focal points for more demonstrations and lots of other actions.

After the action happened, a grand jury was called. You see, there was a sexist perception that it just couldn't have been us who did it, that there *had* to have been men behind it, that there had to have been more going on in terms of a conspiracy or someone to put us up to it or something like that. Because of these sexist assumptions, a grand jury looked into the action.

The thinking of the pro bono lawyers, Fred Boyden and Carl Broege from the Center for Constitutional Rights (wonderful guys who other peace folks had contacted) . . . anyway, the assumption was that the grand jury would subpoena me and give immunity if I talked but jail time if I didn't cooperate, in order to coerce me into talking about who had put us up to it. So I chose to leave town for a number of months and not make myself available to subpoenas.

As I'm remembering, the others who had been arrested at the demonstration were subpoenaed and appeared before the grand jury, but declined to testify. But even after the grand jury, the case just sat there! Eventually our lawyers moved to have it dismissed because we weren't being given a speedy trial.[23] So Judge Constance Baker Motley dismissed the charges against us and nobody ever served time for Women Against Daddy Warbucks.

Another thing in the mix was that the women's movement sort of took off on its own around that time. Most of us got involved in that as much as the antiwar movement. Another thing, though, was the reaction we got from the feminist movement in New York. As part of what we tried to do after the action to further its impact, we contacted a group of feminist activists who'd newly organized under the name "Redstockings." We also visited the consciousness-raising groups of the early feminist theorists.

In both groups, we got a very mixed reaction: "Of course we should be against the war, but when you run into that opposition from the male members of the antiwar movement, obviously you shouldn't be involved with it but should be doing things that further women's agenda more specifically." We were stunned! It just put us between a rock and a hard place! Rejected by the feminists and by most of the men in the Catholic Left.

23. Jill Boskey told Murray Polner and Jim O'Grady on August 13, 1994, that the FBI didn't prosecute because they spent all their time "hunting for the men they believed had directed the women." Polner and O'Grady, *Disarmed and Dangerous: The Radical Life and Times of Daniel and Philip Berrigan* (Boulder, CO: Westview, 1997), 240.

I also interviewed Linda Orell.[24] When she returned her transcript, she commented:

> I had forgotten about the massive chauvinism, even though some of it was probably unconscious, at least some of the time. Something that needs to be remembered: we were Catholics. Catholic laywomen. That carried with it membership in a hierarchy, a caste system, in which women religious—nuns or former nuns—enjoyed more credibility and more entrée into these communities than did laywomen. A married laywoman, as I was, who did not cower in her niche as a married person, was on the lowest rung of all. If those priests had accepted us, it would have been an implicit admission that the hierarchy was evolving or was capable of evolving. In a sense, feminism *did* erode the Church's base, and the priests in the Catholic Left felt it coming.

24. Linda Orell interview, Marquette Archives. Her transcript says, "I was arrested at Rockefeller Plaza with a bag full of the shreds, and that's what I'm comfortable saying."

4

Beating Swords Into Plowshares—
The United States

"They shall beat their swords into plowshares and their spears into pruning hooks; one nation shall not raise the sword against another, nor shall they train for war again."

ISAIAH 2:4

The end of the Vietnam era found the phrase "Catholic Left" applying to more than the Catholic Worker movement. Cohesive and vocal—especially in the numerous newsletters which fly back and forth via mail and Internet—members of the Catholic Left are guided in a loose way by the Jonah House Community of Baltimore.[1]

Jonah House was founded in 1973 by Liz McAlister, her husband Phil Berrigan, and four others.[2] After their civil marriage, Phil Berrigan was no longer a member of the Josephite order, as he had been in his civil rights and Vietnam War resistance days, but he did not apply to Rome for laicization and his friends say he regarded himself as a married priest. The community has changed over the years, but from the beginning has concentrated its work on resistance, specifically at eliminating nuclear

1. The Berrigan Archives at DePaul, the Daniel and Philip Berrigan Collection, 1880–1995 at Cornell University, and the Catholic Worker Archives at Marquette are repositories for these newsletters as well as photos and other documents.

2. See Chapter 2 of *Doing Time for Peace* for interviews from McAlister and the three Berrigan children.

weapons, the exorbitantly expensive means of mass destruction which they see as the underlying cause of the violence throughout the world.

Liz told me that their first vision was to establish resistance communities all over the country.[3] They soon found they were going to so many meetings that they didn't have time for resistance actions themselves, so they developed another model, that of biannual Faith and Resistance Retreats, held in the nation's capitol. One is held shortly after Christmas, at the Feast of the Holy Innocents, and one usually from August 6–9, the days commemorating our bombing of Hiroshima and Nagasaki.

Those who attend meet for two or three days, usually in a church basement, in an atmosphere that feels a bit like a family reunion, with everyone cooking and having fun as they catch up on what's happening in other families and communities. They also study the scriptures, listen to speakers about nuclear weapons and resistance spirituality, and plan a resistance action. In Faith and Resistance Retreats, there is always an arrest component where some "risk arrest," as these peace people euphemistically call nonviolent civil disobedience, while others act as support people. These support people contact relatives, arrange for bail and release, if necessary, and support those who are arraigned and incarcerated. Several of the resisters whose stories are included in this text got their start in a Pentagon or White House Faith and Resistance action.

This model has been adopted nationwide, sometimes by permanent groups called Life Communities, sometimes by Pax Christi or diocesan groups, sometimes by Catholic Worker regional gatherings. For instance, during the eighties, Faith and Resistance Retreats in the Diocese of Saginaw targeted the now-closed Wurtsmith Air Force Base in Oscoda, Michigan. These gatherings were my first post-Vietnam War forays into activism. Besides the DC symbols of US military power, groups witness at the UN complex in New York City, at military recruiting centers, air and water shows, museums which glorify war, nuclear weapons and depleted uranium plants, and army, navy, marine, and air force bases

Faith and Resistance Retreats build community and provide spiritual sustenance for resisters at all levels. They also may become recruitment tools for Plowshares actions, the most serious resistance actions of the Catholic Left. The Plowshares movement grew from an action at King of Prussia, Pennsylvania in 1980, where eight resisters, including Phil Berrigan and his Jesuit brother Dan, broke into a General Electric nuclear weapons plant and damaged a nose cone on a Mark 12A

3. Liz McAlister interview, Marquette Archives.

warhead.[4] Since then, there have been between 93 to 150 such actions, depending on how they're counted.[5]

Following the draft file destruction model of destroying "improper property," resisters symbolically or actually "beat swords into plowshares," most often using ordinary household hammers. In actions heavy with religious symbolism and repeated ritual, they usually pour or throw bottles of their own blood, hang banners naming the sin and identifying themselves, recite prayers, and leave documents that they hope can be introduced as evidence. Because the success of their action depends on secrecy, the Gandhian practice of alerting the police is not followed, but the nonviolent principle of not endangering human life is absolute.

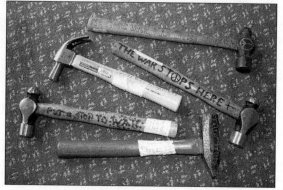

Hammers used in Plowshares actions, 2003. Kevin McLaughlin, OMI.

Plowshares people cut through fences and cross airplane runways, enter nuclear weapons plants in crowded urban areas and missile silo sites in lonely fields, swim out to submarines, take the ramp into naval museums with other tourists, and cut down poles which carry messages to nuclear submarines. And they go to prison, often for one to three years. (Plowshares activist Helen Woodson was released from prison in September of 2011, after serving nearly 27 years for Plowshares and related actions.) Once in a while, the resisters aren't prosecuted and once in a very great while, they are acquitted.

Unlike the organizing around Vietnam era trials, the defendants in the first Plowshares action at King of Prussia faced silence and ostracism, both from the general public and from the peace community, according

4. See Chapter 4 of *Doing Time for Peace* for Sr. Anne's Montgomery's description of that first action.

5. The 150 number refers also to those more accurately called "disarmament actions" because they don't look to the Biblical prophecy for their inspiration. Sister Ardeth Platte of Jonah House told the author in an August, 2010 e-mail that the lower number is probably inaccurate as it's hard to keep track of the European actions.

to Fr. Dan Berrigan's memory. "Every church and religious institution within range of the courthouse closed their doors to them. They finally found a Catholic women's college to house them and their supporters, but when the trial unexpectedly went into its second week, the college's alumnae forced them out into the morally isolated landscape."[6]

Through the years, support has grown, and although the larger peace movement still ignores them, faith-based activists now flock to pretrial gatherings called "Festivals of Hope" and stay for the trials if they can. In fact, as the FBI noticed in the sixties, the trials themselves can serve as recruitment vehicles. Communication among the peace people grows apace. *The Nuclear Resister,* published by Felice and Jack Cohen-Joppa, keeps track of everyone incarcerated for nonviolent civil disobedience in the cause of peace.[7] Frank Cordaro maintains a Catholic Worker news service which spreads the word on upcoming retreats, nonclandestine actions, and trials.[8] The number of newsletters and blogs grows exponentially and the Jonah House archive site is crammed with the results of actions, trials, and incarcerations, with many photos and videos.[9]

The Catholic Left received massive media coverage during the Vietnam War. This is generally not the case with most Plowshares actions, although leaders Phil and Dan Berrigan are sometimes treated as icons. This chapter and others throughout the book provide the reflections of those whose voices are seldom heard. Jerry Ebner explains the theology behind Plowshares actions and describes how he and Joe Gump entered a missile site in Missouri. Art Laffin talks about two actions on the Thames River in the early '80s. Sue and Bill Frankel-Streit recall walking across a huge tarmac at Griffiss Air Force base in the early hours of January 1, 1991. Dr. Barry Roth tells us why he participated with his friend Phil Berrigan in the Aegis Plowshares in Maine. Susan Crane details her growth in prayer as she prepared for a Plowshares action and then tells how easily she and Steve Kelly, SJ, walked into a nuclear weapons plant.

6. E-mail of October 27, 1997 from John Hines to Barry Cort. Hines paraphrased remarks by Fr. Dan Berrigan given at a dinner at the University of Maine Peace and Justice Center.

7. Online: www.nukeresister.org.

8. To join the e-mail list, write Berrigan House, 713 Indiana Ave., Des Moines, IA, 50314.

9. Online: www.jonahhouse.org/archive.

Jerry Ebner

Jerry Ebner and I first met on a snowy morning in January of 1988. A few weeks later, he started a thirty-month prison term at Sandstone for his part in the Transfiguration West Plowshares action in 1987. As a young man, he met Phil Berrigan and began his resistance career. In 2006, he opened his own Catholic Worker house in Omaha, serving formerly homeless men in a personalist way. Because of his hospitality commitments, these days he does only low-key resistance actions with short jail terms.

Jerry: I'd been reading everything from Dan and Phil Berrigan, hearing about these guys. And then I got to meet Phil in the flesh. I had no idea what Jonah House was all about; however, there was a clear invitation to come out. I went for a Faith and Resistance Retreat during Holy Week of '76. God! The night before the action I didn't sleep. I ended up pouring some blood on the pillars at the Pentagon, along with several other people.

Ro: Did you take your own blood?

Jerry: Yes, we did. Very Good Friday. That was the first time. I was a full-time student at Goshen College then, and the trial was the next summer, so I was between school years. I ended up doing thirty days in the Richmond City Jail.

    I wasn't too sure what to expect, but a couple good priest friends were there, Bob Bossie from Chicago and Roy Bourgeois. We were probably the only three white guys out of about sixty. I was lucky to be with experienced friends who I trusted. Without them, I'd have felt pretty alienated and alone. We had good discussions and a lot of scripture study. The action came out of the context of Holy Week and you're in jail with two priests. If you were really Catholic, what more could you want?

    After another year of college, I decided I'd had enough of this fine education in peace studies and needed to put it into practice. So I moved to DC. Ended up doing a lot of support activities for the first Plowshare trial. Then I joined a group of folks at L'Arche in Columbus, Ohio. I met them at one of the Pentagon actions. You always met people from around the country at those actions. Later I lived in St. Francis Catholic Worker in Chicago and at Casa Maria in

Milwaukee, and that's when Joe Gump and I planned the Transfiguration West Plowshares action.

Ro: Jerry, how did your decision to do a Plowshares action fit into your life as a Catholic Worker?

Jerry: My resistance is rooted in the ideals of the Worker. Our founder Dorothy Day was very much part of resisting those forces that create poor people, so she asked questions: "What's the relationship between being a Christian and resisting the state?"

You know, I can't end homelessness by myself, but I can respond to a few poor people by being personally responsible for their lives and for justice in their lives. I believe we can disarm nuclear weapons in the same way if we take personal responsibility to do it.

Ro: Could you talk about the Plowshares concept for people who don't know about it?

Jerry: [Pause.] Well, I'll try. I don't know if I can do it very well. [Longer Pause.] One of the main aspects of a Plowshares action is to keep to the spirit of Isaiah in chapter 2, verse 4, when he talks about beating swords into plowshares. Seeing that as more than a vision for the future. As I understand the Scripture, Isaiah is saying that "they shall beat their swords into plowshares" in a covenant response to God's faithfulness. Often times in Old Testament covenants, God is saying, "I will do this if you will do that." It's somewhat of a contractual agreement, in order to bring peace to the land. God is willing to be faithful, but He is also expecting people to beat their swords into plowshares as a sign of that covenant. As I understand the Isaiahan scripture, peace won't come without people's following through with their faithfulness to that covenant.

Beyond that, there's always the question of the definition of nonviolence. The Plowshares actions have always been very nonviolent in the sense that no people have ever been hurt or injured or even threatened. Not other people, not ourselves. There are no martyrs in this movement by any means; no one wants to get themselves or anyone else killed.

Another big reason for a Plowshares action is to take personal responsibility for these weapons, and that's the Catholic Worker part I talked about earlier. Very few people do. Even the government doesn't say it's responsible. And I mean taking responsibility all along the way, from the action point to responsibility in the court system.

Using the court system to speak about those issues and then also taking the consequences of the jail time.

We don't pay restitution for what we damage, because it's contradictory to damage something you feel doesn't have any moral right to exist and then pay to fix it. To turn the plowshare back into the sword would be violating the covenant.

Ro: I see a big step between recognizing the wholeness of that vision and acting on it.

Jerry: Some of it, for me, was deciding whether it was the right time. And the right community. Doing work in the context of community is real important for any Catholic Worker. About a year before the action, Joe Gump and I joined with a group of people who had decided to come together and pray and reflect about the idea. One thing I'm real thankful for is the process. None of us came into the gathering with their minds made up. Several people eventually decided it wasn't for them, sometimes because of the possibility of long, long prison sentences, but mostly because of things in their life at the time, not the action itself. For instance, no one came to the conclusion that it was not nonviolent.

Ro: And for awhile you thought you were facing fifteen years?

Jerry: Right. And now it's only three, which is nice.

Ro: Why did you choose the Feast of the Transfiguration for your Plowshares action?

Jerry: We chose August 6 as, first of all, the anniversary of the atom bombing of Hiroshima by our government. It's been in my craw for many, many years that no one from the Pentagon, and no one from any White House, has ever told the Japanese people we're sorry or asked forgiveness, even though we talk all the time about how great our relations are with Japan.

Then we saw that Sunday was the Feast of the Transfiguration, and that example of God right in front of His disciples on this earth really seemed to fit. We acted on the exact time of the forty-second anniversary of the bombing of Hiroshima—August 5th at 5:15 p.m., which is August 6th at 8:15 a.m. in Hiroshima.

Ro: Now you didn't know that there was another Plowshares action on the same day?

Jerry: We had no idea, and they didn't either. So that's why they ended up being called Transfiguration Plowshares East and we were West. Wouldn't it have been wonderful if there were Transfiguration Plowshares one through twenty, all on the same day?

Ro: Can you describe your action?

Jerry: Sure. Joe and I arrived at K-9 Missile Site, which is part of White-man Air Force Base near Butler, Missouri.[10] First we attached three banners to the fence. "Swords into Plowshares: an act of healing." "Violence ends where love begins" Joe made a third banner, with pictures of all of his children and grandchildren.

Then we cut the little lock on the fence, entered into the gates, and locked them again from the inside. We walked about a hundred feet to the top of the missile silo which carries a Minuteman II Missile. Now the missile is down in the ground, covered by 110 tons of concrete. These sites are only guarded by electronic surveillance, no military personnel at all. We cut off a maintenance hatch lock at 5:11. This set off an alarm, and they got there at 5:47. But before they came, we were able to cut some cables to the electronic surveillance systems, damage the maintenance hatch lock, and do some spray painting as well.

We were pretty much finished with what we wanted to do in twenty minutes, so we came together again to pray and read scripture. And sing. I'd brought in my guitar so when they arrived, Joe and I were sitting on top of the missile site and singing away. Probably stuttering a bit.

Ro: Now I saw an essay you wrote that said this was "the most joy-filled day of your life." Are you still feeling so joyful about it, now that you're almost in prison?

Jerry: Well, it *was* one of the most joyful times in my life. I mean I'm scared now about going to prison, but when you're on the site, you're not thinking about prison. To be able to actually *do* what we had been talking about and praying about for a long, long time—that was the joyful part.

---

10. Maps showing all one thousand missile sites in the Midwest at that time can be found in *Nuclear Heartland*, available from Nukewatch online: www.nukewatch info.org/. These missiles have since been replaced by 450 Minuteman IIIs, buried in remote areas of Montana, North Dakota, and Wyoming.

I really do believe that people can be about disarmament. Too often we leave the responsibility to other people. I realize that all of the powers—Congress, the president, and the corporations—have got a part to play in the work for disarmament, and they can certainly do a lot. But we *all* have a part to play, in a very personal way.

Now people don't necessarily have to do our Plowshares kind of action. As an example, there are 150 missile silos in Missouri. What if two people would go to each of the 150 and just cut the little lock, which doesn't cost more than three dollars, and go on the site and pray. If they did that all at the same time, it would really shake up the whole state of Missouri.

Ro: Well, the Missouri Peace Planters did something like that, planting sunflower seeds on silos.[11] But are masses of people willing to make that move? You can get millions of people to come to New York and march in a parade. You can get maybe a hundred people to do a low-sentence resistance action and go to jail for a couple of days. Sort of like a day off. You don't find too many people willing to go away for five years. So do people want it badly enough? Are we going to have those mass numbers?

Jerry: I don't know. I hope so, but I just don't know. Eisenhower once said that eventually people are going to want peace so bad that the government will have to get out of the way. And I think that will happen. It's no different in lots of ways than Gandhi going down to the [sea]with a crowd of people, threatening the salt business.

Ro: Well, maybe. [Pause.] What about the idea of noncooperation, of not waiting around to be arrested, like a lot of folks did at the end of the Vietnam era? Waiting around to be arrested seems to be cooperating with the state you are resisting.

Jerry: Well, first, in a Plowshare actions, we're trying to challenge other people to think about it. Our silence has allowed them to be there for many, many years, and we want to take responsibility for them. Being responsible for something means you're going to engage it, stay with it, not do something and run away.

So you go to court. Joe and I chose to do a jury trial. Not because we thought we'd get justice out of the system, but basically because we wanted to be teachers to the twelve people on the jury.

11. See Fr. Jerry Zawada's and Fr. Bob Bossie's interviews in Chapter 9.

We knew the verdict was going to be guilty, because the judge pretty much constrains everything with his jury instructions. We were able to engage the jury, though, and I was even allowed to sing the song we sang at the silo.

Some people have just done nothing with the court system, and remained totally silent the whole time. I think that's appropriate, too. There are all kinds of ways. But I don't understand what it would teach people when you do something and then run. It just doesn't feel right in my gut.

Ro: Well, one could be around to do more actual disarming. Theoretically, anyway.

Jerry: That's true, but it's egotistical. The emphasis then would be on the individual person. "*I'm* the key to disarmament." Bullshit! That's not . . . I'm sorry. Joe and I did what little we did, and that's all it really is, something very modest. The other people in this world have a responsibility, too. It's doing what you do and then admitting it and saying what you did was right. That includes not even going on to another site, although if someone had a plan, maybe they could get to three or four different sites and then stop and wait for arrest.

Ro: Another thing: there's usually not much damage in a Plowshares action, at least the ones I know about. The damage is mostly symbolic and doesn't affect that missile's capability of being released and killing thousands of people.

Jerry: I guess that points to the same thing. The work of disarmament needs lots of creative thinking. In some ways, it's no different than recognizing your limitations in doing hospitality. I can't solve the problem of homelessness, and the world isn't dependent upon Joe and I to disarm it. But if a lot of us would act, I'm convinced we'd eventually be able to disarm the world.

Art Laffin and his wife Colleen are members of Dorothy Day Catholic Worker in Washington, DC. He acted as a support person for the first Plowshares action in 1980 and has been involved ever since, both in actions and as the one who keeps track. He estimates that he's been arrested over a hundred times and has spent a little over a year in jail and prison. Art works against violence in all forms, and after his brother was murdered by a mentally ill man in 1999, Art became even more active against the death penalty.

Art Laffin

When the eight acted in 1980 at the first Plowshares action, they had no idea how things would develop. They acted out of faith and conscience and left the rest to the Holy Spirit. Then other people became inspired by what they had done, and the Plowshares movement was born, with actions mostly in the US but also in Europe and in Australia [and New Zealand.] Gandhi called nonviolent resistance acts "experiments in truth," and that's what the Plowshares actions have been for me and for others.

When someone has done an action using the symbols—basically a hammer—we put it in the chronological list. People learn from those who've gone before, especially to get a better sense of what the trial and prison experiences are like. The trials have changed over the years, as the courts have become more systematic and used previous case law from other Plowshares trials. Now they repeatedly use an *In Limine* motion, which prohibits any affirmative defense. That means that if we mention certain things, we could be in contempt. In some trials there's even a list of words we can't use, like "the Bible," "poor," "nuclear weapons," "US foreign policy." But of course people *have* spoken about those things in court, at the risk of being held in contempt. In some trials there's been resistance in the courtroom where people turn their back to the judge or decide not to continue with the trial and instead begin to read the Scripture, and then supporters do the same thing and sing and people are arrested during the trial.

See, the jail and prison experiences are a way to continue the witness. None of us wants to go to jail or prison. We don't do it to be arrested but because it's the right thing to do. Of course, there's a long Biblical tradition of people going to prison for their faith, and we act in that tradition and are strengthened by it. A great cloud of witnesses has gone before us.

During our Trident Nein trial—my first Plowshares action—the judge threatened us with contempt because we kept pressing to speak about our intent. He sent the jury out of the courtroom and began to admonish us. I remember asking, "If you were a judge in the South during segregation, would you have upheld those laws? Those racist, illegal laws?"

And he said, "Well, as a judge I'm sworn to uphold the law of the land. I have taken an oath and I have to do that." Then he went on to say, "You people may be right. We may blow the world up, but the law must be upheld. God's law is irrelevant; the only law that's relevant here are the laws of the state of Connecticut and the United States of America."

Ultimately, we may be violating the laws of this empire but we're upholding God's law, and that's the primary law. We don't think it's irrelevant at all, so, in a way, we have a *responsibility* to violate these US laws because they're keeping this whole system of empire in place, a system which is causing so much suffering and needless death.

 Dorothy [Day] made the point that during the Nazi era, Hitler brought people to the ovens, but now we have the capacity to bring nuclear ovens to the people. In our first Plowshares action, we actually spray-painted on the Trident submarine "USS Auschwitz," and then on the sonar equipment, "Trident, a holocaust, an oven without walls." Both that 1982 action and the one in '89 were directed at Trident submarines.

The Trident has been called "the ultimate first strike weapon" because it can travel so far and so fast. At the time of our 1982 action, that Trident carried twenty-four missiles, each missile having seventeen individually targeted warheads, with each warhead capable of over five Hiroshimas. And the missile carrying these could go six thousand miles in thirty minutes and come within three hundred feet of its target.

The Trident Nein action had two parts. Some people canoed out and boarded the submarines from the Thames River, and some of us, including me, cut through a fence and then walked to the storage area. We were there for three hours in the early morning. (The mosquitoes were kind of feasting on us as we prayed.) We never planned that we'd be there so long and we kept repeating our actions and praying until they found us.

In the '89 action, I was in the canoe and there were several swimmers. They saw us right away and kept telling us to stop, but I held up a Salvadoran cross and we slowly kept going until we pulled right alongside the Trident. I think the reason there was no force used against us was recognition of the long history of nonviolent resistance in that area of Connecticut, a history that dates back to the late 1950s. After we hammered on the sub, we poured our own blood on the hull and then beached our little canoe on the tail end of it and went up on top and knelt and prayed. Eventually the Navy started spraying the fire hose toward us and demanding that we get off their submarine. But even then, they didn't shoot it directly at us.

I'm sure you've heard some people say that it's a violent action to destroy property. But we say the weapons have no right to exist, and that they're antithetical to everything that God calls us to cherish. As Dan Berrigan said in the Catonsville action, "Better to burn paper than children." These weapons are anti-God, they are anti-life, they're a theft from the poor, and their only purpose is to destroy God's creation.

Ro: What about the people who say civil disobedience hurts the peace movement, gives it a bad reputation?

Art: Well, I have to ask how it does that. It's *God's* movement. It's calling us to respect and protect *all* life. There's Jesus's admonition to love our enemies. And the prophets Isaiah and Micah. And the commandments, "Thou shalt not kill" and "Thou shalt not have strange gods before Me." We shouldn't worship gods of metal!

Plowshares actions are also acts of repentance for my own complicity in the culture of violence as well as prayers of intercession for the victims, for those who have suffered and died because these weapons exist, and because of the misuse of resources, resources diverted from eradicating hunger and poverty in the developing world.

I view them as acts of divine *obedience*, not acts of civil disobedience. The classical definition of civil disobedience is that you break an unjust law to try to change that law. Here we're talking about a conversion of our hearts and a transformation of our world. So, it's about a radical change, not just changing a law.

As I said, I consider these acts to be prayers. But when we did our Plowshares action in '82, there *was* an uproar in the peace community in southeast Connecticut. The Nuclear Freeze Campaign totally distanced themselves from our action. They said it was counterproductive—a setback for the peace movement because it deflected attention from the Nuclear Freeze Campaign. They couldn't agree with our symbols and they even referred to it as vandalism. We tried as best as we could to dialogue with people and then certainly in court to tell why we did what we did. Incidentally, we had a hard time picking the jury. Went through several hundred jurors because everybody was in some way connected to building nuclear submarines. But some jurors were in tears after the trial because although they convicted us, they felt our actions were commendable.

Former Attorney General Ramsey Clark was able to testify about international law and how it applies to nuclear weapons. Our trial judge, after hearing Clark's testimony with the jury out of the room, ruled that it wasn't applicable in our case, mainly because there was no legal precedent citing that nuclear weapons violated international law. We implored the judge to set that precedent, but he declined to do so. Routinely now, Ramsey Clark's testimony isn't allowed by the courts, because we're really asking them to indict the system they are part of. Ultimately, it's the law that sanctions these weapons. The weapons protect the law and the law protects the weapons.

Sue and Bill Frankel-Streit

Sue Frankel converted to Catholicism after college and joined the Dorothy Day Catholic Worker community in DC. There she received what she calls her "real education" and met Bill Streit. Bill Streit was ordained a priest in 1982 and served for several years in the Scranton diocese. He finally opted for a Catholic Worker family life. They now live with their three children and other community members at the Little Flower Catholic Worker in Louisa, Virginia. I interviewed them separately and interpolated some of Sue's comments into Bill's description of the action.

Bill: It was the 1980s, with Reagan and nuclear weapons and massacres in Central America. As a priest, I had my first little arrest in 1985, with Dan Berrigan and others at the State Department. After some seven years of diocesan work, though, I got burned out—physically, spiritually, every which-way. I knew I needed a break.

I had a letter Phil Berrigan had written to me after I'd told him about a nice calm day I'd had at the parish. He wrote: "I don't doubt that taking communion to shut-ins is a good and noble thing, but it's not the cross. The cross is nonviolent resistance to the imperial state. Period." And it hit me like a Zen Satori.

I ended up at Dorothy Day House. I chose it party because they had a chapel and I'd found contemplation and resistance [to be] two sides of one coin. I needed to both pray and to discern what I was doing. The priesthood was very much a part of my identity, but I was having a very difficult time doing it the way they wanted me to.

I met Sue there, and we became very good friends, intimate friends, sharing our visions and fears and thoughts and our struggles. I was afraid of her at first, though; she was so bubbly and energetic and always riding off on a motorcycle with this guy. But after seven or eight months, we finally became a couple, which was just an amazing thing.

Trying to decide what to do, Bill went on a solitary retreat in 1990, engaging in a "week-long wrestling match with God, like Jacob wrestling with the angel." He decided to go back to the diocese but lasted only five weeks.

Bill: I remember a clergy dinner the first night I was back. I'm wearing full collar and black coat. Big long table with chandeliers and servants, and the same terrible grousing conversations. The Bishop called me over after dinner and said they had therapists who could help me to "readjust into being a cleric in the traditional Scranton mold."

A couple of weeks later I called up Dorothy Day House and said, "I want to come home." So I did, but I still had cold feet about the marriage. Then one night Phil Berrigan invites us both to what he calls a Plowshares community. "Personal and political disarmament," he called it.

Well, that was another Zen Satori for me. What I simply had to do. In hindsight I can see I needed to do something sacramental outside of the institutional priesthood to kind of communicate to myself that I was still a priest, and that getting married didn't nullify that. The Plowshares action had that sacramentality for me.

Phil and Liz were our role models, so I was never laicized. Like him, I claim an identity as a married priest. I feel I could step into a church tomorrow and have Mass as if I'd never left. But I also feel that I'm doing more now, living more as the priest I was ordained to be. In the diocese I was ordained to be a manager of an institution. Here I really believe I'm preaching the Gospel. "Using words when necessary," as St. Francis said.

Let me say that doing the Plowshares action together was the *best* marriage preparation! When I prepared couples for marriage as a priest, I tried to communicate a sense that it somehow had to be more than just a double self-absorption. To give yourself to some vision beyond yourselves—a vision of building the Kingdom, protecting life—a vision that *feeds* life. The Plowshares did that for us.

Saying yes to the action freed me up to say yes to marriage, actually. In fact, we got married while we were out on bail. Phil and Liz had advised us to make sure we had a marriage license so we could visit each other in jail and prison. So we were married before a city judge in Syracuse, even though being Catholic Workers and anarchists, we didn't think we needed the State to rubber stamp our union. So for those ten months in prison after the Plowshares trial, we were able to exchange letters *because* we were legally married. Then we had two more months after conviction and of course I've had plenty of prison terms since then, and Sue some short ones, so being married has worked in that sense, too.

Now I know there's been discussion about Plowshares maybe breaking up families and there's always that risk, I guess, that the separation will be too much. Sue and I did our first big action *together*, so both of us know what it's like to be the one in prison as well as the one out. See, sometimes one person is going forward into resistance, and the other one wants to have nothing to do with it. Or it's one person's "job" and not the other's. And that would work at unraveling a relationship. With us, our continuing resistance is one thing that glues us together.

There were four of us: Sue and I and Ciaron O'Reilly from Australia and Moana Cole from New Zealand. We called ourselves the Anzus Plowshares, subverting the nuclear war pact these three countries have. Putting the three countries together, it spells A-NZ-US. The three countries were gathering together to wage war; we represent them gathering to wage peace.

August of 1990 was when Saddam Hussein invaded Kuwait and from being our fair-haired boy, he was turned overnight into the personification of evil. We decided on Griffiss Air Force Base in upstate New York, where there were first-strike capable nuclear-armed B-52s. And the B-52s from there *did* do a significant amount of the bombing in Iraq.

The first time we tried to do the action, and there were just too many guards around, so we backed off. Afterwards, we had some really challenging times as a community, trying to work with Moana and Ciaron. Went through a lot of our issues, so when the action happened, we were really very solid. During the stress of the trial, we did okay because we'd formed a good community after that first challenge.

We finally did the action on New Year's Day of 1991, the World Day of Peace, according to the Pope. It was a great action, even though we were kinda surprised when we learned we were facing fifteen years! Ciaron and Moana cut through a fence and went to the runway and sprayed it with Day-Glo paint: "No more bombing of children." Then they started taking up the runway—the over-run of it, not the middle, in case a plane needed to make an emergency landing. See, the cardinal rule of nonviolence is to not put any human life in jeopardy, and we knew that if the Air Force found out that somebody was on the runway, they'd close it. So this would be comparable to . . . A lot of our discussions talked about what we would do if we'd been in Poland in the 1930s and '40s. Would we take up the tracks? So that was the symbolism of Ciaron and Moana going to the runway.

Meanwhile, Sue and I were driven to the other side of the base. We cut through three fences on our way to the B-52s. The third fence said, "Danger: High Voltage." I touched it with bolt cutters and didn't feel anything, so we cut through it and went through. We found out later on, in Air Force testimony, that the fence sets off an alarm in a guard tower. But it didn't go off. They test that fence all the time and it worked before and it worked afterwards. But it didn't work then. Like many of these Plowshares actions, something of the miraculous happens and the waters part. And so we walked through and went to a refueling plane, a KC-135, and we poured blood and hammered on that, and left our leaflets and an indictment, indicting them of war crimes.

We still really wanted to reach a big B-52 and to get to them, we had to walk across this tarmac, and it was . . . Picture a parking lot big enough for a B-52 to turn around in. Over to the right was the security building with lights and jeeps and then over to the left were hangars with huge lights, like baseball stadium lights. We learned later that's where they load on the nuclear bombs.

Sue: We had walked and walked and walked to another fence, and another fence, and finally onto that huge tarmac. "Where are the guards?" And they just didn't come. Anyway, we kept walking across the tarmac in the dark—I was holding on to Bill's arm—and then all of sudden we were standing under the wing of the B-52. We were there!

After just a little while, the guards saw us and came, of course. That's the only time I was really afraid, when they got out of the jeep, pointing their guns at us. We were in a deadly force area, which gives soldiers the right to shoot to kill, no questions asked.

Now we had this agreement that when the guards come, we'd kneel down. And Bill kept going, carefully placing out all the statements around the plane. I'm like, "Okay, Bill! Now is when we kneel down so we don't get shot." [Laughs, somewhat nervously, at the memory.] They walked us across this empty field, guns pointing at our backs. I had a few minutes where I thought they were going to kill us right there. There was no one there to see them and they were really irate!

Deadly Force Sign. Elmer Mass Collection, courtesy of DePaul University Special Collections and Archives Department, Chicago, Illinois.

Bill: They came out cussing. We tried to tell them we were peacemakers, and that we'd come there on the World Day of Peace, but they told us to shut up. But then we began to sing, and . . . they stopped yelling. So here we are in upstate New York, and it's quiet and cold, and we're walking across this huge space with nothing in the air but our voices, singing "Peace is flowing like a river."

Meanwhile, Ciaron and Moana are still out on the runway. Ciaron and Moana told us later that four or five security cars passed them before they were caught in the headlights. Anyway, they took us to this outdoor pen and did the most complete frisk I've ever had, and then handcuffed us. I turned around and see fifteen MPs with M-16s trained on me. Somehow it was just too funny, to see all those guns, so I smiled this big smile and said, "Happy New Year, everyone." Slowly the mouths opened and the guns began to fall.

Barry Roth

Dr. Barry Roth practices psychiatry in Brookline, Massachusetts. In 1991, he and Phil Berrigan and three others completed a Plowshares action against an Aegis-equipped Cruiser docked at the Bath Iron Works in Maine. They worked aboard the ship for over two hours, pouring their own blooding, hammering on the covers of launching systems, hanging origami cranes, leaving indictments, and even ringing the ship's bow bell to announce the dawn. They were finally arrested, arraigned, indicted for criminal trespass, and jailed for several days before being released unconditionally. Six months later, their charges were dismissed, literally on the eve of trial.

Aegis Plowshares, 1991. Courtesy of Jonah House.

Barry: These things have been close to my heart for years. I mailed in my draft card in April of '68. I met Dan Berrigan when I was an undergrad at Cornell. I went to the trial of the Catonsville Nine. So these things had been close to my heart for a long time.

My heritage is Jewish. My principal practice had been Buddhist. The people I had been most often involved with in this world for the last fifteen years were the radical Catholics. What's true is true. Different people have different ways of understanding that and talking about it. But I don't think there's a Jewish truth, or a Catholic truth, or a Hindu truth, or a Moslem truth, or a Buddhist truth, or a Native American truth.

Presently, my primary spiritual guide is an indigenous woman, recognized in a 2,700 year lineage, and also in Tibetan Buddhist lineages. She has told me the "Grandmothers" came to her very strongly and urged her to tell me to bring forth the Jewish contributions for global healing. She has instructed me to do Jewish practices every day, first thing in the morning, from Deuteronomy, Exodus, and Numbers. These practices follow more than 3,350 years of oral Torah, in the lineage from Moses.

[When I participated in community in the Aegis Plowshares action], we weren't clones who didn't have independent thoughts, but we were of one mind and one heart. It was Easter Sunday and nobody was there, other than ourselves and the Spirit. You never know what you're going to find. But I was pretty clear how I was going to behave. And I was pretty clear about how the people I was with—[Phil Berrigan, Daniel Sicken, Tom Lewis, and Kathy Boylan]—were going to behave. I was hoping we could follow through with what we intended and be true to our intentions. That was the main thing.

After some hours, [Phil and I walked to the Bath Iron Works guard station to announce our action.] I was in the police cruiser, not handcuffed. That I recall! The cops were talking to each other on their two-way radio. "These are nonviolent people, and they're here because they don't believe in violence and don't believe in killing." Then the [officer] I was with said, "If more people felt like that, our work would be a whole lot easier."

At the arraignment, the judge remarked that "One of their number—[referring to Phil]—was the conscience of a generation. I can't believe they won't come back for their trial if we release them now." When he heard that, Phil leaned over and said in a low voice, "You'd better watch it when they start complimenting you."

The trial date kept getting postponed and postponed; and in September the CEO of Bath Iron Works resigned in a contract bidding scandal. We were to go to trial the next month. About four in the afternoon [the day before the trial was to start], we'd finished our discernment about what kind of a case we'd present, and I called the press to announce a press conference the next morning.

"Haven't you heard?" the reporter said. "The charges have been dropped."

Recently I looked at some of the newspaper reports from that time, and the prosecutor was quoted as saying, "We don't think it's in anybody's interests for us to pursue this anymore." I think they were embarrassed. Bath Iron Works wasn't that far from the Bush residence in Kennebunkport, you know, and they were already in the news with this CEO resigning.

Ro: Yes, the trial publicity wouldn't have helped him. Especially with Phil in the action. Dr. Roth, as a psychiatrist, are you aware of any peace resisters who've done significant jail time and have been psychologically damaged by their prison experience?

Barry: Not really. Dan Berrigan would point out that when people get killed in war, people just take it as a matter of course; but if people get hurt in peacemaking, that's considered some kind of exception. When I came to act, I had to weigh the damage to my soul by not acting versus the possible risks of acting. And at that point, I couldn't *not* act. You see, we can get hurt if we do something, and we can get hurt if we don't do something—so we might as well try to do what we think we ought to do. When do we move from "my [own, not so significant] pain" to noticing the pain of the world? And what do we do about it? Every thought, every word, every act—it all matters. The purpose of life is to be able to love and give and do, and whether one defines that as sacrifice or gift makes a big difference. Despair is self-indulgent. There's just too much to do.

Susan Crane

Susan Crane is a member of the Jonah House resistance community. She's been in four Plowshares actions. Here she describes her first Plowshares, Jubilee Plowshares West. She and Father Steve Kelly, SJ, chose to act on August 7, 1995 to mark the 50th anniversary of the US bombing of Hiroshima and Nagasaki.

Susan: I was teaching school in California when I first heard about the Plowshares. For several years, I'd been going to actions at Diablo Canyon [Nuclear Power Plant] and Vandenberg Air Force Base and the Lawrence Livermore Lab, where the next generation of nuclear weapons is designed. The Ash Wednesday and Good Friday services and actions at Livermore Lab got me thinking, and for the first time, I really began to understand collective sin. Nuclear weapons are a visible icon of collective sin.

I'd spend a weekend here and there in jail, but I felt very complicit in our government's construction of nuclear weapons. I wanted to do more and Plowshares appealed to me. I very much liked the idea of actually beginning to disarm the weapons.

Then I met Steve Kelly and he was interested in a Plowshares, too. Up to then, I'd always accepted the nonviolence code for a particular action, but I didn't want to distance myself from people in other countries who were so oppressed that they'd take up arms. What it might mean to live my whole life nonviolently had never occurred to me. Then I met Steve, and he said, "We want to do this action right."

The actions that I'd done up to then involved planning, developing a leaflet, doing press work, making banners and props, thinking creatively, and generally having a good time. So that's what I had in mind when Steve said "Do it right." But he was thinking of something entirely different. As it turned out, the "doing it right" took over two years!

It was during those two years that Max Ventura and I went to Livermore Lab on August 6th, Hiroshima Day. We brought white paint and some thick plastic cutouts in the shape of a person. Walked right past the guard post, into the lab area, and painted around the plastic on the sidewalk. That left an outline to remind [people] of the shadows that were left in Hiroshima when people were vaporized in 1945. The guards told us to leave but we just kept painting until eventually we were arrested and taken to the Santa Rita jail.

When I'd spend these short times in jail, I'd usually be put in solitary because I was experimenting with noncooperating. I wouldn't change my clothes, didn't cooperate with a strip search, basically tried not to cooperate with my own oppression. So they'd put me in what they call "Administrative Segregation."

When you're in solitary, all the normal things you do are gone, so I'd just sit there and think. Finally, I thought maybe a good thing to do would be to pray. But I realized I didn't know anything at all about praying.

So I started asking everyone I knew: "What exactly do you do when you pray?" Most people didn't have much of an answer. It's a pretty intimate question, I guess, and I'd just hear generalities. One woman taught me some things about Buddhist meditation. I was going to a Methodist church at the time, and the pastor there had some things to say, too. I talked to Benjamin Weir who had been held hostage in Lebanon; he gave me a copy of his book, *Hostage Bound, Hostage Free*, and suggested that I focus on Romans 8:39, where it says that nothing can ever separate us from God's love.

Finally Steve Kelly said, "Well, [the Jesuits] have a course where you can learn how to pray. Just like you learn how to do push-ups, we have these exercises you can do to learn how to pray."

I thought, "Wow! I really want that." Steve set me up with Father Bernie Bush, SJ, and he guided me through the Spiritual Exercises of St. Ignatius. I met with Father Bernie every other week for a year or so, and did these exercises.

What a change in my life! You know, it just . . . I became a better teacher, I became more nonviolent, and I finally started to understand prayer. It's as if all this time I'd read about water and heard people talk about it, but had never been in it. Now I was in the water. All this time, people had been talking about prayer, and prayer finally became real for me. At the same time, I realized that God and nonviolence are the same. And how we're on a journey to nonviolence. What a preparation for my first Plowshares!

In the summer of 1995, Steve and I were finally ready. Lockheed Martin had a big plant right in Sunnyvale, California, building the D–5 missiles for the Trident submarines. That's where we chose to act. We had to figure out how to get over this big fence that surrounded the plant, and then we had to figure out how to get into the building. The month before the action, we were driving in the parking lot with Phil [Berrigan], looking at the building, and I told Phil I just didn't see how we were going to get in. He said something I'll never forget. He said, "Well, you do the best you can, and you leave the rest to God."

We went in around 8:30 on Hiroshima Day. When I got on top of the fence to climb over, I saw people standing around outside the building. Smokers on a smoke break! So we get down off the fence and walk towards the building. We looked pretty much like every-body else, with a clipboard, and [wearing] slacks. As we walk up to the building with this group, a big bay door opens right in front of us. So without breaking stride, we walk right into the building. I don't know how or why but it . . . it just opened!

We walked down a hallway, and we looked in different rooms. Finally we found a door that plainly said, "D–5 Trident Missiles." We walk into a big warehouse area, with tall ceilings. A guy with a pneumatic tool is working on some metal, and he tells us it's part of the missile. We said, "We have come here to disarm it, and convert it." And we pull out our hammers and our baby bottles of blood and start to pour the blood and hammer on the missile.

The guy's just sort of watching us, so Steve says, "We mean you no harm, but you should call security." We keep hammering, and he's still just watching us, so Steve said it again 'cause we didn't want the guy to lose his job. We saw another missile across the aisle, so we started hammering on that one, too and then Steve found some plans.

We put them on the floor and wrote "These missiles kill children," and added our bloody handprints. Next, we laid out the Plowshares banner and pictures from Hiroshima. Then we knelt down and said the Lord's Prayer.

When I looked up, there's this whole circle of workers watching us. One guy came up to us, and whispered in our ear: "You have shown a lot of courage." Then the security guards came and then we were in jail, you know, and finally went to court.

Nowadays in Plowshares trials, you can't bring up the affirmative defenses. Can't even say the words. We were found guilty of two felonies. Once you're found guilty, the sentence is based on the amount of damage that you've done, so we were looking at a lot of time, because they said we'd done $400,000 damage. (Even though the amount hadn't been proved, that's what they were saying.) But the judge only gave ten months and two years of supervised release.

I was sent immediately to Dublin, right below San Francisco. You know, it's a funny thing. While I was there, I felt peaceful and content, and even happy. Doesn't that seem strange? Here I was, in what's considered the worst place to be—in prison—and although I had difficulties with this and that, I was content. I thought something was wrong with me, but Fr. Bernie assured me that suffering and joy can exist together, and that God's consolation can be with us in prison, maybe even *especially* in prison.

Not long after I was released, I became a Catholic, and then moved to Jonah House. So many of my heroes have been Catholic, and when I'm in prison, it's so good to plant my feet firmly in the Mass and say, "This is mine!"

How do people's hearts change? I know, for me, things happen, and I often don't respond right away, and then two years later I think, "Oh! That's what it means! That's how we're supposed to live!" For example, after the second Plowshares action—the Prince of Peace Plowshares in Maine—the marshals shipped me to a jail back in California. Turns out the policewoman who was booking me had been working at Lockheed and heard about that first action. I asked her what she thought about it. "I'm not working there anymore. I'm working here." So our Plowshares action caused her to rethink her job.

In prison I talk a lot to my fellow prisoners about faith and international law and about the economics of war. I always tell them why I act, why we hammered on the A–10 or the war ship or the Triton missiles. The women understand the economics because they've been at the bottom themselves. So when I talk about the money spent on wars instead of schools or medical care or job programs or roads, they know that it doesn't make any sense. We take better care of our weapons than we do of our children! We're now spending $32,000 a second on war-making, and the schools I taught in didn't have money for proper books or enough teachers.

I talk about depleted uranium any chance I get and in fact, one of the [Plowshares] actions we did was about depleted uranium. People are really aghast that our government is poisoning our own soldiers. When I was in prison in California, I was talking to some of the guards about why I was in prison [for the depleted uranium action], and they said, "Well, you should talk to the woman who runs the commissary, because she was in the Gulf War and she's married, and she's been very sick." So I did. I had a book about its use in Iraq and I showed it to her. She opened it up, and went right to congenital deformities and started to read about them. It just made me cry.

Susan's last Plowshares action was in 2009 when she and four others entered the Bangor, Washington Trident base, just twenty miles from Seattle. This base houses more than 2000 nuclear warheads and is home to 24 percent of the nuclear warheads in the US arsenal. Bangor alone has more than China, France, Israel, India, North Korea, and Pakistan combined. Each of the new 24 D–5 missiles on a Trident submarine is capable of carrying eight 455 kiloton W–88 warheads and each warhead is about thirty times the explosive force of the Hiroshima bomb and costs approximately $60 million.[12]

The five of them—Fr. Bill "Bix" Bichsel, Lynne Greenwald, Fr. Steve Kelly, Sr. Anne Montgomery, and Susan—called themselves the Disarm Now Plowshares. They walked for several hours through the woods, until they reached the MLA (Main Limited Area) where they cut the fence with bolt cutters and were soon apprehended, cited, and released. The youngest of this group was sixty, the oldest eighty-three.

12. Online: www.globalsecurity.org/wmd/agency/3351mw.htm.

Disarm Now Plowshares at day four of their trial, 2011. © Leonard Eiger.

Almost a year later, a federal grand jury returned indictments on four charges, one of which carried up to ten years in prison. On December 13, 2011, a Tacoma-based jury found the five seniors guilty of trespass and three felonies. They served prison terms of various lengths, but none as long as ten years. Susan was returned to the Dublin facility where she'd been after her first Plowshares.

Philip Berrigan died in 2002, and Father Dan Berrigan is in his early nineties. Warfare, terrorism, and nuclear weapons continue to plague the planet. The Atlantic Life Community and the Pacific Life Community continue to meet regularly for retreats and civil disobedience actions. "The vision of Isaiah remains," Father John Dear, SJ, writes. "People will beat swords, bombs, and nuclear weapons into plowshares until war is abolished once and for all. Only then will the movement end, when everyone finally accepts the wisdom of peaceful nonviolence. Until then, we will continue to resist."[13]

13. Father John Dear, SJ, e-mail to author, May 10, 2012.

An Interlude

"Sleeping Beauty"

Judith Malina

The feeling of captivity began when the door clanged shut and 'till the moment I stepped out into the street from prison, I was not myself but under a spell. One cannot act but only be acted upon: not move, but be moved. It is the spell of Sleeping Beauty, of Brunhilde, of all princes transformed into beasts and toads. It is also the nonfictional story of all slaves, all the oppressed, and of all prisoners.[1]

---

1. *The Diaries of Judith Malina, 1947–1957* (New York: Grove, 1984), 444.

5

Beating Swords Into Plowshares—Europe

European activists soon followed the US Plowshares model. Three years after the first action at King of Prussia, Pennsylvania, Dr. Wolfgang Sternstein and three others entered the US Army Base at Schwabisch-Gmund and incapacitated a Pershing II missile launcher. Since then Plowshares actions and others which nonviolently involve damage to "improper" property have occurred in Australia, England, Germany, the Netherlands, Ireland, New Zealand, Scotland, and Sweden.[1] Some of them identify with the faith-based US Plowshares movement; some, such as the massive Trident Campaign in Scotland, have adopted their own culture of resistance, which allows for varied kinds of participation. US resisters have much to learn from their confreres in other lands. In this chapter, you will hear the voices of Ciaron O'Reilly and Deirdre Clancy of the Pitstop Plowshares at Shannon Airport; Jane Tallents, Ellen Moxley, and Brian Quail of Scotland; Frits ter Kuile of the Amsterdam Catholic Worker; and Hanna Jaskolski and Dr. Wolfgang Sternstein of Germany.

Ireland

While many Plowshares actions do only symbolic damage, actions in Europe often inflict real and substantial damage, including the one in February 2003, named the Pitstop Plowshares by participants but "the Shannon Five" by the Irish press.

1. I have retained the US spelling of "Plowshares" throughout, except in footnotes, where the inconsistency would provide an incorrect citation. My apologies to the European activists who spell it "Ploughshares."

CIARON O'REILLY

Ciaron O'Reilly has participated in three Plowshares actions on three continents and communicates worldwide via the internet. He was visiting his family in Australia when I was in Europe, so I interviewed him later by phone. In 2010 he moved to London where he continues his resistance with the London Catholic Worker.

Frank Cordaro, Steve Jacobs, and Ciaron O'Reilly blockade the gates at 10 Downing Street, 2011. © Marie Albrecht.

Ciaron: Three weeks after our [Shannon] action, three commercial airlines transporting troops through Ireland pulled out, and the US ambassador said it was specifically in relation to [our action and Mary Kelly's a bit before ours] that it happened. Also, [the plane] was the only piece of US military equipment that I know of that was turned around by the peace movement, that didn't make it to Iraq, but was sent back to Texas.

Ro: Harry Browne says that the repair estimate Boeing submitted to the US Naval Systems Command for both your and Mary's actions was $2,715,000.00.[2]

2. Harry Browne, *Hammered by the Irish* (Oakland, CA: Counterpunch, 2008) gives full details of the action, including accounts of the three trials.

Ciaron: Yes, it was substantial. Christians are supposed to have stewardship of property and so one would wonder—whether it's Moses smashing the tablets or Jesus overturning the tables or people burning their draft cards or people burning child pornography or throwing heroin into the river—if they can be charged with criminal damage. These things are contraband, really, and the value of property is only relevant to how it nourishes and sustains life. If it threatens life, then one has to disarm it.

So of course it's great if there's an actual element [in a Plowshares,] but it's the symbolic dimension that's the most significant. The actual part is two bits of metal relating to each other—a hammer and a war plane—but the symbolic nature is a group of people coming together, forming community to disarm, and speaking to hearts and minds and free wills. What we did at Shannon Airport is still speaking in Australia, four years later and twelve thousand miles away. I only wish it had spoken louder in Ireland.

To be serious about waging peace, we have to take some of the risks of those who wage war. As Frank Cordaro points out, if one percent of the people who marched against the Iraq War had gone into nonviolent resistance to the point of being imprisoned, and the other 99 percent had stayed in proactive solidarity and fed the cat and dealt with hysterical parents and paid the resister's rent and so on, then these arresting governments, including Ireland, would have had major problems.

Folks ask why we do this when—so far at least—only the US has dropped nuclear bombs, and that was against two huge Japanese cities in 1940. And I tell them about the first time I was in prison and my "cellie" was a bank robber. He'd say that the best use of a gun in an armed robbery is when it's not fired. And it's the same with Trident warheads and other nuclear weapons. They're used in the same way, as a threat, to keep the US empire in control of the world.

DEIRDRE CLANCY

I was able to meet with one of the Pitstop Plowshares while I was visiting Ireland in 2007—Deirdre (Dee) Clancy of Dublin. In her Masters work in Women's Studies at Trinity, Dee had studied liberation theology with Mary Condon and learned about Phil Berrigan. Disturbed by the inequalities of life in her newly prosperous homeland, she spent a year

and a half working in the corporate world in Sweden, but realized that
if she continued on the treadmill, [she] wouldn't have done anything
to make the world a better place. The devastation of the UN sanctions
on Iraq affected her greatly as did the looming war against that country. She returned to Dublin and began attending liturgies at the Dublin
Catholic Worker.

A month and a half before the "Shock and Awe" bombing that began
the Iraq War, Dee and four others broke into a hangar at Shannon Airport
and damaged a US Navy plane which had made a "pit stop" in Shannon
on its way to the Mediterranean Ocean. Joining her were Ciaron, Damien
Moran, Karen Fallon of Scotland, and Nuin Dunlop from the US.

Dee: There was so little happening in terms of resistance in Ireland, and
I felt we had to do *something*! We needed an action that actually
damages the war machine, to show that you can have a very concrete
effect on weaponry and the logistical elements of the [Iraq] War. Of
course none of us was naïve enough to think that one action was
going to get rid of the problem.

I remember it was me who actually suggested maybe doing a
Plowshares action. Ciaron had shown some footage of the Catonsville Nine, and it really affected me that a group of people would
do something so risky. Before I knew Ciaron, I would have thought
that only extraordinary people did things like this. It wasn't me, only
other people, people who were remote from my reality and who
had heroic qualities, and so on. I now know that not to be the case.
Having said that, there are some extraordinary people who do these
actions—the Berrigans, and people I really look up to. But knowing
the way our group was, and how imperfect we were as a group and
as individuals—I mean, there were just so many flaws there—yet we
managed to get through three-and-a-half years [of action and three
trials] and get the first unanimous acquittal.

In a sense, if we can do it, anybody can do it, and I really feel
that. Because there was something that carried us through. I believe
it was grace or the Holy Spirit, because there's no way we could have
gotten through it without imploding [unless we had] some sort of
spiritual support.

Ro: Did you ever feel like backing out?

Dee: Yes, I almost did back out on a few occasions, especially when there
was conflict in the group. But the issues transcended the personalities.

I mean, I love them all to pieces and everything, but I still feel I wouldn't work with a couple of them again. We were capable of much messiness, and much craziness, but also much hilarity and laughter. I guess the Holy Spirit must have a sense of humor to have put the five of us together for such a long time.

Ro: Someone I recently interviewed said, "You know, we seem to have our theory of nonviolence worked out pretty well politically, but not personally."

Dee: That's exactly what it is. At times, I was kind of disillusioned, I suppose, by the idea that things could get very aggressive in an antiwar affinity group that believed in nonviolence, sometimes even get physically aggressive, I'm afraid. I just couldn't reconcile that with the philosophy and spirituality associated with nonviolence. I actually wondered whether the antiwar/peace movement maybe even attracted people who had things to work out within themselves. I think people go in with very good motives and . . . but nobody's motives are 100 percent pure, and it's important to realize that, and also to look into one's own.

Ro: Here's Ciaron, so tall, with those dreads and that charismatic personality. And then three young women and a young man join him. He seemed so typical of the strong men in the resistance.

Dee: People seemed to have a misconception that we were somehow the Manson Family: Ciaron was the leader and we were all following. It was actually very far from the truth. It just happened that we all came together, and because Ciaron is an excellent public speaker with a lot of experience, he can draw in a crowd very, very well.

Ro: Did you maybe romanticize the actions themselves, particularly after seeing the Catonsville movie?

Dee: I don't think so, because Ciaron talked a lot about what prison was like, and I think I knew that prison wouldn't be a particularly romantic experience.

Ro: But the idea of the breaking in at dawn, that seems a bit David and Goliath to me.

Dee: There is an element of that, yes. But I think there's a difference between romanticizing something and being inspired by something, as I was with the Catonsville footage. What I was inspired by was the use of prayer and the Word of God in such a way that [the action] was a result of a reading of the Gospels. I remember suggesting a Plowshares in October, after one of the liturgies. And Ciaron took out his famous hammer that's been used for several actions.[3] I think it's notched up x amount of millions in damage. Then a couple of other people joined the discussions. Of the people who initially joined, none of them ended up taking part, but around that time, Ciaron met Damien Moran, who was a seminarian with the Holy Ghost fathers. He was quite young, in his early twenties.

Highlander Karen Fallon and Nuin Dunlop, a US citizen then living in Dublin, joined the group in January. The five of them spent a few days together at Glenstal Abbey in the West of Ireland and early in the morning of February 3, they began their witness.

First, they cut through a fence to enter the base and crawled across the runway. While some of them built a shrine in front of the hangar to symbolize their intent, Deirdre spray-painted "Pit Stop of Death" and "R.I.P Phil Berrigan" on the hangar. Then they broke into the building and took hammers to the plane, frightening but not injuring the one guard. When the Irish garda arrived, they found five people on their knees praying. Their written Statement of Faith said they were "inspired by Brigid and Irish traditions of healing and peacemaking."

Pitstop Plowshares pray with symbols of their action, Glenstal Abbey, 2003. Dave Donnellen.

The people and the press in Ireland were strongly against the Iraq War, but this action confused them, in part perhaps because they couldn't equate Catholicism and direct action. Even in the Irish Left,

3. The hammer had been used in the Anzus Plowshares in 1971, and in at least three other disarmament actions in Great Britain (ibid., 59).

public opinion generally turned against the Shannon Five, in contrast to the US activists who traveled to Dublin to support the group during what became three trials.

Ro: Did you pay bail so you could get out of jail and plan the trial?

Dee. Yes, eventually. Karen and Ciaron had the toughest conditions; and then with Damien, myself, and Nuin, it was slightly more lenient. I paid mine myself. That was important to me, actually. There was no support system for nonviolent direct action in Ireland, so I tried to make sure I had resources from my own earnings to do me for a year, which is how long we thought it would take.

It turned out to be three-and-a-half years. We had legal aid. If you're not rich, basically, you can get legal aid in Ireland. If you were going to pay your own legal fees, I'd say you'd be into six figures for each one of us. The system here is that your solicitor does much of the background work, and the barrister speaks in court. Each person is entitled to a junior barrister and a senior barrister. Nuin and I had the same senior and junior barristers, Karen had her own two barristers, and Damien and Ciaron had the same [two.] So we had three sets of legal counsel, possibly the best legal team [one could] assemble in Ireland today, for a case of this nature.

Our solicitor, Joe Noonan, is highly regarded and he's a committed person, and we also had the top barristers in the country. I think something resonated with them. The ideology that they subscribed to would have drawn them to our case as well, and they were always so respectful to us.

For awhile, Ciaron thought at least one of us had to defend ourselves [as so many Plowshares people do], "just to be authentic." I can see why you'd want to do that if you weren't surrounded by a committed legal team, but we were. And I really felt from the outset that we really had a really good chance, if not of an acquittal, of a hung jury. I really felt that quite strongly.

Ro: Now the first trial resulted in a mistrial, and the second was even more fraught.

Dee: Oh, yes! The first judge didn't allow our witnesses. The second judge allowed our witnesses but ruled out our defense, which was "lawful excuse." Without that defense, we just had no . . . it was unlikely a jury would find us not guilty.

After two weeks of the trial, our solicitor learned that the judge actually *knew* George W. Bush. He'd had his photo taken with him when he was a governor, and he'd been invited to both presidential inaugurations. [The judge] was very embarrassed by the whole thing. He discharged the jury and stormed out of court, but he forgot to put a gag on the media, which as a judge he could have done. So the newspapers had it all.

Then we had the third trial. Kathy Kelly [of Voices for Creative Nonviolence] came over for all of them and we had Denis Halliday.[4] Jimmy Massey, who was in [Iraq] Veterans Against the War, came for the second two trials. Kathy gave a very moving testimony, and it probably had a huge impact on the jury.

We had these brilliant barristers who gave these amazingly moving speeches. I had really high regard for my senior barrister, Michael O'Higgins, and I just knew he was going to give a brilliant closing speech. Karen's senior barrister was Brendan Nix, and his closing speech was this impassioned . . . At one stage, he said, "You know, my client Karen Fallon and her colleagues have been accused of being political throughout this trial. Well, so what? Let me read you the greatest political speech of all time." And he proceeded to read the Sermon on the Mount.

At the end, there wasn't a dry eye in the courtroom. And Michael O'Higgins's closing speech may have influenced the jury even more. It appealed to the mind as well as the heart, in equal measure.

Ro: So amazing! Can you describe the acquittal?

Dee: The jury had retired the day before, and this was the next morning. I remember we were standing outside. Logically, rationally, I felt the trial went very well, because of how wonderful the legal team was, and because I think we ourselves testified quite well. Also, the judge gave us our "lawful excuse" defense, and we were thrilled with that, but we'd come to court with our bags packed for prison.

Then we were called in. The clerk was given the envelope [from the jury] and opened it. Ciaron O'Reilly was first on the list. There were two counts for each of us: one for the plane, and one for the window of the hangar, which was broken in order to put our arm in and open the door. I heard the clerk say . . . God, even when I think

4. Halliday, an Irish citizen, was the United Nations Humanitarian Coordinator in Iraq from 1997 until 1998, when he resigned in protest over the economic sanctions.

about it, it's . . . It's like it happened yesterday. "Ciaron O'Reilly: not guilty, count one; not guilty, count two." We all knew, then, that if Ciaron was found not guilty, everybody was. [Tearful.]

We . . . we were sitting there in disbelief. Then I remember Nuin just heaving with tears. She'd had such a fraught time in Ireland, and it was a big release of tension. I was crying as well. There was also a sense of . . . you know, sometimes you're a bit jaded, and then suddenly something happens and you realize that there's real goodness in people and that there's goodness in the world. I'm sorry, now, for getting emotional, but . . .

Ro: Well, it's an emotional thing. It's the not-crying that can be the problem.

Dee: Yes, that's true as well. [Long pause.] Afterwards was just a haze of . . . We stayed in the courtroom for about twenty minutes and then we went outside with the supporters. Everybody was given a bunch of flowers, which was really nice. There was an agreement that one of the women would read out the statement for the press, so I was given that task.

Now it was quite funny, because the media had no interest in the trial as it was happening, absolutely none. They reported nothing, really, and the small bits they did report were all the prosecution side. Suddenly, when the acquittal happened, they all just descended on the Four Courts! When we got outside the gates, they were all there, pinning us up against the wall and not giving us any room. It was really overwhelming, and another lesson on the fickleness of the mainstream media. As Ciaron often says, "Why do we insist on talking about them as if they're a public service?"

You know, I don't think I've really processed the whole journey within myself. For the three-and-a-half years, I managed so well in many ways; I had the advantage of being Irish and knowing the landscape, having somewhere to live, being able to get work most of the time, and so on. But it's had some effect on my life that's not so good as well. Yet, if I say that, does it show a lack of faith in the action? I *do* have a faith in that action, and in the end that faith was proven to have a basis. Even if we hadn't been acquitted, I still would've felt justified in what I did. But the acquittal was just . . . the icing. It was. But in trying to live a normal life, whatever normal is, you know, it's important to acknowledge that it does affect aspects of your life.

Ciaron had said there's a phenomenon of people feeling a bit lost after the whole process is finished. A sadness, too. Nobody really understands. Once the court process is over, the support falls away, so it's quite lonely. Everyone in the Pitstop Plowshares has been through a version of this experience, in one way or another, and it has been very vivid for all of us. It's the elephant in the room, and as such, it needs to be talked about in the movement. But I'm lucky in many respects, and a week from now, I'm heading down to Glenstal Abbey for a real retreat.

Ro: I guess you could say you don't get home free.

Dee: You don't. Is it worth that? Do the lives of Iraqi people deserve my attention as much as my own happiness and my own fulfillment in other aspects of my life? In my view, they do, and I probably haven't given enough to the people who are oppressed by Western imperialism. I'm not a Kathy Kelly, and I'm not somebody who's given up my whole existence to this. If I could make that leap, maybe that would be the best thing. But those three years were very fraught, I'd say. [Long pause.] I'm sorry. I didn't mean to get too emotional about everything.

Ro: You need to be emotional about it. It's your life! We're all humans, and if we're good at being humans, we cry. [Noise in room gets louder.] Dee, we're going to have to quit because of the noise. I've really enjoyed talking to you.

Dee: Well, it's been good for me, too. In my view, analysis and reflection are just as important in the movement as going DIY with the wire cutters and hammers.

Scotland

Shortly after my meeting with Dee, I met three amazing resisters at a Glasgow conference convened by the Scottish Campaign for Nuclear Disarmament (SCND).[5] One of them was Brian Quail, another Jane Tallents, a third Ellen Moxley. All of them are both members of SCND and of Trident Plowshares.[6] The latter is a direct action group that, since 1968, has focused on Faslane, a base which is home to the UK's Trident

5. Online: www.banthebomb.org.
6. Online: www.tridentploughshares.org/index.php3.

nuclear submarine fleet. Both groups share the goal of removing nuclear weapons from Scottish soil, with SCND working through legal political channels and Trident Plowshares coordinating direct action, including the year-long blockade called Faslane 365 which occurred from October 2006 to October 1, 2007. That campaign involved 131 autonomous groups and resulted in 1,150 arrests.

BRIAN QUAIL

I remember Hiroshima. The universal jubilation, the feelings of great joy. Even the Glasgow tram cars had big signs—VJ, VJ—Victory in Japan!

I was seven years old, and I asked my mother about the bombs. Now she was a university graduate and an intelligent person, but she had no idea what was involved. She told me how things are made of atoms, which were not dividable, and then they discovered a way of splitting the atom. I think she had visions of people gently dematerializing and going up to Jesus, like dust motes in a sunbeam, you know. She had no notion of the heat of a blast.

Secrecy was the absolute policy at the time. There were no pictures at all of the human suffering of Hiroshima, only pictures of the mushroom cloud. And distant pictures of the city, looking like an archeological site. No pictures at all of the actual human impact. Those came out thirty years later, when those films were declassified in America and then the government began to systematically destroy them. The Japanese had this project called the "Ten Foot Society" where you donated money to save ten foot of film.

I saw a film [about Hiroshima] here, shown by the Campaign for Nuclear Disarmament, and . . . Oh, my God! I had to leave the room and splash cold water on my face because . . . Oh, the sights! A little girl with her breast beating like a captured bird. Her eyelids were open and there was this horrible hole where her eyeballs had melted. And then you saw someone with pincers extracting this disgusting white maggot from her arm. I don't know the physiology, i.e., why irradiated flesh putrefies so rapidly, but it . . . it was horrendous. Thinking about those pictures, I'm still upset.

That was the beginning. When I was at school, we'd go to meetings in Glasgow. This was the tail end of the good old days of street speakers and soapboxes. I got caught up in a group of Glasgow anarchists and someone gave me this book called *We of Hiroshima*. The author is Endo, a Japanese man. That book convinced me, finally, that nothing, nothing, nothing in the world justifies this. Absolutely nothing!

Ro: Brian, have very many people seen these films? If they have, you'd think everyone would be in the peace movement!

Brian: I don't think the masses of people have seen them. So a lot of it is just not knowing. Or not wanting to know.

And the words: "deterrence," "capabilities." So abstract! The whole nuclear thing is conducted in this vicious framework of abstraction and dehumanized language. Confucius was asked, "How would you bring justice to the state?" And he said, "By calling things their proper names." There's no such thing as a "nuclear umbrella," for instance. Poppycock! It's an *atom bomb*! It's a weapon of mass destruction.

Ro: Yes. The words hide. Can you tell me what people are doing in Scotland to oppose the Trident nuclear submarines you've got here?

Brian: Well, originally, the Americans had a Polaris base here, at Holy Loch. That closed over fifteen years ago, but not because the Americans converted to peace. They just didn't need it any longer because their new missiles have a longer range. But the British have their so-called "independent" deterrent, at Faslane Trident Base, twenty-five miles from Glasgow, on Loch Gare.

The Americans gave us a deal. They gave us the Trident technology, and we gave them Diego Garcia, an island in the Indian Ocean. A very strategic position and a lot of the bombs [the Americans] dropped on Iraq and Afghanistan came from there. Now the Diego Garcians weren't asked about this, of course; they were dumped in Madagascar, all three thousand of them, and the Diego Garcia islands are nothing but a huge American base now.

The Campaign for Nuclear Disarmament in Scotland was founded in 1958. I got involved when they started a permanent Peace Camp at Faslane. It's been going for twenty-five years now, a permanent physical witnessing against Faslane, on the side of the road just opposite the base. They pay "peppercorn rent," a token rent of a pound or two a year and there's water and sewage and so on.

Trident Plowshares started in 1998. That came from a slightly different angle—using nonviolent direct action as a political tool, which was very successful in the American civil rights movement. In particular there was an action around East Timor, where the British were supplying Hawk aircraft to Indonesia. Angie Zelter and three other women—Jo Wilson and Andrea Needham, and Lotte Kronlid—went into the base and caused a million pounds worth of damage. They were called the Seeds of Hope Plowshares. And they were acquitted by the court!

I got enthusiastic about [Trident Plowshares] because it was to do with action as opposed to aimless talking and meetings and resolutions and debates. It's been half a bloody century of discussion and debate. I don't want to debate nuclear weapons. I just want to stop it. Debate's a cop-out!

Ro: Have you yourself done any direct action?

Brian: Yes. I've been in jail five times but just for short periods. For blockading the gate at the base. Most people go to jail but some pay the fine. Or because of personal circumstances, you might do community service, like work at a charity shop. I go to jail if I don't have anything else hanging over my head, but my personal circumstances are a bit changed now. I'm a single parent with a five-year old boy. When he goes to nursery I can do community service, but it would make jail very difficult, you know. It seems to me everyone can do direct action to whatever extent he or she can. Or do support for others.

Trident Plowshares is totally committed to nonviolence, and this is reflected in the attitude of the Strathclyde police. Over the years we've built up a very good relationship with them. Still, I don't want to paint just rosy pictures because when push comes to shove, the police will support the existing powers.

I remember when I was being taken to one of the police stations in the area. The policeman said to me, "You must think that because people don't say anything, they don't appreciate what you're doing here. A lot of us understand why." Now I don't know to what extent he was talking about himself—he wouldn't particularize—but he was a very interesting lad. Part of it may be that the base is guarded by the MoD (Ministry of Defense) and there's a certain amount of antipathy between the proper civilian police and the base police.

Ro: Now you've told me you're Catholic. How do the churches react to the nuclear threat, both in general and in particular?

Brian: Well, you may remember that in the '80s the pope issued a pretty powerful statement against nuclear weapons. But have you ever heard a sermon in church on nuclear weapons? Only once did I hear one, only once! By the late Cardinal Winning, was it?[7] Way back in eighty-something.

Why is it that the pro-life movement isn't really pro-life? Pro-life is from conception to death, and if you're against the bomb, it's because you're pro-life. They've highjacked this term and it annoys me, to be honest, because they focus entirely on the question of abortion. Not that this is unimportant, I hasten to add. But why be so passionately concerned about defending the rights of unborn babies, but once a child is born, if it's a Marxist baby or an Iraqi baby, you can bomb it? That just doesn't make sense, doesn't make sense at all.

Of course, it's really a political thing, isn't it? To be fair, the peace movement is associated with kind of Left radicals, which are not very sympathetic, generally, to the anti-abortion thing. So they polarize each other.

Many, many years ago, Bruce Kent said the churches are sleeping giants.[8] Well, the gentle slumbering and snoring continues. We have not yet galvanized the religious community. I think it is a question of respectability. The churches see themselves as respectful members of society, and if they were to identify too closely with the peace movement, that would be slightly distasteful. I remember a Church of Scotland Moderator coming to visit the Faslane Peace Camp. There was a wonderful photo in the papers of the Moderator standing with his cravat, smiling away at these archetypal hippies squatting behind the peace camp. It was an absolute study in noncommunication. The guy meant well, but it was just two different worlds.

The churches have always seen their existence as symbiotically linked to the state, so they are atrociously uncritical of the state's use of violence, and they've compromised this so often in the past that it's become ingrained. Their survival is linked to the survival of the state, and there you have the whole business.

We now have a Scottish national parliament that's against Trident. It's a slender majority, but it's the first time. There's massive opposition to both nuclear weapons and nuclear stations in Scotland. And the SNP (Scottish National Parliament) can carry that [to Westminster which has the final say.] Maybe I'm an eternal optimist, but I

7. Cardinal Thomas Winning was Archbishop of Glasgow from 1974 until his death in 2001.

8. Bruce Kent is a former Catholic priest who was active in the CND.

look to the changes in Scotland as having a really seismic effect in the nuclear issues. Beyond our borders.

The question of Trident is a bit more difficult. The physical facts are that you cannot take Trident from the Clyde and put it, let's say, in Portsmouth or Davenport. You can't move the weapons storage which they've got in the Clyde. The whole of that mountain contains two hundred atom bombs, the greatest nuclear arsenal in Europe. You can't transfer that to England because there are no mountains to put it in. So a nuclear-free Scotland [would mean] a nuclear-free Britain. I think we have a slim chance now, though, and it's time to keep up the direct action pressure to prevent it sliding back into endless verbiage. Bugger the existing power structures! You stand where you stand and you say no.

JANE TALLENTS

For several years, Jane Tallents served as Vice Chair of SCND, which includes several MPs and other prominent people. But as a member of Trident Plowshares, she's also a veteran of more than forty arrests for nonviolent direct action. At the time of the interview, Jane was helping to coordinate Faslane 365, a year-long campaign where autonomous groups would come to close the base with a day-long blockade.

Jane: I've been at Faslane for twenty-three years now, and I sometimes feel a bit . . . well, not burned out, but boiled dry. People tell us we just keep doing the same thing. That's right, but if it's the right thing to do—and it still *is* right to do everything we fucking well can do, whether it's lobbying the politicians or getting publicity, or doing direct action in the streets—we need to keep doing it.

I was first arrested in 1982, I think. Sitting in front of a very large bulldozer at a construction site, where they were trying to build a factory for a nuclear-tipped torpedo. That was the plan then, to make every weapon nuclear, so they were busy everywhere.

What a liberating experience it is being arrested! You suddenly realize you can actually say no to things. And that, if the law seems wrong, you can break it and feel okay about it. But that's a big step for lots of people. When we're doing [nonviolent] trainings and workshops for people doing it for the first time, I try to remember back to that first time for me and tell them how good it will feel. I also tell them that I still get butterflies. I think I'd stop doing it if I didn't, 'cause if you do it mindlessly, that's not meaningful.

I used to just sit in the road and wait to be moved. But these days we like to sit there as long as we can, right at the gate. That's what Faslane 3-6-5 is, basically. Different groups do lock-ons with a plastic tube, a wide plastic drain pipe. We put our arms in it and lock ourselves together. Then you use a carabiner, you know, like the clips that climbers use. You have a loop around your wrists with this attached to it, and you just clip yourself to the other person. Now if you choose to let go because you've had enough or there's an emergency vehicle coming or something, you can unclip yourself, but the police can't pull your arms out. In the old days, they'd just drag people to the side of the road still locked on. But that could break the blockader's arms, so now they're not allowed to do that.

Actually the police at Faslane have a special Protestor Removal Unit, which comes to cut us out. They have to first cut a hole in the pipe and then cut the clips or the tape, and they pride themselves in being able to do that pretty fast, so we try to keep one step ahead of them and find new materials that make it more difficult. Like if you add to your plastic pipe a few layers of tar paper and some rope and some concrete and some metal and some . . . oh, as many things as you can think of and lots of different materials, the police have a harder time of it. The longer you can keep them from moving you, the better it is because you prolong the blockade.

Ro: Do you ever have trouble with violence at Faslane? With people who don't keep to the nonviolence vows?

Jane: I think in Faslane 3-6-5 it's been okay. One group of people had made some lock-ons with some bits of sharp metal in them. Not to make it dangerous but to make it more difficult for the cutting team. When the police cut the lock-ons open, they thought the sharp edges were deliberate, and we had to work hard to convince them that the potential danger wasn't intentional. After that we put a message out to make our lock-ons difficult without making them dangerous. Quite a fine line.

Two years ago, we had a blockade a few days before the G8 Summit and there were lots of groups coming in with not necessarily a commitment to nonviolence. We worked very, very hard at making it clear that ours was a nonviolent protest, and if they didn't want to stick with our guidelines not to come. We had teams of peacekeepers in place ready to intervene if there was any situation that looked like it could turn violent. But our message was heard, and the day passed off peacefully with the police not even trying to break up the blockade or arrest anyone, except a couple of people who climbed on the fence.

There's always a heavy police presence at the gate because the Faslane 3-6-5 blockades are open in that we put them on the website. The police can log on and find out what's happening and when, so they're always there when they're expecting us. Some actions have been "unannounced," as we say. Actually Trident Plowshares have done some of the Faslane 365 blockades, and mostly we've done those as a surprise. But you need both kinds—both the publicly scheduled and the unannounced.

Ro: Are most of the arrests and the sanctions and fines and prison for the unexpected ones?

Jane: Not particularly. It doesn't seem to make much difference. The way the courts have responded to us has really changed through time, though. When I first moved to Faslane Peace Camp in 1984, they mostly *did* prosecute people. Took us to the Sheriff court, which is kind of a second level of court. We'd have a chance to put all our arguments, and we were generally found guilty and given a small fine.

Then we went through a period with the prosecutor deciding not to prosecute. He said, "It only encourages them. Just ignore them and they'll go away." Which, of course, we didn't. Then as Trident Plowshares began, another [prosecutor] came. He saw it as a personal mission to try and stop us, so he prosecuted huge numbers of people. One time, we had 385 arrests, and he actually prosecuted 200 of those through the district court, which is the lowest level.

The majority of people plead not guilty. We don't feel guilty, so we hear all the evidence against us, and then we put out our reasons. Everybody puts their own defense, and it's fantastic! They oppose nuclear weapons for every moral and political and personal reason! People sing and read poetry and fold paper cranes and laugh and cry, all of that in front of the court. It's really powerful. And powerful for the people who testify, too, because when they have to actually explain their reasons for resisting in court, it's a . . . it's a recommitment.

At the end, you hear them say, "When's the next protest? I'm coming back!" So the court scene kind of fires everybody up. During breaks, the activists all come together, and then we dish out the leaflets for the next action. We have a community there in the court, and it's clear where the power really is, even if we're found guilty.

Jail is usually just a few days for not paying the fines. We support everybody, whatever stand they take. Some people need to plead guilty because they can't go to jail for all sorts of reasons. There's no kind of hierarchy to that. When I know I'm going to jail, I work my socks off before I go to court to get everything caught up. A few days in prison can be restful. There's no e-mail, there's no mobile phone, and you can't do all the things you've "got" to do, so you get to sit back and read a book.

The proposed renewal of the Trident system has helped get us back onto the political agenda. A majority party here in Scotland has an anti-Trident policy and even though it's debatable whether they have the powers to close the base, they're going to see what they can do. Actually, the final decisions are made at Westminster, not in Scotland, although people are trying to change that. And there, they have a three-line whip, which meant that all the parties' members are expected to vote with the party line. Well! Nearly a hundred [Westminster] Labour MPs rebelled against that and voted against replacing Trident, which is a huge rebellion.

In the area around Faslane, there's a member of the Scottish parliament who will always stick with the Labour party line on Trident. She says it's all about the jobs, you know, and that if we cancel Trident, all these jobs will go. And of course we care about those people's jobs, too; we want them to be converted into good peaceful jobs with lots of skilled labor. So that's an issue—looking at how to retrain and provide good jobs.

She always says to us, "Oh, morally you can't justify nuclear weapons, but putting that aside . . ." I'm sorry, you can't put morality aside. There's no credibility in anything you decide if morality doesn't come into it. So we will continue to work on her.

I work in quite a number of different organizations. They're all very different in the ways they organize, and they've all got value. The CND is very structured and they have "positions" and write papers and have conferences and that kind of official way of working. Then other parts of the peace movement are more nonhierarchical and decentralized. Generally we all get along. I work a lot with CND, but I also think direct action is really important and I get a bit fed up with people who say, "I'm only part of the respectable way." [Mimics sarcastically.]

I go to Parliament and listen to their debates on Trident, but I've also blocked the road outside Parliament. Once we blocked High Street with a 24-foot model of a Trident submarine. Sitting with me was Rosie Kane, an MP who chose to join the direct action with us instead of being in Parliament that day. So sometimes the divides aren't that clear, and there are activists who are voted into the Parliament and remain activists.

When we set up Trident Plowshares, we hoped there would be lots of people who would take part in what we call major direct actions. Going in and trying to do as much damage as you can. Actually stopping the system. Now there are only a limited number of people who are free enough to be able to risk that long of time in jail. And committed enough, to be honest. It was a good try, good to put it out there and test the water. A number did step up, like Ellen Moxley and Angie and Ulla, but it's limited.

What we discovered along the way, though, was that there were *loads* of people who would come and do a blockade and risk a small fine. So that's where our strength is, and that's why we went for the idea of Faslane 3-6-5. Lots of people came and did a little bit, rather than a few people doing a big thing.

Ro: In the States, most of the Plowshares people come from a faith-based perspective and frankly, they're often pretty much ignored by the people who don't share that faith.

Jane: Well, I think that's what's really good about our movement. We embrace everybody. Trident Plowshares isn't faith based. Now there are affinity groups within it which are and affinity groups with all sorts of different kinds of takes. And different faiths, even nuns. We have a Buddhist group coming to Faslane in a few weeks. I'm always up at Faslane making tea and doing things for the Christian groups, but I'm a pagan. I'll work with anybody and everybody who's up there opposing nuclear weapons, whatever their reasoning, and I think it's important that the reasons are not kind of weighed up against each other.

In big blockades, we've had hundreds of people along, with Trident Plowshares joining CND. The big blockades are *amazing!* Socialists at one side of the gate, shouting slogans, with Clergy Action on the other side doing a church service. Another group dancing and singing and somebody meditating in another spot. All those things work together, with no friction between them and no competition.

I like the way [Faslane Peace Camp] works nonhierarchically, and shares out the tasks. Some places have administrators who do the office work, with the activists outside, and different groups having different status within the larger group. But we think it's important that the ones who give the speeches also empty the toilet and chop the potatoes. Actually, it's really good to be grounded, and it's good to share all those things around and trust, you know, that when you're in jail, other people will take on those roles.

I remember when I had my first baby, people said, "Oh, you'll stop doing all this now." Which seemed ludicrous 'cause to me children are all the more reason to do it. Now I stayed active—you can sit on the phone and do legal support while breast feeding, and so forth—but I didn't do the traveling bit.

Then in 2000 there was an opportunity to go to a Peace Action conference in the States and talk about Trident Plowshares. The kids were old enough then, so I decided it was my turn. I'd only flown once before, so this was an epic journey for me, to fly across to Albuquerque.

We went out to Los Alamos one day. People came from a whole lot of countries, including two people from Japan, who were there when the bombs were dropped. We stood in this hot, desert undergrowth, very close to the old wooden building where the bombs had actually been made. I mean, even now the hairs on the back of my neck stand up when I talk about it. We'd been given permission to be there, and the Los Alamos security people stood around us in their black sunglasses and their bristling equipment, and we did this very simple ceremony with huge bowl of sunflower seeds, one for every person that has died at Hiroshima and Nagasaki!

What we're doing here now—Faslane 3-6-5—was known at first as the "mad plan." [Laughs wryly.] Trying to blockade every single day for a year. Well! We got more people than I would have possibly imagined. Usually not large groups, but we've shown that very small groups can actually be quite effective, and we're planning to have a big one at the end that we're calling simply "The Big Blockade."

A year was exactly the right amount of time. Lots of groups have come back a second and third time and people that come with one group have convinced another group to come. It's really important to have new people with new ideas and new energy, especially young people, but I think you also need a bit of continuity. I'm now doing things with people who weren't born when I started all of this! In fact my two kids are now involved.

Direct action's always part of it. It raises the profile, of course, but it does more than that. It kind of strengthens people's resolve. When you go to see your MP after you've been lying in front of the gates, somehow the horror of nuclear weapons sits differently in your heart. So when you talk about it, you give a very different message.

For me, the bottom line in nonviolent direct action is that it's personally the right thing to do. So many of the local people just accept the nuclear base at Faslane and want everything to return to normal.

My message is that it *isn't* normal! It's not normal to have weapons of mass destruction on your door step. In 180 countries in the world this would be considered a very *un-normal* way to live. So we're trying to get them to actually think about what's there. The Faslane 3-6-5 direct action campaign has put us into a dialog with the local community on a level we've never had before. I've lived there twenty-three years, and my kids went to the local school, so I know lots of people locally, and I can explain to them that the Swedish kids who've come all that way to protest don't just come for a holiday. The nuclear weapons are in our backyard, but what the local people need to realize is that the whole planet is the back yard.

For now, our job is here, and again, at the moment, we've got a particularly good political chance. Some people say, "Well, now that we've got an anti-Trident party in power, we should be respectable and lobby and not do that direct action stuff, because that just gives us a bad name."

I say, "Hey, wait a minute!" As long as there are nuclear weapons on Scottish soil we have a job to do here. And [direct action] is part of it.

ELLEN MOXLEY

Ellen Moxley, Angie Zelter, and Ulla Roder—the Trident Three—completed one of the most audacious of the Trident Plowshares direct actions. Born in China, Ellen grew up in California, but she's now a Scottish citizen and a fervent nationalist. She's been working with the Trident Plowshares campaign since 1998. Ulla Roder is a peace activist from Denmark who has participated in several of the Trident Plowshares actions. Angie Zelter, originally from Norfolk, England, calls herself a "global citizen." She has coordinated major international peace campaigns, including the Snowball Campaign in the 1980s, which encouraged thousands of people to cut the fences around US military bases in the United Kingdom. Her latest campaign takes her to Jeju Island in South Korea, where activists are nonviolently resisting the construction of a US naval base.

Ellen: It was the eighth of June 1999. A beautiful, beautiful night on Loch Goil. Angie Zelter and Ulla Roder and I went down to the loch and rowed out to the lab barge–called Maytime—on a little boat we'd managed to get. We were after the computers on the lab which monitored nuclear submarine activity. Our affinity group was lurking in the bushes along the shore and David Mackenzie was there, taking pictures.

Ellen Moxley carrying dismantling tools, 1999. © David Mackenzie.

We thought we'd be stopped halfway to the barge because, you know, it was a nuclear installation. But we got all the way out and climbed up to the deck on a metal ladder. Angie discovered that one of the windows to the laboratory was half opened, so she crawled through and opened the window for Ulla and me.

Before I went in, though, I hung our banners. My partner Helen [Steven] had made a lovely banner which showed a bunch of rainbow people pushing a black bomb into the sunlight. Because the first thing to do is to identify that you're a nonviolent group and why you're doing it. We laid the big thick book of Trident Plowshares Guidelines on the table in the laboratory along with our own individual statements, including a description of what happened after Hiroshima.

Trident Three banner, 2012. © Ellen Moxley.

Then we went to work! Tossed everything in that laboratory out the window and into the loch. Absolutely everything! Computers and fax machines and CDs, everything except the drinking fountain and a first aid cabinet. As one of the witnesses for the Ministry of Defense said, "The place looked sterilized." We had cleared everything totally out and got rid of "the infection." Then we went up to the top deck and tried to get into this little office there, but we couldn't, so we sat down and ate the sandwiches and grapes Helen had sent out with us.

Our own boat had floated away, even though we thought we'd moored it to the barge, so we just waited. And waited. Waited about three hours for the MoD policemen to arrive. Finally [the people on the shore] phoned the press and told them to call the MoD and they finally came.

They were very friendly. "Oh yes, we know Trident Plowshares." When we came down to their boat, they made us a cup of tea. We told them what we had done and why, and they were very amicable. They looked around the whole platform and took very careful notes. Then we went to Coulport and were charged. We refused to go on bail because we would've had to sign an undertaking which said we would not commit further "malicious damage," and we said it wasn't malicious damage but a disarmament action. So they said, "Right. You're in Cornton Vale until you get a trial."

That was four months. It wasn't too awful, actually. We had separate rooms but were in the same unit so we could still see each other. We immediately got vegetarian food, too. (They have a lot of vegetarians inside.) We got quite a few questions from the other prisoners, and they seemed very sympathetic. Even the wardens. We got endless flowers, endless cards. The one thing we couldn't have sent in was food because it could have heroin in it or something. And all the post, of course, was opened to make sure there wasn't cocaine on the seal.

We had lots of visitors, and Helen and Dave Mackenzie organized the visitor's rota, which was just this enormous bureaucracy. Helen was also trying desperately to get Danish language speakers for Ulla, and still had her full-time job at the Scottish Center for Nonviolence, and she . . . she was just going crazy! She became very white and very tired and said to me once, "I'm just not coping." Finally she got some compassionate leave from the Center, and from inside, I also got her a Teasmade, so she'd get her tea in the morning.

People on the outside do harder time, you know. Endless people would come wanting to visit me, so she'd provide food for them. She made huge, huge pans of lasagna, and cut them into slices and froze them. One of the visitors was a total vegan, and in fact wouldn't even eat cooked food. Helen finally said to her: "Just go out to the garden, find what vegetables you like and bring them in and eat them."

Ro: Good for her! Can you talk about the trial?

Ellen: It was four weeks long, the trial was. We admitted to everything, of course. Angie, who's a pro at this sort of thing, had gotten Francis Boyle to defend us.[9] Ulf Panzer also testified. He was one of the judges who had sat outside the gate at the Mutlangen Pershing missile base in Germany and got other judges to sit outside with him. Angie knew all these great witnesses from her other resistance work.

The pivotal point was whether the Sheriff, Margaret Gimblet, would let us use international law as a defense to counter what the Ministry of Defense was saying, that we had committed "malicious damage." She was thinking and thinking—a very reflective, lovely woman—and all the Quakers were standing outside the courtroom

9. Francis Boyle is a professor of international law at the University of Illinois. His *Protesting Power: War, Resistance, and Law* (New York: Rowan & Littlefield, 2007) has been used by resisters in their trials.

holding her in the light when she was making this decision. Well, she came back in and said: "Yes, I'll hear the international law argument."

Angie wrote her own defense and was allowed a laptop in her room [in the jail]. She didn't mind that Ulla and I had lawyers, because that spread the message a little bit further. I had a very fine guy whose name is John McLaughlin and Ulla had John Mayer. (John Mayer has since published a book about this action: *Nuclear Peace: The Story of the Trident Three*).

At the end, the judge decided that because of the international law argument, she was going to instruct the jury to acquit us. So we were acquitted! We've heard since that the jury said that they were going to acquit anyway, but having the judge say it really cinched the case.

Ulla Roder, Angie Zelter, Ellen Moxley, "Victory at Court," 1999. © David Mackenzie.

Now this didn't mean that nuclear weapons were outlawed in Scotland because the government then said: "This has to be taken to a Lord Advocate's reference." Months and months and months later, it came to a hearing, and obviously these advocates were being leaned on. They said that it may be decided that nuclear weapons are illegal when they are being *used*, but the fact of the *possession* doesn't mean they're illegal. Though the 1996 International Court judgment *did* say they were illegal, so . . . Anyway, this was the British government.

Ro: So they wiggled and said that the weapons are legal until they're deployed?

Ellen: Yes. At that time you make a decision as to whether they're illegal or not. John Mayer is trying to get the Scottish Parliament to create a law which says they're illegal under *any* circumstances. The Lord Advocate's reference has said that Scottish law is part of international law and therefore it has to correspond. But even though we have our own parliament, Westminster can make decisions about defense, and that's where the catch comes in. So the Scottish Parliament could say no to the whole thing up here and the British could still set it aside.

John Mayer thinks, though, that if the majority of the MPs in Scottish Parliament pass this law, it'll be difficult for Westminster to override it. That's what we're hoping for. Do you have any acquittals in the States?

Ro: Sometimes the charges are dropped, or they aren't charged, but acquittals of any kind are highly unusual in my country, even for misdemeanor trespass actions. How do the people in the more moderate action groups—say, Faslane 365—feel about the radical actions?

Ellen: They usually feel very good, yes. Everybody does what he or she can do. An awful lot of the Faslane 365 people had jobs and couldn't afford to get arrested. It's been a tremendous movement. I had my doubts when Angie started Faslane 365. She asked everyone she wrote to get a hundred people, and I thought, "Right. Yeah." [Laughs.] She expected us to go around door to door with leaflets, and that's just not how you act in the Highlands. But I got this little group of thirteen together, and we went down and it was a wonderful experience. They loved it, they felt it!

The people who blockade feel as if they're doing something with their bodies against Trident, too. So very rarely do we hear people say, "Oh, you people are the exhibitionists. You do the big stuff." When I was in prison and seeing how enormously tired she was, I *did* say to Helen that I won't do a big one again. I think my decision is absolutely right. Angie agrees that the big stuff has to be left to the younger people. *If* they want to do it. If they can and want to do it. But we don't want prima donnas in the peace movement. I think that's why 365 emerged, because it's something small people with jobs can do, you know?

Ro: People came in all different ways, didn't they, like choral groups and the academics that came with their folding desks.

Ellen: Yes, and everybody has a say. You know, another lovely thing about Plowshares is that it has a wonderful sense of humor. For example, our group—the Horties—did an upside-down can-can at our

[Faslane 365] blockade. We were on our backs at the gate and then locked ourselves together.

Ro: Oh, that's wonderful, to have fun like that when you're resisting. What else do you do to keep up the hope?

Ellen: Well, it *is* easy to get discouraged, even with a great peace group. Because somehow people don't see the connections between nuclear weapons and their standard of living, can't see that the schools, the national health service—everything—could be better funded without the Trident. So we just have to keep on making those connections.

You know, I'm reading a new book, *Bury the Chains* by Adam Hochschild. It's about the abolition of slavery. For *fifty* years, they worked at abolishing the slave trade. They went thousands of miles up and down the country. Holding meetings, getting money, getting signatures on petitions. Having freed slaves speak about their experiences.

This little group of twelve men in a London pub came together faithfully and talked about what to do and who was going to do it, and how they were going to raise funds, and so forth. Gradually, gradually they succeeded. Finally, finally, finally, after fifty years, they got abolition.

In 2001, Ellen, Angie, and Ulla received the Right Livelihood Award. This award was established in 1980 by Jakob von Uexküll as an alternative to the Nobel Peace Prize because he wanted to "recognize the efforts of those who are . . . coming up with practical answers to challenges like the pollution of our air, soil and water, the danger of nuclear war, the abuse of basic human rights, the destitution and misery of the poor and the overconsumption and spiritual poverty of the wealthy."[10]

I also interviewed another courageous European Plowshares activist, Susan van der Hijden, a citizen of the Netherlands whose Plowshares action was in England. Susan spent some time at Faslane in 1998 when the peace camp was still muddy and fairly primitive. In 2000, she and Father Martin Newell of the London Catholic Worker disarmed a convoy truck being prepared to carry nuclear warheads up to Scotland. She was "on remand" in jail for seven months while awaiting trial. A

10. Online: www.rightlivelihood.org/award.html.

jury found them guilty, but they received only a year's sentence and the judge released them with "time served." As Susan told me, "It felt like we were acquitted!"[11]

The Netherlands—Frits ter Kuile

I first met Frits ter Kuile when he visited the US for a national gathering of Catholic Workers, bringing his verve and particular kind of Dutch humor with him. Later he escorted me to the European Catholic Worker gathering and provided leads to the interviews on the continent. When he was young, he resisted registering for the mandatory military service which was in place at that time in the Netherlands.

Frits: To be a CO, you had to write statements and go to a board with military and psychologists. I was not into having my conscience judged by people who were prepared to kill other people, and I didn't want to serve in their system [by doing CO work]. So I did not apply for CO status.

In 1984, they sent me a letter, and I didn't reply. I was living in a peace camp then, near a nuclear missile base of NATO. There was this urgency of resisting. What Gandhi and Martin Luther King said: "Fill up the jails!" Also, when you are young, you like to be a hero. When they'd arrest me for protesting, I'd say, "I am Frits Men." Not giving my last name but calling myself "Frits the Human Man." They'd take my fingerprints but they didn't connect them to this man they were wanting for draft dodging. One day, though, while I was chopping onions and carrots, the police checked the list of who was camping and off I went.

Then you pray hard. First, they brought me to a military prison and put me in isolation. They don't want you in the general population because they think you might be a rabble-rouser and con-taminate others. I did not walk around corners in square angles and stomp my feet the way the military wanted me to, but I tried to be okay, to cooperate but not go into a total crazy military way. If they say empty your dustbin, then I emptied my dustbin. I cooperate to a very high degree and I help all their prisoners, so the guards and the prisoners like me. Prison is a dark place with many people unhappy and broken and hurt. To be able to bring some mediation or just

11. Susan van der Hijden interview, Marquette Archives.

another way of seeing things, to pull people from their heads full of misery into . . . to open up the sky a little bit, I think that's a very important part of the witness.

For a week they brought me to a psychiatrist every day, and he kept asking me to sign a paper so I could get S5. Now S5 means you are totally unstable, mentally unfit. If you agree that you're cuckoo, you're a free man. But then you can't become a teacher or a government employee or a judge—or anything. So each day I said to him, "No! No! I am not cuckoo! Guys who shoot other people who they don't even know, they are the cuckoo ones."

Then they transferred me to a really, really old civil prison, built around 1896, and after three months, the trial came. Jesus says, "Don't worry about a trial," so I didn't. Why have a lawyer? Jesus didn't talk about lawyers. I was thinking, "God will touch my tongue."

But I had friends outside who wanted to use the trial to witness for peace, and I said okay, so they organized a lawyer and witnesses. One of the witnesses was von Meijenfeldt, a well known retired general who was very sharp against the military. Another one was Tinbergen, a Nobel prize winner on the economy. He spoke of the link between the war machine and poverty. And the third one was Rene Shaeffer, a Dutch national who survived the bombing of Nagasaki as a prisoner of war.

There was good media coverage 'cause those friends, they know how to do it, you know? They used this opportunity to bring up the whole issue of the nuclear race and poverty in the world and stuff like that. The trial lasted only a day, though, and then I went back to prison.

There were like 150 people at the trial, and my father, too. "Wow! My son is not a donkey who is fighting windmills alone. He's a bit nuts, but here are respectable people with gray hair." He thought they were normal people like he thought he was. So he slowly started changing. A little later he gave a talk at his Rotary Club concerning conscientious objection and his son being in prison and refusing to cooperate with the system. So he came quite a ways in accepting and even telling others about what I did.

A couple of months later, for the appeal, I had to appear at the high military court in The Hague. All these military brass judges are sitting at this big table, very imposing. I look at this table and the paneling on the walls. It's all tropical wood and I know they chopped forests to make this. So when they asked me if I wanted to say something, I talk about tropical forests and deforestation, not defending myself at all. But afterwards, the presiding judge and the secretary of the court, they came to visit me in prison, and we had a good conversation. My lawyer said he'd never heard that happen before.

But still, they gave me the standard thing, which was a year in prison. I served forty weeks. In Holland most prisons are one-man, one-cell, which I really like, you know, because I like to work in prison. I study Russian, I read books, and I write a lot of letters.

What I discovered is, the government tries to squeeze you in and block you out, but a letter to the editor or to people from prison has much more attention than just Frits who wants to save the world. So I wrote a lot of letters and it was heyday of the peace movement so you get a lot of mail. I corresponded with 434 people. Got a callus on my finger from all this correspondence. Then when you get out, all these people know you, so I biked around Holland to visit many of them.

God was with me then. Some draft resisters or conscientious objectors were broken by the government, but they didn't break me. I met so many people, and then later when I asked for help on other projects—like to Kosovo or walk across America through the desert or do this Catholic Worker house here in Amsterdam—people say, "Hey, there's this Frits! He lived four years in the peace camp, sleeping outside in the winter, and he went to prison. He really tries to live what he says!" So I got a lot of support, and God was with me.

Ro: How did you become this Frits, coming from [what sounds like] a traditional family?

Frits: I don't know. That's a miracle. Why did my brother not and I did? The [liturgical] reading this week is from John where Jesus says, "You did not choose me, I chose you." So maybe Jesus called me, you know? I [used to think] the Bible was for hypocrites like our Prime Minister, for people who just *say* they're Christians. I thought it was just soft stuff, or only good to roll joints, 'cause the paper is very thin. Then I learned that Bob Marley gets his inspiration from the Bible. Bob Marley, the Rastafarian prophet from Jamaica. He touched my heart and his music brought me a different message from God and the Bible. Then St. Francis, 'cause he was in our house. My mom likes St. Francis, but I didn't as a kid. To get me to Sunday classes, they had to drag me to the car. Last Sunday we had the First Communion of my daughter, and my mom said, "Well, well, well!" [Laughs.]

When I was sixteen or something, I rolled into the squat scene. There's a lot of thinking in the squat scene that I'd never heard of in my conservative circle. All these little anarchist booklets and papers. You pick up on whole other ways to look at the world and how it came to be that we are haves and others are have-nots. But my friends that had dropped out, most of them became junkies or living lives that I didn't want to go into. I did a lot of drugs, too—no heroin, though. But after I started university, I realized these stoned people get awareness but they don't do the revolution.

I studied half a semester at university and then I thought, "I'm going to save the world by dissent." This was in '83 with the cruise missile deployment bases and the peace camp. I was twenty-one and then the draft thing happened. After I got out of jail and biked around, I went back to the peace camp until Reagan and Gorbachev signed the INF Treaty in December of '87. Then on the first anniversary of the treaty, we scaled all these fences and banged away at some cruise missile doors to turn them into cellars for raising mushrooms. We did considerable damage, but not in the millions, just like ten thousand or twenty thousand dollars.

They let everyone out pretty soon but Kees Koning; he was kept because of another action—spray painting a plane bound for a war in Turkey. (Turkey was fighting against the Kurds.) I had [the Plowshares] book by Art Laffin with me in the cell, and as I was leaving I opened the food hole in Kees's door and shoved it in to him. When he got out and saw me, he said, "We need a real Plowshares. I'm going to do one on New Year's Eve."

Now this was just before Christmas. I said "Kees! Wait! Plowshares is by consensus with a community. Preparation and prayer and all of that." But he said he was going ahead alone, and then he asked a physician friend [Co von Melle] to take his blood for the action. Then the friend wouldn't let him go alone. He went with him.

So there's these two old guys, both in their fifties, and they do the action. Kees was not into symbolic damage, and it was a good hit. They harvested military tools from the vehicles and he had a really good hammer. So these two established men, not just some rowdy activists, they beat the shit out of a military plane. After these actions, the press was discussing this arms sale and it was discussed in Parliament, too. So that's what Art's book did, passing from one to another. Phil Berrigan came over for Kees's trial, but Kees is dead, now. In 1996.

Once I beat up a bulldozer and a big truck. Slashed all the tires. I think that's even slightly more Plowshare than the one of Kees and van Melle. The government needed a bigger runway for the big transporter airplanes for the missiles, so they had to chop down all the trees. I knew that part of the forest, and I thought, "Somebody needs to speak up for the trees!"

I had my axe and I scaled the fence and went to this bulldozer, and I swung my axe and the axe goes "Dup!" It bounces back. And I think, "Shit! These tires are really tires!" So I scaled the fence out again and I go to a farmer, a good farmer, and I asked him to sharpen my axe. "Good luck!" he hollers as I go back. Inside again, I go "Bussh!" and the tire goes "Hiss!" Very loud because it's a quiet night. I slash all the tires. I thought they'd arrest me [right away], but they didn't, so I scaled the fence back out because I had to work the next day.

I ring up the press from this farmer's house and say what's happened and after I finish work the next day, I go to the military and turn myself in. They've arrested me so many times that we know each other. I think I only got six weeks for that slashing.

Ro: What do the Dutch think of the property violence?

Frits: Ahh. The eternal controversy. Is it property or is it improperty? Is it okay to stop the engine pulling the train to Auschwitz or should you let it roll? That splits people apart. Some think it's very good. One religious, an older Grey Nun, said on TV, "We support this fully!" And other people, say, "No, no! We live in a democracy, and you have to write letters to the editor and vote for the right parties and then everything will be fixed."

Ro: Have most of the people that you've worked with been faith-based?

Frits: No, and that has been the hard thing. 'Cause the others don't understand that you block the road or you cut the fence but at the same time you're nice, you're polite and friendly to the soldier. They think you're nuts. Left-wing atheists tend to treat the soldiers and the police as enemies. But today many people are not looking at soldiers as enemies, they just don't believe in God. I like it more when it's Christians, or other religious people, Buddhists or people who have the same ideas. To win the opponents over, as Gandhi said, not win over them.

Frits traveled to the United States in 1988, spending Lent at the Nuclear Test Site near Nevada and meeting Catholic Workers and other faith-based resisters.

I went to a trial of Phil Berrigan in Norfolk and saw Catholic Workers there, too, and they did good stuff.

In 1992, I walked across the United States and I met even more Catholic Workers. We started in St. Mary's, Georgia, at the Atlantic Trident Base. Then to Redstone Arsenal in Alabama and then Amarillo and Los Alamos and on to the Nevada test site. It was a nine-month walk, with between twenty and seventy of us at various times. From Vegas to the test site there were thousands and at the test site there were like 10,000. Some Belgians walked from New York on the more northern route, and in the end it all converged. On the day in early October that we walked into Las Vegas, Bush signed a moratorium on nuclear testing, so that was very nice. So you think, "Well, we stopped the cruise missiles from coming into Holland and now we stop nuclear testing." It's nice to see sometimes a little result on doing stuff.

Back in Amsterdam, Frits learned of the Jeannette Noel Catholic Worker Huis, named after a beloved Catholic Worker from Massachusetts and New York. After a trip to Kosovo with a Peace Team organized by War Resisters International, he moved into this Worker and has been there ever since.

Frits: At the time, I was really committed to celibacy. And no kids, no kids. Then after like eight months or so, came Aiyun to our house. She was illegalized and pregnant. I fell in love with her next day. And I thought, "Oh boy! That's not going to work, you know?" An illegalized woman from China who doesn't know Tolstoy." Still I loved her, but I only gave her . . . she could hold my little finger but that was it, you know. Then Jia Jia, the little girl, was born. When I held this baby in my arm, wrapped in stuff, I'm thinking, "Ah, this poor little baby. What's going to happen to her? She has a hard life ahead."

This arrow went "Whirr!" right into my heart, and I thought, "Well, it's okay to give love to a baby, you know. Won't do any harm, only good." So I started doing lots of stuff with Jia Jia and was sort of a father figure, but still celibate. I don't marry Aiyum for like three years. Finally she says, "Okay, Frits, either we marry or I move on with my life."

Well, my heart fell out and I realized I couldn't live without them. I'd been thinking: "I'm a strong, detached celibate hero guy who is doing lots of good work!" But when I look in the mirror, I see that at center I'm so ultra-attached. So I proposed and Aiyun says, "Ha, ha!"

And now we have another child—Onno, a little boy. I stopped

the whole protest side to get married. I'm not . . . I don't feel the soil is fertile for civil disobedience now. Also, it doesn't fit in my life at this moment. I very much enjoy the children, and it's so short that they are small. To go away for a month is—whoa! I couldn't leave my wife with all that responsibility. Maybe when Onno, my little boy, is bigger and goes to school by himself and understands why I would go to prison . . . But for now, it's time for toddlers.

Frits ter Kuile, 2008. © Jim Forest.

Germany

HANNA JASKOLSKI

I interviewed Hanna on May 22, 2007, in Cologne, Germany, meeting her first in the huge Cologne cathedral, massively bombed by the United States during World War II and now beautifully restored. A leading figure in the German anti-nuclear movement, she has been jailed several times for nonviolent direct action. She also challenged Cardinal Meisner during a Mass for NATO soldiers, celebrated at the cathedral.[12]

Hanna: My parents were Christians, and as Christians should be, they lived for justice and peace, for poor people. I was very much impressed by the memories of my father who took part in World War I. He told us how he would stand face-to-face with the enemy—the so-called enemy—but he'd shoot into the air.

Ro: Do you remember the bombing of Cologne?

Hanna: Yes. I was eight years old. For two years after, I was convinced that I might die any night. I was ten when the war ended, and then I learned about the reason for this war. I learned about the Holocaust. I also learned about Hiroshima and Nagasaki, and this was terrible for me. I compared it to my own traumatic experience except that so many of the Japanese didn't survive, and if they did, they were very, very sick.

Ro: Even some peace people in the States call World War II "the good war" because it did stop the Holocaust, finally, and it did stop Hitler.

Hanna: I am convinced that there are no good wars. Every war will produce hatred, and this will lead to more war. All of life is destroyed through war. How can anyone call that good? Also after a war there is a lot of sorrow. I and my family experienced hunger and cold, and every war produces deprivations like that. Also, after every war, there is more weaponry, and this weaponry becomes more and more awful.

When I was growing up and studying music, I read a lot about nuclear weapons and realized how dangerous they were for the world. Then I married and had four children and this was a big task. When the children were teenagers, I started to be active and went to protests and gatherings and signed petitions.

Ro: When were you arrested for the first time?

Hanna: This was the eighties at Linnich, near the Rhine River, where the underground central command building of NATO was under construction. Forty meters under the earth. A nuclear war with the Soviet Union would have been led from that central command.

---

12. My sincere thanks to Ariane Dettloff who served as both translator and transcriber when Hanna and I talked. Dettloff's translation was done in the third person; I have changed it to first person to match the other interviews.

This was when I first practiced civil disobedience. We went over the fence. I first started to climb with a ladder, and then like a monkey, without a ladder. There we experienced some hard things. The police dragged me a hundred meters over the ground and even through water, and they were very rough and saying bad words to me. They were very angry, yes. They were furious because this had happened again and again and again. But from the people who were with me, I learned how it is possible to de-escalate situations like that, so at the end we had good communication with the police.

During the trial I put questions to the judge, which is usually not allowed; but he answered them, and he was moved. He said he didn't like to judge me as guilty, but he would have to say I was because otherwise he himself would be judged.

Ro: Did you go to prison for that action?

Hanna. Not for that. It was very difficult for my family to accept that I did dangerous and illegal things, so at first I paid the fine and didn't go to prison. They were against nuclear arms, though, so after many talks, it became easier to convince them. The wars in the world got worse and worse, and they finally said that I could go to prison. My first prison time was when I de-fenced the depot of the American nuclear weapons here in Germany.

Some people say it is problematic to destroy things like a fence. Now I'm well educated in nonviolence, and generally it doesn't fit to destroy things; but I had no problem destroying the fence because this fence is unjust, and what happens behind this fence is unjust. My cutting was not unjust. Gandhi said you always have to publish injustice, to bring it out into the public. Actions like the de-fencing do that.

Ro: What about the Gandhian principle of announcing the action ahead of time?

Hanna: We *do* announce the actions ahead of time, but we don't say where or when. If we did, it wouldn't be possible, so we have to be a little bit tricky. Nobody is hurt, and we don't reach the weapons; we destroy just the fence and enter. The last tine in 2005, we had only three people, but once we were twenty-four.

The first time I went to jail was in November 1998. The sentence was for twenty days, but after nine days my husband paid the rest of the fine. Because I had to go to another jail for another action. They pushed me out of one jail into the other one for twenty days more. In the end, I came to know three jails.

I also went to jail resisting the so-called civil use of nuclear power. I wrote on a container for nuclear waste. "Mothers against nuclear madness." People know about nuclear energy, but I'm astonished always that so many don't know about all the nuclear weapons that are still here.

In March of this year, I went to Faslane in Scotland. Eighteen people did a blockade—put pipes around their arms and locked themselves together—so the police had to carefully cut them apart. I decided not to have my fingers locked in the pipes because I am a musician, and I was afraid they might be hurt. It is always allowed within those actions to be honest and to confess that you are anxious. Sometimes people draw back, even at the last minute, and that's fine. During this action I played peace songs on my recorder whilst sitting on the street leading to the military base.

Everyone there was thankful for our protest, even the police and even the taxi driver who drove us. He wouldn't take any money. One of the four nuclear submarines was going to and fro as we were protesting, with the weapons all ready to be fired, and the people there don't want those underground boats with nuclear weapons in their neighborhood.

Ro: Do the newspapers cover your actions?

Hanna: Often it was in the newspapers, and four years ago the German television came to the jail where I was and made a half-hour film. We learned afterwards that 300,000 people watched it.

Ro: Can you talk about challenging the Cardinal at the cathedral Mass where he blesses the NATO soldiers?

Hanna: Yes. In the Cardinal's sermons, he would say that the weapons were safe and to the NATO soldiers: "You are the biggest peace movement in the world." Unbelievable!

Our group is called "PaXan!" Pax is a Latin word for peace, and "Pack's an!" is from a German word meaning to seize something, or roughly, "Do it now!" It's a play on words, like "Seize peace." Every year since 1997 people are protesting outside the cathedral. People from Pax Christi—the Catholic group—and other groups and single persons, too.

At our vigils I play to accompany the singing. Once I played the tiny piccolo recorder. It's very loud, and you can hear it from far away. Sometimes I play a trumpet because that's loud, too. We always tell [the police] about the vigil beforehand, and they know there will be music with instruments. So the vigil part is legal.

Twice, though, I went into the cathedral alone and did an action by myself. The first time, in January 1998, I sat down on the floor. There was no service going on, so I didn't disturb anybody, but one of those church officials closed the doors so the public couldn't enter. I played peace songs on my recorder and I had a candle, and a sign, "I believe in nonviolence" in German and in English. I did what is always done in church—playing peace songs, lighting candles, praying for peace—and therefore it was difficult for the priests. They didn't know how to handle me. They told me to sit in a pew but I said, "I sit on mother earth to heal her." Then they telephoned their chief—the Cardinal—and in the meantime, I played my songs. This lasted for forty-five minutes. I told them I would leave when the hour I had promised myself was up. But they didn't wait. Four policemen came and they dragged me out and to the police station where they noted my name, address, and so on. After that I was free. No real arrest.

Then after the terrible war in Yugoslavia, I decided to make a bigger notice. There were bombs falling on Belgrade, cluster bombs also, and the soldiers who maybe had dropped the bombs were praying in the Cathedral in a special Mass with the Cardinal, all sitting together in the front.

Because they fly so high in the sky, they didn't see any blood, didn't see the wounds, didn't hear any crying. I thought, "I must show them blood. And maybe throwing a glass would make noise like a cluster bomb."

This was in January 2000. At the beginning of the service, not the sacred part. I came early and was sitting near the middle of the cathedral, up close to the front. I waited for a moment when it was completely quiet, then I ran up and threw the glass bottle with my blood, and shouted the fifth commandment in German and in English: "Thou shalt not kill!" As loud as I could. (I wanted to shout in French, too, but my courage left me.)

The ushers came very quickly and just picked me up and carried me outside. They swept up the glass right away, but the trace of this blood was over five meters long, and all the soldiers had to step over my blood to go to Communion. But for this, I wasn't arrested.

This was very spectacular, and it was a high point. I don't think I'll ever do it again, but we still demonstrate outside every year.

Ro: Hanna, how did you become so courageous?

Hanna: I get courage from other people who have done similar things. As a young girl, I heard about Sophie Scholl, the woman who was executed for fighting fascism, and I say to myself: if anything unjust and terrible like that should ever happen again, I would like to be as courageous as she was.[13] For some, it is difficult to go on with this protest without seeing any real success. For myself, success is not the most important thing. I do the right thing because I am convinced. You know, my business card . . . it has a bird on it. Um . . . what is the name of the Hiroshima bird?

Ro: Oh, an origami peace crane.

Hanna: Yes. On the card, there's a picture of a peace crane, a symbol for peace without nuclear weapons, and on the card is written, "I am woman—a mother, a musician and a peace activist." I explain to people that I change from one role to the other, depending on what is most important at the moment.

I have lost many friends from former times because of these peace actions and being arrested. Many people can't accept this, but it's the price of peace. In spite of these "crimes," it is not difficult for me to live as a normal woman within society.

Hanna Jaskolski, 2007.

DR. WOLFGANG STERNSTEIN

Dr. Wolfgang Sternstein was another contact Frits ter Kuile made for me, and I spent an enjoyable two days with Wolfgang and his artist wife Gisela. Wolfgang is known throughout Europe for his brave and principled opposition to nuclear weapons; in addition, he is a distinguished

---

13. Sophie Scholl was a member of the White Rose, a nonviolent resistance group in Nazi Germany, consisting of students from the University of Munich. She and five others were executed in 1943 for distributing anti-Nazi pamphlets. One of their group, Alexander Schmorell, has been canonized by the Russian Orthodox Church.

Gandhian scholar. His interview recalls adding activism to his academic life, first in the ecological movement of the seventies, and then as a nonviolent resister in the German Plowshares movement, where he dismantled trucks which carried Pershing II missile components. His retelling of the nationwide campaign against these missiles shows that massive nonviolent civil disobedience can result in significant victories. Dr. Sternstein concludes with an explanation of some aspects of Gandhian thought; his charming wife Gisela has a last word.

Wolfgang: A special aspect of the German situation is that the ruling class is not so arrogant—not so self-confident—as in the States. In the States, politicians always think they know what's best and think it's always best to stand for law and order. But German politicians, because of our past history, realize that much injustice *can* be done by the state. That experience is very deep in the character of the people, so the police and the politicians and even the justices—the whole ruling class—are very cautious, especially when the people are acting in nonviolent resistance groups.

During the Nazi era, any resistance groups were shot or executed. The lesson of that time is that resistance is sometimes badly needed. United States has its tradition of nonviolent action and civil disobedience, but today it seems to be worse for you than it is for us here.

My father fought with the Nazis. He was not a big shot, only a little party member, but in his family he behaved like Hitler. I experienced violence on a rather high scale during my childhood. So to understand the origins of violence, to learn how to overcome it, that became a theme for my life.

I was lucky, really lucky, to meet my wife Gisela very early, when I was nineteen years old. If you experience violence, your body and your soul will not forget it, and Gisela was very, very important in helping me to get out of the violence in myself. I also learned that it is important to study and work on the outside on peace issues, so I received my doctorate in political science, with a critical study of Marxism.

I had a theoretical approach, but I also developed an interest in practicing nonviolence from Matahma Gandhi and Martin Luther King, of whom I am very fond. They can teach everyone! So it was a great event to be part of a resistance movement against the nuclear power plant to be built on the Rhine and to try there to keep the action nonviolent. Probably 100,000 people were engaged, and initially they were not nonviolent at all, so I got a lot of experience in conveying the idea of nonviolence. Now the violence in my youth had made me a very timid and shy person, so I was scared to utter anything in public. But after a long time and much failure and often praying, I was finally able to talk about nonviolence to many people.

It was a hard struggle with police there, and we were all sometimes in great danger from the water cannons and horses, but we were successful and the nuclear plant never opened. It was stopped by the brave resistance of the people of the region.

The police and the politicians in Germany are very careful. They try to avoid violence, and therefore we have a similar interest. Many of the police in Germany are also against nuclear weapons; I think the majority of them are. I know the highest police officer in this region. He is a very fine character, and he wants to avoid violence by the police. That's very important, especially in the Plowshares actions. Before our first Plowshares, I sent a letter to this high officer, along with a little booklet explaining why we were doing the action. He said, "What they want is not bad, but my task is to prevent them from doing it." You have very different interests, of course, and you have to realize that and work to create understanding on the opposite side. I think we did a lot to encourage this, and you *have* to do a lot. We can't think they'll always understand what we do, because they won't.

Ro: Did you have spies infiltrating the German peace movement?

Wolfgang: Some, I think, but they didn't do any damage. Because of our Gandhian way, which is to make everything open, what can they spy on? That's really the best strategy to deal with spies—having no secrets.

Now with Plowshares actions it's different. To be successful with a Plowshares action you need a part of it to be secret. How to balance, how to be as open as possible but not to tell everything—when, which day, and which place—you should not tell those details to everybody.

For our first Plowshares, we had a long march before the action. Ah! It was a great adventure, I can tell you! All the way from the coast of the North Sea to the site here in Schwabisch-Gmund. We'd march all day and then every evening we'd meet with local peace groups, telling them about the action and spreading the message of nonviolence and especially [about] actions of civil disobedience. On the whole march there was always a police car following behind us, and the people would ask how we could do the Plowshares when it was already openly announced.

And we answered: "You will see. We will be very quiet, very quietly quiet." And we succeeded! Because there was a secret part of the action, a secret preparation. See, the Gandhian message is to be just as open *as possible*.

In the beginning we were ten and we ended with three—Herwig Jantschik and Karin Vix and me—and then Carl Kabat came from the States and made four. Phil Berrigan had come to visit first, with Anne Montgomery. Phil gave me some very good advice on how we shouldn't be depressed when people drop out, and how to do it and so on. Also on the importance of solid preparation for the action. Otherwise you run great risks.

Then Carl came and he brought us a banner which had been used in several Plowshares actions. At that time, my wife asked him to join our group, because we had so little experience and he was an old fighter. An old fighter. When he said he would be with us, I was deeply moved. It's all very hard, because you're under such awful stress. You cause such high expectations in the groups who are supporting you and in the larger peace movement. If you fail, they would think you're a little bit silly or you are doing the action just for show.

The hardest for me was when friends came to me, very good friends. They implored us not to do the action and said it would hurt my family and the peace movement. They said it would be labeled as vandalistic and that we would be called terrorists. So to keep to the aims and the conviction after that . . . that was awfully hard. My family was great! I wouldn't have the power to act if my wife and children were not so much supporting me.

To tell you some details on the secret part, the ones who were going to act went off on a different route than the marchers, and the large group was not informed because we were in fear of a spy. We walked six kilometers during the night, carrying our heavy metal tools, and came to the action site on December 4, 1983. I carried a big hammer for destroying the windows and the dashboard [on the truck which carries the Pershing missiles].

We cut through the fence of the US Army base. There was only one guard. (Usually there should be two, but one of them was smoking grass and was sleeping in the driver's cab.) We put our banner up and our witness statements to explain our action.

After we disarmed the truck, we sat down and sang some peace song, and it was very emotional. Then the soldiers came and we expected to be beaten very hard. But nothing of that kind happened. Instead, they looked at us with a . . . a mixture of astonishment and admiration, especially the Blacks. I didn't expect that, but then we realized that they know we are fighters, too, and that we both take risks. So we are comrades to them in a certain way.

I was rather sure we would get two or three years in prison, but it came out that we only got a fine. We have so many rights in the courts here in Germany. For instance, we can talk in court about our motives and our aims, and about international law. The judge isn't allowed to stop us, as they can in the States. The court was convinced that what we did was right, so he decided to give a symbolic fine—a symbolic punishment for the symbolic action—and no damage restitution. We also had the good lawyers, and we tried to explain our action clearly, and the press coverage was great.

The company which repaired the truck sent us a bill, but we explained we couldn't pay it because we were convinced that we did the right thing, and I think they thought the unrest of having a civil trial to get the repair money wouldn't be so good for their image, so they let it go. Same for the US Army.

But I want to put this Plowshares into context. In the early eighties, there was a big resistance movement in Germany, with many demonstrations and symbolic actions in the struggle against the deployment of the intermediate range missiles in Germany—the Pershing IIs and the cruise missiles. There were about one hundred Pershing IIs around Stuttgart and about hundred and fifty cruise missiles in the Hunsruck, which are mountains in the middle of Germany.

Quite a lot of actions took place during October, 1983, including a human chain 108 kilometers long, between Stuttgart, the seat of EUCOM, and Neu-Ulm, one of the Pershing II sites.[14] Nevertheless, on the 28th of December, the first Pershings arrived, and all of a sudden the whole movement crashed down. Just went to nothing.

But this breakdown was not the end. There was a small group, not more than four students of Tübingen, who said, "If the danger is as great as we were always telling the public, then we have to go on with acting. If not, we have to confess our error. If we believe the first

14. EUCOM (United States European Command) is the US joint command which covers all of Europe, most of Africa, and parts of the Middle East. Its headquarters are in Patch Barracks, one of four US military installations in and around Stuttgart. Online: www.eucom.mil/mission/background/history-of-eucom.

to be correct, we have to try our best to move the missiles away, to get rid of them."

So they started a new movement. They moved from Tübingen to Mutlangen and set to work. It was a very small beginning, and I can tell you, it was hard work to get a new movement going when people all over the country said all the protests were in vain and were depressed, depressed, depressed.

The movement began just as a little creek, not even yet a stream. But because they were such tough and determined people, the creek began to swell and it became a river. They called it Campaign of Civil Disobedience for Disarmament and they allied themselves with the international Campaign for Nuclear Disarmament (CND). CND was founded in Great Britain by Bertrand Russell and others in 1958, and it received much popular support, both there and in Europe, as people became aware of the dangers of nuclear weapons.

The main part of it was civil disobedience to remove the new weapons. That made it different from the original mass actions. It had a new quality, and finally there were thousands of people who were going to act in this civil disobedience movement.

That part of the nonviolent resistance in Germany, I think, was more important than both of the Plowshares actions. They were of great value, but the Campaign was necessary, and I think it was the main reason for the success of it all. As you know, the missiles were finally disarmed with the INF Treaty in 1987.

Ro: So the second phase of the movement was more concentrated on CD.

Wolfgang: Yes, indeed. We used the affinity group system that we learned from the States, with five to fifteen persons who prepare for action, act together, and stick together in trials and jail. The Tübingen students who moved to Mutlangen formed a frame for other groups. We had groups of physicians, groups of artists, of seniors, and so on. It was very impressive. All the actions were taking place at Mutlangen, in front of the site where the Pershing IIs were deployed. There was only one street to this site, so it was possible to blockade it.

Ro: Was this when the judges did their own civil disobedience action? I remember reading about it in the Jonah House newsletter.[15]

Wolfgang: Yes. On January 12, 1987, not long after our second Plowshares action. They met here in this house, and I prepared them for

15. Online: www.jonahhouse.org/archive/UlfPanzer.htm.

the action. Twenty judges, and with supporters they were forty, so we had a full house!

I wonder whether such an action would ever be possible in other countries. Naturally it had to do with our Nazi past, when so many judges became willing executors of the Nazi ideology. But it was difficult. People who stand for law and order were going to transcend the line between the criminals and themselves. You can't imagine how difficult it was for them! Then there was a quarrel. Some of them said, "We can't do it without announcing it to the authorities." Others said "No, no!" So we were talking until about 4:00 in the morning. Finally we came to the conclusion that it must be announced publicly but not to the authorities. So everyone knew, but the government didn't believe it. They wanted to ignore it, but they couldn't.

In the blockading statement, Judge Ulf Panzer wrote,

> Fifty years ago, during the time of Nazi fascism, we judges and prosecutors allegedly "did not know anything." By closing our eyes and ears, our hearts and minds, we became a docile instrument of suppression, and many judges committed cruel crimes under the cloak of the law. We have been guilty of complicity. Today we are on the way to becoming guilty again, to being abused again. By our passivity, but also by applying laws, we legitimize terror: nuclear terror. Today we do know. We know that it needs only the push of a button and all Germany, Europe, the whole world, will be a radiating desert without human life. It is because we know this that we have to act. Many of us judges have organized "Judges and Prosecutors for Peace." We have raised our voices in warning against nuclear death. We have worked with local peace groups, advertised against nuclear armaments, demonstrated and submitted resolutions to our parliament . . . Our warnings have died away unheard. That is the reason why we today block the US air base in Mutlangen. We hope that such an action will be heard more loudly than all our words before.[16]

But then five hundred other judges and lawyers joined them in a newspaper advertisement, so it was not possible to remove them. The judges were taken to court and got a fine, of course, like everybody else; but to give them more punishment was impossible because so

16. Online: www.nuclearfiles.org.

many people were joining them. And they were all allowed to keep their offices. This action made a lot of impact on the public.

There were a lot of other blockades, too, and one of them, called "Promiblockade," was famous all over the world. ("Promi" means prominent people.) Even in Japan there was press coverage of this blockade because it included famous writers, like Heinrich Boll and Günter Grass, and actors and artists. Almost everybody on the Left wing in Germany was taking part in this blockade.

Even that group had the nonviolence training, which you really need because there were always conflicts within and between the groups, and especially between the groups and the organizers. Because in Germany you still have a residual culture of violence with some of the people heirs of the bad heritage from the Nazi past.

Ro: How do you keep them out of big actions?

Wolfgang: Ah, that's difficult, but it is possible. You must announce your action and say, "If you will take part, you have to pledge to fulfill the nonviolence guidelines and do the training program, and be a member of an affinity group." That gives a certain control. But in spite of this announcement beforehand, some of them caused us a lot of troubles. It was hard work to keep them nonviolent.

The second Plowshares action was at the height of this civil disobedience campaign, the 12th of December in 1986. In the months before, there had been blockading, every day blockading. We had a very hard process in the second action. Lots of conflicts in the group and great difficulties in finding people who were able to do such a risky action. Finally we formed a group of four people—two women and two men—Heike Huschauer, Suzanne Mauch-Fritz, and me from Germany and Stellan Vinthagen from Sweden. The action took place where we did the first one, and we were happy to be able to succeed again.

This time it was more secret. We cut through the fence again, early in the morning. There were no guards this time, but we saw someone driving by, so we were worried that we'd be detected very soon. We found one truck and we went into action and destroyed the electricity supply and a crane behind the cab. We also cut this very strong cable between the cab and the carriage where the missile launcher was. My task was to jump on the electric armament behind the truck cab, open it, and destroy it. I'm for real action, risky actions [that do real damage]. When everyone's talking about symbolic acts, I can still hear Phil Berrigan saying, "We need a hammer."

We used our blood as a symbol. I am a little bit reluctant about this. In the US, the symbolism in the Catholic religion will be understood, and you can transport it to the Plowshares milieu. In Germany, this is difficult because the movement is so secular. But the other members of the group wanted to use it, so I agreed because it connected us with the Americans and with the larger Plowshares movement as far away as New Zealand and Australia.

Suzanne Mauch-Fritz and Heike Huschauer, 1986. © Thomas Pflaum.

The response of the army was very different from the first Plowshares. This time, officers rushed to the scene in their car. The doors burst open and six or seven of them sprang out and began abusing us with very hard words like "You motherfucker! I was in Vietnam!" One of them cried, "I know how to handle people like you!" And he began to attack one of the women who was trying to read a statement.

You know, at those moments sometimes you get the inspiration you need. He was tearing down the banner which we put at the front of the truck, and I said to him, "Don't touch anything because it is all evidence, so you have not the right to touch it."

Ro: Brilliant!

Wolfgang: Yes, in the moment you find the right words. Then it was interesting. His *comrades* stopped him! A moment later, they rushed into their car and drove away and called the German police, as they did in the first action. Now it's different if you go into the base at Mutlangen, where the missiles were actually deployed. Then they will easily shoot. We just went into the barracks where the trucks were parked [which carry the missiles].

Very similar to your civil rights movement was the peace movement here during the eighties. The general public was realizing the real danger to the existence of our country in case of nuclear war in the middle of Europe. There would be nothing left. No Europe.

We succeeded in conveying to almost everyone the motives and the aims of our struggle. We contributed to the end of the Cold War because public opinion came to be so against the weapons. First there was the INF, the Intermediate Range Nuclear Forces Treaty, signed in 1987.[17] That was the beginning of the end of the Cold War. That led to the reunification of Germany and so on. So it was a very central thing, a very good thing and very worthwhile, with results.

But even if there were no results, I would not regret anything I did. Because you have to plan and to perform your actions in a spirit that it is worthwhile even if there are no results. Of course results are always there. Sometimes you just don't see them.

After the missiles left, Dr. Sternstein built a Hope and Resistance Network, a sort of European Plowshares movement, with Per Herngren of Sweden. They had about a dozen actions in the UK, Sweden, the Netherlands, and Germany. But the distances and the language barrier made working together difficult, and the group is no longer meeting.

Wolfgang: Now the Trident Plowshares at Faslane in Scotland have taken it up. Sometimes nonviolent civil disobedience goes underground, but it has influence and it keeps going. It's a very fine experience when you see other people taking up the theme and the issue.

17. The treaty eliminated nuclear and conventional ground-launched and cruise missiles with intermediate ranges. By the treaty's deadline of June 1, 1991, a total of 2,692 of such weapons had been destroyed: 846 by the US and 1,846 by the Soviet Union. Online: www.fas.org/nuke/control/inf/index.html.

Everything here has changed since 9/11. For example, the EU-COM was in former times very easy to get into. You just had to cut the fence and go in, but now they've made a fortress out of it. Also, they announced that there's an area around EUCOM that is illegal to enter, but there is no fence around that area, nothing to show where it is.

Ro: So you could just wander in unawares and be in trouble?

Wolfgang: Indeed. They tell us that terrorism is the reason for making this big area illegal, but in reality it is to prevent demonstrations. Because now they can easily throw you out without any warning. They know, of course, that they are doing something illegal, so they said, "Here's a place where you can demonstrate." It's very far from the main gate.

Ro: We have those, too. Ironically, they're called "Free Speech Zones." It's always this little pen far away from what you're demonstrating against.

Wolfgram: Here, too, our rights are reduced, step by step, and the German authorities go along with the United States. We are challenging this ruling in court.[18]

Ro: Oh, good! Can you talk about the de-fence movement? I think it's such a clever name!

Wolfgang: So do I. The method was originally invented by the Dutch resisters. I developed a different model which we used at least nine times at EUCOM and twice where the last twenty nukes on German soil are deployed. It's a German military installation and in case of war, these nuclear bombs will be in the hands of the Germans. I think that is against the Non Proliferation Treaty, because we belong to the non-nuclear states.

I thought we should be able to get rid of them, so I began to organize this campaign of de-fencing EUCOM. Beginning in 1990, we did nonviolent resistance by cutting through the fence and proceeding on the site to occupy it symbolically. I thought it might grow bigger and bigger, but it didn't. We tried to do one action every year but in the long run, we were not successful in broadening the campaign. The peace movement is fainting—so weak—so now we are in the situation of starting all over again.

18. In a 2008 e-mail, Dr. Sternstein wrote, "We won! The courts have decided we have a right to rally and distribute leaflets at the main gate of EUCOM."

The spirit is gone. The Mutlangen group is gone. Burned out. But even the highest politicians have said they want to get rid of the nuclear weapons in Germany, and the people, too, in surveys. In 1990 a public opinion poll found that 80 to 90 percent of the people are against nuclear power plants and against nuclear weapons. In this respect, we succeeded in a certain way, even if the movement is quiet.

There's always the double aspect: how to overcome violence in yourself and in society. Those are the main questions of my life. When you look at the facts of the military system, of the industrial system, you cannot avoid realizing that there is no hope for the human family any more. That's a hard hard thing to realize, especially if you have children, and grandchildren. What will be their fate?

Perhaps our generation can manage to muddle through before a nuclear war occurs. But when I think of China and India . . . they are on the way to industrializing their economy and it will come to the point where they will be in conflict with all the other imperial powers—with Europe, with the States, with Japan. So I see a very dark future for mankind.

There are other dangers, for example the terrorist one, the clash of civilizations or religions. And the ecological problems. If you look realistically at the world scene, you will realize that there is no hope.

Ro: So do you just say everything is lost and therefore let us enjoy the day? *Carpe diem*?

Wolfgang: "Let us enjoy life." That would be the conclusion by many, many people, but I don't think so. I learned from Gandhi a very good quotation. I'm afraid I cannot tell you in English, but I'll sum it up. Gandhi says everything that is done for good in the world will stay, and everything that is done from evil will be lost. Every evil deed will just disappear, because it has no real existence. If you look from the perspective of eternity, it has no existence. On the other side, everything that is done with good motives and good aims and good methods—that will be preserved for eternity. That makes me sure that everything we do will not be lost.

Ro: But if there's no world, where is all this good going to *be*?

Wolfgang: Well, it is my belief that this world is only one of millions of worlds, of planets. I don't know. I'm not God. He knows, but I believe there is a reality behind ours, a reality behind what we see and touch and smell. I think we get part of this reality when we try to cling to the truth, what Gandhi called *satyagraha*. When we use the force of love, the force of truth, the force of God within us. If you are able to act out of this spirit, then what you are doing will not be lost because it is part of what is real.

That is my conviction: I think this reality is the eternal one and what we are experiencing is transitory and will pass away. If we do the right thing, we become a part of this permanent reality, and that is the goal we have to strive for.

I learned this from Gandhi. He opened my eyes to this reality, so I think, in the end, there is no reason to despair. Not at all. You will suffer a lot when you see that this world is going to be destroyed, but nevertheless, I'm convinced there is no reason to despair.

Ro: I'll sound Manichean here, but if good will be in the eternal world, why not evil?

Wolfgang: The way Gandhi puts it is that in the ancient Indian language, Sanskrit, you have a term Satja which means "truth" and also "that which is." Asatja therefore means "untruth" and it also has the meaning of nonbeing or "that which is not." If untruth is seen as not existent, the victory of truth is not in question. Truth is that which is and can never be destroyed.[19]

Ro: Evil or untruth is then nonbeing.

Wolfgang: Nonbeing, yes. We have no evidence for that. It's just a belief, but if you really believe in the existence of truth and the nonexistence of untruth, then it came out that all the untruth, which is surrounding us—the military system, the political system, the economic system— all that is not really existing. If you take the stand of eternity, it has no existence. It will be like the smoke over the fire, it will pass away.

Ro: Okay, that I can understand. Thank you. Now you've been a student of Gandhi for a number of years, haven't you?

Wolfgang: Oh, yes! I've just finished writing a book, *Gandhi and Jesus: The End of Fundamentalism*.[20] Gandhi liked the Sermon of the Mount very much. He really understood what Jesus meant by the love of God, the love of the enemy, and the love of the neighbor.

19. Portions of this explanation were taken from an interview of Dr. Sternstein printed in *Lebenshaus Schwäbische Alb*, April 8, 2008. Used by permission.

20. The book has been published in Germany and will soon be available in an English translation.

But Gandhi knew that its not enough to be a believer. You need a method of conflict resolution and that's what he did. He transformed the Christian belief into such a method. A fortunate progress, a great progress towards political methods of conflict resolution, I think. Unlike in the churches, it becomes real. It is not far away and it's not only to be passive or just to show your love. You need to combine strength and love.

Gisela: For us, no matter what we do, we are always together in our hearts. We can develop this practice of nonviolence by doing it. So we can all be creative, not only in painting and writing but in the connections between human beings. God is everywhere—in you and in me—but we have to act in order to recognize this. Then we must practice it every day. Gandhi says that to practice nonviolence you can't stay home. You have to be among the people.

Gisela and Wolfgang Sternstein, 2007.

6

School of the Americas Watch

The annual School of the Americas (SOA) protest has become a fall rite for thousands of faith-based peace and justice activists. They come by bus and bike, by train and car and air. They unite in protest at the gates of Fort Benning in Columbus, Georgia in a vigil to close the SOA, the US Army School which trains soldiers from other countries. Since 1946, the school has trained over 64,000 Latin American soldiers in counterinsurgency techniques, commando and psychological warfare, military intelligence, and interrogation tactics.

In one of its many attempts to blunt the force of the citizens' campaign, the US Army has changed the name to Western Hemisphere Institute for Security Cooperation (WHINSEC) but opponents still call it SOA and say it stands for "School of Assassins." In response to congressional calls for reform, WHINSEC now requires eight hours of human rights training, but US Army Major Joe Blair, a former director of instruction at the School, has said, "They teach the identical courses that I taught . . . and use the same manuals."[1]

SOA graduates have been linked consistently to human rights violations and to the suppression of popular movements in Central and South America. School of the Americas Watch (SOAW), the campaign to close the school, says it's responsible for the deaths of thousands of peasants over the years. They point as well to the assassination of four US women missionaries; six university Jesuits, their housekeeper and her teenage daughter; and Archbishop Oscar Romero, all in El Salvador in the '80s, and Guatemalan Bishop Juan Gerardi in 1998.

1. Online: www.soaw.org.

At the heart of the campaign is former Maryknoll priest Roy Bourgeois. When he was a missionary in Bolivia, Fr. Roy learned how US foreign policy favors the rich and how its army trains soldiers in other countries in techniques used to torture and kill their own people. Then in 1980, Archbishop Oscar Romero's conversion from timid priest to prophetic champion for peace prompted him to ask that those who have a voice speak for those whose voices have been taken away.

Father Roy decided to be that voice. In 1983, he and two others went to the SOA. They sneaked onto the base and up a tree and broadcast the last words of Bishop Romero into the ears of 525 El Salvadoran soldiers who had just started their training at the School. For that broadcast, the three protesters served a year and a half in prison.

Then in November of 1989, Roy and the world learned of the murder in El Salvador of six Jesuit priests, their housekeeper, and her daughter. A Congressional task force determined that nineteen of the twenty-five men who killed them were graduates of the SOA.[2] Roy began the campaign in earnest by traveling to Columbus, renting a small apartment near the base, and starting to fast and to vigil. He was joined at first by only a few, but the vigil grew into a campaign, and today thousands gather in Columbus each November to honor those killed by SOA-trained personnel and to work for the closure of the school.

During the yearly vigil and at other times as well, activists "cross the line" into Fort Benning and are arrested, tried, and imprisoned. Since 9/11, the security at the base has markedly increased. Formerly the protesters had been able to walk peaceably into the base, holding crosses bearing the names of those slain by SOA graduates and singing "No Más, no More." Most would walk out when asked to leave. Those who wanted to "risk arrest," as the organizers say, would stay on the base and be removed by bus and processed. They would typically receive "ban-and-bar letters," which denied them entrance to the compound. Now all those wanting to be in the solemn procession or the festivities which precede it must go through security gates similar to those in airports, and the gates to the actual base are locked. Instead of ban-and-bar letters, those arrested usually receive at least a three-month sentence. After a record number of arrests in 2002, the numbers have greatly diminished. Those "crossing" have to find other ways of getting into the base—usually by crawling under the fence, and it's become both more tricky and more ritualistic. Since the beginning, SOAW has provided tactical and

2. Ibid.

moral support for the prisoners of conscience, making sure everyone receives thorough nonviolence training and other kinds of preparation, helping them with bail and trial work, and supporting them during their prison stays.

The campaign continues throughout the year. They travel south to persuade Latin American countries not to send soldiers to the US for training and attempt to minimize US military involvement in the hemisphere in other ways. So far, Ecuador, Nicaragua, Venezuela, Argentina, Uruguay, and Bolivia have agreed. Volunteers and SOAW staff lobby Congress to pass legislation to permanently close the school and campaign throughout the United States to gain support for the cause. WHINSEC fights back with a "Strategic Communications Campaign Plan." In 2005, Aaron Shuman, on trial for a line crossing, entered into the court record copies of this plan, which he had received while acting as a journalist. The plan showed how the school tracked Fr. Bourgeois's activities, sent prefabricated letters to newspapers to counter negative views of the SOA, and otherwise worked to destabilize the SOAW.[3]

While the lobbying and protests in Washington have become an important focus, the annual protest at Fort Benning calls to the peace people as a grand family reunion. The city sees the protest as a convention, so the visitors get convention discounts at hotels and restaurants and a general air of festivity prevails, even as counter protesters hold competing rallies.

Until recently, a consortium of Jesuit colleges would hold a day-long teach-in on Latin American affairs on the Saturday before the vigil and busloads of university students would come from across the country, celebrating together at the end of the day with a rousing bilingual Mass. There's always entertainment and a street fair with activist groups renting tables to display their messages.

Martin Sheen at SOA protest, 2004.

3. "More than an Image Problem," *National Catholic Reporter*, February 18, 2005. Online: natcath.org/NCR_Online/archives2/2005a/021805/021805t.htm.

On Sunday the mood changes and the crowd lines up for the solemn vigil, with short speeches from notables such as Martin Sheen and the families of victims, followed by an orderly procession.

For hours a voice sings out the individual names of the dead, and the crowd responds "Presente," as the protesters slowly move towards and then past the gate, leaving their crosses and other mementos on the gate and the surrounding fence. The few doing civil disobedience crawl into the base through a hastily dug hole and are immediately apprehended. The vigil traditionally ends with puppets from the Bread and Puppet Theatre in Vermont.[4]

Author at School of the Americas gate, beginning of SOAW vigil, 2004.

Puppets at SOAW vigil, 2011. Jean Bassinger.

SOAW counts over 200 convicted prisoners of conscience. In recent years, Judge G. Mallon Faircloth has presided over their trials, usually held the next January after the big November action. Sentences vary

4. Bread and Puppet is a politically radical puppet theatre, active since the 1960s and currently based in Glover, Vermont. They participate in demonstrations for social change and frequently give workshops on stilt-walking and creating papier-mache puppets.

greatly. Once in awhile charges are dismissed or people receive probation, but the current standard sentence for first-time offenders is from
three to six months. Repeat offenders get longer sentences.

This chapter presents interviews from several of these prisoners of
conscience, including one of founder Roy Bourgeois by Nicole Sault and
the late Father Lorenzo Rosebaugh's description of the first and most
striking SOA action. Rebecca Kanner, a Jewish activist from Ann Arbor, recaps how the fall protests and the resulting trials work.[5] Kathleen
Rumpf tells how she and others changed the SOA sign at the entrance
to read "School of Shame." Other narrators include Missouri Catholic
Worker Steve Jacobs and Lisa Hughes, who was living at the Portland
Catholic Worker when I interviewed her. Tina Busch-Nema, another
SOA protester who is a former Sister of Notre Dame, tells of her efforts
to brighten the lives of the women prisoners held in the Carswell, Texas
hospital prison. The chapter concludes with a thoughtful interview from
a couple who wish to remain anonymous.

Roy Bourgeois

Roy: We are a product so often of our past experiences.[6] I grew up in a
very conservative area of the country, in a small town in Louisiana.
Was basically a Sunday Catholic. Went to public school and then
went off to college where I got a degree in geology, hoping to get rich
in the oil fields of Venezuela.

Back then they said the enemy was Communism. (Now it's terrorism.) I didn't question our leaders in Washington who said we
were going to be "liberators" in Vietnam, so I went. Vietnam was a
turning point in my life. Losing friends and being wounded there—
death being so close—really forced me to look at my faith more seriously. A chaplain suggested I write to the Maryknoll community, so I
did. In a sense, that started my coming back to life.

Those seminary years were formative. I was introduced to the
Scriptures and challenged by my peers. After three years in seminary,
I went to my first demonstration. We blockaded the White House

5. See *Doing Time for Peace* for five other narratives of SOAW actions: Becky
Johnson, Kathy Kelly, Rae Kramer, Ed Kinane, and Ann Tiffany.

6. This interview by Nicole Sault was originally published in a longer version
in July 2007 online: webzine.thesocialedge.com, a Canadian social justice webzine
edited by Gerry McCarthy. Used by permission.

with other veterans and some of our seminarians, and I spent a night in jail. I look back on that first protest as a sacred moment. I had so much to learn, but my faith was telling me that I would be speaking out against war and killing.

I went to Bolivia after ordination and the poor people there introduced me to my country's foreign policy and what it meant to be on the receiving end. We'd meet in their small faith communities where liberation theology was giving hope. The indigenous of Bolivia had such a wonderful spirituality, so connected to Mother Earth. They realized that Mother Earth had all these resources and blessings, more than enough for everyone to live comfortably and in peace. But it ended up in the hands of this small elite. Wealth and power have become gods (in the US) and it's all very connected to the poverty in other lands.

After Roy learned about the 1989 massacre in El Salvador, closing the school that had trained their murderers became his life work. Ten friends joined him that first year; now thousands gather. He sometimes still witnesses alone at the entrance to the base.

Roy: In solitary witness I find great meaning. When we do actions alone or with a small group, we are approachable. People stop, and I have resources for them. It's important that we think about how to be creative peacemakers. The message of Jesus is a simple one—that we can arm ourselves with love and do good things in the world. Whether we speak out as individuals in solitary witness, or add our voice to thousands, like in the November action, it all contributes to that goodness.

Now I know people are afraid. When I was in El Salvador, I was very fearful, because they were killing and disappearing so many people. But here in the United States, what do we have to fear? I know some fear being arrested, and I remember feeling that fear. I've spent over four years in federal prisons around the country, and I've learned that prison is really nothing to be afraid of. It's a hard place to be. Difficult. But once you face that, you realize that you can turn the experience into something very positive.

Some feel it's a waste of time. But when they bring us to trial, we put our country's foreign policy on trial. We have interviews with the media, and we try to break down the ignorance that's such a big enemy in our country. Many people have been awakened in the process, including ourselves.

What's important is for all of us to ask a basic question: What can I do? It might mean going out to a street corner with a sign. Maybe by yourself, or perhaps with a couple of friends. It might mean circulating a petition in your workplace, or with your family. It might mean knocking on doors. We have to step forward and say, "Not in my name." We can do that wherever we are.

We all make choices. The three of us who did the first action [broadcasting Bishop Romero's sermon from the tree] went to prison for a year and a half. I have never regretted that time. It was our most creative action and it made sense. But while it made sense to me, it didn't make sense to some friends and relatives, and I was criticized.

I think what most of us are most afraid of is that criticism. We're afraid to be called names, to be not loved. That's what we have to come to grips with. I've lost people I thought were good friends, because my going to prison was an embarrassment to them. But if we're going to be warriors for peace, we're going to upset people, and lose friends.

When we first started here [at the SOA protests], I'd get death threats. We carry these makeshift coffins, during our protests in November [and one threat said], "If you leave your apartment and attend this here protest, you gonna end up in one of those coffins!" Well, it's something you have to think about, but it doesn't prevent me from joining the protest. We have to muster up the courage and not allow others to paralyze us with fear.

Most of the time, now, I'm traveling around the country, accepting speaking engagements. But you know? I'm learning to appreciate silence and solitude. [The last time I was in prison], I went on a work strike, so I was put into solitary confinement, and I spent the last couple months in this six-by-nine cell. I was allowed three books at a time, one of them being the Scriptures. Friends sent me a steady flow of books by the mystics—St. John of the Cross, Thomas

Merton. I went through some dark nights of the soul, but I felt God's presence in a very deep way.

When I got out of prison I felt I wanted more solitude. Perhaps God was calling me to leave the world of activism. So I went for five months to a Trappist Monastery, to discern and to try it out. I found out, though, that I wasn't called to be a full-time contemplative, that my life really was in the world, working for peace, struggling for justice. I did learn that I need solitude and prayer and silence and nature, but it's got to be integrated into my active life. Most of us need that quiet time, to sustain our hope in this work for peace.

In 2008, Roy gave the homily at the ordination of a Roman Catholic woman to the priesthood, Janice Sevre-Duszynska, a former SOAW prisoner of conscience. Subsequently he was asked to recant his support of women's ordination. He refused and was excommunicated. In July of 2010, "feeling it necessary to avoid any appearance of endorsing his views on women's ordination," his order revoked its $17,500-a-year funding support for SOAW. The campaign continues.

Roy Bourgeois dancing at the end of the vigil, 2004.

Father Lorenzo Rosebaugh, OMI

Fr. Lorenzo: We did that action at SOA in 1983. Before [SOAW] got official. With Roy and Linda Ventimiglia. We bought army uniforms and dressed up like soldiers and put names on them of people from Latin America. Gave ourselves pretty high ranks, and I even cut my beard and got my hair looking tidy.

First, we snuck through the woods and up behind the barracks, with leaflets that had Bishop Romero asking the Salvadoran soldiers to put down their arms. They thought we were for real, so the men all stood up, and Roy said, "Attencion!" Then he gave them orders to pass out our leaflets. [Chuckles.]

But one of them got scared and ran off and came back with this American and a police dog. So we were taken in, but the army couldn't arrest us on the base, so they just wrote us up and kicked us out. The next day was a Sunday. We decided to pass out the leaflets in front of the chapel. The chaplain was really angry and he got us tossed out a second tune.

Then the third day, Roy came up with this idea of getting a big speaker that would blast into the barracks. We got a recording of Romero giving his last homily. At eleven o'clock at night, we snuck through the woods and climbed this tree. (We'd practiced all of this and were wearing spikes and carrying a homemade ladder.) Roy lugged up this big boom box and when the lights went out in the dorm, we turned it on, and [the guys] heard their former bishop's voice blaring at them, calling the military to put down their arms.

Here's a translation of part of what the foreign soldiers heard from their murdered archbishop:

> The peasants you kill are your own brothers and sisters. When you hear the voice of the man commanding you to kill, remember instead the voice of God. "Thou Shalt Not Kill." In the name of God, in the name of our tormented people whose cries rise up to heaven, I beseech you, I beg you, I command you, stop the repression.

Fr. Lorenzo: All the lights went on and all the guys came running out. They're looking all around, and this message is repeating and repeating. "Stop the killing, stop the killing." Then cars and jeeps started pulling up and dogs started coming over into the woods where we were. We'd put some pepper down at the base of the tree so that when the dogs sniffed it, they'd keep going. That was Roy's idea, I think, maybe learned when he was a kid in Louisiana. Well, it took them quite awhile to find us, and all the time Romero's message just kept repeating itself. Finally somebody flashed a flashlight up into the tree and saw us. And then again they tossed us out. They were really upset with that one and said we'd be turned over to the FBI.

We decided we might as well do one more thing, so we organized people from the town and had a vigil in front of the base commander's house. That was the fourth time we got tossed off. A couple of days later we're having a meeting real early one morning, at a house we had rented. I see a car pull up and then another one and before we know it, [FBI] guys are coming in at both doors and we're arrested.

We just . . . We didn't cooperate. They had to drag us off to the car and into the jail. Word of all these actions had been in the news, and when we got to the jail, the inmates were looking out their windows and applauding!

Our sentence was a year in federal prison. Roy went up to Sandstone, and I ended up down in New Mexico, at La Tuna. Linda went to a women's prison in Lexington, Kentucky. Her work was to assemble something that was to do with the war situation and she refused. It's sad but we've completely lost track of her; she was one game lady.

Rebecca Kanner

Rebecca Kanner has been involved in the SOA Watch movement since 1997, first as a prisoner of conscience and now on the Labor Caucus and Legislative Working Group, as well as other committees. She lives in Ann Arbor, Michigan, where she's active in the Interfaith Council for Social Justice and works part-time for the UAW and the People's Food Co-op. During the summer, she does farm work on a CSA farm. In prison, they called her "Rebel."

Rebecca: Interfaith Council brought Father Roy Bourgeois to the Michigan Theater, here in Ann Arbor.[7] Just meeting Roy, you can't help but want to be involved. So a group of us went down in 1997, and that was the year [the protest] really exploded in size, with about 2,000 people. We got there on Friday, and at first it was a small

7. The Interfaith Council for Peace and Justice (ICPJ) is a non-profit education/ social action organization in Ann Arbor, Michigan. See online: www.icpj.net.

gathering, and just filled with gray hair. But by Saturday, the students started coming in.

The staff did nonviolence training and explained what the scenario was, that we would walk two-by-two into the base and everyone would be carrying crosses with the names of people who were killed. That was difficult for me as a Jew, that the movement was so rooted in the Catholic religion. So I raised my hand and said, "What if you don't want to carry a cross?" They told me I could be a peacekeeper, but it seemed there wasn't room for other scenarios that year.

"Presente," 2011. © Calvin Kimbrough.

As a peacekeeper, I walked down the side of the procession, and despite feeling a little outside, it was a very, very moving experience—a holy experience—to walk into the base while we were hearing a beautiful voice chant the names of the people who were killed. Everyone would pray "Presente" after each name. It's meditative, too, and it was a beautiful fall day with the trees changing colors. We walked in about three-quarters of a mile, and then they stopped us and put us on buses and took us to a fenced-off area.

They searched everyone individually and took away all the literature in our pockets. (This all took hours 'cause they weren't prepared for so many.) Then we all went one by one in front of military police and other personnel, and they took our information and gave us a sheet of paper saying we'd be banned for a year. The next winter we found out via registered letter that we'd been banned for five years! I think 601 people crossed the line that year, and a lot of them were students with different addresses, so they didn't even get their registered letters.

In '98, the numbers had grown again. I had come down wondering if I was going to cross the line. So many issues went into it, you know. Like my life here in Ann Arbor. (At the time, I was doing environmental education for the Ecology Center.) I had also been wondering about not giving names when we were arrested [like in other protests, where people practice jail solidarity]. I'd called the office and they'd said no, that with true nonviolence you go into it willingly and give your name, and that it was a bit dishonest not to.

I said, "Well, I don't really want to be a martyr and give six months of my life." And guess who I was talking to and didn't know it? Roy Bourgeois! And he'd spent four years in prison! So I was thinking about all of that, and I didn't sleep on that first Friday night in Columbus. Finally on Saturday I decided not to cross, and it was . . . um . . . it was a really hard decision. As it turned out, that year they didn't arrest anyone. They just put them on a bus, gave them a piece of paper, and took no names. So I could have had a free pass! [Laughs.]

So then the next year, '99, I thought they'd do the same thing, so I crossed and again, they just put us on a bus. But it felt a little like . . . you know, what's the point? It's a game. A dance, with our part and the military police part.

Ro: You didn't carry a cross, did you?

Rebecca: No, no, I didn't carry a cross, but the people I was with did. Then they also started putting some names on Stars of David and having other religious symbols, too. It's amazing how things have changed and opened up since '97. I think the SOA Watch movement is a wonderful movement because it's flexible. There are lots of debates and people deal respectfully with the differences, so it's all an empowering process.

In 2000, again I crossed the line and got on the bus and was processed for hours and hours. They were much more sophisticated than before. They had a computer and they could see right away that I had a five-year ban-and-bar letter, but they released me and I went home. Then in March, I learned that I'd been indicted. My first response was, "Well, I'm ready for a change." So I went in with an open mind. Went to [SOA Spring] Lobby Days in DC and met a number of my codefendants.

I know many people do it from religious convictions, but for me, it was a very tactical thing, a step in getting the school closed. To get the Congress and the President to change their mind, we have to create the movement, and I see civil disobedience as one way to grow the movement—a very, very effective way! Organizing helps it grow over the years, but so does the power of every single individual who goes to prison.

I don't really like being the center of attention, but I saw that people need a personal story to learn from. Going to a rally in Columbus isn't a story, but going to trial and prison is. I decided to try to reach two groups to get them more involved in the movement—the Jewish community and the labor community. I had an interview and a story in the Cleveland Jewish News and *Solidarity*, the UAW magazine, did a story on me, too. (I'm a UAW member in my work at the Ecology Center.) Then the UAW vice president—Bob King—began going to the protests, and the UAW involvement has grown until they were at least seventy UAW members there in 2004. From all over the country.

Back to the trial: I pled "not guilty, stipulate to the facts," and that gave me time to explain why. I talked about the concept of *tikkun olam*, which is Hebrew for "the repair of the world." As the Chassidic Rabbi Nachman of Bratslav wrote, "If you believe that you can cause damage and ruin, you must believe that you are capable of repairing the damage."

Then I talked about Rabbi Abraham Joshua Heschel who walked with King at Selma. He called that walk "praying with his legs," and I said that's what it feels like when we walk onto the base, a very holy, spiritual time, like praying with our legs.

Our lawyer had set up the statements like a mosaic, with each of us coming at it in a different way. A retired business person talked about the economics; a Catholic Worker working in land use and affordable housing talked about housing issues and the money that could be spent other ways. Then people who'd been to Latin America told stories of people there, so the victims themselves were brought into the courtroom.

We were all thinking we'd get a three-month sentence, like the group before us, even though they had a different judge. Sister Dorothy [Hennessey] was the first person called for sentencing. At that time, she was 88 years old. An amazing independent woman! The judge sentenced her to six months of house arrest. Six months! We all kind of gasped! Then she basically said, "Don't condescend to me. I want you to treat me like everyone else."

Well, that just threw him. This was Judge Faircloth, and this was his first SOAW trial, although he's done them ever since. After a long pause, he said, "Okay, six months."

Ten of us were able to ask to go together to Pekin, and we got that, so I went in with tremendous, tremendous support, and I never felt nervous. My nickname in prison was "Rebel." Part of it was my attitude. They need to keep control because there are so many more of us than of them, but they know they don't have much control over those of us with only federal misdemeanors because when our time is done, our time is done. (They can control the others because most prisoners go to halfway houses when they leave, and the authorities have a say in when and how they leave. But to us, they really can't do anything.)

So I would be strong when I talked to them, and they didn't like that. At one point, I started a signature petition over the issue of laundry. A friend said right away that my starting the petition would be seen as "instigating a riot," so I stopped it within three hours [so I wouldn't be transferred]. But they already knew! From a snitch. Today I understand the dynamics better. People are in for years and years, and just as in real life, there's good people and there's bad people. People can get extra privileges if they snitch. Everyone knows everything, and the snitching and the gossip are part of how the guards keep power. I had thought there would be real solidarity of prisoners against authorities, and there isn't.

Plus I was already in trouble because I wouldn't pay my $500 fine. There are very few times when you can say yes or no when you're in prison, and I wanted to say no to having it come out of my commissary account. So they put me on "refusal status." I *was* paying; it was just coming in from the outside, not from my commissary account. Anyway, they put me in solitary, in a room with glass windows and a bright light shining on my bed night and day. They also docked my pay, so I only got $5 a month to spend on commissary. (I kind of liked that room, though, because it had a door I could actually close.) Then they moved me into [even harsher detention] because of a misunderstanding on my part; I could only leave for work and meals and had to go to certain bathrooms and a certain shower. Couldn't listen to my radio or watch television. Saw the other SOA folks only when I ate. No visitors, so my parents couldn't come anymore. It's hard for moms when their kids go to prison, even if they're forty-three, as I was.

I ended up writing complaints, anyway, because I wanted to learn the process—how you fight it, even if you're never going to win. First, you complain to your counselor. Then you go to the warden of the prison, and then you go up to the regional and you get your answers back. So I went through those steps. Every time they found against me. But I have a whole notebook of documentation.

There were some good things, too, like our poetry class! The teacher was from Bradley University, and it was wonderful! But other classes, like the GED program . . . If you don't have a copy of your high school diploma, they'll stick you in the GED class. And they're horrible! They don't teach you; they just put you in a room with a book. They get money from the government for each person in the GED program, so it's just a money-maker.

You can get very fit in Pekin, though. I took three aerobics classes a week, and I didn't watch much TV, except *West Wing*. Now, watching what you want on TV isn't that easy. Most of the battles are over what's on TV. In Pekin, they have this calendar where you sign up to choose. But the people were very respectful of the nuns, so they'd give up an hour of their TV time to Sr. Dorothy so we could watch Martin Sheen on *West Wing*.

After I got out, I did a lot of work with SOA Watch. I went down to Georgia in 2002 when over eighty people were indicted. That was the first year they kept all the people over night in jail and the first year they each had to pay a $500 bond. If you multiply 500 times 80, that's a lot of money! And it has to be cash.

So the SOA Watch Legal Collective was busy making phone calls to families, and some of the families . . . you know, here's a stranger on the phone who says, "Your son's in jail! Can you please wire $500?" Some of the parents didn't even know their kids had come to Columbus. I talked to one dad who was all worried about the dangers in prison. I was able to calm him down a little on that, but that's the first thing anyone thinks about when they hear the word "prison." So the parents need support, too.

Many of the people that year just crossed on their own, so they didn't have anyone except SOA Watch working to get their $500. That's why planning and affinity groups are so important. The people in the affinity group who aren't arrested can make these calls and get the money.

In fact, the supporters are just as important as the prisoners of conscience, if not more so. When someone's in prison, they can't really do much work. The people on the outside are their coattails, talking to the press, getting people to write letters to the legislature and to the prisoners, setting up lobbying visits, getting more people to go to the protests. All sorts of support for the action. The prisoners may be up on the stage, but the supporters should get the glory!

Kathleen Rumpf

Kathleen Rumpf participated in antinuclear campaigns as an early Plowshares activist but is best known for her efforts at jail and prison reform, both in Syracuse, NY and nationally. Here she describes a 1997 SOAW action that happened separately from the November vigil and resulted in a one-year sentence.

Kathleen: There were five of us on the ground: Father Bix (Bill Bichsel, SJ), Ed Kinane, Mary Trotochaud and Sister Marge Eilerman. We altered the sign at the entrance to Fort Benning so it said "School of Shame" and "SOA = Torture." I brought blown-up pictures of the death scene of the Jesuits and the four church women who were murdered. We'd made crosses representing every country that sent men to be trained at the School of the Americas.

Altered SOA sign, 1997. © Sr. Jackie Doepker, OSF.

Charlie Liteky and Christopher Jones climbed these tall, tall trees, and chained themselves up there on deer stands. We stretched a banner between two trees behind the Welcome sign, and hung banners down the side of the trees. Initially we were just charged with misdemeanors and released on our own recognizance. We appeared before a federal judge named Robert Elliott. Ninety years old. Had pardoned Lieutenant Calley from the My Lai massacre. (Not only pardoned him but golfed with him, 'cause Calley still lives in Columbus.) Judge Elliot had blocked Dr. Martin Luther King from marching in Columbus, saying that allowing him to march would deny the civil rights of the people who didn't want him there. What a sense of . . . of full circle.

A few months later I heard on NPR that they had decided to charge us with a felony. So I decided to be a good girl and not get arrested again. Most of the other folks in our action went back to Fort Benning for the annual November march to the gates, and they were re-arrested and re-indicted for the felony.

Here I omit Kathleen's saga of paperwork gone awry, a cruise with her mother "to try to mend family fences," and being arrested on the ship when it docked at Miami. Seems the prosecutors at Columbus had put out an erroneous warrant for her arrest as a fugitive!

Kathleen: They didn't allow me to take my wallet with my ID or my legal papers. They gave me three strip searches and an orange jumpsuit, and mailed my clothes to Syracuse, so I had not *one* thing. They refused to call the FBI in Syracuse so [they] could explain. I always have such a strong spirit, you know, but this involved my mother, because they'd come right into our stateroom, and it wasn't fair to her. When I saw the judge more than a day later, he did a little checking and then released me on my own recognizance. But here I am in an orange jumpsuit and no underwear! They just opened the door and said, "See ya!"

This is three days before Christmas! I had no I.D., no nuttin'! I'd also had a knee replacement, so I was on a crutch, and only those plastic prison shoes on my Fred Flintstone feet. But I found a place that let me use their phone and finally a niece picked me up, and I went back to Georgia for my arraignment. At the trial, my defense was that I had "committed art" by telling the truth. It was a wonderful trial. Powerful! So much conversion happens in the courtrooms. I was very much aware that we were in the South and wondered how I could communicate our reasoning to [the jury]. Then I remembered a parable, so I went over to the jury box and talked about a village.

Here's more or less what I said: "Every day, the women in this village would go to the river and wash their clothes on the rocks. One day, the women saw a body out in the river, floating down but still alive. Well, a few of the women jumped in to rescue this person. The following day, there were a few more bodies in the river. Every day, more and more bodies were floating down the river.

"Just like in Georgia, when something happens, people get together and arrange to feed people and find them some clothes and a place to stay. Many of the people in the river were children and it soon became the work of the whole village to save these children.

"Well one day, instead of jumping into the river to retrieve the children, one woman started walking upstream. And the women in the river yelled at her? 'Where are you going? We need you! We've got to save these children from dying!'

"She yelled back at them, 'I'm walking upstream to find the bastard who's throwing them in.'" When I stopped, I was crying, and some of the jury were, too. It was . . . I felt God's presence so strongly within me. I was wasted, but I was at peace. I had told the truth.[8]

Steve Jacobs

Steve Jacobs and others founded the St. Francis Catholic Worker in Columbia, Missouri. For years, until an apartment complex near the gate of Ft. Benning was torn down, St. Francis would rent an apartment there and host a temporary house of hospitality. Everyone was welcome to stop by to use the restrooms, meet with friends, warm up with a bowl of chili or a coffee. Some of my SOA interviews took place in an upstairs room in the apartment, with the chants of the solemn procession in the background.

8. Calley has moved to Atlanta since this interview was recorded.

Catholic Worker House of Hospitality at SOA, 2004.

Steve: I was in the Navy from 1973 to 1976. Worked in a psychiatric hospital in Philadelphia. I saw the horrors of the war up close, and it really tore me up. I lost my faith in patriotism and nationalism as virtues and . . . was just functioning in a moral vacuum. I knew what I didn't believe in, but I needed to find out what I *did* believe.

Finally I went back to the Gospels that I was taught as a child. I saw that Jesus rejected violence and realized that Jesus lived under a military occupation that was every bit as ruthless as any communist regime I'd been taught to fear. His teaching to love one's enemies was the big stumbling block, but I knew that Gandhi and Martin Luther King, Jr. had given us examples and that enemies had been changed by seeing people's willingness to endure violence. The social changes that came through nonviolence appealed to my intellect and validated my sense that I was on the right track.

I realized if I was to live what I believed that I had two choices. I could make an accommodation with evil and quietly serve out the remaining time in the Navy, or I could apply for CO status. So I went through all the paperwork and interviews, and I got it.

Met Phil Berrigan when I was going to the University of Missouri, and he told me about Dorothy Day and the Catholic Worker and said it was much easier to hang onto these essential teachings if you lived in community with like-minded people. So that was it. That's when it started. We were able to start the Catholic Worker in Columbia, Missouri, in 1983, and we've been there ever since.

At the SOA strategy sessions in 1999, they had asked people to do what's called a Gandhian Wave—actions in wave after wave after wave, at least one every month. You form an affinity group in your own community and think up your own action and prepare for it there and then come down to SOA at different times of the year. The first wave action happened right after Judge Faircloth found a bunch of November line-crossers guilty. Right then and there, several people drove into the base and tried to dig a grave on the lawn. This way it wouldn't be so ritualistic and we'd keep them on their toes.

In April of 2000, three of us from the CW in Columbia went down and recreated the assassination of Bishop Juan Gerardi, the Guatemalan bishop who was killed by an SOA graduate. Maureen Doyle and Chrissy Kirchhoefer and me. Our plan was to lay "his" body in the doorway of the building that had trained the soldiers who did it. I was to be the priest (Chrissy borrowed some priest garb from her brother) and the two women wore black mourning shrouds and white masks. We used fake theatrical blood and had half of a cinder block as our prop, because that's what they used to kill Bishop Gerardi.

So we did it. They put some of the fake blood on the block and some on my head, and made my head look as if it was bashed in. We'd contacted a reporter at the *Columbus Ledger-Inquirer*, and she'd agreed to meet us at the SOA building, but she'd come early and when we got there, she was inside talking to Colonel Widener, the SOA commandant. Within two minutes after I lay down, Colonel Widener was outside, berating us for our "inappropriate behavior." The reporter was taking notes, and he sort of played to her, I think. "All you had to do was come inside. Any American citizen can take a tour."

He kept asking us our names. Dead people don't talk, so I didn't respond, and Chrissy and Maureen didn't, either. Maureen's job was to read from the *Nunca Mas Report*, Bishop Gerardi's document on the human rights abuses in Guatemala. (The publication of all that documentation was what got him killed.) But she didn't get very far, because the commander had taken the stage himself, rattling on and on.

After he asked me my name for the third time, I opened my eyes and I said, "My name is Bishop Juan Gerardi. One of your soldiers killed me two years ago." Then I went back to being dead. Finally they handcuffed us and walked us down to the police station on the base. One of the military policemen asked me how many times I'd been arrested on the base, and I told him five but that I'd never been prosecuted.

Then they put us in a holding cell which had a big window in the door. Everybody who walked into the lobby could see me standing in the holding tank with my bloody-looking head, and my black shirt and Roman collar. The bloody concrete block they put on top of the front desk, I guess to tag for evidence. So here's this broken, bloody concrete block and this guy in the holding tank. But pretty soon they released us with just another ban-and-bar letter.

We went out to eat with Roy [Bourgeois], and on our way to the restaurant, we spotted these three big crosses out in a back alley, by a dumpster. I'd guess they'd been used for Easter services. The largest one was at least twelve feet tall and covered with lilies. All kind of wilted and a week old. Chrissy said we ought to pick up one of these crosses and leave it by the entrance to the base, right by the welcome sign. So we did. We put a message to Colonel Widener on the cross and also a big photo of Bishop Gerardi.

After we got back to Missouri, Roy called us. "The cross wasn't there but fifteen minutes before about ten cop cars came—four or five Columbus City police cars and then five or six military police cars. They all stood around talking about that dangerous cross."

I guess they fiddled around with the envelope for awhile. Didn't know if maybe they should call the bomb squad, but finally they opened it and saw the message we'd left for Colonel Widener. "You thought it would be more appropriate for us to have a dialogue with you. But where was the dialogue between Bishop Juan Gerardi and the Guatemalan soldiers that you trained here at the School of the Americas?"

Steve Jacobs, Catholic Worker house near the SOA gates, 2004.

I crossed again the next November, and they finally sent me a summons for all the line crossings that they'd let go before, so I got charged and Judge Faircloth sentenced me to a year in prison.

Ro: You know, Steve, you're sounding so matter-of-fact about it all. As a Catholic Worker, you do all these thing—you do resistance and you serve soup and you work on community and you buy food for hundreds here at SOA. Do you ever take resistance for granted, like Catholic Workers take cooking for granted?

Steve: Not really. The whole process of resistance sort of forces you to focus your attention. It's unusual for individuals to actually address national problems, and most people have decided that they can't personally address them in a way that calls into question the legalities. That's what we want to do, you know. And the theater we use, the language we use, the criticism of the government . . . it all forces you to articulate why you're doing it. Also, you try to do it to so that the message is not lost, so that people really hear you and don't think you're just a bunch of flakes who think hurting people is wrong.

You know, we haven't succeeded, even with all our getting arrested. But it's important to continue to do those acts of resistance so that the world doesn't change your heart. And as long as it doesn't do that, as long as there are people trying to act Christ-like, then Christ is still here, doing those things. And the dream of loving your neighbor as you want to be loved still lives.

Lisa Hughes

Lisa Hughes's stay in prison propelled her to the Portland Catholic Worker, where she provided hospitality to recently incarcerated women. We met and talked there in 2004. Since then, she's worked on an organic farm in New England and participated in other worthy work adventures. In April of 2012 she left for Zambia, where she'll work as a nurse with HIV-positive women.

Lisa: On my first visit to El Salvador, I listened to the stories of the people and heard the results of my tax dollars at work. A huge wake-up call! When I got back to my little Kansas City apartment, I realized it could house three families by Salvadoran standards. The only thing I could think about was going back. So I studied Spanish for two months in Guatemala and then went to El Salvador in January of 1991. Stayed there for two years, working with health promoters and living in a tiny repopulation settlement.

And oh! I just learned so much about living my faith on a daily basis, reading the Bible "from my heart," as a friend once described it. I also learned so much from the Salvadorans about hospitality and valuing relationships over things or work. I . . . I just felt at home there in so many ways.

It was also challenging in ways I'd never known. Helping communities to organize and care for themselves in any way, including caring for their nutrition and health, was "Communist activity" in the eyes of the soldiers. The volunteer health promoters I worked with took personal risks. So I had to learn to tell half-truths to the soldiers and hold back information when it was crucial to a person's safety, and that was challenging.

It was also the beginning of standing up to authorities in the face of injustice. I ran out of money in 1993, so I came back home for a year. That was a difficult year, trying to meld back into this society after such a change in values, so I eventually went back to El Salvador for three more years, working with the Mennonite Central Committee.

When I came back for good, I moved to Portland to be near family and then in 1999, as a continuation of my time in El Salvador, I began attending the SOAW protest at Fort Benning. The first two years we could go onto the base and just receive a ban-and-bar letter. Then in 2001 they put up the fence. I didn't want to go around or under, but I was angry that they'd thwarted our ability to walk peacefully onto the base.

Towards the end of the day, I was moved to action, and I talked it over with my affinity group. The army had put up the fence about five yards beyond the white line [marking the base perimeter] that they'd painted for our benefit. So there was this ambiguous area that was over the line but not beyond the fence. Three of us decided to sit in this area, past the expiration of the permit, which was 5:00 p.m.

For the five hours or so it took them to figure out what to do with us, they kept the gates closed and began clearing the gates and fence of all the crosses, photos, posters, flowers, peace cranes, flags, et cetera that were part of the memorial we erected to the martyrs killed by SOA graduates.

SOAW memorials, end of vigil, 2004.

But we'd just replace whatever they knocked off and finally they stopped. Mostly we just knelt and prayed. For hours. Finally, around 10:30 p.m., the gates opened and six young MPs came running out. They put us face down on the ground, cuffed us, and practically carried us to the cars—one MP for each protester—with only commands coming out of their mouths. (I think it was a training exercise.) We were released at a gas station around two in the morning. I was the only one who was prosecuted. (This was still in the days where they prosecuted only some of those who crossed.)

Trial was just an amazing education on our judicial system. I'd watch and listen as Magistrate Faircloth would engage people in conversation and seem to be having a pleasant exchange. And then he'd just turn on them in an absolute display of power. *Abuse* of power! He was very age-ist also, letting priests his age say all kinds of things but jumping all over younger people who would challenge him in similar ways. He got so upset with a few young people that he sentenced them to six months for a first-time offense instead of the usual three months.

I'd like to believe we reached him on some level, but it felt like he was playing with us, like a cat with a mouse. All through the trials, I kept thinking, "If this is how he treats educated, middle-class white people with lawyers and media presence, how does he treat people of color, immigrants, those without much education or legal counsel?"

People would be testifying from the deepest parts of themselves, and Judge Faircloth would seem like he was interested. Then suddenly he'd mock them. Was it when we were starting to touch something in him that he would do that? You'd worked so hard on trying to see him as a human being, and then you'd see the abuse of power.

I was on trial with thirty-six others and though I "stipulated to the facts" and assumed I'd serve prison time, he acquitted me, stating that kneeling and praying was not a crime. (I think that acquittal was setting the precedent of the fence being the legal boundary because many who got past the fence had just knelt and prayed, also.)

I was back the next year and having learned how easy it was to go around the fence, I did that. I crossed holding hands with my mentor and dear friend, Ann Huntwork. First the army processed us and then the federal marshals. The marshals go through all these questions; what kind of car I drove, where I hung out, who my friends were, all my family's names. They wanted a release on financial and medical records.

Nobody knew whether you had to give that information or not. The marshals got so angry! I answered the questions about my family, but I wouldn't list my friends. They said, "Well, every question that you refuse to answer is left blank, and that makes it more likely we won't release you." I mentioned something about El Salvador, and they said, "Do you have a passport?" Like I'm gonna flee. Like they didn't know we do this on purpose, to go to trial. I remember one marshal, though, who said, "I don't really want to do this." I told him he did have choices, that he could get another job.

When they took us to the jail, they put us in shackles. On our ankles and then around our waist, and then handcuffs, and they chain it all together so you can't move. Some people who'd had marshal's uniforms on at the hangar had sheriff's uniforms on at the jail. Later I learned that sheriff's deputies can be deputized as federal marshals, but it was really weird to see the same people in different uniforms.

Then they interviewed us again and put us in a cell and gave us our prison uniforms, which were like scrub suits. The great thing was the Puppetistas were outside of the jail with the puppets, and they were hammering on the drums and yelling encouragement up at us.

The women were housed in the Columbus Stockade, where the last legal hanging in Georgia took place. It was just freezing cold! They gave us only these thin cotton sheets that were like mesh, so we tried to use our towels as blankets. We didn't have socks and we really froze! Some of the older women actually had cognitive changes, because they were using so much of their energy to try and stay warm.

While we were waiting for arraignment—over five hours—we had thirty-five women in a cinder block cell that was about seven and a half by ten. No even enough room for all of us to sit on the floor, so we had to take turns sitting and standing. But even though we were that close together, we were still freezing. All the Sheriff's officers are wearing their thick heavy coats inside, because it was so cold, and we're sitting there in those little scrub-type uniforms. We tried to do back rubs and did a lot of singing and prayer circles, and walking meditation. Of course people had different faith backgrounds, and what was soothing to some was not to others, so we had a good lesson in the oppressiveness that Christianity can be.

When I finally went to sign my court papers, I couldn't write, my hand was shaking so bad. The judge asked me what was wrong. I told him we were freezing and hadn't had any food for twelve hours. Finally at 5:00 in the morning, we got a bit of food—some sort of salad on a sandwich and a carton of milk, and some cookies. I was prepared for prison; I wasn't prepared for county jail.

Ro: Did you post bail?

Lisa: Yes. Now bail is supposed to be for anyone who is a danger to the community, or a flight risk, and of course, SOA Watch protesters are neither. SOAW tried to argue that, and the court wouldn't agree, so we each had to pay $500, ten percent of a $5,000 bond. SOA Watch raised that money really quick. Then the next year they upped it and everyone had to pay $1,000. So now it's deterrence by pocketbook.

At the arraignment, they gave us a trial date of January 26th. And that seemed so soon! That year there were . . . oh my gosh! Eighty-five of us. We knew Bill Quigley couldn't do it for eighty-five people, so I recruited a lawyer from my church named Bill Conwell. Because I'd been on trial before, and wasn't working at the time, I got involved in the working group for the trial prep. Doing conference calls and sending out packets of information to other people on trial.

We had two trials because there were so many of us, and I was there for both of them. But that second year, I decided not to speak. That brought real anger from the judge. I didn't feel angry at all. I had just decided that I wasn't going to engage in it as if what I had to say really mattered. I responded when they called me, and I affirmed, but I just stood silently at the podium and didn't take the stand.

He tried to engage me, again in that mocking way. "I assume you're choosing not to speak and not that you're deaf." Then he totally misquoted me from the first trial and did four or five things to try to make me angry so I'd say something and I just wouldn't. And I really wasn't angry. Instead I had this sense of peace. After he convicted me, I read a very short statement, including the names of my family that were killed in El Salvador.

It's interesting: Where I used to have to really work to find places to talk about my times in El Salvador, once I was going to prison, all kinds of groups wanted me. And the media pays more attention to you if you've gone to jail; in fact, that's one of the main reasons for doing it. After this trial, the *Kansas City Star* did a huge article. The reporter did a lot of research on the SOA and focused on the issues instead of the person, which was great.

I reported to prison on April 6th, to Greenwood, Illinois, not far from St. Louis. My folks drove me down. I'd talked to three SOA Watchers who'd been here, so I was prepared and they had people in the prison looking out for me.

I worked in the kitchen and when I wasn't working, I was mostly writing letters. I received over five hundred pieces of mail, a third of those from people I didn't even know, and I answered them all. By hand, of course. I think I read thirty-some books while I was in there, and I learned to play Scrabble pretty well. Walked the track a lot. But it's pretty tough to occupy your time when you're not a TV watcher. A lot of women end up either sleeping or sitting in front of the television all the time. At Greenwood, you sit in a room with the door closed and hear it through a head set.

Oh, I missed color! I remember once we'd had this parent-kid craft thing [on visiting day] and a friend found some scraps of construction paper in the trash can. It was a huge find, scraps of paper in all these brilliant colors. I wanted to frame the color. Really, though, I didn't have a hard time in prison. Not at all like that bad time in the Columbus jail.

Tina Busch-Nema

A former Notre Dame sister, Tina is now married with three children. In 2006, she participated in her first SOA protest, crossing the line with sixteen others. She was sentenced to two months in Carswell, a medium security prison which also serves severely ill prisoners in what Tina and others document as minimal care. I interviewed her by phone in 2007, shortly after she was released.

Tina: My son, who is eleven, goes to peace vigils with me. One day before the SOA action, he said, "Mom, if you have to go to prison, I'll be a little bit scared and a little bit proud." So I always remember that.

My husband has not been supportive. We have a really strong relationship, but he's a Hindu and he doesn't believe in any kind of spirituality. (Gandhi is good for some other family but not his.) So trying to explain to him that this is how the Gospel calls me, that it's what I see as necessary, it's uh . . . we've been struggling. It's been good in the sense that this has caused both of us to kind of look at ourselves. I don't know where it goes with him, to be honest with you. But we've been taking the risk to talk more. He's a scientist. He sees things pretty much in black and white, and I can't promise him that I won't do it again. In the end, if he's able to be in a relationship with me with that much uncertainty . . . it's been hard. Coming home has been traumatic for me.

You know, in many ways, I'm more a Notre Dame sister now than when I was in the community. I see resistance as a journey of faith and an act of love rather than an act of anger. The whole idea of living out of nonviolence . . . I've worked on political campaigns, so I know what it is to be driven by anger, and the absence of that anger in the SOA witness stuns me.

It took a lot of prayer [to decide to do the SOA action]. "God, if you want me to do this, you have to take care of my kids." And all sorts of people offered: people in my home school group, people in the various parishes, Quakers, other friends. My mom and one of the Notre Dame sisters were there with them, night and day, whenever my husband would go to work. The children were never, ever in need of anything.

I'd been very nervous about the action in the beginning and felt like I was going to throw up when we first crossed into Georgia. But then on Friday when I met the people who were going to team cross with me, a lot of the fear dissipated. Students, elderly people, priests, nuns—everybody was supportive of everyone else.

Somebody—I don't know how or who—made a hole in the fence. In a wooded area, probably about fifty yards from the gate, so it wasn't in plain sight. While the funeral procession was going on, the sixteen of us met at a café close by and then attorney Bill Quigley very quickly led us through the procession to the main stage on the trailer. There they gave us popsicles. (My last meal was a banana popsicle.) And then two by two we went through the hole in the fence. Very quickly before the hole would get closed up.

One of my friends had gone to Honduras in June for the twenty-fifth anniversary of the Notre Dames' presence there, and she brought me a handful of soil, in a little baggie. I brought that into the base with me and also the cross [commemorating the murder of] the brother of one of our Notre Dame Honduran sisters. I wanted to mix the soil of the suffering poor with the soil of the people who were causing the suffering, and one of the young men who crossed with me, Nathan Slater, kind of shielded me so that I could pour out my soil [on the grounds of the base] before they grabbed me.

The base police handcuffed us and put us on a bus and then drove us further onto the base to do the real processing. Someone from SOA posted the bond and they read us our rights and let us go. So we were the first group who didn't spend the night in jail. Actually, what they did was illegal because you're supposed to have a bond hearing in front of a judge and we didn't have that; they just took our bond money. By the time everyone got processed, it was dark. They put us on the bus again and dropped us off at the Civic Center parking lot, and that was all prearranged, too. SOAW had even told my support people so that worked out well.

The trial was on January 29th. When I was first writing my statement, I was just going to tell the judge how wrong it all was. Kind of like I had earned the right to lecture. [Chuckles.] But I realized that everything that happened, being in Honduras and crossing the line and being on trial, and going to prison—they're all consequences of loving, so that's more what I talked about. I wanted the judge to know that I had kids and that being on probation would be the best thing for the family. My six-year-old daughter had slipped into my suitcase a picture she'd drawn a picture of an Indian woman. (My husband is from India.) I gave it to Judge Faircloth. He didn't blink an eye. "Two months."

I didn't go into prison until the end of March. That waiting time just dragged on and on and all that time I didn't know where I was going. When they finally told me I was going 750 miles away to Carswell in Texas, to what they call a medium security prison, that was really out of left field for everyone at SOA. And for me. Not only because it was so far away from my home, but also being sent behind a fence. Usually Class B misdemeanors, which we were, go to a work camp with no fences and no locks.

We finally found out why. Since May 2006, the Bureau of Prisons puts the name of everyone sentenced into a computer in East Prairie, Texas, and the computer just spits out who's going to go where. No more trying to get you within 500 miles of home. I think the fact that they didn't have any PSI [pre-sentencing investigation] on us made it worse; the computer maybe bumped us up a notch on security because it didn't have any information. Of course I googled Carswell right away, and I also called Kathleen Rumpf, who had been there, and she told me that it was a difficult place, that she had a hard time with it.[9]

It was so hard to say goodbye to my kids, probably one of the most gut-wrenching things I've ever done. My friend Cynthia and another Notre Dame drove me down. She'd been six months at Pekin, and her final words to me were, "Tina, keep your heart soft. Just keep your heart soft."

There's a part in the Harry Potter books where they talk about the "dementors" and how they try to suck out your soul. Well, the farther I got into the complex of Carswell, the more I could feel them trying to suck out my soul. Trying to scare me and intimidate me. Treating me like a nonperson. I remember telling the man at the gate my number—924-4020. (I still remember it.) He said, "Okay, that's right." I just jokingly replied, "Passed the first test," and he said, "Ma'am, this is not a joke. You are the property of the BOP." In the holding area, they stripped me and gave me new clothes. I got two left shoes, kind of boat tennis shoes with the soles completely out and bare on the bottom.

Then they started getting nasty. The man who was my "counselor" was an ex-military Marine—very angry, very derogatory—probably one of the saddest men that I've ever met. He threw me the rules and regulations. "Read these." Then a woman took me across the campus to a big high rise. She opened a door and said, "I'm not walking up all those stairs. Just go up and walk in." So I'm going up four flights of stairs all alone, not knowing at all what I was walking into. Honestly, it was gut-wrenching.

9. See Kathleen Rumpf's interview in Chapter 5 of *Doing Time for Peace*.

The campus has the high-rise where I lived and also a hospital
of sorts. In the high-rise, there's a fifth floor for people who are in
chronic care—people who have strokes, cancer, chronic diseases of all
sorts. The fourth floor is a med-surg floor. The third floor sometimes
has a doctor, and always a nurse. A lot of people who are just coming
out of the hospital are on that floor. Also in that main building is
the dining room with the kitchen just thick with rats and mice and
roaches. I know 'cause I worked there.

When I was there, Carswell housed over 1700 women, and there
are more now. Over fifty percent of us were healthy women, and we're
the ones who basically run the place. They also have a UNICOR business—answering 411 directory assistance cell phone calls. After I got
out, I learned that cell phone companies make a whole lot of money
on prison labor. It's outsourcing, right here in the United States, only
with prisoners and UNICOR.

So many of the sentences at Carswell are really long ones. A
ten-year sentence for an elderly woman is . . . you may just as well say
it's a life sentence. There were some women there who had murdered
people, but I'd say over 80 percent were nonviolent offenders, many
because their grandson or their children were dealing drugs out of
their house. They wouldn't testify against their relatives, so they're
sentenced under conspiracy laws.

The pill lines would go on forever because so many people were
very ill. And they don't get good medical care at all. For example,
I got food poisoning while I was there. Couldn't keep any food or
water down for four days, and they still made me go to work. At one
point, I was crawling up the steps 'cause I just had no reserve. My
mom got mad and called Senator Obama's office and got them to
investigate and finally the prison staff gave me a couple of days off.

Ro: Most of the women there don't have that kind of power.

Tina: Exactly. There's a young woman there now who had been in Dan-
    bury. She's only twenty-three. They found out at Danbury that she had
    a nasal polyp that was cancerous. They waited seven months and then
    sent her to Carswell, and by that time her cancer had spread to her brain.
    Then they waited a whole 'nother month and only did surgery because
    she woke up one morning and couldn't see out of one eye. They put a
    plate in her head and another one in the palate of her mouth. Then it
    took them two months after the surgery before they even started any
    radiation or chemo. The care they give—it's horrendous!

But I want to tell you about the peace cranes. When I finally had those two days to recuperate from being so sick, I still couldn't do much, so I started folding peace cranes. (Before I left home, I had sent some origami paper to myself in prison.) Soon some of the women wanted to learn how to fold the cranes so I taught them. Then I got permission to go to the chronic care floor and teach the women there. We named it the Carswell Peace Crane Project, and everyone just started folding, folding, and folding. After my paper was gone, we used colored paper from magazines and sometimes paper that could get through from my friends on the outside.

Of course the officials started getting nervous about it. I was up on the fifth floor one evening delivering some origami paper. One of the guards saw me up there and took my ID and told me, "You're out of bounds. You're going to the SHU." Even though I had permission to be there. Well, I don't know what kept him from doing it, but after berating me for a good twenty minutes, he gave me back my ID and said, "Take this elevator all the way down and turn right and go into the SHU." But he didn't go down with me. So I just . . . instead of going down to the SHU, I turned left instead of right and walked away. Nobody took me, so I didn't go.

Ro: Well, he had to know that you could do that.

Tina: Yes, you would think so. What they ended up doing with those cranes . . . The day after I left, they had Family Day, and they hung all the peace cranes from a tree, hundreds and hundreds of them. Then they taught the children of the prisoners how to make the peace cranes and let the kids take them home with them at the end of the day. So that was one wonderful thing that happened.

Here's this little piece of paper that has no power, but when people fold it a certain way . . . And I had told them the story of Sadako and the 10,000 cranes, and so they knew if you fold cranes, it brings peace. They wanted peace in their world and in their prison, and in their families. So that was an amazing example of how God works.

Judy and Charles

One couple asked that I use pseudonyms for their interview, in fear of professional reprisal, and I agreed. While anonymity is common in social-science work, this is only the second time I've received this request in thirty-five years of recording oral history. (The first request was in 1987, from a war tax resister.) I've also made a few factual changes to preserve their privacy. Their interview, recorded together, raises important questions about the kind of nonviolent resistance SOAW uses.

Judy: We're Ohio people. Went to preschool Montessori together in Cleveland and then Charles moved to Indiana. We didn't meet again until I was twenty, and I heard him in a presentation about the World Bank.

Charles: Judy was the first girl I ever kissed.

Judy: In preschool. [Laughter.] We actually didn't start dating, though, until after we got arrested at SOA. We were married after we got out of prison.

Ro: How did you two come to embrace SOA Watch?

Charles: I like to say that Judy started being political and then moved to being radical. I just started out radical. [Laughter.] I guess I came through globalization issues and through viewing the School of the Americas as the military wing of globalization.

I realized fairly early in my life that there's a strict definition of normalcy, and that in many ways I didn't fit that definition. I remember at one point realizing that Pop Tarts were awful for one's health. And just feeling betrayed by the American way of life, which seems all part of a corporate propaganda mill. I got into trouble even as a kid and then went into one of those full-time counseling places when I was fifteen. Against my will. I felt oppressed there and that led me to empathize with other people who are oppressed. Then I probably started reading Chomsky or something.

We did something a little different for our SOA action. Ever since the fence went up and the gate was locked, people have been wondering how to get around it, and we decided the best way for us to help would be to break the lock on the gate and then lock it open with a U lock. So then folks could just go through the gate instead of having to climb under it.

Judy: We didn't feel drawn just to crossing the line with everyone else. We wanted to push the envelope. You know, I think that within the SOA Watch movement—and maybe the greater peace movement, too—there's a tendency to fall into habits, you know, and to like actions where you'll know basically what's going to happen.

When you're doing civil disobedience somewhere else, it's usually not that planned and predictable. You enter into this chaos and say, "I subject myself to the chaos for a bigger purpose." In the SOA movement, there's less chaos, and we know the possibilities. So in some sense that comfort in tactics . . . We think that ideally some group of people every year will do something a little different, just to push us and make us think about it differently. Obviously, though, common sense still reigns in this pushing-the-envelope concept. Like we wouldn't go in with machine guns or anything.

Charles: We felt our action was nonviolent and in accord with the nonviolence principles and guidelines. We were only trying to make it easier for other nonviolent activists. And it almost worked! But the gate kind of stuck and wasn't wanting to push all the way open. They didn't see us cut the gate, but they saw us start to push it, and we weren't able to get the U lock attached in time. In fact, they locked the gate closed again, using our own U lock.

Judy: It *could* have worked because a U lock is long, so it gives you more space, and they're really hard to cut. They're used extensively at globalization protests, and of course we use them all the time as bike riders.

We had Class A misdemeanors and all the rest of our SOA "class" had Class B, so they did a pre-sentencing investigation for real on us and we thought for awhile that we might get eighteen months, but instead we got six, plus probation, the only ones that year that got both. And we paid our fines because otherwise they would have sent us back to prison. That was kind of rough. People helped us some, but most of it we paid ourselves.

Ro: What did your parents think?

Judy: My parents had been expecting me to get arrested. When they got the call from jail, they were like, "Finally! She's been trying to get arrested for we don't know how long!" I feel that sometimes, with young females in these protests, the cops won't arrest us, but they'll arrest the guys next to us. That had happened with me a lot, so my parents weren't surprised at all. They were very supportive, but my mom says she cried a lot and didn't sleep for six months.

Charles: Longer than that, like two years.

Judy: Yeah, 'cause the whole process is so long. The trials and then the pre-sentence investigation, then prison for six months, then probation.

Considering how young we are, it was a huge hunk of our lives. So my parents were supportive but stressed out.

Charles: My folks were . . . I didn't . . . I didn't tell them beforehand. They would have been very antagonistic to the idea. They found out when the lawyer called them from jail. Now they've gotten used to it, and they're very supportive. The other day, we were talking to this guy at church, and my dad brought it up and prompted me to tell the story. He seemed proud of it, which is a big step. But at first they were freaked out and they didn't . . . It was bad. We had a meeting with my extended family, and I talked about capitalism and the World Bank and . . . They just didn't know what to do with that information. But through the prison experience, my parents and I really came together as a family. They really supported me when I was in prison and I . . . I hadn't expected that.

I was sent to a minimum security prison, but there was a max right next door. For me, it was really bad at first. I was twenty-one, and it was like everything I had was taken away, and I had to figure out who I was. Without reference to friends or family or clothes or . . . or anything. It's like you have to discover some inherent property about yourself. At first I didn't know what to do with myself, and I just sort of tried to be invisible and it was awful.

I had started reading the Bible before going in, and while I was there I read it all through to the end. Through the prophets and so forth, I really came to understand what Jesus was saying. (Well, as much as anybody can understand what Jesus was saying.) That was just what I was looking for! It marked a sharp divide from childhood to adulthood and was very much a coming-of-age for me. Very much.

Ro: Were you kind of a loner in prison then?

Charles: As much as that was possible. Men . . . when pressure forces down on them and authority tightens, they lash out at one another. So it's difficult to get close to men in that kind of setting. Then there's this subtle taint that corrupts all thought in prison. People are given to conspiracy theories and just all sorts of crazy, outlandish . . . just crap, you know. I looked for community, and I found it in the church in a lot of ways. And I had a friend, an everyday American type of guy. A business guy about two years older than me. We just talked about everyday type stuff, but it was a lot of fun. He was a good guy. Really normal, which I liked. [Laughter.] Then also getting nice letters from Judy.

Judy: Yeah, when they were nice. [Both laugh together.]

Ro: Charles, did you ever go into isolation, into the hole?

Charles: No. But I could have, because I got into a couple of fights. My bunkie and I . . . there was sort of both a race and a class tension because I was definitely this suburban white kid who didn't know anything about anything. Mostly issues of space. Finally he blew up, basically. "Am I gonna have to kick your ass, white boy?"

"All right, old man. All right!" Because he was like a forty, fifty year old guy, you know, but really strong. He actually beat the crap out of me, and I just kept getting back up. But after the fight, he said, "We're square" and we did the fist knocking thing, and we were fine after that. I hid my bruises, and [the guards] never found out.

Ro: Judy, did anything like that ever happen to you?

Judy: Not at all. Prison's just a different thing for women. Plus I think we went into it with two very different mindsets. He lost it at the beginning and for me it was okay at first. I made friends. I started crocheting, I read lots of books and just tried to make the best use of my time. I got excited about my job driving a forklift. I was even able to take some college classes, correspondence style, which was unusual for [my university]. Of course I couldn't do the usual things—type on a computer or e-mail my professors. Instead I sent handwritten papers through the mail. But they didn't take away my scholarship, which was nice.

Plus I was there during the summer, so I could go outside and walk the track. I'd say the first three months weren't that bad. But then around the fourth month, I remember feeling it was never going to end. Then it became an identity issue, sort of. I was losing it, losing myself or my mind or something. Then I'd ask why this was happening to me, when all the other women have been there forever and will still be in prison long after I'm gone.

So after about four months, I started to withdraw, and it wasn't as easy for me to socialize. I began to become . . . uncomfortable in my own skin, I guess. Then I got sick. Something hit the camp. I'm a vegetarian, and I was trying be a vegetarian in prison and, you know, nutritionally it's nearly impossible. You can get enough caloric intake, but you can't get enough *good* stuff. I don't think I realized that it was slowly wearing away at my body, so when this flu or whatever it was hit the camp, I got *so* sick!

I'd never been even close to being that sick in my whole life. I passed out on the floor. I was pale and shaky, and they did all these tests and took me off work assignment, and it was just really bad. My body had totally given out on me, and it was just horrible. But when the six months was finished, I got out and two weeks later I felt fine. A little skinny and malnourished, but otherwise I was okay.

That experience really shocked me, though. I went in feeling so invincible, as young people are prone to do. I met women in prison who had serious health problems, and I'd wonder how they ever make it because after four months, I was so sick I couldn't work. A lot of the women probably come from the projects, with Fruit Loops and high sugar, low-nutrition diets. They come in like that and just continue it. So why couldn't my body handle it? Rather than becoming accustomed to it, mine just broke down.

Also, I got at least a little bit into that fog that often happens in prison. I think the fog problem is at least partially a nutritional issue. You're not so far into the fog that you don't even know you're in it, but you can't focus on things. You're trying to read your book and you can't get into it and you don't care about anything and . . . Everything just feels really gray. So it's kind of a depression but it's also . . . It's not that you don't want to feel, you know. I *wanted* to feel. But I just couldn't.

Ro: That prison fog I've heard about scares me more than anything else because I can get into a fog sometimes just from regular life, you know.

In unison: Yeah.

Judy: That whole thing was a wake-up call. I know now that I'm definitely not invincible. And however strong my will is, that doesn't mean I can just plow through everything and be fine. I've had other bad things in my life that had made me realize that I wasn't invincible, but in some senses they'd made me think, "Okay, I made it through this. I can do anything." But that fog . . . It was a lot of work to get through it.

There was another difference between my experience and what happened to Charles. Where I was, the women knew about the protestors, and they were always talking about them. For example, when I first got there, everyone was trying not to cuss around me just in case I was this very young nun. [Laughter.] I was so set apart at the beginning.

After awhile, though, they began treating me like all the rest of the prisoners. Whereas they had stepped lightly before, *now* I could do stuff wrong, just like everybody else. In prison, there are these wild, emotional responses to what seems like a small thing. And now it was being directed at me and not just this weird anthropological thing that I was watching. That kind of pulled me into the population, which in a sense . . . There's something wrong with the fact that I went in thinking I was different. And everyone treated me like I was different, so for awhile it didn't really sink in that I *wasn't* different, that we were all just people together there in the prison.

Ro: Judy, this is kind of a dumb question, after what you've said, but can you remember any things that were pleasant?

Judy: Well, on the day-to-day, I loved driving the forklift. It was kind of cool to learn a bizarre new skill. In terms of things that were fun or interesting . . . After awhile I started pulling little pranks. There was an education director, and she . . . she was just this cruel machine. Periodically, she'd put up little quotes on the board. So one day she puts up a quote by Malcolm X. Something like "Education is the key to success" or some other trite thing.

Well, I thought that was really tokenizing and irritating, so I got a bunch of other Malcolm X quotes and put them up underneath her quote. All sorts of things about capitalism, the prison system, white people, whatever. Well, she's freaking out! That was the most entertaining thing I did the whole time there. It went on for two weeks and I never got caught.

I also could have been to the hole for this big meeting we had. We were teaching [the women] how to do media work, so they could send out press releases about medical mishaps, and teaching them ways they could talk to the media and how to write to their representatives about things that affected them.

We had this huge workshop. We billed it as something else, like teaching people about writing legal appeals or something. My friend [who did it with me] was a lawyer. I don't know why the guards didn't show up for this meeting because two-thirds of the camp came! There were like two hundred people in the room, frantically taking notes. I mean we weren't allowed to even write a petition, let alone do training like that. That meeting was definitely "instigating a riot," so I surely would have gone to the hole if they'd caught me. But they didn't.

Finally it was over. Charles and I got out the same day. His parents came and my dad and sister picked me up, so both our families were there when we first saw each other.

Charles: At first, we were kind of shy with each other. We'd been through a lot of stuff and had a lot of arguments. For one thing, I had become a Christian in jail, and she hadn't.

Judy: There was a lot of conflict.

Charles: And a lot of misunderstanding on both parts.

Judy: So few people in prison maintain the relationships they came in with. For us it was only six months, and we had all sort of things working in our favor, and it was still really strained. Charles was having all these ideas that were developed in this very male-centered world. And I'm having all these ideas that were developed in a very female-centered world where a lot of women had been abused or raped. We're having very different ideas about male-female relations, and it wasn't like, "Oh, how interesting that you feel that way!" It was more like, "How could you ever come to a conclusion like that? You're insane!" It morphed into those sorts of interactions by the end.

Even after we were getting along well again, it was just hard for us to get back into life, you know. Like we couldn't get jobs. We couldn't manage our time at all. For about three months, just fulfilling our basic needs seemed to take all our time. It was really ridiculous. When people say it's easy to just get back to life, I think they're totally bullshitting.

Ro: Yeah, probably. Will either of you be going to prison again for nonviolent direct action?

Charles: Sure, but not for SOA. I don't regret what I did, but I think there are far more immediate [issues]. SOAW is an excellent bridge for white [women and men] to become involved in global solidarity, but I don't think it's the end issue. If I was going to go to jail, I'd go to jail over something more immediate. We use SOA as a bridge [to other issues] when we talk to churches and other places.

Judy: I probably wouldn't do the SOA again, either, not because I regret what I did, but just because I wouldn't repeat the same act twice. You know, we've both been reading a lot lately and thinking about various things. I've been reading about religiously inspired violence in various religious groups, be they Christian or Jewish or Muslim.

It's interesting to think about the ways in which our motivations are similar to those of a lot of terrorists, whatever that means.

You see Timothy McVey or the people who shoot the people at abortion clinics or a suicide bomber from Hamas . . . They're all saying it's okay for them to break the law because there's a bigger issue. Which is exactly what a Christian pacifist does, right? This is certainly not to say that what the Christian pacifist is doing is wrong. Or that's it's right, either. But I do think that, instead of always thinking about how we're different, we should think about how we're similar. If we did that, we'd learn a lot in terms of the way we do civil disobedience but also [about] the sorts of movements that we're involved with and drawn to.

It seems the peace movement has become very narrow. When I say narrow, I don't mean narrow in tactics. We need to be more creative in tactics, but I don't mean that at all. It's rather that there are certain cultural things that we associate with the peace movement which ultimately might be a white American cultural thing. That [kind of thinking] has caused a lot of the civil disobedience movement, I think, to be funneled into a very specific style of activism which ultimately can be very exclusive. Exclusive of all sorts of people. It doesn't relate to the reality of, say, the Zapatistas or a lot of other social movements. Now the Zapatistas have sort of a violent side to them, but I wouldn't call them a violent movement in general. (For instance, most of the time they carry wooden guns.)

It's not so much that my concern is that we're too dedicated to peace. I think that our dedication to nonviolence is great, and that the way we think of nonviolence as a process and as a goal in and of itself is great. But we need to think about what it is that we're building up around. Are we making nonviolence an idol? And if nonviolence is an idol, and then we've built a pedestal for the idol based on all these weird cultural things that we've developed to associate with the peace movement, are we forcing ourselves into something that pulls us too far away from mainstream culture? Or maybe in another direction pulls us too *close* to mainstream culture in . . . in the arbitrariness of some of our rules or understandings.

Charles: I want to say something related to the duality of terrorists and pacifists. Most people don't become involved in this movement. Most people are moderate, and they don't take stands about things but try to be the middle ground, right? You saw that in the German Christian

Church. People defined themselves vis-à-vis Nazi Germany and then their being moderate was saying they wouldn't [forcibly] baptize Jews. When your middle-of-the road is defined against a terrible evil, your moderacy itself is evil.

It takes courage to call the world insane, and there's a duality between us and the terrorists in that we both reject the world's standards. And that's dangerous. I think that there's a reason why people don't take extreme acts of one sort or another. People often base goodness on normality and conflict avoidance. Now that's a false peace, but I think it's the reason people don't like extreme acts of one sort of another.

Judy: People outside of our two camps see that and we don't. We can't learn from that because we have a narrowness, or a lack of vision. So I think the next development in the peace movement—whether you want to call it the peace movement or something else—will be to challenge and examine our assumptions and what we've built up around our identity and try and learn more from other groups. The reason the peace movement is the *white* peace movement for the most part has a lot to do with this. We've constructed too much around our own cultural conceptions.

So I don't know. I think what I would go to prison for hopefully would be something that would be a part of that expansion of our understanding—our understanding of peace and our goals and how we're going to go through this process. Because even though we're so focused on self-transformation, we're only transforming ourselves in this narrow way. A greater transformation needs to happen, and it isn't going to happen insofar as we're focusing inward. We need to focus more outwardly and look at other movements and other things if we're really going to grow as a movement ourselves.

Tom Cordaro has posed some of the same questions that Charles and Judy grappled with. Tom is the Director of Justice and Outreach Ministry at St. Margaret Mary Parish in Naperville and a Pax Christi USA Ambassador of Peace. See his blog on the Pax Christi Minnesota website: "Now We See in a Mirror Dimly," at www.paxchristimn.org/2012/04/01/for-now-we-see-a-mirror-dimly-tom-cordaro/.

7

Behind the Bars

While the narrators in other chapters talk about being behind bars, those in this chapter speak even more specifically about their prison times. We begin with Jeff Dietrich, a man of many experiences. David Gardner and Renaye Fewless, two young people who lived at the LA Catholic Worker with Jeff and his wife Catherine, tell of their first imprisonments. Lisa Hughes shows how she became a friend to her fellow prisoners and Doris Sage describes how prison life is circumscribed, even in a minimum security prison, Fr. Lorenzo Rosebaugh, OMI, reminisces about several prison experiences, both here and in Brazil. Father Steve Kelly, SJ, tells why and how he practices noncooperation when imprisoned and Bill Frankel-Streit provides a startling comment on Steve's stance. John Heid, a veteran of many arrests and incarcerations, concludes the chapter.

Jeff Dietrich

Jeff Dietrich, 2004.

Jeff Dietrich has lived at the Los Angeles Catholic Worker for years, cooking soup on LA's skid row in what locals call the "hippie soup kitchen," weathering all sorts of community-living storms, and frequently doing time for resisting war and the politics which work to the detriment of the poor.

Jeff: As the latest Iraq War was starting, a number of us felt called to keep having some kind of witness. We felt that if we didn't, we'd be like the quiet Germans of Hitler's era. It's not that our feeble efforts were going to stop it, any more than Franz Jägerstätter and the White Rose could stop the war machine of Nazi Germany.[1] You felt like it was immoral to keep on with business as usual, even if that business was feeding the poor and running a soup kitchen.

Ro: Jeff, you seem tired. Is being tired, perhaps, the essence of a life spent resisting?

Jeff: Maybe it is. Anybody who does this for any length of time kind of hits a wall. You constantly come up against your own delusions that you're really going to address the problems of the world. Particularly since 9/11, we've had to retrench ourselves. Yet we don't have the luxury of despair. We have to remember the duty of hope, as Dorothy [Day] would say.

Also, what else am I going to do? What else *can* I do or what would I *want* to do? I'm certainly not going to leave the Worker and get a job somewhere. I can't get terribly enthusiastic, but I won't abandon hope and I won't stop doing what we're doing. It's just . . . it's part of our faith commitment, part of who we are.

We're not going to make a difference. Except maybe. Maybe, maybe . . . the hope is that this tiny seed of something that we do will come to some kind of fruition someday. As the Gospels and Dorothy always said, we're the planters, not the harvesters. The next generation reaps the fruit of our planting, so thank God the young people still come. Because of that, you still carry some hope that you yourself might see some fruition.

Ro: Dorothy would also say that the suffering of jail is what will redeem the action.

Jeff: Of course. That's basic old-style Catholic Church. That's where I'm coming from, and that's where she came from. Like my mom always said when I was a kid, and things weren't going my way: "Offer it up."

---

1. Franz Jägerstätter was an Austrian Roman Catholic farmer and father who refused to serve in the Nazi army. He received no support from his church and was executed for his pacifism in 1943. His fate became known in 1964 when US sociologist Gordon Zahn published a biography, *In Solitary Witness*. Years later—in 2007—Pope Benedict XVI declared him a saint.

Jail is part of the calling! If you're going to do this, you've got to take your turn in jail. You don't just work with the poor and do charity. Part of the mission is addressing the root cause of poverty and standing in solidarity with those who suffer all over the world. Those of us who live in simplicity—live in *comfortable* simplicity in this country—have got to once in a while detach ourselves from that and stand in a place poor people are relegated to. So you take your turn in the jail. I know I'm pretty reluctant to do it, but it's an essential part of what we're about.

Ro: When you're here at the Los Angeles Worker, there's so much going on. When you're in jail that stops. You have a completely different kind of schedule, a completely different life. How does that play out?

Jeff: Well, it's not inappropriate to think of it as a Catholic Worker vacation of sorts. I've been very fortunate, I guess, in that I haven't had any physical confrontations with people in jail. For the most part, people have been pretty friendly. The closest I ever came to being physically accosted was some years ago in the LA County Jail, and it was pretty terrible. The environment was awful, with like three hundred people just packed into this enormous room for four days. Lights on all the time. People sleeping on the floor. Lots of fights.

One young man came up to me and said he wanted my brand-new running shoes, and I'm afraid to say that I gave them to him. The odd thing was that by the next morning he gave them back to me. Apparently, he was gambling and got quite lucky, so I got my shoes back. Since then, if I have them, I never wear good running shoes to jail.

Ro: Do you ever get written up?

Jeff: This last time—or the time before, I guess—I declined to work, so I did spend some time in the hole. Refusing work is the ultimate noncooperation. But being in the hole is not bad, certainly in the federal system. You're inactive for 24/7, but you can get books and writing material. Actually, the hardest thing about being in the hole isn't being alone, it's the fact that you have a roommate and you're with a roommate *all* the time.

In the two weeks that I was in the hole, I had four different roommates. And mostly they wanted to talk! And talk. So you find yourself being like a counselor or a psychiatrist, listening to everybody. Personally, that's not my . . . I don't like that. I would prefer to be alone. In general population, you're only with your roommate and locked down when you're going to bed, so it's not quite such an intense personal encounter.

Also, you worry more in solitary. Wherever you are in jail, you're always reviewing your past life and your actions, but your friends aren't there to support you, so you're just constantly wondering if you did the right thing. "Here I am, just this puny guy." God! It just seems so self-righteous. You really need community to do what we do, need to affirm each other that we're doing the right thing. When you don't have that, it's lonely and isolating and very difficult to continue with confidence in your "deviant behavior." So you constantly have to turn to prayer and Scripture. And that's a good thing about being in jail: it gives you a lot of prayer time, and a lot of time to reflect on the Scripture.

David Gardner

David Gardner came to the Los Angeles Catholic Worker (LACW) in June of 2002. At their "hippie soup kitchen," David served many of the same people with whom he shared his first jail term. We began our interview by looking at his arrest citations. One was for an Iraq War protest at the Rose Bowl Parade when he spent the day in the drunk tank with football revelers. The second was for saying the rosary in front of the Federal Building. I asked him if he had knelt to say the rosary, and he replied, "I'm not *that* Catholic!"

The third was again at the Federal Building, when the Catholic Workers blessed it with holy water and were arrested when they tried to enter the building without going through the metal detectors. Again, no jail time. He was finally sentenced to the LA County Jail for an action on Ash Wednesday of 2003, just before the latest Iraq War.

David: There were about two hundred people at the action, with maybe fifteen to thirty getting arrested. It was at the height of the civil disobedience against the war-to-be, so we had great media attention. Now these people all had jobs; they were what we'd call "real people," not Catholic Workers. Their lawyers went in and got this deal: for the first-time offenders—the majority of the group—the charge got dropped down to an infraction, which is like a parking ticket, with a suspended fifty dollar fine.

The people with priors got forty-five days in the County Jail or 600 hours of community service. I got counted as a prior because I'd had those three previous arrests. (Jeff's and Catherine's priors were long computer sheets, like accordions.) The long sentence was because the DA wants to look tough on crime; however, County's so overcrowded that we knew we'd be out way before that, and we were. Only eight days.

That's another way the poor get screwed. The jail's so full of nonviolent offenders that the Sheriff kicks people out left and right, and the DA knows this. But it's your sentence that's on your record, not the time you actually serve. So poor people have a conviction record that doesn't match their actual crimes, and the DA looks tough.

David Gardner, 2004.

You know, I was scared of the LA County Jail, but I'd learned a bit from other Catholic Workers who'd been in County before, and I'd also talked to some of the people we serve. So I kind of knew what was going to come down, or thought I did. Even so, I've gotta tell you—I got the "s" scared out of me in County!

I walk in. It's my first dorm, one hundred fifty people. They know who the fishes are, because you don't have any property with you. (They call the first-timers "fish," because you don't know what you're doing yet.) This guy comes up to me and goes, "Hey, I'm Kevin. I'm the rep for the Woods." White people. W-o-o-d-s, as in peckerwood. (I learned that later.)

"Hey, you ever been here before?" I said I hadn't.

He goes, "Well, shut the fuck up and listen to me." See, Kevin was basically the head of the white people, so he was the one to show me the ropes—which toilets were for urinating and which for defecating, which sink was for spitting, which for washing your face, which one was for cooking your Top Ramen in. Different hygiene things.

Then other things, like if a Black man is taking a shower, as a white man I have to wait. If another white man or a Mexican is in the shower, then it's okay for me to go in. Then I asked him when the

Jewish services were. I'm not Jewish, but I know the rabbi [for the jail] and he's a great guy.

Now I didn't know this then, but on Kevin's back was this big swastika. And he's like, "What? Are you Jewish?" "No, no! I'm Catholic!" But my question didn't get me any points.

Now in this dorm was this guy they called Bishop. An older Black guy. Bishop saw me reading a Bible, so he invited me to a prayer service. It was very . . . uh, touching because all of a sudden, it was okay to pray together. White people and Mexicans and Blacks.

In that dorm there's four groups: the Blacks; the Sureños or Mexicans from Southern California; the Paisanos, which are Mexican nationals and Central Americans; and then the Woods or white people. The Woods, the Paisanos, and the Sureños were kind of tied together and on friendly terms, but I was not to make friends with Blacks. Every rule seemed to be, "Avoid the Blacks." Like there were phones for them and phones for the rest of us. Chairs with marks on the back. When the newspaper came in, one of them said "Black" and the other one said "Sureño." When we lined up for lunch, the Mexicans got the best position in line; the Paisanos the second best, Woods third best, and the Blacks the worst. The deputies recognized that system, and they knew who the reps were. In fact, the deputies expected the reps to make everybody shut up.

Ro: Like the kapos in the concentration camps.

David: Yes. Pretty soon I was moved out into another dorm, and this one was more like what you'd see on TV. A double-decker gangway with a row of about ten cells that should have four guys in them but unfortunately had like nine. The head white guy of the bottom level took orders from the head white guy on the top level. And the head white guy on the top level, he was an Aryan Brotherhood. You know—skinheads, swastikas, and all that. The rep on the lower level was a drug dealer who was older and kind of respected and a pretty good guy. Didn't have that neo-Nazi stuff, and didn't use the N word. Same kind of rules here [as in the other dorm], but here we had our own cells, with a toilet and shower.

Then I got moved again and became a trusty. The trusty dorm was pretty cool. I guess the big touching thing was that I made friends there; they were really nice to me and offered me food and stuff. Because they were trusties, they had everything! One guy worked at the library, and he got me a book. One guy worked in the laundry, so we had extra towels. Our clothes actually got washed every other day and we got an extra set of underwear! All these luxuries.

I ended up writing letters for this middle-aged man. He had a little Nazi tattoo and was missing a couple of teeth, and he was illiterate, so I wrote letters to his girlfriend, his mom, his sister, his daughter. All to the same address, a little trailer park up in Lancaster. I'm completely dyslexic—never did good in English class—and I couldn't believe he wanted me to do it.

In every dorm there were the hard-core criminals who tended to have the Nazi tattoos and had already done time in State and that kind of put them in the leadership. The ones I associated more with were the first-timers, the minimum security boys, basically all in for dope.

Ro: What did your parents think of all this?

David: My parents were divorced when I was pretty young. My mom is completely against it, and so is my grandmother, who we lived with after the divorce. My dad . . . [long pause] passed away a few months ago. He told me, "I understand this war is really bad, and I understand you're angry about it, and I understand that it's hard to get media coverage for your protest, so sometimes you have to get arrested in order to get on the TV."

I said, "Well, Dad, we didn't call the press. Nobody saw it except for Catholic Workers and about twenty people kind of associated with us."

"What did you do it for, then?" And that was actually the hardest one to respond to, because he made a little too much sense! It was kind of hard to give him that "Well, we're called to be faithful, not effective" line. But he understood, finally, and I think he was proud of me.

Ro: Hmmmm. Did the jail experience change you?

David: Well, in the weeks afterwards, I didn't feel quite right. I was edgy and angry and wasn't as willing to show my emotions as before. You know, you kind of put on a persona when you're in prison, trying to look tougher than you really are. I'm not really a tough guy; like, I was pushed around a lot in grade school, that kind of thing. Maybe that's part of my pacifism: violence never really worked in my favor, anyway.

But the learning: I guess ultimately being in jail just kind of added to my experience and my understanding of the people I serve on Skid Row. You know, when you tell people that you serve the homeless, you complain that they do time for jaywalking or for having a shopping cart. And the people say, "Well, at least in County Jail, they get a roof over their head and free meals."

Now I can tell folks that I've been there and I'd rather sleep on the streets. The food's better on the streets, and you're safer. It's just as cold in County because they've got the AC running too cold all the time. County . . . County is just not a good scene.

Renaye Fewless

Renaye Fewless was arrested in Los Angeles in 2000, a few years before David. She had traveled alone on the Greyhound from Michigan to California, leaving right after college graduation, to do a summer internship at the LACW. Her arrest group was trained in nonviolence and solidarity techniques and was able to get their charges dismissed, a practice common with resisters in the '80s but rarely used today.

Renaye Fewless, 2007.

Renaye: It was when the Los Angeles Rampart Police were at their worst. Collaborating with the INS (Immigration and Naturalization Service) in framing people and then deporting them. So the [protest planning] committee for the DNC [Democratic National Convention] decided to do an action against the Rampart Division. About forty of us blocked off the stairway to the main entrance of the Rampart Police Station. We all had gags over our mouths to symbolize those who couldn't be heard.

Five of us from the LA Worker were part of this larger group, and we all practiced jail solidarity so none of us brought our ID, and we didn't give our names. Our lawyers were set up ahead of time. The plan was that each of us would have a trial and legally they only have so many days to do that, but not giving our names slowed the system down big-time.

We were in jail for an entire week. They took everything from us, and I remember always being cold with only a tiny, thin blanket.

No sheets, no pillows. Some of us kind of rigged up the toilet paper as a pillow.

They isolated us from the other prisoners, though, so we didn't really experience what they did. For three days I went to court but never did give my name. Going to court was really traumatic because we only had one set of clothes, with only two pair of underwear, and you wanted to have clean underwear for court.

See, you were strip-searched and cavity-searched every time you went. That was really humiliating. There were so many people at a time, probably about fifty. You had to take off all your clothes and then lean against a wall with your hands on the wall and your legs spread, and they'd use flashlights to look in your crotch. It was . . . it was really, really terrible!

All the time the search was going on, they'd be saying horrible things. One day they kept telling us how bad we stunk. Well, you could take showers and they give you some kind of cheap deodorant, but it didn't work, you know, and you couldn't wash your clothes. And you've been over in court all day and you're all nervous and worried. Here's all these women, spread open, and they're telling us how bad we stink. One lady kept spraying air freshener on us. If you said anything, she'd get more degrading, so you were better off just taking it quietly.

I remember in the court house there was a glass cage, and it made me feel we were like animals, waiting our turn in some kind of pen. The good thing about going to court was that we got to mix with the general population. That was fun, although a lot of people resented us. The jail had shut down all the TVs during the Convention and a lot of people blamed us for that, but it was really because the authorities didn't want the inmates to know about us. In fact, that's why they isolated us.

Lots of prisoners were really supportive, though, because they lived in LA and were victims of the system on a daily basis. Especially the prostitutes. In fact, most of the women we met were prostitutes, and I realized that most of the crimes were economic crimes. Being there was really eye opening, a first-hand experience of *so* many things.

I told my mom and dad beforehand, of course, and they were upset. And terrified, just terrified. (They were even terrified that I took the bus all the way to California.) My sister turned eight while I was in jail, and I was able to call her. It was during her party so all my aunts and uncles were there, and they learned that I was in jail. It's a big stigma in our family to be arrested. Now my mom's proud, though, because she understands.

We had meetings all the time in jail and tried to use the consensus model. That was a new thing for me, too. And fasting . . . After talking about it for a long time, we started fasting—or some of us did—as a technique to get more bargaining power in the courtroom. But I couldn't fast completely! I just thought about food *all* the time!

The jail staff would entice us with candy bars and stuff. Normally, you'd have to pay for the snacks, but when we were fasting, the guards would bring in bags of junk food. And I got hooked with a whiff of Cheetos. [Laughs.] So my name became "Cheeto Cheater."

The guards got very scared because of the fasting. Different people came in to rationalize with us. And then one bossy woman tried to bully us, but enough people had done jail solidarity before, so . . . We were very strong in the unit, and we knew our rights pretty well because we'd had all kinds of training.

We sent out statements, and whenever the lawyer came to see us it was always a great big deal. A lot of people were vigiling outside, actually camping out there, especially after the Convention ended. I could see them from my room. They had candles and signs and life-sized puppets and posters with our code names on them. My code name was "Stir Fry." (I have no idea why I picked that.) My friend Jessie Lewis from the LA Worker would hold my sign up all the time, and it made me feel really special.

We also used our code names with each other in the jail so we wouldn't give our real names away. The courts wouldn't use them, of course; to them I was just "Jane Doe Number Six."

I don't know the details about how we got out or why they dropped the charges; we never really had a trial where we all had to appear. I guess the lawyers worked something out and they finally gave in. Our supporters gave us this great "get-out-of-jail-free" party, and I wasn't even hungry, just excited to finally be out!

Ro: What advice would you give to people who might be thinking of getting arrested for the first time?

Renaye: Stick with the Catholic Workers. I felt so trusting of them. Protesters can get hurt, so I took very seriously everything I learned at the training during the DNC. I particularly remembered the part that said not to let anyone get separated from the group. They tried that several times while we were in jail, but we stuck together and it worked.

Ro: Going to prison to protest injustice and war . . . What do you think about that now?

Renaye: I think it's something that needs to be done, but I don't feel drawn to do it. It was very hard for me to be in jail and I couldn't . . . I don't think my personality is such that I'd be a gift to the prisoners, like some people are. But I'm really glad I went to jail because you learn firsthand what it feels like. Even though we were treated better than other people, and we had a lot of power and knew what our rights were, it was *still* bad!

When I was growing up, my parents were careful, and I was sheltered. Now I think that's good to do to your kids, but there were so many things I didn't know about and so many things happened to me that summer at the Los Angeles Catholic Worker.

You know, I went almost right from college to jail. College is kind of a created world. It's controlled by adults, and it doesn't seem real in some ways. I learned so much more in LA with the Catholic Worker than I did in college. I was just a sponge, soaking it all up. And going to jail was part of that learning.

Lisa Hughes

Lisa Hughes, 2004.

During Lisa Hughes's six months in a minimum security camp for an SOA action, she grew close to the women with whom she was imprisoned. Her story illustrates the presence resisters can bring behind the bars.

Lisa: The women at Greenwood are just incredible! For instance, a group of Christian prisoners presents every new prisoner with a welcome gift. (They keep a little fund.) Four pre-stamped envelopes, some paper and a pen, shower shoes, shampoo, lotion, and . . . you know, the things that you might not get to buy right away. Or ever, if you don't have money for the commissary.

When you first come into Greenwood, you're given this white jump suit, and everyone else is in greens. So it screams, "New person!

New person!" All sorts of women welcomed me and gave me gifts: a coat, extra PJs, a set of long johns, a nice bar of Irish Spring soap. But the best present was a green jump suit, so I didn't have to wear the white one.

Ro: Did you feel that anyone was checking you out romantically?

Lisa: No. I never experienced that at all in prison. Other SOA'ers have, I guess, at some of the bigger prisons. Janice, one of my friends there, was feeling threatened at one point, because some women felt like she had told on them. She hadn't, but they thought she had, and so they were threatening her. But then they found out she wasn't the one who told on them after all.

And get this! One of the women actually went up to her—at church, in front of everyone—and apologized and gave her a hug. That was a huge thing, a really huge thing, to see in prison. This woman had totally been in the wrong and way out of hand, and she admitted it—not just in private but in front of everyone.

I was able to relate to just about anybody, even the pretty tough ones. I think most people were in for drug crimes, but there are also a lot of white-collar crimes. Embezzlement, that type of stuff. The most amazing thing, I think, is that people in prison rub shoulders across class lines, across racial lines. People you would never have crossed paths with otherwise. You're living under the same roof, sharing a room, eating the same food, showering in the same showers, so you can't help but see the common humanity. And I learned so much from them!

One highlight was my exposure to Native American spirituality. I had a really tough time with the Christians in prison. I went to Mass every Sunday and to a Bible study class but there were all these divisions among the Christians, all kinds of splits over types of worship. Some people didn't like the traditional one so they started their own. And they were the most judgmental people there.

There was also a chance to model nonviolence in prison. I'm thinking particularly of the case with my friend who had been threatened. On her alley, there were some people who were hollering sexual comments down to each other. This is how she said it to me, "There were some Black lesbians who were da, da, da . . ." So I had a talk with her and said, "Your issue with them is not that they're Black or that they're lesbian, but that they're loud and they're sexually explicit with their words. Which doesn't necessarily go hand-in-hand with them being Black or being lesbian." You know, just kind of pointing that out.

Then I had another friend who said to me, "They need to have a whole separate wing for lesbians."

I said, "Well, maybe they need to have a separate wing for people who want to be sexually active. A lot of women in here wouldn't call themselves lesbians, but they're choosing to be sexually active with other women while they're here, and then there are other people in here who are lesbians but are not choosing to be sexually active." So, you know, just kind of helping people separate out these differences.

There was also an instance with my friend, Tina. You know, the guards just love it if you get in a fight, because then they can send you out to medium security. So a couple of times, one of the guards kind of egged Tina on. I tried to explain to her: "All he wants is for you to respond in the way that you're tempted to respond. He's got that power over you and then you end up being transferred."

There was another time when there was almost a fight in the cafeteria. Over chicken wings. (All these things sound so trivial on the outside but on the inside . . .) Now I knew both of these people. One was Black and one was white. So there's also the racial thing. And with both of them it was kind of a pride thing, not to back down.

Mindy comes out of the kitchen and sits down. I'm between her and Tina and Tina's leaning around me, saying [sotto voce] "white bitch" and stuff like that.

I said, "You know, Tina, you've got a choice here."

"What? What's my choice?"

"I'm not saying Mindy was right. I'm not saying that she wasn't being unfair. But at this point, you can either let it go or you can end up being moved." Because she was right on that brink of hitting Mindy. I think Tina would've had to give the first blow. (Mindy was a middle-class, white-collar crime sort of person, and much more in control.) Well, Tina listened. She didn't hit her.

She had a really long sentence, and she had said, "I never make friends with short-timers because you just pick up and leave." Then when I was leaving, she started to cry, and said, "I swore I wasn't going to do this." I don't think anyone needs to be kept so long. Three years, maybe. Five years, max. Anything beyond that just doesn't serve any purpose.

How does it help anyone to separate a mom from her kids for years and years? Terrible things happening to the kids. One woman's daughter was sexually abused while she was in prison and she couldn't even hold her and help her through that.

Ro: Do you keep up with any of them?

Lisa: Oh, yes, I'm still in contact. A few of the women in there have no financial sources, and I'm able to send them some money, and then there are a few I just keep in touch with because we were friends. Just the other day—this just broke my heart—we sent them our [Catholic Worker] newsletter, and on our wish list we had put stamps. Stamps are one of the few things of value in prison that you have access to, so my really good friend went up and down her "alley," which is like thirty-two beds, and collected stamps. They sent us twenty stamps.

I remember one young woman named Tara. She was about to get out. Her parents and everyone she knew were involved in drugs. She's twenty years old, she doesn't have her GED, and she's dumped back on the streets. You know, no matter how much motivation she has, she has no support at all.

Lisa carried these stories with her. After she was released, she moved to Portland, Oregon, and started a Catholic Worker house to provide a home for women who had recently finished prison terms.

Doris Sage

Doris and Dan Sage had long been activists in Syracuse, working both professionally as disability advocates and on justice issues through the Syracuse Unitarian Universalist Fellowship. In 1997, after they had both retired, they were incarcerated together for crossing the line to protest the School of the Americas at Fort Benning, Georgia. Doris went to Danbury.

Dan and Doris Sage, 2005.

Doris: We still go to the SOA protests, but I know I'm not well enough to go to prison again. I remember what it was like, trying to get [the right] medication! You see, I've had high blood pressure for years and had been through a lot of different medications, and this one was working, so they promised in court that they'd continue it.

Then in the prison they tried to substitute. I finally reached a friend from church and she couldn't reach my doctor so she called the Republican representative here in Syracuse. Someone in his office wrote a letter to the prison on United States government letterhead, and the very next day I got the Procardia medication that I needed.

Another time, I needed to refill a couple of the prescriptions, so I stood in the line. The physician's assistant took my name and looked in this huge tray of medications and pulled one out and put it in my hand.

I said, "What is this?"

He said, "Take it!"

I said again, "What is it?"

He said again, "Take it!" It didn't look like anything I'd been taking, and I was ready to bolt. Then he asked my name again, and he'd given me somebody else's medication!

Ro: Holy cow! Now, you said before the interview started that you had a vindictive counselor . . .

Doris: Vindictive. That's a good word for him. He was . . . was well recognized as one of the most diabolical. Actually we [prisoners of conscience] weren't treated as badly as some of the other women. When you see them being harassed and ridiculed and put down, and they already have low self esteem . . . you know, it was cruel! He was ex-Vietnam military. I could never make a bed that'd suit him, so I always got demerits on making my bed, and when you get demerits, your whole room doesn't get benefits. Even today, when I'm making the beds here, I think of him. I think prison work with women appeals to men who have issues of control. That's one of the perks of prison work at Danbury.

But despite all this, the women prisoners made family in the prison. Like on my 69th birthday. See, among the things you're not allowed to do in Danbury is give a gift because that could be payment for something. And no hugs. Because they wouldn't know whether an embrace is comforting to another woman or the beginning of a fight. Or a lesbian relationship.

You're not allowed to celebrate anything at Danbury, either, but they did on my birthday, anyway. The morning of my birthday, I'm going through the breakfast line, and the woman dishing out Eggos goes [hums birthday song.] Under her voice. And the guard shuts her up! Singing not allowed. At breakfast, Megan [Rice, one of the other SOA women] had a little bouquet on our table, in the lid of her water bottle. And the others had splurged on mangoes. (You don't get fresh fruit unless you buy it in the commissary.) Then my son and his family came to visit, which was wonderful.

Later in the day, the women gave me a birthday party. Our friend Carla could make lotions and creams with Vaseline, cocoa butter, and other ingredients you could buy from the commissary. She had a special way of whipping them up and cooking them in a microwave. So there on the table is a jar of Carla's cream, in a crocheted basket that she'd made. Crocheting was one thing the women could do. They couldn't knit but they could crochet.

Megan wrote a poem, and oh . . . she brought champagne! [Laughter.] You could get ice, and she made up a juice cocktail of some kind with pop and that was our champagne. A woman made notepaper with pretty torn edges and little bits of dried flower behind some wide Scotch tape. I can't imagine where she found the tape because it's illegal. Or where she kept the dried flowers through all the inspections. She took the paper from the GED program and made envelopes and glued the envelopes together with toothpaste. You're not allowed glue or paste or anything like that, but toothpaste works just fine. (That's how you get your pictures up on your locker.) They were just the most wonderful birthday gifts on this, my Danbury birthday!

Father Lorenzo Rosebaugh, OMI

The late Father Rosebaugh's memoir, *To Wisdom Through Failure: A Journey of Compassion, Resistance and Hope,* was published in 2006.

Fr. Lorenzo: I learned a lot about prison during those ten months in solitary in the Wisconsin state prison system [for the Milwaukee Fourteen action]. Almost every single person that I ever saw in solitary was on some kind of drug, you know, to keep them calm. When you'd come back after a meal, there'd be all these pills in little containers, to keep us halfway quiet. I never took 'em. The guy next to me, I swear they drugged him so deeply he never woke up. They'd clang on his bars for him to take his food.

After I got out, I lived and worked in the inner city of Milwaukee for about three years. We had a little place called The Living Room, for men on the streets. And a job cooperative, too. During that time, I hitched all over and rode my bicycle all over the Midwest. That was really good, as far as I was concerned. Then I hitchhiked all the way down to Brazil, learning Spanish and Portuguese on the way, which was really a good experience, but hard.

I went to Recife, and before I knew it, Bishop Dom Helder Camera called me . . . well, called the Oblates in, my order. He was looking for somebody to do street work, because he'd had a man die right at his door from eating dirt. The Bishop went to get him a cup of coffee and when he came back, the guy had dropped dead.

The Bishop said, "I don't know what to do or how to do it, but whatever you do, I will support you." So that's how it was. I was about five years living on the streets. I didn't live out of a house or nothin'. (Went to meetings with the other Oblates pretty regularly.) A Mennonite came down and joined me, and we slept with the street people and made the soup. One day, for no reason at all, the police came, jumped out of their Volkswagen bug, and tipped over our big pot of soup.

Then several weeks later, we were going to a market on a Sunday morning. We had this big vegetable cart, and they stopped us and accused us of stealing the cart. They took us way out in the outskirts, to a jail for robbers and thieves. A horrible place! They stripped us of all our clothes and tossed us into a room with about thirty people. Everybody else was nude, too, and they all looked like they were starving.

Two prisoners were like trusties. They got to wear jumpsuits and eat special food and were real healthy looking. Their job was to beat up anybody who got out of line, and that's the first thing they did to us—beat us up, using karate kicks and hits. Then they got huge plates of steak and ate in front of us.

After they ate, they told us we had to dance for them. In the nude! They told the other guys to sing for us. Then they tried to scare us by saying these guys hadn't seen a woman in . . . "They're going to have a feast tonight with you nice gringos!" I didn't think it would ever happen, though, and it didn't. Later a couple of other guys were brought in and they really got beaten. Tortured, I'd say.

Anyhow the Oblates started looking for us, and the Mennonites, too, and Dom Helder called up the military and said they'd better do something about the two missing missionaries. So we were out in about four days and we got the story out through the Archdiocese.

And then! We got word that Rosalynn Carter was coming to Recife! We somehow got hold of her through the Embassy, and we had about forty-five minutes with her and the Vice President's wife. After that, Mrs. Carter came out with a strong statement, saying to the Brazilians that they wouldn't get any more money if they didn't change their system. So it really . . . It made an impact.

But they're still doing it today. I was in federal prison for a year, in downtown Chicago, after an action at Pantex in Amarillo, Texas, when they were making nuclear bombs. My last time. And I saw them beat the heck out of people there, too. One of them was just a young kid—about nineteen, I think. So it goes on. It goes on.

Father Steve Kelly, SJ

Father Steve Kelly, SJ, and Father John Savard, SJ, in front of San Francisco Federal Building, 1989. © Father John Quinn, SJ.

Fr. Steve Kelly, SJ, has been a priest since 1982. He works full time in resistance, either at Jonah House or on the West Coast, where he and others have reinvigorated the Pacific Life Community. He's participated in numerous Plowshares actions, including the Disarm Now Plowshares in

2009, and always carries his resistance into the prison, so that means he spends months at a time in the SHU (Segregated Housing Unit), known in some prisons and jails as the hole. His interview begins with why he resists and continues with details about how this works out behind bars.[2]

Fr. Steve: I'm trying to be a Christian, and I think there are just two essentials for that: the cross and community. The cross, of course, has to be redeemed from Constantine. The first-century Christians understood the cross as [resisting] the state, which was terrorizing people to make them stay in line. I see it that way now. As Phil [Berrigan] would say, "We're all in minimum security," with the state's carrot and stick coercion.

One of the toughest decisions I made in my entire life was when I was in El Salvador. I'd been there a year, and I started to see real people, much different than an abstract "abolish nuclear weapons." I saw that all their problems were coming from our county, the font of violence, with the nuclear threat at the bottom of it all. In the end, I decided to come home to resist because I saw that in resisting nuclear weapons, I'm doing what a good pastor does for his people—putting myself between the weapons and the people, to protect them.

Part of what's going on here, for me, is the Church's role in this and how the Church has gone to sleep. In the nineteenth century, the sleeping giant woke up in regard to slavery. First, it was just a few people, mostly in churches and synagogues. People told them, "Look! Slavery is an economic institution, and it'll always be around. That's just the way it is." But some people kept saying no, until finally it changed. There's a tremendous hope in that. For me, the purpose of the Plowshares movement is to wake up the sleeping giant.

I'm always trying to stir up trouble. But the action itself is only one percent of what's going on. The way to that destination is equally as important as the destination itself and that's where the community of the Church comes in. We are not individuals, we are members of the body of Christ, made to act together and to need each other. Our culture gets way, way, way away from this. So it's difficult, initially, to get with people and start cooperating to build community. Now I've heard of Plowshares where people have seemed to agree as they're

---

2. For more on Fr. Steve Kelly's prison resistance, see the cover story "Prisoner for Peace" by George M. Anderson, SJ, in *America*, Oct. 17, 1998.

going into it and then fall apart during the trial, or afterwards. How do you prevent that?

That's why the process is so important. In any sort of war resistance, people have to work on three actions. The first is the disarmament itself, violence converted into something beneficial for humankind, something benign. The next action is to convince the judge or a jury that what we did was right. So the courtroom is a second action. It's one of the more dangerous rooms of the Pentagon, an extension of the Pentagon's agenda as the moral and legal legitimator of nuclear weapons. We try to put the whole system on trial, but here in this country, we're often prevented from putting on a defense. The third action is the jail time. Another witness. You enter a place where you're not ever in control. So it's another action, to take on a dehumanizing system that is very much an extension of the system outside. They can only run the prisons through coercion and incentives to those who cooperate—carrots like visiting and phone calls and commissary and better housing situations.

Prison is really a colonization of the mind, so I continue to resist in prison. I will not take part in the state's attempt to change me into a contributing citizen, so I don't program at all. Won't do any work and refuse the tests—urine or a DNA sample or a Breathalyzer—and so I get sent to SHU right away. Refusing gives me a chance to say, "I'm not here for this. I'm here because I'm against nuclear weapons." Of course they think it sounds crazy at first, but after awhile, you hear, "That guy locked up in the hole? He's against nuclear weapons."

I've lived months and months and months in the SHU. Without any good time, without any commissary, without visits, without phone calls. When you go outside, you have these little kennel cages, with cyclone fencing. There might be two of you in a walking cage, about twenty to twenty-five feet. Back and forth. Back and forth. But that fresh air makes a big difference!

Ro: Does your health suffer?

Fr. Steve: I've sometimes lost my wind, and when I was in for three years, I really felt unhealthy. But I do calisthenics in the cell, and my yoga.

Dorothy [Day's] got me through a lot of time in the hole. Her writing was probably the most . . . the most compassionate reading I could do. She threads our humanity through the most bleak situations, so that helps to keep one's heart a heart of flesh rather than growing colder and colder and more withdrawn. I live by her phrase,

"Our problems stem from our acceptance of this filthy, rotten system." When we begin to accept . . . If you cooperate in prison, your whole sense of who you are as a person begins to deteriorate and you start to see yourself as an object of the state. That's what I mean about "colonizing the mind."

Ro: How do you spend your day when you're in detention?

Fr. Steve: Actually, there's not enough time for all I want to do. I sleep in two shifts, getting up around 3:30 a.m. the first time, when the guys come around doing the count. Start the yoga at that time, then prayers, then breakfast, usually shoved through the door. (The Psalms are a great solace in the SHU because they cover a whole gamut of emotions and it's important to stay in touch with that.) Then I clean up a bit and spruce up the cell. I don't make the bed on their terms, but the way I like it.

Then they ask us if we're going to go for an hour of rec, and I decide whether to go or not, and after that some exercises or maybe some paperwork. I usually do serious reading in the mornings, then sleep my second shift before lunch if I can, but people are always at the door bothering you—for count, counselors, unit managers, all these people. The talk goes on and on and on. You're listening to it and trying to read at the same time.

After lunch, I exercise, and then I calmly try to do both serious writing and letters. Mail is . . . in the course of a week, it's not unusual to get sixty to eighty pieces of mail. This last time, when I was in for three years, Ardeth Platte was very helpful; I'd put an address at the top of a letter and give it to her and she'd envelope it for me and mail it out. I used any kind of paper I could get hold of, even the backs of envelopes.

When you have a visitor in SHU, there's a long complicated procedure. First, the guard comes by your cell. (With the Feds, they might warn you over an intercom. "Kelly, visitor! Be ready in x number of minutes.") Then two guards come, one with the key to the "wicket," the drawer-sized flip door in the lower part of the cell door, and the other guard with shackles, manacles, and handcuffs. They chain you and then unlock the door. The two guards take you to the outer door of the hallway, then through another sally port to leave the SHU building. Then there's another locked gate and then a walk to the visiting room and a strip search. Finally the visit itself—a half hour—and then the same procedure again, with the escorts and the chains and the three locked doors.

After dinner, sometimes they take you out for a shower in this complicated locking-up way. Sometimes a cart comes around with pencils or toothbrushes and things like that. Then finally some light reading just before bed. In the SHU, you live in a very grey, sensory-deprived world. Phil [Berrigan] taught me to read mysteries and novels. I don't mean trash, but pulp basically, like murder mysteries, to feed your imagination. State segregation is extremely noisy; the federal SHU is a little more quiet and it's easier to get to bed at 11:30 or so.

Ro: Now you said you don't even have a watch. How do you keep track of time?

Fr. Steve: That was an ongoing project. There are audio cues. All the counts and shift changes. A new rule covers up all the windows in the federal segregated units, so now everything is only black or white or grey but the inside lights go out around 11:00, so if you have some sense of circadian rhythm, the cues are there.

Ro: Do you get depressed, being so sense-deprived?

Fr. Steve: You know, if I'm obsessing about something that isn't going my way, there's a tendency to get a little depressed. I see depression as anger that's had to grow cold, that can't quite get out. But I don't have a lot of those bouts, and can bring myself around by correspondence or reading.

Ro: How does the Jesuit order relate to you?

Fr. Steve: Just for advocating, you hear words like "maverick." When you're thrown into jail or prison, it's "loose cannon." I've had tremendous personal support from individuals, though—writing me and sometimes visiting—and that's just plain wonderful. Officially, both the Church and the Society of Jesus can't come out and say, "Oh, it's just wonderful to break the law." Although we have a great tradition of it, in both the Gospels and throughout the history of the Church.

Ro: Do you carry your noncooperation into probation, when you're finally released?

Fr. Steve: I always refuse supervised release, so I usually get added time for that. At the beginning, after arrest, I refuse to either put up bail or to be released on recognizance, so unless there's no bail, I stay in prison from the time I'm picked up or arraigned. You see, the conditions for that release are that you can't do this activity that you're saying is such a great witness. So the clock starts right there, and all that counts towards your sentence.

Then at the end, I tell them I'm not going to cooperate with supervised release, and I won't give them an address. So they have to either keep me in or tell the judge before release, and the judge can decide whether to release me.

Twice I went underground for nine months at a time. In 1996, I avoided the marshals in order to complete the next Plowshares action, so time was added on to my next sentence, for that probation violation. The next time I was released I told them point-blank: "I'm refusing supervised release." They even tried to make me get on a certain bus, but they couldn't, so finally they just let me out of the truck at a bus station. The coercion has an end. They are limited but they don't want you to know that.

Bill Frankel-Streit

Although everyone in the circle of faith-based resisters who knows Steve Kelly admires his resistance stance, I have sensed that some don't think the privations are worth it. So I was surprised to hear Bill's story.

Bill: I was sent to Fort Dix. As soon as I got off the bus, I got taken into a separate room and interrogated. They had sensed similarities between myself and Steve Kelly, who had just been there—repeat offender, peace activist, and priest. Steve Kelly, they said, turned the whole place upside down. See, Steve just totally noncooperates.

This guy from prison administration said that five hundred prisoners were looking at Father Kelly. In so many words, he said that if all of them would do what Father Kelly did, the prison would be in big, big trouble. They were freaked out the whole time he was there because just one man—Father Steve Kelly—was holding that possibility out to the other prisoners.

They pleaded with me—and I'm not exaggerating—they were practically on their knees, saying, "Just program. Don't turn this place upside down." You know, the powers put up the propaganda that nonviolence is ineffective, but I don't think the authorities themselves really believe that. They just want *us* to believe it! So of course I had to tell this story all over the compound.

See, when you're in federal prison, you'd think the big decision was done and you've lost your freedom, but there are constant little decisions. I respect both ways of doing it, whether somebody resists like Steve Kelly or doesn't.

Overall, Phil [Berrigan] didn't refuse in prison. He felt to be among the population was important, and he actually felt that refusing in prison was clouding the issue, that it was then crossing over to prison reform or focusing on the prison instead of focusing on the bomb. So, when you've got people like Phil Berrigan who didn't resist and Steve Kelly who does, you've got heavies on each side. It comes down to what one's individual conscience says. I have the utmost respect for anybody who goes to prison, whether they cooperate or not.

Sketch of the view from his bunk, 1991. Bill Frankel-Streit. Elmer Mass Collection, courtesy of DePaul University Special Collections and Archives Department, Chicago, Illinois.

Eventually, I felt I had to follow in [Steve's] footsteps. I wrote to [my wife] Sue and she was very encouraging and felt it was great to love somebody who could live that freely. I went to the hole for six weeks and actually, it wasn't any big deal. They can't do anything more to you and that's the freedom.

After about two weeks, a lieutenant came. First he was the good cop, but then he turned bad cop, and he said, "Well, if you don't leave, I'll give you a direct order to leave and if you disobey, I'll write you up another shot."

I said, "The only sanction you have is to put me in the hole, and I'm already here." Then the stupidity of what he said dawned on him, and he stomped away without a word. As Janice Joplin sang, "Freedom's just another word for nothing left to lose."

John Heid

John Heid spent high school and college in a Capuchin Franciscan seminary. After years in DC with the Community for Creative Nonviolence [CCNV] and Anathoth Community Farm in Wisconsin, he now lives at Casa Mariposa in Tucson and works as an advocate for children in the foster care system.

John Heid, 2005.

John: In the beginning, I was absolutely opposed to direct action. I thought it was wrongheaded because it only made people angry. See, I was then owning a lot of responsibility for other people's reactions. Later, I became familiar with the idea of creative tension in non-violent action and understood how anger can be used to foster change.

I needed to be nourished into confronting injustice, and I was lucky to get [that nourishment]. When I crossed the line the first time, in 1984 at Grifiss Air Force Base in Rome, New York, I was guided, gently and slowly, by an affinity group that included family and children. That's when I got this toolbox notion. In our country, one of the tools [for social change] is direct action. So let's use every tool in the box.

I remember my very first night in jail. It was later than the Grifiss experience, I think. Brian Flagg and I did "Ash Wednesday at the

White House." The theme was that the poor were being reduced to ashes, and we could all be reduced to ashes with a nuclear war. So we walked through the White House tour and [threw] ashes on the pillars on the Pennsylvania Avenue side. (I suppose that would be more difficult to do today.) Of course, we were immediately decked, and that's the first night I spent in jail—in the Central Cell Block in DC. A crash course. A real initiation.

What I remember most was the din. So many men in a place so dark I could barely see. It was in the basement and it was hot. A real Dante's Inferno, with cockroaches and moaning and suffering, suffering, suffering all around me. I don't remember being scared; I just remember a basement and noise.

I don't remember a trial. Maybe the charges were dropped, as they often are in DC. After that, I started spending time in Jonah House and eventually moved over there. Then I did a Plowshares—my only Plowshares—at General Dynamics' Electric Boat. Greg Boertje-Obed and I stayed in prison for five and a half months before the trial because we refused to pay bail. Finally, they agreed on personal recognizance and we got out. That incarceration time was an enormous mixture. Kind of a lockdown situation with a lot of sensory deprivation.

It caught me. I got very . . . I didn't recognize it at the time, but I became very depressed. Very down. And that translated into some anxieties, anxieties that I carry to this day. I wasn't assaulted by anyone, or threatened, but those months were soul-challenging times.

You know, I'm a very hyper person. Always, always busy, whether I have lots to do or not. In jail there wasn't enough to stimulate me in the day-in and day-out, and I allowed myself to glide downwards.

But the turning point . . . I heard from Father Carl Kabat, who was locked up, too [for a Plowshares], and the letter was very to-the-point. "You need to start taking care of yourself." What he meant was to take a break, read lighter books, that kind of thing. He reminded me that I *was* working and [resisting], simply because I was in prison.

Then a friend sent me a subscription to *The New York Times*. He knew I needed something to engage me, and it did. I used my excess energy reading the *Times*! Now I always tell people that the biggest obstacle in prison will probably be flat-out boredom, and that your most difficult cellmate is going to be yourself. Because you're faced with who you are and who you aren't, without the boundaries of everyday life in the other world.

When I went back to prison after the [Plowshares] trial, I did much better. I began to run a lot. In fact, the other prisoners called me the "Jericho Man." Also, the men I was with—not activists, necessarily—taught me how to do time. At first, they were stand-offish because of my vocabulary, but then we started taking some classes together and they realized how poor my math was, and that was the great equalizer. The guys could help me with math, and I could help them write letters.

Once I had as a cellmate a man who I later found out had killed someone. (One of the unwritten rules about prison is that you don't ask a guy why he's there, but eventually I learned.) If you know your cellie's a murderer before you even learn his name, you're always doing a realignment of perspective, trying not to let that bald word stand in your way. Because clearly his whole life is defined by that moment. Everything. Whereas in the other way around, you see the person rather than the defining word and you find yourself thinking of the circumstances that led up to that moment. I saw this in my cellmate, Eddie, who was about as hard a man as I'd ever run across. Just a teenager with a crusty streetwise exterior, which he was trying to toughen up because he knew he was facing life.

Now the man he had killed had a common name, and it happened that a major car dealer in the Boston area had the same name, so we'd hear it often on television. A couple times, when that name came on, I'd see tears in his eyes, and finally I got the nerve to ask, "What is it about that name?"

He said, "It's the name of the man I killed." Young man, high on drugs, and going to get more by any means possible, hits an old man and flees. Old man dies a few days later and young man lives with that for the rest of his life. [Long pause.]

Once, after I got out after serving seven months as a combination sentence for both SOA and ELF, I was thinking of another action.[3] And my partner at the time, Jane Hosking, said to me, "What do you think about spending as much time out of jail as you just spent

3. Project ELF (Extremely Low Frequency) was a transmitter system built to send one-way messages to submerged British and US submarines around the world, allowing Trident ballistic missiles to get close enough to targets to launch a nuclear first strike. After years of legal protest and civil disobedience by thousands of activists in both Wisconsin and Upper Michigan, Project ELF was closed in 2004. For a concise history of actions against these miles of transmitter wires, see Nukewatch, "Project ELF Closes," *Nuclear Resister* 135 (October 15, 2004); online: nuclearresister.org.

in jail?" So now that's become kind of a guideline for me. You see, at one point in my life, I felt like a resistance machine. In the late '80s, I was getting arrested roughly every six weeks and spending time in jail for about every five arrests. (I didn't keep track.) But after a couple years of that, I realized it wasn't fidelity as I understand it.

So you try to talk sense to people. When I was in DC, I'd spend hours with young folks who had come from the Midwest to the Pentagon. They'd hear all these fiery presentations by people like Mitch Snyder of CCNV. He'd say, "You gotta do it." Their souls would be churning inside, and they'd look for someone to just kind of walk them through it.

I'd tell them that to the best of their ability, one has to try to come to both peace and discomfort with it, as dissonant as that sounds. I don't know how many arrests I've had. Forty? Fifty? It's never gotten easier. There's never been a time before an action where there hasn't been tension, anxiety, concern—that kind of discomfort.

Then I tell people what happened to me after doing the Plowshares action, when the vacuum-sealed door of the prison slammed shut behind me and I walked into that cell and heard the electric lock. I remember saying to myself, "It's you and me now." The media may or may not cover this. My family may or may not understand. My support community is there for me, but they're *there* for me. Bottom line, it's me and you."

Yes, let's be honest about our fears. And yes, there's a sense of needing to do this, and let's be honest about that. But when the door clicks shut, it's you and your Creator, if it's a faith-based perspective, or it's you and yourself, period. If you cannot silence your need to do it, then you need to do it. Do it because you cannot *not* do it, as Dan [Berrigan] would say, but not because you think your action is going to change things in itself.

Our culture is so focused on results. Everything we do is supposed to be a positive, productive solution to a problem. And of course life isn't that way. So I remind folks that everything we do, period, has an effect, whether we know what it is or not. We can control what we do—maybe not over the way the bell sounds in someone else's ear, but in what bell we ring.

An Interlude

"Let's Fill the Jails"

Martha Hennessy

Martha Hennessy is the granddaughter of Catholic Worker co-founder Dorothy Day, herself no stranger to prison.[1] Born in 1955, she grew up in Vermont and still calls the state home. When she was young, Martha was jailed for three months for her part in the massive Seabrook protest against a proposed nuclear power plant. Following in her granny's footsteps today, she travels frequently to Catholic Worker houses, to war-torn countries as an ambassador for peace, and to protests against war and nuclear weapons across the US. I last saw her at a blockade of the Creech Air Force Base in Nevada, where they push the buttons for drone warfare in the Middle East.

Martha: I'm still trying to come to grips with Dorothy's Catholicism—
    what it meant to her and what it means for me. I can't disagree more
    with the Catholic Church in terms of its attitudes and actions with
    regard to women and children and the situation in Central and South
    America. But then I think about Dorothy being "a devoted daughter
    of the Church." She . . . She came away with what was important.
    And [my mother] Tamar the same, with these gems she remembered
    from her Catholic upbringing. You have to hold on to those things.
    Right now, I'm going through a process of rediscovering what faith is

1. For Day's early prison experiences, see her autobiography, *The Long Loneliness* (New York: Harper & Row, 1952).

about and how it sustains us. Where is the hope? Why keep trying? All I can say is there is a force within me that will never give up.

I was born into activism, you know. When I was fourteen, my brother Eric went to Vietnam. That was a huge wake up for me in terms of what was going on in the world and how it could impact on one's personal life. Thirty years ago we could all protest and have a great time and then some of us would go to jail. During the Vietnam War, my mom would drive us to New York for the marches. Of course, it meant a lot to Dorothy to know that we were anti-war, but we were in a difficult position because Eric didn't perceive what we were doing as supportive. It was a good experience for me to feel both sides, though, to see how we're all victimized. And still today, with the young people in Iraq, doing that horrible work—if you want to call it work and then their families waiting back home. But protest today is certainly not a pretty picture, with all this corralling and "free speech zones." The information we're getting is much more controlled, and they keep the wars from being in our faces the way Vietnam was.

I think we're aware that our government is doing wrong, most of us, anyway. But we don't –or feel we can't—do anything about it. Millions of people all over the world protested before the Iraq War started and it still happened! Where is Congress? Where's the media? Have we ever had this level of connivance in reporting?

We should be filling the streets, protesting the dreadful things that are being done with our tax dollars and supposedly in our name. I'm grateful and proud that I had the experience of prison. It helped form me as a person, and I know now that I had the courage to stand up to this very scary authority and that I could survive it. So let's fill the streets! Let's fill the jails!

8

Challenge and Change

The narrators in this chapter all speak of challenges and the changes these challenges wrought in their lives. Brian and Liza Apper found a ministry to the police through their peacework, Marian Mollin a life in academe. Father Larry Morlan finds that, for him, God appears to write in crooked lines. Frank Cordaro, for years a priest, has weathered many a storm. Scott Albrecht and Mike Sprong learned valuable lessons about themselves while in prison. Stephen Vincent Kobasa responded to a challenge that resulted in his leaving his life as a high school English teacher.

Liza and Bryan Apper

Liza and Bryan Apper and their children are a Catholic Worker family in Fresno who learned at the LA Catholic Worker, then moved to their

own ministry, which now includes serving both prisoners and those who guard them. Liza begins her interview by describing how she was changed after her first arrest, at the Seal Beach Naval Weapons Station.

Liza and Bryan Apper, 2004.

Liza: The scariest part about going to jail the first time wasn't the jail part; it was knowing that my life would be different from then on. You cross a cultural divide and you can't go back, because you become a part of society that had been closed off to you. We were with the marginalized, not just talking about them.

Sometimes the correctional officers try to act like we're really not one of "those people." But we always made a really big effort to be with the other inmates; I'm not arrogant enough to think that we *are* the same as the people we go to jail with, but I try to enter into their reality. So that's one reason we don't cite out on bail—so that we can be the eyes and ears of people who are voiceless.

Like when I was in jail that first time, I was shocked that the toilet was in the middle of the [cell]. The detectives at the booking desk would just look right in at us women. So I stood directly in their line of vision and looked straight back at them, and they turned around. Ashamed, maybe. Often, though, we were the ones ministered to. Most of the time, in fact.

Bryan: I remember being squeezed into this absolutely filthy pen at Inglewood with about a hundred people, almost all African-Americans. They had absolutely no trouble understanding why we protest. In the poor communities around the world, the bomb has already gone off. That's a stark contrast from some of our fellow-travelers in the LA Catholic Worker who had spouses or friends working in the war industry. Their sympathy was all for the engineers with their big salaries. We were even banned from a parish once, not allowed to talk about what was going on in our own back yard.

Liza: We always took our children to demonstrations. Bundled them up and had doughnuts and big thermoses of hot chocolate. Every Friday for a couple of years, we'd pile them into the car and leaflet at the Rockwell Plant. Employees would say "Aren't you concerned for your children out here?"

We'd tell them, "We think the weapons you're making endanger our children far more than a morning vigil does." We were arrested there only once and that was because we went into the plant. They tried to cite us out, but we refused, and the detective said, "Well, then, your ass is going to County. Do you know how people are in County? Mother rapers!" (I think he meant rapists.)

But we've never had any trouble with inmates at all, even at County. It's the correctional staff that has been difficult and uh . . .

fearsome. We had one in Orange Country who was like an Ida Lu-
pino character in a prison movie. Everybody was afraid of her. And it
was weird. I heard her get a call from her family, and she was talking
real sweetly to her children. But when she got off the phone, she was
the worst thing on wheels.

As a result of this woman and others, I really hated correctional
officers. Absolutely just hated them and was just very hardened. I'd
seen—not only in jail, but on demonstrations—officers stepping on
people's glasses, beating prisoners, those kind of things. It wasn't until we had our Catholic Worker soup line in front of the jail [here in
Fresno] that my attitude changed.

We started with coffee and donuts. We know what it's like to be
bumped out of jail at 2:00 in the morning, with no resources, but we
couldn't go down there then, so the second greatest time they release
people is between 7:00 and 9:30 at night, and that became our target
time. A couple of days a week, at first somewhat randomly.

We served not only people visiting prisoners or getting out of
jail but homeless people, too, and one day this fellow named Clifton
came, with his little shopping cart. He was about eighty years old.
Looked like you'd go "Whoosh!" and he'd just fall over. He said to
us, "I need to know when you're going to be out here."

"Well, Clifton, what days are good for you?"

He said Tuesday and Thursday, so that's what we do now. Now
Clifton had been the CEO of Community Hospital in Fresno but had
left his job in the seventies and spent about thirty years on the street.
Alcoholism. He died a couple of years ago in the hospital which he'd
supervised. Wasn't that ironic?

Anyway, we discovered that everyone needed something more
substantial than coffee and donuts so we began serving soup. That's
when the sheriffs got nervous. Very nervous.

I got nervous, too, because I didn't want to deal with them.
[Laughs.] They thought their jail stretched out to the curb. Now in
Fresno, it's legal to give things away on the sidewalk, but the sheriff
would harass us until we started working with the city about it, and
it was eventually okay.

Well, one night, this lieutenant came out, like he usually did, for
a coffee and a little conversation. Then he took us over to the car and
in the trunk was a twenty-five pound bag of pinto beans. "Ma'am,
could you use this in your soup?"

Then a month later a man came to our line who was being very verbally violent. This same lieutenant came out with two of his men, and he says to me, "This is an arrest situation now. But I won't do it if you don't want me to. It's your call."

I said to myself, "Wait a minute! Twenty-five years of civil disobedience and no one has ever told me, 'It's your call.'" I told him we'd like to take care of the man ourselves, and we did; we got him calmed down. About six months later, that same officer tried to take his life. One of his fellow officers asked me to write him a letter.

Well, I didn't know what to say so I kept putting it off and putting it off, but finally I did. I talked about those two incidents, and how he had respected our work and us and how he was there for us and we wanted to be there for him. A bit later he showed up on our soup line with clothes and blankets.

"Can I see you once a week, ma'am? To talk about God?"

I said, "Sure." Then I thought, "Oh my God, what did I do? A correctional officer and a Catholic Worker. What do we have in common?"

So that's how it started. It led to a real change in him. And in me. Inside the jail, things started to open up, too. And *we* started to open up. God showed me through that experience that the Body of Christ includes everybody, not just the ones we think belong there. That officer was as poor and bereft as any homeless person.

One thing led to another, and now I've taken training to be a volunteer sheriff's chaplain, working with officers. It's interesting to see that their belief system is as varied as anybody else's.

Even before I started inside the prison, Bryan started a group [that goes inside], called Matthew 25. They're Catholics, all volunteers working out of the Cathedral, and they visit prisoners and also do Eucharistic services. It's big now, over a hundred people.

Bryan: Liza works with the guards, and we do individual visits with inmates. We make priests available to hear confessions, and we supply Bibles in English and Spanish, rosaries, rosary pamphlets, and daily prayer books in English and Spanish if people want them.

Before this, the Christian ministry in the jail was mostly evangelical, and some of them were openly anti-Catholic. Now the jail is strictly enforcing its policy of respect for all faiths. Like if I'm doing a Bible study in a high-security pod, where they're not able to go out for services, I don't identify it as Catholic ministry. We're just available for anyone's needs. Our services are one hundred percent bilingual, even the songs, so that helps to break down some of the racial barriers.

Liza: Not that there aren't problems. Some of the officers themselves talk about racism in the department and racism between the officers and the prisoners. But they trust me, and it fits into my life in pursuing justice, because one of the most unjustly treated groups is police officers.

They have a seventy percent divorce rate. They have domestic violence issues. High suicide rate. If they seek help from a staff psychologist, it goes in their file, and a lot of them can't afford to go outside the department for help. If they go to a chaplain, sometimes the information gets out, so there's a really high level of mistrust.

I remember a speaker bashing the police at a Livermore demonstration three or four years ago. He was saying the police represented George Bush and just went on and on. Afterwards I went up to him: "You know, you don't know what any of those officers are thinking. We may have an officer here who's in total sympathy with us. All you did was create a divide, and you've blocked any chance of conversion." Before I'd left for Livermore that day, one of the men in the Fresno Sheriff's department told me he'd be praying for me, because I was "doing God's work."

Marian Mollin

Marian Mollin grew up in the suburbs of New York, the daughter of affluent and educated Jewish parents. Idealistic even as a youngster, she was drawn to activism after graduating from Cornell. She lived a full-time resistance life for ten years, subsisting on odd jobs and frequently being arrested. A re-examination of her life sent her to graduate school in 1992. She wrote a dissertation on women activists during the Vietnam era and then joined the faculty at Virginia Tech.[1] Her *Radical Pacifism in Modern America* provides the peace movement with important historical context.[2]

1. Marian Mollin, "Actions Louder than Words: Gender and Political Activism in the American Radical Pacifist Movement, 1942–1972" (University of Massachusetts–Amherst, 2000).

2. Mollin, *Radical Pacifism in Modern America: Egalitarianism and Protest* (Philadelphia: University of Pennsylvania Press, 2006).

Marian: In April of '83, I moved to Minneapolis and right away I started organizing for the Honeywell Project. They had this huge demonstration and hundreds of people were arrested, so that was my first real arrest. That fall, we blockaded the main corporate offices and shut down Honeywell for the day, and at that one, the police chief arrested his own wife!

Actually the first time I was arrested at Honeywell, we were acquitted by a jury. Pretty amazing! We didn't use a technical defense, just moral suasion. The second time, though, I was found guilty and spent forty-eight hours in jail. What I remember most about that first time in jail was being really lonely because I was kept in isolation the whole time. And yet with a complete lack of privacy! No bars on the door, but people were always looking in this glass window and could see me on the toilet and lying on my bed.

I also remember feeling really nervous the first time I went into a courtroom. I'm very soft-spoken, usually, but I discovered, over time, that the courtroom was the one place where I could speak out clearly. It felt like an acceptable venue for my outrage.

After I came back East after Honeywell, I started getting arrested a lot more. Continued going to the Pentagon with the Atlantic Life Community. I was raised Jewish, very secular Jewish, but there was something about how the Catholic radicals practiced their nonviolence that I found really appealing. They seemed so centered and so totally committed to nonviolence. I had the sense that they wouldn't freak out in a crisis, that you could count on them to act in certain ways. So solid. And they'd been doing it for years!

Marian's longest time in jail was thirty days in Massachusetts for crossing the line at a company that made missile parts.

Marian: I knew they'd only let you keep the clothes you wore in, so I put on like four pairs of underwear and multiple shirts and socks. I was nervous but also kind of excited because at that point I considered myself in training to do a Plowshares action, and I knew I needed to do some jail time to see if I could do it. And also to prove that I was committed.

That thirty days was an okay time, like a retreat time in many ways. Actually what made it okay was my extra underwear! One of the first women I met was a prostitute who'd just been picked up for probation violation. She had only what she was wearing, so I gave her some of my underwear, and she became my best buddy.

A lot of the women were doing what was known as "fine time," like me, which was paying off your fine at the rate of $2.50 or $3.00 a day. Unlike me, who just had a little fine, some had $500 fines, and they were poor and couldn't pay, so they were there forever.

Being there by choice made it a lot easier for me to hold onto my sense of inner dignity, no matter what guard was yelling at me. See, being in prison for me was an act of agency, whereas for the other women there, it was the exact opposite.

I continued to live as an activist for ten years. I was still preparing to do something bigger and was actually in a process to do a Plowshares action. But I didn't go through with it. One weekend, one of the people took me aside and told me that I wasn't Christian enough.

Oh! I was really insulted at the time! Maybe he was afraid that if something really terrible happened, and I had to spend years and years in jail, I wouldn't have the spiritual fortitude to do it. Thinking about it now, though, I think he was trying to say that I wasn't ready—that I was doing it for the wrong reasons. And in retrospect, I *was* wanting to do it for the wrong reasons. I wanted to earn a credential, to show my commitment. That isn't the right reason to do a Plowshares action.

Ro: You've probably heard Rachelle Linner's remark, that doing a Plowshares action gives you a plenary indulgence. (That's an old Catholic word for getting enough grace to guarantee heaven.) The "big thing"! You get all the grace you ever need if you do a Plowshares. The metaphor also speaks to elite or hierarchical thinking.

Marian: Oh, it's very hierarchical. I wanted to be in the inner circle of this community where the way you get respect is to get arrested. I wanted to show that I was just as worthy as anybody else. In retrospect I'm glad he said that, but at the time I sure wasn't.

Oh! Let me tell you about my favorite arrest! I shouted down the first George Bush. And he heard me! It was right after the first Gulf War. Bush was speaking at the Yale graduation, and a group of us got tickets. My friend Vincent Kay and I got all dressed up. I had a banner pinned under my skirt, like a slip, and at a certain point, I whipped it out, and we started yelling at him.

We were close enough to the front that he actually stopped. The Secret Service guys quickly whisked me away, of course. Carried me so I couldn't walk. All these parents were yelling, "Why don't you drop her?" But guess what!? The police officer didn't come to court so the case was closed.

Ro: Neat! What made you decide on graduate school?

Marian: Hmm . . . Well, when I was twenty-two I thought political work would make my life fulfilling. Later I decided it was a necessity, like breathing oxygen. Still later, I realized that yes, you need to breathe in order to live, but this breathing wasn't enough to make life fulfilling.

Also, it was really hard to do this kind of work as a single person. I was getting arrested several times a year, and each time had the potential of jail, so I couldn't hold a normal job. For ten years, I cobbled together these little jobs so I could leave if I had to, and it got really exhausting.

Marian did a lot of internal searching and external researching and decided to become a historian. She was accepted at the University of Massachusetts in 1992 and received her PhD ten years later. She told me her standard of living actually went up in grad school as her stipend raised her above the poverty level and stopped her tax resistance.

Ro: Have you ever regretted moving back into what some people call the real world?

Marian: Sometimes. I miss the community and I miss the sense of political purpose, even though I really love my work. It's so . . . so different in so many ways. Like . . . one thing that's stayed with me about the prison experience is the gut understanding I learned about power. Going to prison—even for that month—made me realize that some things are . . . are just out of my control. I had no power, no power at all. And if you haven't experienced that in yourself, I don't know if you can ever get it. Not completely.

Father Larry Morlan

I met diocesan priest Father Larry Morlan in the winter of 2005 while he was on sabbatical and living in the Chelsea Hotel in Manhattan. At the time of the interview, I felt a strong connection to him but then we lost contact for several years. I finally spoke with him by phone in April of 2012; a paraphrase from this conversation concludes his interview.

Fr. Larry: 1980 started me off. Draft registration. I can see myself still in my parents' living room on a Saturday morning. It was the first time I'd really sat down and read the Gospels, and when I came to the Sermon on the Mount, Jesus just . . . He felt real. So no draft registration for me! Now you gotta know that all my family were Republicans and when I was a kid I was hanging out campaign literature for Nixon on the doorknobs of unsuspecting Midwesterners.

Anyway, I went to my spiritual director and he introduced me to Gandhi, and it just so lined up with the Gospel, you know, that you do a good thing with complete disregard of the consequences. Because the good thing has a value and energy that resonates in the universe—in the world, in your soul. You do it because it's good and then let it go.

Then my director also had the great good sense to suggest that I go to Davenport to hear this couple speak. It's Brian [Terrell] and Betsy [Keenan], and they're talking about Dorothy Day. "Wow! Why have I not heard of this woman before?"

That year—1980—was something else! Romero was killed, the Maryknoll women were killed, Reagan came in, and nuclear war's right over our shoulder, you know. So I didn't register for the draft, along with some other men, and my parents kicked me out of the house and I lived in my car for the whole summer and did some resistance over at the Rock Island Arsenal.

Then the next fall, I'm sitting in my seminary dorm room, and I see this photograph—no article, just a photograph—with a little caption about these priests who had hammered on a nuclear weapon. I thought, "Swords into plowshares. It's perfect! If you want to organize your life around Jesus, can you imagine a better symbol to organize yourself around?" Boy, I was in trouble then! [Laughs.]

So then I'm in St. Ambrose seminary, and I become a really manic organizer. In my last year there, I organized hospitality for some Buddhists and others who were walking from California to New York for a UN Conference on Disarmament. They give this big presentation about nonviolence in the chapel, and my Bishop is there—Ed O'Rourke. Afterwards, he takes all of us seminarians out for coffee and pie, and I asked him what he thought about the presentation.

I can remember it word for word. He said, "These people don't realize they're pressing the free world to commit the greatest sin of social injustice possible, the sin of unilateral disarmament." From then on, it was a rant. He just went on and on and. He was monopolizing the whole conversation, but finally I got in: "Bishop, can you imagine Jesus pressing a button that would indiscriminately wipe out civilians?"

"Yes!" he says. "In the name of freedom, of course He would."

So. I took a year's leave of absence after I graduated, which turned out to be ten years, most of which was in jail or prison for the first of the two Plowshares actions and other resistance.

My first jail sentence was in 1983. We came out [to Washington, DC] for the Holy Innocents Retreat. People were going to do a theater piece, early in the morning when the workers were coming into the Pentagon. I was to be a spray painter, painting "Herod" and "Reagan" on the pillars at the river entrance. Phil said we were just stage hands, providing the scenery. "The actors will take the bust, so don't worry!"

Pentagon Action at the Feast of the Holy Innocents, 1983. © Tom Lewis. Elmer Mass Collection, courtesy of DePaul University Special Collections and Archives Department, Chicago, Illinois.

So the next day we did it. We got the letters on all right, even though some of them were out of order at first. Right away, though, we're busted. On the 17th of February, 1984, I go before Judge Elson, and he says something about "white-collar terrorists" and sentences Martin Holliday and me to six months.

My dad was pretty pissed off. I said he should be happy that I have a white-collar job. "White-collar terrorist!" [Laughs heartily.] Dad wasn't amused.

I was twenty-four years old, and it was the first time that I'd been in jail. The DC jail was grueling, just grueling. Hellish. I remember when the marshals finally moved me to downstate Virginia. They turned on the radio to this horrible oldies station—I mean like oldie, oldie, oldie, oldies. And I hear "What a Difference a Day Makes!" Here I'm handcuffed, with shackles on my ankles and around my waist, and I'm just shaking with laughter! Because the DC jail had been just a dungeon! The worst prison, though, was after the Silo Plowshares [in 1986]. I was at Marion for four years, and at that time it was under twenty-four-hour lockdown every day.

Ro: Wasn't it on the Amnesty [International] list for denial of human rights?

Fr. Larry: It was. Human rights groups said the lockdown was an excuse to do an experiment. Of course, the BOP said it wasn't, that it was because of a riot when guards were killed. Well it *was* an experiment! Trying out all these high-tech things that are now in place, not only in prisons but in county and state jails because [the methods] have all filtered down. Marion was a Level Six prison—the only one at that time—and now most federal prisons are run along those same standards and so are the county jails, which at least used to be more friendly.

I made friends during those years that I still correspond with. And the first priest chaplain there was wonderful towards me. He kinda broke the rules so I could help him with the liturgy. Most of all, he gave me access to the Blessed Sacrament, so that I could receive it every day, which was really extraordinary.

Then Frank Cordaro came and he was still in the priesthood at the time. The chaplain stashed a bottle of wine in the guard's office, and we'd get a little dixie cup of wine every day and Eucharistic bread so Frank would say Mass after the ten o'clock count every night. Those were really power Eucharists.

All this would completely be impossible today, I'm sure. Even then, it was very much underground. But I remember one of the guards saying to Frank, "So you're hitting the bottle again, Father?" So they knew. The irony of this . . . When Father McSorley was captured by the Japanese, they always provided him with enough wine to say the Eucharist.[3] In a land that didn't know Christianity, our priests got more respect than the priests captured in our own system.

Phil Berrigan had visited my parish in Rock Island during his last Lent and he gave me his, "Let's you and I take a little walk, buddy!" That's what started both of my Plowshares, so be scared if that happens because you know you're going to get hit. He was already suffering from the . . . the fuckin' lung cancer that killed him.

Oh, dear! Excuse me for my language. I still use that word way too much, from all those years in prison! But that brings back another funny story! After I got home from my first jail stint, I'm eating my first supper with my folks, and I say to Mom, "Could you pass the fuckin' mashed potatoes?" My dad went like "Wha' . . .?" But my mom just hooted. [Laughter.] I was dreadful! But that's all you hear in jail.

Oh, my mom . . . During that long sentence for my first Plowshares, my mom was diagnosed with breast cancer, which she eventually died of. But that initial diagnosis while I was in prison, those were some of the worst times, the darkest times. When my mom was . . . it was . . . It was hard to pray, and it was hard to keep going. I felt so bad that I couldn't be there for her. [Larry falters and I turn the tape off. Later he signals me to turn it back on.] When she was better for awhile, she was able to visit me and she asked what she could bring.

"Mom, you can't bring me anything in. It's against the law."

"Oh, come on! If you could have one thing, what would it be?"

And I told her what I would most love would be some egg foo yung. So my mom and sister get some egg foo yung and wrap it up in a big baggie. She . . . she put it in the part of her bra where her breast was before they cut it off. And she smuggled it in! Somehow I got it from her and a friend of mine took it back to my cubicle. I will never ever forget that meal! [Long silence.]

3. Fr. Richard McSorley, SJ, (1914–2002) was an outspoken and respected advocate for peace and civil rights who had been imprisoned by the Japanese during World War II. A friend and confidant of the Kennedy family, he founded two Catholic Worker houses in Washington, DC, and also the Georgetown University Center for Peace Studies. His statement, "It's a sin to build a nuclear weapon," was widely publicized; online: www.johndear.org/articles/death.html.

Ro: Was she still alive when you finished that long sentence?

Fr. Larry: Yes, I got out in '90 and she died in '93. I was working in a parish then—still not yet ordained—and they let me take a leave of absence, so I could be with her and nurse her and that was just incredibly powerful. I was able to keep her out of the hospital and she died at home, so I was able to give back to her something that she gave to me.

[Tape off again for a short, private conversation.] I was ordained by Bishop Myers in 1995 and three years later I did my second Plowshares action, at Andrews Air Force Base (AFB).

Gods of Metal Plowshares: Sister Ardeth Platte, Kathy Boylan, Father Larry Morlan, Sister Carol Gilbert, Father Frank Cordaro, 1998. © National Catholic Reporter.

I remember that we used to have prison visitors at Marion. One guy was always probing, always asking me questions. I told him one time, "You know, I think my purpose here is to be helpless." That's very Gandhian, I suppose, now that I hear myself saying it out loud again. It's a lot like what Dostoevsky has Father Zossima say: "Fall prostrate unto the earth and kiss it." It doesn't make any sense. It's complete absurdity. But it kind of sums up the whole thing—that prostration of loving the Word and loving the world, loving its dust and its substance. That helplessness has always seemed to be the posture of resistance at its very best.

When I caught up with Larry seven years later, he told me that after the Chelsea Hotel stay, he and a friend started Casa Romero, a house of hospitality for young Latino men who were thinking about the priesthood. Dan Berrigan gave the homily at the Mass for the blessing of the house. Although he had a spiritually nurturing relationship with a community of cloistered Dominican sisters in the South Bronx where the house was located, finances were always precarious, with much begging and dumpstering, and eventually Larry returned to the Midwest.

He served in Peoria parishes for some years until his bishop finally told him, he "didn't fit into the diocese." Now he said he's "waiting permission to make the next move, which is to explore joining a religious community." Just before we concluded the conversation, Larry said, "I'm lonely. It's . . . it's much worse than I can say, worse than anything I went through in prison. Everything seems to be uncertain, to be like . . . like dust. But what I *am* certain about is the Cross and being a disciple and priest of Christ Jesus."

Frank Cordaro

In his thirty-plus years as a resister, Frank Cordaro, a Catholic Worker from Des Moines, has crossed many a line and been imprisoned for ac-

tions in DC and in the Midwest, including a Plowshares action in 1988. I interviewed him first in 1989 and then again in 2005, and this chapter combines words from those two meetings.[4] Frank was ordained a diocesan priest in 1985 and resigned in 2004. He told me he misses the priesthood but not "the inner conflict that I put myself in and the heartache that it gave me."

Frank Cordaro arrested at an anti-NATO protest. Obama campaign headquarters, Chicago, May 14, 2012. © David Goodner.

4. Portions of this interview are included in a different form in *Voices*, 370–79.

Frank: I was a real Neanderthal when I was a kid. Would have easily fought in Vietnam. See, there are basically two types of deviants in high school, the juvenile delinquents which everyone can pick out—the guys who smoke and leave school—and the ones who beat the system. They're the officers in all the clubs, so they run the school and can get out of all the classes they want. That's what I was, a jock and a play-the-system kind of guy. With my Dad being the Athletic Director, it wasn't hard. Same in college, from 1969 to 1973. Still a jock and president of my fraternity. However, I was also going to daily Mass.

Ro: What would you have been, Frank, if your Dad hadn't passed away?

Frank: I . . . I don't think that I would have gotten into this stuff at all. Probably been a coach, a great coach, like my Dad. My Dad was the most important person in my life, and he died on Easter Sunday morning of my senior year. A great man. But his dying did more for our family then anything he ever did in life. Because we came together much closer, and my mother just blossomed into a full human being. I've been gifted with lots of breaks and lots of love and attention, but my real strength comes from my family.

While in college and later in seminary, I was five years as a charismatic, which is very vital. I read those Gospels as stories and let them speak to me. Then there was a summer I spent in the Bronx when I finally began to question the Cold Warrior mentalities I'd grown up with. One thing I learned in the Bronx is that I ain't Black, and there ain't nothing I can do about it. I'm Catholic, I'm middle class, I'm educated, I'm from the Midwest, and I'm a white male. Where can I stand with some integrity and be a Gospel person with all those things going against me?

Well, I found that place in the Catholic Worker. It's the only place I know of where it's possible for me to read what's going on in the culture and also address it through an encounter with the homeless. They're your avenue, your authenticity.

It's difficult for Americans to see the truth. In so many ways and on so many levels. We're so dummied up with the nationalistic jingo and mythologies of war and fear, so crazed in this consumption society. Our ignorance lends itself to great arrogance, as we are demonstrating globally. So the Catholic Worker world, with its works of mercy, is a reality check. It helps us get in touch with the truth.

See, Catholic Workers address the issues of society in a personalist way. The works of mercy are our work: feeding the hungry, clothing the naked, sheltering the homeless. Another work of mercy is visiting the prisoner. You can't visit prisoners any better than being one of them and you do that by being arrested for resisting the war machine.

After several false starts, Frank joined the priesthood, becoming a diocesan priest and still trying to live a Catholic Worker life in some way. From 1985 to 2004, he was pulled constantly between pastoral and resistance work. This narrative highlights parts of his long resistance story.

Frank: See, unlike most of the other priests who did resistance, I was a resister first, and then came into the priesthood. My first arrest was a blood spilling on the pillars of the Pentagon in '77. First time I ever saw the Jonah House people, and those folks were a natural for me. I was going to base my life on the Scriptures, and these guys seemed to be living it in full measure—no holds barred. I knew that was what I wanted to do with my life.

But this first blood spilling . . . I had lots of second thoughts, but there I was at the Pentagon, and I did it. Screaming out, "The Pentagon is the temple of death!" The sound would reverberate up those large pillars. Then out of nowhere comes these storm troopers, maybe seventy strong. Blue jumper suits. Large clubs. Complete helmets. These two Black guys take me to a bus and we're still screaming, but as soon as we're settled, these guys take their helmets off and sit down. "We're real glad you guys keep comin' here because these people are nuts. And they *will* use nuclear weapons."

At the trial, I'm just out of seminary, so I give this theologically sound little talk, and then the judge says, "Thirty days!" I was shocked! Most people had just been getting time served. So right away I learned that there's no telling what might happen when you stand before a judge. If you're going to do the crime, be prepared to do the time.

The whole thing [at the DC jail] was just an eye-opener in so many ways! A completely African-American world. I remember seeing a guy who was dressed up like a woman. He tied his shirt around his waist in a little knot so that he showed his midriff. He walked with slippers and wore a red scarf, and his hair looked feminine. Frankly, I thought he *was* a woman. We were treated well by the Black inmates, though. After two wars, many of them were familiar with us demonstrators.

I've done lots of stuff over the years but being in Des Moines, and so close to the SAC [Strategic Arms Command] base, that's sort of been my focus. SAC is the main command post for nuclear war, where all the planning takes place, the total workbook on how to go to nuclear war at any given moment, at any given time, at any given level. These plans include first strike preemptive nuclear war and are completely contrary to the conditions that the bishops put forth for the moral acceptability of deterrence.[5] The first time we went onto the base, we said a rosary—the whole fifteen decades—and no one arrested us. But we've done lots of things since then.

One time . . . God, when was it? In December of 1980, we edited the billboard in front of the SAC base. Their motto was "Peace is our Profession." A hundred of us showed up for a prayer service, and then ten of us crossed out the word "peace" and put the word "war" in its place and doused the sign with blood. All the TV channels were there, and eventually I did six months in Leavenworth for that sign.

Ro: Getting up to edit that big billboard . . . I'd say you were part of the theatrical arm of the resistance movement.

Frank: Well, it's good theater and it's also good liturgy. A message is much more palatable if it's delivered in an exciting and inviting way.

Ro: But what about the "ashes at the White House" story? That was theatrical but I'm not so sure about the message. Can you tell that story again?

---

5. SAC, US Space Command, and US Cyber Command have since been merged into USSTRATCOM (United States Strategic Command), a unified command which controls space weaponry, defensive computer network operations, and nuclear weapons. It also provides a host of capabilities to support the other combatant commands, including strategic warning; integrated missile defense; global command, control, communications, computers, intelligence, surveillance, and reconnaissance (C4ISR); and measures to combat weapons of mass destruction. Online: www.stratcom.mil/history/.

Billboard at SAC base, Offut, Nebraska, December, 1980. © Des
Moines Catholic Worker.

Frank: Well . . . sure. But it turned out to be more comedy theater, I guess.
Let's see. [Pause.] It's November 1979. I'm not a priest yet. Jimmy
Carter's pushing the SALT II treaty, and I somehow get an invitation
to the White House! I'd already had that blood spilling and I'd been
arrested at Rocky Flats, but I sent the White House my Social Security
number and got a security clearance, much to my surprise. Begged the
money and flew out and spent the night before at Jonah House with
Liz McAlister and Phil Berrigan, trying to figure out what I should do.
We settled on ashes, so I got some out of their fireplace, put them in
a plastic bag, tucked it down inside my pants, and went on down to
the White House.

That's quite a trip from Baltimore into DC. Right through some
of the meanest neighborhoods in the world. And then within a few
blocks of the White House, it all turns into an open museum. Everything's clean and white marble monuments.

I was the first person in my family ever to be invited to the White
House, and I'm going to try to challenge the president. With these
ashes in my pants. So I'm tense as a cat while we're waiting in the
basement of the White House. (It isn't a basement at all but a major
mansion in itself. One room had all these gold plates.)

Finally, they take us upstairs and I jockey a good seat—third row
center aisle, maybe fifteen feet away from the president's podium. The

first guy who speaks is Ziggy [Zbigniew] Brzezinski and he goes on for about forty-five minutes about why they need the SALT II treaty. Mooning would have been an appropriate gesture for the baloney that was coming from him, but of course you don't moon the national security chief.

Then some other guy gets up, a Texan with a drawl. Former chief of staff. Military person, but in a tie and suit. Goes on and on about not trusting the Russians. Finally, after this warm-up, I hear "Ladies and gentlemen, the President of the United States!"

At this point, there's all these bleeps and intensive TV lights. See, any time the president goes up public, all three major networks cover. The intensity of the media around this man is amazing. Then we're all clapping including me, and after that, everything kind of goes into slow motion.

I'm so nervous that I . . . "Hey! This is the White House. I'm with the President of the United States. Maybe he's right, and I'm wrong." Then I go into what I call willful doing. "I'm an actor. This is a play. The president has a role, up on the podium, and I've got a role, so we'll play it out."

I unbutton my pants, 'cause the ashes are underneath, you know. And then everyone sits down and I hit the center aisle. I grab the ashes out of my pants and take a step towards the podium. From the back, you'd see a man who's hunched down and taking a step in front of the president, so it looks like he's going to pull out a weapon.

Now I'm an Italian-American, but this was nine days into the Iranian crisis, and if you look real quick, I could look like an Iranian. So I took that step towards the president, and I'm sure everyone's heart just fell out of their chests. If you wanted to, you could have picked them up and put them in baskets. I immediately turned around 'cause I didn't want to personally confront the president, but just to stand in front of him.

Then a number of things happened simultaneously. The crowd, who just a moment ago was holding their breath, saw that I was an opportunist to the full extent and started to boo me. All these people were dressed to the hilt, and trying to act so suave and debonair. But instead it sounded like a baseball game: "Sit down, ya' bum!"

My voice is kind of high normally, but I'm nervous, so it's even higher. [In a high-pitched tone.] "Friends! SALT II is a lie, and Jimmy Carter's lying to us. These ashes represent the dead from the first strike." And I pull the ashes out. Now they've been in my pants all morning, so they've condensed with the moisture, and they come out like clumps of clay, you know. And I'm looking at them [hits himself on the head]. Boing, boing! These ashes represent . . ." To add injury to insult, my pants start to come down and everyone starts to laugh at me. Then, quick as can be, this Secret Service guy comes and grabs my arm. "There, there young man. You're all right. Just come on out here." Like I was some kind of loony.

Of course, no one heard me. No one heard a word I said, but the TV picked it all up and later a woman from Iowa got up very politely and said, "Mr. President, I'm like that young man from Iowa who was dragged out of here. No one in the peace movement can support a treaty that allows for first-strike weapons." So the media people got my name and statement from her.

That night it made all three major networks. Walter Cronkite mentioned my name, and it was all on the front pages . . . a front page picture in the *Washington Post,* the *New York Times*, and papers all over the country. The prophet Isaiah never got that kind of exposure.

But they didn't even press charges. First, the secret police wanted to know if I was crazy. Secondly, they wanted to know if I'd planned to do any harm to the president. But rudeness is not necessarily an illegal act, so they let me go. The last thing this Secret Service guy says was, "Well, I guess you know this means you'll never get invited to the White House again."

Ro: No matter how many times I hear it, this is still an amazing story![6] But I see it as still part of the same symbols—always blood or ashes, or blood *and* ashes.

Frank: Well, I think the primary symbols of resistance are the risks the people put themselves in and the suffering they're doing. Blood and ashes is part of what it's all about. So is crossing lines. That's what I get into—crossing lines—and that's what we do all the time at SAC. You couldn't get a more abstract and pristine civil disobedient act. Draw a line and put your body across it. That's the statement. No blood. No ashes. No property destruction.

It's orchestrated. One judge said he was "tired of the charade. It's not just you protestors; it's the SAC people, too. You make it look like a Christmas holiday." And it *is* joyful! I'm not saying it's the only

6. This White House story is favorite open mic entertainment at Catholic Worker gatherings.

way to do things, but why not make it as life affirming as you can? Why not make it an entry for people to get into civil disobedience?

Ro: Frank, how do these more measured actions fit with the more theatrical ones of your youth? Or maybe I could better ask how your ego— or maybe your self-righteousness—fits in with your resistance story?

Frank: Well, my ego and self-righteousness and my white male privileged status is a cultural problem. It's not unique to Catholic Workers or to resisters. Any male in this culture has to live through this shit, layer after layer. And oftentimes we don't do it well. Growing older and more mature, seeing life in much more complex grays, dealing with my own mortality and my own string of failures in life—the things that come to everybody—all this has helped me a lot.

That being said, as a Catholic Worker and a resister, when I was younger, I was much more sure of my positions, saw things more clearly in black and white. But most of that bravado-ism was a cover for a young person who hadn't walked the walk enough to claim it for himself. I knew it was the right way, but until you actually live in this skin and do it for awhile, even if it *is* the right way, you can't claim it as your own. It'll ring tinny.

In time, you eventually become comfortable with it and won't have to prove it to anybody. The day you stop having to prove anything to anybody is the day you've proven it to yourself. Then you really *are* the person you say you are. Now that I'm in my fifties, the real task is to make sure the person inside me is really the same person I profess to be outside. And that's an issue that all males are going to go through in this culture, when they hit a certain age.

Ro: I think we all need to go through this, male and female. Trying to make my insides and outsides match is kind of the project of my life these days.

Frank: Well, It's my project, too. It wasn't when I was younger. My project then was to live the Way and to knock down anyone who was trying to stop me from doing it, especially authority figures. I don't need to do that anymore. For a number of years, I considered myself a student of the Catholic Worker movement and the Berrigan brothers. Well, I'm not a student anymore, I'm a practitioner.

This is who I am. It's a sobering thing, the older you get. You know, I haven't paid taxes and Social Security since college. I don't have any kind of retirement plan. Now, that's all romantic when you're in your twenties and your thirties, but now I'm in my fifties, and there's a certain concreteness to that decision. It really is a statement of faith to say, "Well, I'm going to live differently and trust that what I'll need will be there when I need it. The Catholic Worker movement is my social security plan."

Ro: I see. As a Catholic Worker, you also have the time and the support to do resistance. Other people may not have either. But when you were a priest, you had some problems with your parish obligations, didn't you?

Frank: Well, that was part of my eighteen-year experiment: I wanted to wed a resistance lifestyle to the priesthood. Phil and Liz raised a family doing resistance, and that's a lot harder than being a priest. So I'm thinking that, as priests, we should be able to come up with models of priestly ministry that incorporate resistance.

As the years went on, it became clear that when I was in jail, I really couldn't pastor. So I kept fostering the idea of a team ministry, yoking myself with another priest, taking on a full-time pastoral position together. And it would have worked; I'm sure of it. When I presented this to the diocese, it became clear they didn't want that to happen. [Laughs wryly.]

That was when I resigned my position as a pastor of the parishes in southeast Warren County, and went and did a Plowshares action. I left without permission to do the Gods of Metal Plowshares action at Andrews Air Force Base in Maryland, in May 1998.

Kathy Boylan and Fr. Frank Cordaro pouring blood on a B-52, Andrews AFB, 1998. © National Catholic Reporter.

But I came back to the diocese, after serving six months at Yankton [Prison Camp] and renegotiated with two different bishops to stay. Lasted until 2004 when I resigned for reasons which had nothing to do with the bishop or my ongoing problems with the institutional church.

Living a resistance life as a priest is hard, but it's hard for everyone, so you've really got to do it in community. Community fits the pattern of faith people; the New Testament is written for communities. Even to have the courage to be prophetic, you can't be a loner, even though there are a few oddballs who will do it on their own, and God bless them. This lifestyle, which I believe is apostolic at its best, has got to be communal.

Ro: What do you tell people when they remind you that what you do isn't effective?

Frank: Being effective isn't my first priority. It might be my third or fourth priority, but being faithful is my first priority. People would say, "You could do so much more for the peace movement on the outside." Which when I was a priest I knew was not true! Because when I was on the outside, ninety percent of my time was pastoring people. Which is great work, and I'm not complaining. But I certainly wasn't pushing the peace stuff.

Yet when I was in jail, there was a platform. People were listening. I'd write letters and hundreds of people would get these letters. There would be a certain *consciousness* that I was in jail, and literally, I would reach more human beings with my peace message in jail than I did when I was just being a priest in a parish.

So that never was a convincing argument for me. Now if I was working full-time peace stuff, going around giving talks and stuff like that, there might have been an argument for that. But it didn't apply to me.

Ro: But isn't all that mostly preaching to the choir?

Frank: Sure. The converted are always my first audience. The whole of the New Testament was written for the converted, you know. It was meant to sustain those who already believed in Jesus but needed to be encouraged and instructed on what believing in Jesus was all about. But true conversions don't happen with a good sermon or speech, they happen person to person by the witness of one person's life to another person's life. So it's the being locked up itself that speaks the loudest.

We just . . . I don't have all the answers. I'm going to try to be in the right place so I can follow the people with the right answers, but I don't have a silver bullet that's going to turn this thing around. It ain't gonna come from me. Or anybody who looks like me. The best thing we can do is create the environment for those who are out of the loop because of *our* wealth and ill-got privilege. The best we can do is create the ground for our kind to be receptive when the message comes from the bottom up. That's the classical place where Gospels come: the bottom up. That's where the true Jesus energy comes from. The best we can do from the top is to create the space so we can hear it.

When I act and go to jail for it, I act as a broken person. I also know that a significant amount of the violence that I'm addressing on the outside is also in me. So it's a catharsis thing, an exorcism. It's trying to get rid of the violence in you as you address the violence on the outside. Our efforts at this point are puny. Pathetic. And we make mistakes. Lots of them. But we have to keep trying. Keep trying.

Scott Albrecht

I interviewed Scott Albrecht in May of 2007 at the Euro Catholic Worker gathering in Dulmen, Germany. An American, Scott lives on Lynsters Farm, a Catholic Worker community not far from London. He and his family and their community provide hospitality and care to immigrants, many of them seeking asylum from repressive regimes. His prison story could be anyone's, living anywhere.

Scott: I used to work with nuclear weapons, and I trained to be a marksman with the US Army. Basically I was [living] the doctrine of mutually assured destruction—MAD—until I was taught the doctrine of loving one's enemies. At one point in my life, I was willing to kill people. I never did, but my willingness to work for peace should be as strong as my former willingness to work on behalf of the government.

So I think of my actions for peace now as a form of penance. You see, I became a Christian while I was in the military. When I told the base chaplain I wanted to be a CO, he told me it was okay to fight in order to protect America from the "godless Russians," and that David and Saul fought wars in the Old Testament. So I [quoted Jesus] to him: "Formerly, it was an eye for an eye, a tooth for a tooth, but I tell you to love your enemies." I said I was now a Christian and couldn't kill.

I had absolutely no support from other Christians, and I was nineteen, and I . . . I wasn't very strong. I stayed in the army. First they said they'd put me in Leavenworth, but instead they just took away my security clearance for working with nuclear bombers, and put me in the snack bar.

Ro: Well . . . better, huh? Can we fast forward to your current life?

Scott: Sure. I lived in London with my family for seven years, waiting to open a Catholic Worker house. We ended up with two, Lynster Catholic Worker Farm and Dorothy Day House, which is in the most deprived area of London. The Catholic Worker allows me to live a contextual theology, one suited to white, male, privileged people who are complicit in violence throughout the world. As an American living in England, I have a double responsibility because the English government stands shoulder-to-shoulder with the US.

During that seven year period, we did a lot of resistance. We did actions at Northwood Military Headquarters. (That's the nerve center for British involvement in Afghanistan and Iraq.) Twice we were arrested for pouring red paint on the signs at the entrance and kneeling in prayer with pictures of Iraqi children. We also went to the Ministry of Defense during the Feast of Holy Innocents, marked the building with ashes, and dug graves. We consider it one of the works of mercy, burying the dead, or remembering the dead.

Our third place was the DSEI Arms Fair.[7] We poured fifteen liters of red paint on the doors at the entrance. So the Angel of Death would pass over without anyone dying, like in the Old Testament. We didn't use blood because we couldn't find a doctor or nurse to [take it,] but Geoff Hoone, who was the Minister of Defense, had to walk through all that red paint.

Ro: I've heard that the symbol of blood doesn't "sell" as well in Europe as it does in the United States.

Scott: Well, blood is the symbol of life and it's also the symbol of death. Red can also symbolize danger. In court for a Northwood case once, we were able to cross examine two policemen. I asked the first one what red meant to him and he said, "Nothing, absolutely nothing."

---

7. DSEI stands for Defense Systems and Equipment International and it sells £6 billion worth of weapons in one week. Six billion British pounds is approximately $9.5 billion. (Added by Scott during transcript review.)

But the second policeman opened up the whole trial by saying that blood meant danger to him. "It means warning. It means someone could be dying." It looked like an accident scene where the action took place, and he was very moved by it. Nevertheless, we were found guilty. But the symbolic nature of the red paint all over the place worked really well.

People talk a lot about the difference between effective actions and symbolic actions. Most of the actions I've done are symbolic. At the DSEI Arms Fair, an effective action might have been to lock the doors so people couldn't go in. And I'm aware that even effective actions just close something down for a brief time or maybe put a plane down for a month. (I know from having worked on aircraft that you have to cannibalize from other planes to do the repairs.) But even that [kind of] action has a symbolic value, as well. Also, you have to ask how effective it is when they can just replace [a certain] plane in the fleet. But that doesn't mean I don't believe effective actions should be done.

Ro: How do police treat you when you're arrested?

Scott: The British police are really good, compared to the American police. I've been smashed down to the ground and had wrist bars and arm bars and arm locks and things like that, but on the whole . . . Well, at the last action we were threatened with pepper spray. We knelt in front of the gates at Northwood. I managed to walk through the gate before one of the soldiers inside knocked me to the ground with a rugby tackle. Then two others dragged me through the shrubs and threw me back out. Now if that had happened in America, we would've been arrested and maybe given a $5,000 fine and six months in jail. At Northwood, we weren't arrested, and that happens quite often. In the last four years, no one has been arrested at the Ministry of Defense for marking the building with ashes, even though they've called it "criminal damage" and asked us to stop. They always arrest us for red paint, though.

Ro: When you were found guilty for the paint action, you did spend some time in jail?

Scott: I did, yeah. It was only two days, but I . . . I found it difficult. But that's because—I'll be honest with you—because of the violence that had been meted out to me as a child. I'm aware of that now, but I wasn't when I went into jail. These things only come up when you're in a violent situation, I think. It had never bothered me when I was just held at a precinct station for a few hours or something.

The jail experience was hard. I didn't expect to go, and I was just wearing sandals and a tee shirt. I had to report to court at twelve, and I thought I'd just refuse to pay my fine and be finished in time to pick up my kids at 3:00. When I refused, the judge said, "You leave me no choice, Mr. Albrecht, but to put you in prison."

In prison . . . [long pause] you could smell the violence all around you. I don't know how else to say it. You could feel it in your bones, you know. The violence of the guards didn't bother me so much. I knew a lot of them were ex-military, and I kind of had a banter with them. But the other prisoners . . . When they come up right in your face and say, "You got a cigarette, mate?" Or "What are you doing here?"

I told them I did a peaceful protest. I was . . . I'm not saying everybody would be intimidated, but I was. Especially one evening. I was lying in my cell, and people were passing things back and forth outside the windows by tying strips of cloth together. They'd put maybe a pack of cigarettes or drugs or something on one end, and they'd swing it from window to window on the outside of the building.

They were trying to swing things to me, and I wouldn't swing it. I wouldn't grab the end and swing it on to the next place. Then I could hear people yelling, "Who's in cell 232?" Yelling and swearing: "I wanna know who the fuck's in 232!"

Somebody yelled, "It's the Yank!" And then I heard . . . Somebody picked up a metal rubbish bin and banged on the wall adjacent to my cell. Banging and banging and banging. And I thought, "Ah, geez, this is gonna be hard. What's gonna happen in the morning? Are they going to pour hot treacle on my face?"

Ro: Because you didn't cooperate in passing stuff along?

Scott: Yeah. I didn't want to pass on anything that might have been drugs. And I just wanted to keep to myself. Well, nothing happened to me the next morning, which was good, of course. And I received a beautiful postcard that really lightened my heart. But when I got out, I asked myself some really serious questions about my suffering, if you want to call it suffering. Why did it hurt me so much to be in for a short period of time when other people go in for long sentences and come out okay?

Through counseling, I started exploring my relationship with my father, my relationship to violence, my relationship to fear, to power, and all these issues, you know. So for me the challenge now is to be able to do it again and pay that bigger price of going to prison. I'm not going to stop because I have the pain about my childhood.

My group therapy folks said to me, "Why don't you confront your father about these things?"

And I said, "Oh, he's too old, and he'll never understand. He lived in a generation where violence was accepted. All the kids in our neighborhood got beaten up." But they kept asking what the real reason I didn't confront him was. Over and over, in this counseling session. Finally I started crying and said, "Because I'm afraid of him."

Now he's seventy years old and half my size. A little, weedy guy. He used to be a big, strong man but now he's half of what he used to be. And I'm *still* afraid of him. It's an awful thing. I'm sure I'm not alone in this, but certainly [this experience has] helped me to say that I'm not going to make my children afraid of me. I've got three sons, and I don't want them to be afraid of me. I know how long-lasting that fear will be.

Lynster Farm Catholic Worker Community, 2012. Justin, Francis, Maria and Scott Albrecht; Angela Formby, Miriam Johansson. (Missing from photo are two Albrecht children. Names of back row omitted for security purposes.) © Maria Albrecht.

Mike Sprong

In June of 2000, Bonnie Urfer of Nukewatch and Catholic Worker Mike Sprong put the ELF nuclear submarine communication system temporarily out of commission by cutting down the poles carrying the transmitter wires. This was the fifth time since 1984 that the now defunct ELF transmitter had been shut down by activists who simply walked up to the supporting poles and cut them down with handsaws.

Bonnie was sentenced to six months in prison, ordered to pay restitution of $7,492.44, and given one year supervised release. Mike was sentenced to two months imprisonment and the same amount of restitution, and supervised release.

Bonnie Urfer and Mike Sprong silence Trident, 2000. © Barb Katt.

Mike: At first, the idea of going to jail was difficult, to say the least. See, growing up, I'd spent a lot of time trying to avoid jail. Had a juvenile record, and was in lots of trouble, and knew folks who'd been to jail. But from the time I stepped into the door of the Des Moines Catholic Worker in Iowa, I knew I was home. My life could have gone either way, and I choose to see walking in that door as divine providence. Catholic Worker became my vocation and part of that vocation is resistance, which usually means jail, at least sometimes.

At the Catholic Worker, for the first time in my life, there was community, and that's what it's all about for me. To me, resistance is a natural by-product of the life of faith and community and service, so the choice to engage in nonviolent resistance also came easy, because I knew I wouldn't be alone.

The choice of going to jail was harder, because of my growing up. When I was with my mother, we lived as if life was one long series of disconnected events. I decided I didn't want to live that way, didn't want life to seem random. In a certain way, there's a discipline that comes from community and from this holistic and connected life. And

I was good clay: got into it when I was only eighteen, so I didn't have a lot of predispositions. Plus I had excellent teachers.

After Des Moines, I lived at the Community for Creative Non-violence (CCNV) in DC for a goodly amount of time and then came back to the Midwest. I traveled around to the different Catholic Worker houses and finally settled into rural South Dakota where Beth Preheim and I married and started our own Catholic Worker presence in Yankton.

There's a federal prison here, bucolic in its veneer. It was built on the campus of what was Yankton College, the first college in the Dakotas. (I guess it's a sign of the times that in the 1980s the college went bankrupt, and the Bureau of Prisons bought it up and turned it into a federal prison camp.) Yankton also has our only state hospital for people with chronic mental illness, and then there's also a state trusty facility. So Yankton, a town of 13,000 people, has 2,000 people who are either receiving long-term hospitalization or are in prison.

Our Catholic Worker house does hospitality for women and children visiting loved ones in one of those facilities. You know, prison is a stigma for so many families who come to us, and once they hear that we've done time, too, there's an affinity.

We're in a small community. I remember a social gathering in the '90s. Some people told me they worked at the prison camp, and I said, "Someday I'll be taking you up on your hospitality." Nervous laughter and then they walked away from me.

Sure enough, a couple of years later, Bonnie Urfer and I cut down the ELF poles, and I end up in Yankton and so I'm one of their charges. And they were so utterly disrespectful! Yankton's not like a real prison where they have physical barriers to keep you in line and isolate you. Without the barriers, the guards can be very petty and they often harass people. Kind of like the bully in high school.

Ro: What did you learn personally from your prison time, Mike?

Mike: One thing for sure: Any personal belongings that you can divest before doing a big action, do so. Because they'll take anything they can get their hands on. If it's a dime on the dollar, they'll take it. I owned private property and had restitution and it was tough. So I really urge folks to divest, no matter how they do it.

Ro: Do people feel complicit when they pay the restitution, say to avoid losing their car?

Mike: Well, without going into details, I've made enough compromises to know how dirty it feels, especially when you've had the courage to stand up in the court and say, "I'm not going to pay," standing on conscience. Look, if somebody pays the restitution, I certainly wouldn't condemn them. "God bless you for being able to get out there and do anything at all." The days are so dark now that all of it's good. So my standards are low.

I think ideally this is where community and connection come in, once again. Most recently, I've come to know the Benedictines who live close to our Catholic Worker house, and am mindful of how personally poor they are. As a community, they're quite wealthy, but individually, they're quite poor. And I think that's really a key—to have all the property owned in a community or in a land trust.

Basically, what you do then is take stuff that you've sort of depended on for economic security and put it in the hands of other people, asking them to steward it and trusting that they're going to let you still take advantage of it. It can work well.

Now if you give something to somebody, you're actually burdening them, so for them to take on co-responsibility with you is a great way for people to support resistance. Of course, if the system wanted to, they could come and get [the supporters] too. Subpoena them, or do whatever they want, you know? They know who's who, or they can find out very easily. So believe me, the people who take the property are in just as neck-deep as the resister.

You know, there's a trick we try to play on ourselves, and that is, if you're not perfect, you shouldn't do these sorts of things, shouldn't be involved in resistance. But that's just a trick. We're flawed and we're going to make a lot of mistakes along the way, but that's no reason not to resist. There's never a good day and never a good time and it never going to be easy. But if we wait until we're perfect and everything's perfect, it's never going to happen at all.

Before our Silence Trident action, I got things as much in order as I could and I still had problems. Beth and I had less community than we do now, and she was by herself for the whole time that I was in. It created some resentment, because some stuff wasn't getting done. I'm sitting in prison, telling her, "Come on, you've just got to work harder!"

We were wrapping up the book publishing.[8] We do a lot of classic Alinsky-style community organizing with local issues, whether it's land justice for tribal people in South Dakota or trying to limit the growth of corporate factory farms. Beth was responsible for all of it, not to mention that our house is ninety years old and out on the prairie, and we grow a lot of our own food and keep our house warm by very labor-intensive methods. Our lifestyle is . . . it's just not "convenient," so one person can't possibly do it all. But I was sometimes extremely impatient with her, and she saw me as just sitting in jail, reading and writing letters.

One should never underestimate the ability to have an inflated ego when you're in prison. Too many people are writing you from Sweden telling you how wonderful you are, so you get an unbelievable sense of entitlement, and it's easy to forget the hard time the folks at home are doing.

Ro: Other cautionary tales from that time?

Mike: Oh, yes! See, I didn't make myself vulnerable enough. My attitude with people who were in charge of me—my keepers—uh . . . Let's say there were moments when I didn't exactly shine. At Yankton, they're used to people being extremely submissive, because they've got them over a barrel with the drug treatment and possible reduction in their sentences. People really kiss ass, and it works and I think the guards maybe expect it.

I got hauled into the office for what I'd write in my letters. They did the whole thing: big light shining on me and six or seven guys asking me questions. Tried to say that I was planning to commit a crime because I was writing letters to people about resistance actions. Then they'd imply things, like that they might stash something in my locker—you know, like contraband—and then I'd really be in trouble.

They were just messing with me. I don't think they ever really would've done it, but I was paranoid enough that it got to me. And instead of just maintaining a placid position, I came back at them: "I know this person and that person in this community, and if you do that, I'll tell them what's going on here." A real tit for tat thing, instead of just smiling at them.

---

8. Mike and Beth had Rose Hill books, a Catholic Worker publishing company, from 1993 to 1999. Paul Magno at The Catholic Worker Bookstore in Washington, DC, currently handles the Rose Hill imprint.

I got on the phone to Beth as soon as I got [out of the office] and I knew they were listening. "Call Jerry Wilson and tell him what's happening here." (He's the publisher of a local magazine and a friend of mine, a peace activist.) So it was who can out-do who and of course, they're in charge.

Every time I had a visit I was strip-searched, and they always did the body cavity. (I didn't just "win the lottery" as the guys say and get a body cavity search once in a while.) And I got shook down every couple of days. That's where they search your dorm for contraband. At least once a week they were hauling me into the lieutenant's office.

And it was just attitude. Just my attitude. I should have just been quiet and let them do [this harassing]; made myself completely vulnerable and quiet. Instead, I was trying to show them how important I was.

Now this went on for about a month, and . . . I became isolated. I was too hot for the rest of the guys, and they resented our dorm getting shook down all the time. I had really taken the wrong attitude. So, yeah, I'd definitely do things differently.

First, I'd have more people to help Beth out with daily life and not underestimate how grueling it can be. I'd learn and practice a daily structure and become a more disciplined person before I went into the prison. And when confronted by those authorities, I'd take on a truly disarmed demeanor, not try to be the big shot.

I'll be back to jail sometime. These things happen in cycles. The last ten months in my life have been plaster and nails and house renovation, and that's been a real stretch for me, because I'm not a handy person. It's taught me some patience, and some sorely needed humility, too. [Laughs wryly.] But I'll be back. I don't know when or how, but I will.

My wife, Beth Preheim, is very clear. People ask why it's mostly straight, white men who are doing civil disobedience and ending up in prison, and she says that's because "privileged white males are the ones who belong in jail." It's guys like me who belong there.

Mike Sprong, 2005.

Stephen Kobasa

Stephen Vincent Kobasa has been active for years in the Atlantic Life Community. He sees his resistance as curating, naming something correctly to make the historical record more accurate. Stephen graduated from Fairfield University and attended Yale Divinity School and then the University of Chicago. For years he taught literature at Kolbe Cathedral High in Bridgeport, Connecticut. After a principled decision not to worship Caesar by displaying the US flag in his classroom, he now teaches by writing for local and national media. He continues to "confront the distorted histories" with his activism.

Stephen: Fairfield in the '6os: The pre-Vatican II structures were still largely intact. Required Mass attendance. A dress code. Curfews and bed checks. An ancient Jesuit was the floor prefect. He'd dutifully go from door to door, you know, and check that there was a body in each bed. So people would hop from bed to bed and just lie there quietly until he counted them and then sneak into a bed three rooms down. So there'd actually be maybe only six people on the floor, and he'd count forty.

    There was a kind of terrible innocence in those times. For instance, in the library, the books listed on the Index were kept in what they called "the Cage." One night, a group of "nameless students" clambered in and took all the books out and put them up on the shelves.

    By the time I graduated in '69, those ancient rules were all swept away. But there was a kind of precision in that world, so it gave you something to resist. When that was swept away, the lines of resistance were also damaged, I think.

Ro: How did that restrictive atmosphere play out in your life?

Stephen: Oh, I think it was a gift to me. Not to everyone. It was erased with such callousness, you might say. There were people who had lived under those rubrics for so long, and they weren't given any way to make the transition, so for some, it was earth-shattering. It lacked charity, as the old vocabulary had it. I mean, those things needed to be changed; they needed to be taken away. But with some . . . some compassion.

After much thought and study, Stephen decided to seek conscientious objector status instead of following the lead of most of his classmates who took refuge in the student deferment. His draft board never acted on his application.

Stephen: They just wouldn't do anything. You know, I guess that was the primary lesson. That even when you confront the system on its own terms, they're still in control. They didn't do anything, so I put my draft card in an envelope and sent it back. It was painful and frustrating to go through this whole process, but there was a grace in what I learned about my own Catholic tradition by going through it. Especially at a time when the church appeared to be largely on the side of the war makers. Also, I was no longer under any illusions about what the system would allow. The system always operates on its own sense of expediency and self-interest, never out of conscience or moral imperative.

Ro: What did your folks think about your application?

Stephen: Um . . . [Long pause.] Well, they were worried about the impact it would have on me afterwards, in terms of professional choices or, you know, reputation in certain circles. But I remember that my aunt said, "You're blood." Meaning that the relationship of blood cancelled out any other insanities that I might be guilty of.

My father was harder to read. He was a World War II veteran. He went ashore on Omaha Beach in D-Day Plus One, and he'd survived a year in Europe. He talks about it a lot, much more now than he did then. And the more I learn, the more I realize how he was marked by it. I think, though, that enough skepticism came out of his experience that he understood.

After Fairfield and Yale, Stephen spent some time with the Committee of Social Thought at the University of Chicago, an experience he said was "extraordinary." Then he learned that the academy wasn't where he needed to be.

Stephen: What I didn't know became clear; what I needed to learn still lay in wait.

Ro: Do you ever miss not going into college work?

Stephen: Um . . . [Long pause.] The fantasy, you know, tends to recur, but it's only a fantasy. In some more desperate moments, I've realized that I might have lived a life that was absolutely different. Some people go into the academy to spare themselves. Not because they're callous, but because they're frightened. Sometimes people see glimpses of the horror and just can't bear it, so they can hide themselves that way. And there *is* something to escape from! It does get unbearable sometimes. I think people get burned out in various ways, and there are other escapes than the academy, as we know.

Ro: You know, I just learned you were a poet.

Stephen: Well, that's a heady claim. [Chuckles wryly.]

Ro: Well, let's say, then, that you write poetry. Did you ever write any poetry in prison?

Stephen: No. That's interesting. I've never found . . . anything there. [Pause.] Much of what I've written, I think, has been acts of self-defense, preserving one's sanity in the face of the madness. About the war, especially. Or wars, I should say. And even when it's gone off on tangents that seem less than political, it's always had that cast. But I don't have the discipline of the vocation. To keep going back, going back, and keep writing and writing. For me, it emerges in moments; I see things and then something comes to me. I wish I could do more of it. I . . . [Very long pause.] I'm lazy, I think, in some ways. But that's a choice, too.

Ro: Yes. For all of us. Now you're a member of the Atlantic Life Community (ALC). I'm wondering how one becomes a part of it.

Stephen: Well, you show up. [Laughs.] You persist. That's how it happened for me, although it took awhile for me to feel like I was a part of it. My Catholicism has become progressively more important to me, so that also certainly led me there, as I returned to the discoveries I made at the time of the conscientious objector choice. The ALC is sometimes reluctant to define itself, but it's largely a Catholic community, in both the lower-case and upper-case senses. I think because of the Plowshares tradition, there was a sense at one time . . . not that this was always made palpable, but that there was a certain hierarchy of witness. Not that people were being set standards—unless you do a Plowshares action you don't qualify—but clearly the threshold had been set fairly high. But I learned that there was a place within that community for a variety of voices and that the callings were varied and manifold. People worked to recognize that the people who did support were all part of the resistance and part of the community, too, and the actions would be impossible without what they provided. [Break in the recording. When it resumes, we're talking about his resistance focus on the Enola Gay exhibit at the Smithsonian.[9]] You know, I'm interested in the way history is used to justify the crimes of the present. Who controls the past controls the future, so you twist the past to control the present, as Orwell tells us. Therefore, places like museums seem to be particularly crucial—as crucial, in some ways, as the actual weapons themselves. We have to confront the distorted histories.

One of the first of these actions along these lines was in '88 or '89 at the Nautilus, the first nuclear-powered submarine, which is docked up at the Groton Naval Submarine Base [as a museum.] I have some deep feelings about places like that, especially where children come.

This action was also on Hiroshima Day, like the later one at the Enola Gay in the Smithsonian. Four of us went on board the submarine with a banner that read, "Hiroshima is here." Again, being a faithful curator and naming it correctly. Of course we were arrested rather quickly.

I'd been fascinated to discover that the Enola Gay still existed. Exhibiting it was just too ominous for words. And they weren't doing it to declare their guilt, so there was a clear sense that the exhibit needed to be addressed, in a direct, physical way. Attached to that was what I had begun to learn about my father's own experience of the war and in particular what the Enola Gay meant to him. How it had become [for him] a version—a terribly perverted version—of salvation.

So my father had the choice between the lie or madness, basically. And that was the horrible insight. Knowing, too, that many other men were in his position. So I wrote about that, and published two essays around the time of the action and afterwards.[10] [Draws a deep breath.]

---

9. The Enola Gay was the B-29 bomber that dropped the first atomic bomb on Japan, on August 6, 1945. In 1995 the cockpit and nose section of the aircraft was put on display at the National Air and Space Museum of the Smithsonian.

10. Stephen Vincent Kobasa. "A Machine for Lying: Reflections on the Enola Gay," online: www.jonahhouse.org/EnolaGaySK2.htm; and Kobasa, "More Lies

That's really what brought me to the Enola Gay exhibit in the summer of 1994, with Kathy Boylan [of the Dorothy Day Catholic Worker in DC] and Anne Quintano [of the Kairos Community in New York]. We knew the War Resisters League was sponsoring some larger demonstrations, and we decided to separate ourselves from that, for both philosophical and logistical reasons. (We wanted a more focused action and one that had a larger chance of success. If we were in a large gathering, the heightened security would make what we had planned more difficult.)

We decided we'd go in after that public event, sometime in July— July 7th, I think. We simply entered the line as tourists. At that time, there was only a section of the plane [at the Smithsonian.] I remember being stunned by how small it was, you know, given the scale of the [nuclear planes] that we've created today. You'll remember that they called the bombs "Big Boy" and "Little Man." "Little Man" was the Hiroshima bomb. They were doing experimental comparisons.

Ro: Is that why they dropped two?

Stephen: Yes, I think so. Truman's point was, "We had them so we used them." Of course that was a sin, a deep sin, so we marked the plane with the symbols of the deaths: blood and ashes. For us, the blood and ashes completed the exhibit, or corrected it. We didn't see ourselves as doing damage. What we went into was a damaged exhibit. When we finished, it was repaired and truthful. That's why I call it curatorial work.

They cleared the place pretty quickly after the action happened and then shut the exhibit down for a period of time. Which was good, in terms of physically stopping the lie, even briefly. Of the trials I've been a part of, this trial was one of the more compelling. The prosecutor was thoughtful, not malevolent, and it was one trial in which we actually got to talk, so that was good. (After it was over, the prosecutor sent me a photograph a tourist took, showing me dumping the ashes.) We all thought it was going to mean significant jail time, but in the end, I was only sentenced to house arrest and confined by electronic bracelet.

That house arrest was worse than jail in some ways, though, because the whole family was imprisoned. They were face-to-face with

from a Machine: Revisiting the Enola Gay," printed in "Resistance Reflections," *The Nuclear Resister* 134, August 1, 2004.

it on a daily basis, you know, getting the phone calls at three in the morning when the monitor wasn't registering the signal, and so forth. What Hamlet says about the world being a prison, that was it! Some dungeons are just darker than others. It's your imagination that forms the prison, makes the invisible walls.

After that? We did an action again there last summer, but only two people were arrested, and now the entire Enola Gay is down in Texas at a new facility, the Udvar-Hazy Center, National Air and Space Museum, in Houston. In some sense, the protests themselves are now part of the history of the plane, and that's . . . Not that I feel like the demons have been entirely exorcized. I think the only way to do that would be to drag the plane out in the desert and let dust storms scour it away to a shell. But I think I've done what I was called to do. It's not that the story's over, but my part in it is, and now I can move on.

Ro: Where do you see yourself moving?

Stephen: [Long pause.] Well, I think in part it's to a more clear sense that what's futile is often necessary. By "futile" I mean the sense by which the society measures success and failure. A lot of what we're engaged in looks to the general perception as if it's failed. I guess I'm still working toward the realization that there's a different standard at work here that looks towards . . . [Another long pause and I interrupt, shamefully.]

Ro: Looks towards eternity?

Stephen: Well, maybe at least looks out of the time that this culture says is the only thing that matters. I think that's partly why one persists. Because it's right. I think we're never absolutely free of ours fears about lack of success.

I have persistent fears about my own mortality, so I wonder who will carry on when our generation has all died. What choices will our children have? One of the first things I learned was how great an impact resistance *does* have on our daughters.

In that Nautilus action, we went in as a family. Clare was about three, so Anne pushed her up the ramp in the stroller and then I ran off and did the action. When the police brought me out in handcuffs, Clare just began to scream—out-of-control crying—because she couldn't come to me. We'd tried to anticipate everything but hadn't thought of that—that a child's grief and anguish would be provoked by not being able to go to me.

For both of them, as they grew up, there was never any question that they wouldn't honor my decisions. Of course, it's never been set up that in order to please me they have to do as I do. I think Clare and Rachel realize that the work that Anne does at the clinic—all her work as a nurse—is as much an act of resistance as anything I do. She's worked in Guatemala, she's been in Frontier Nursing Service, and worked with migrant workers. For over twenty-five years, she's been at a community health clinic in an underserved area of the city. The whole idea that health care is a right, not a privilege . . . If her life is not resistance, nothing is resistance.

Anne Somsel and Stephen Kobasa, 2005.

In October of 2005, six months after we talked, Stephen was asked to leave his position as teacher of English literature at Kolbe Cathedral High School in Bridgeport, Connecticut. The reason? He refused to permanently display the US flag in his classroom. In a valedictory published in *The Catholic Worker*, Stephen wrote:

> For me, an essential element of the mission of Catholic education is to offer evidence of the practice of nonviolent peacemaking and principled resistance to nationalism that have been nourished and expressed within our tradition. It is impossible for me not to see an act of discrimination against my long held religious beliefs in the invention and application of this policy

requiring the flag in my classroom. Its unique and arbitrary standard, along with the extreme penalty attached to refusing it, creates the unmistakable impression that national loyalty is being valued over faithful obedience to the Gospel. . . . On October 13th, I removed the flag from my classroom for one last time. That afternoon, the principal asked me to return my key. Students and colleagues embraced me throughout the hours between those two moments, reminding me of why I came to teach in the first place, and of why I am leaving now. It was my last lesson for them, my last lesson from them.[11]

11. Stephen Vincent Kobasa, "Allegiance to Conscience," *The Catholic Worker* (January–February 2006) 2. In the introduction to the essay, he wrote, "The history below is drawn largely from a letter that I sent to Bishop Lori of the Diocese of Bridgeport, CT. That letter was never answered."

9

The Prophet Priests

These five narrators, all Roman Catholic priests, don't fit the traditional model of harried pastors who worry about keeping enough parishioners in the pews to pay the bills. Instead, they seek to serve a global community, urging it to heed the Gospel message of peace. Profiled in this chapter are Jesuit "Bix" Bichsel, diocesan priest Peter Dougherty, Priest of the Sacred Heart Bob Bossie, and two Franciscans—Lou Vitale and Jerry Zawada. All of them feel the tensions between a hierarchical church and the call of conscience. All of them, in their strikingly individual ways, are prophets for peace.

Father Bill Bichsel, SJ

"Bix," as people call Father William Bichsel, SJ, was born in 1928 and joined the Jesuits in 1946. He helped to start the Martin Luther King Center in Tacoma in 1969 and later cofounded the Tacoma Catholic Worker. He's also been arrested more than forty times for protesting the politics and policies of his government. After spending about two years of his life in prison, he again said yes to incarceration in 2009 by taking part in the Disarm Now Plowshares action at Bangor, home of the Trident nuclear submarine.

Fr. Bix: I was born and raised here in Tacoma, on 27th and G Streets, and I now live on 15th and G Streets, so basically in my long life, I've moved a mile. [Chuckles.] I joined the Jesuits just out of high school. The guy who kind of steered me to the novitiate was Larry Donahue, who was in and out of the Order a couple of times. He died in 2003, but he's still part of my fond memories. I have so many close friends who have left the Jesuits that I refer to them as "graduates."

In the fifties, I went to theology school in Frankfort, and then was Dean of Students at Gonzaga for awhile. When you don't know what to do, most people go back to school, so I did, too. Boston University. Those were two great years for me, from 1966 to '68. Most of the people in my class were Jewish, and I met some good friends. Got involved in the peace movement in Boston, the anti-Vietnam demonstrations, and the burning of draft cards. The murder of Martin Luther King . . . all those thing touched me very deeply.

But, anyway, I went back to teach at Seattle Prep. It was an upper echelon school, and I wasn't prepared for that. Didn't do well at all. Before, when I taught in high school, I always prided myself on my control. We used to knuckle the boys on the head if they got sassy. (You'd be sued for that now.) But now I had changed, or was trying to change at least, to a less violent, less scrappy man.

It was a very tough year for me. Wrong place! I started drinking pretty heavily and life was bad. I was thinking about leaving the Jesuits, but I didn't even have the oomph or esteem to do that. Finally in March, the Provincial asked me to serve at St. Leo's in Tacoma, during the summer. I said, "I'll leave tomorrow!" So I came down to Tacoma in April in 1969 and I haven't left since, except to go to prison.

Being at St. Leo's was great. We established the Martin Luther King Center and a Native American Center, and we got into housing, opened up a farmers' market, and started a counseling center for gay and lesbian people. Good years. People look at those as the golden years, from about 1972 to 1977. They were struggling years, too, because I wasn't always that well received, you know.

Eventually, Bix took a sabbatical. He told his superiors he'd do "theology of the road" and after six months hitchhiking around the country, he spent some time on Fort Belknap Indian Reservation. Then in 1979, he helped to rehab two old duplexes and joined them together to form Guadalupe House, started the G Street Community, and lived in community with people suffering from mental illness. In 1989, the community became the Tacoma Catholic Worker.

Ro: When did you really begin the peace activism?

Fr. Bix: My first action against the Trident at Bangor was on August the 9th, 1975 or '76, while I was still at St. Leo's. They called for a group of volunteers to carry a replica of this big Trident submarine through the fence. I remember we were in a kind of meditative silence, and the Buddhists were drumming, and I looked at a picture of the ruins of Nagasaki, and when the guy says, "Are there any volunteers?" I raised my hand. That first arrest started me on my way. A life-changing experience.

There were seventy-two of us and the replica was 600 feet long. Made out of inner tubes, stuff like that. People had worked all night, diligently cutting out a big section in the fence, dodging the patrols on the perimeter road. Anyway, at the given time, the fence went down and we walked straight through. We were all arrested immediately but just booked and mugged and given ban-and-bar letters. Not prosecuted. After that, my actions continued at Bangor.

Ro: In the new millennium, nuns get sent up for three years for cutting down a fence.

Fr. Bix: Yeah, now it's different. Real different. Other actions back then: Once a number of us got into boats and invaded Bangor Submarine Base from the Hood Canal. What was really amazing was that when we got in there, we were arrested by guards from Pan Am! They were very polite, and said things like, "Sir, would you mind turning around while we put your handcuffs on?" I did a ten-day stint in the King County Jail on that one, and in 1980 I served a four-month sentence at Lompoc Federal Prison in California. Then there were other shorter sentences for trespass that were served in the King County Jail in Seattle.

At that time, Ground Zero had formed with Jim and Shelley Douglass. Once I got six months in a Ground Zero action and was sent by rail all the way down to L.A., cuffed all the way. They'd free one handcuff so you could you eat your lunch.

What I remember especially about the LA County Jail was my first night. They dragged a man out of a cell and kicked the hell out of him. Women guards as well. I couldn't believe it! [At intake], they had us all strip and throw all our clothes into a big pile, and then they deloused us. With a spray hose. They were really fooling around with it, getting a big kick out of where they hit 'ya and stuff like that. All the guards carried big, rubber-headed flashlights. "Flashlight therapy" they called it 'cause they'd use it as a billy club.

After we became a Catholic Worker, some of us got very involved in Central American issues, in Nicaragua and El Salvador. Roy Bourgeois came out here in 1994 and he called on us to fast on the steps of the Capitol in DC, trying to close the SOA. So I went. That was a grand time for me, during that forty-day fast.

Then that November was the first time I went down to Fort Benning, Georgia. At that time, there were just twenty of us protesting outside the base. Five of us went in. We were dressed as construction workers with orange vests and hard hats, and we had chains and locks in our pockets. Even though they knew we were coming, we got all the way into the SOA building, and put the chains through all the doors except the last one. The guard came out and we told them we were from "security," but he finally wised up and called the MP's and they took us away. The FBI released us after eight hours, but again, only with citations.

The next day Fred Mercy and I took a taxi into the base and poured blood on the SOA sign. Again, we were arrested and held for hours, but didn't get a court notice. The next November, in 1995, ten of us went into the base again and re-enacted the 1988 Jesuit massacre with the housekeeper and her daughter. I finally got four months for that action.

Father Bix continued his SOA actions, going down to Fort Benning every year and in 1998 he was sentenced to a year for what he called "felonious hand print" and six months for an earlier trespass. His attorney appealed and was able to get the sentences running concurrently so Bix just served a year.

Fr. Bix: They never let me say Mass [at Sheridan, FCI in Oregon] but we bootlegged it a couple of times. My first time there we smuggled in a tape of the School of the Americas. Hid it in the chapel, underneath one of the statues. They used the chapel for movies when it wasn't in operation for services, so for awhile we had classes on the SOA.

Until the chaplain discovered us. Or maybe we got snitched on. But I was in there with some great people! Got to be pretty good friends with Tom O'Connell, who was quarterback for the Buffalo Bills. Tom would just shake his head at us resisters. "Doing all that stuff, that's against the law!"

Father Bix had visited Hiroshima in 2009, and that's when he decided to return to nuclear disarmament, protesting both at Bangor and at the Oak Ridge, Tennessee, nuclear weapons facility. In prison in 2011, in his 83rd year, he wrote:

> I shuffle around the common area, and I thank God for being here and for the peace I experience. I am not anxious or overly concerned about anything . . . [I have] things wrong from head to toe, move slowly, tire easily, and take a half ton of pills to prolong breath and life [but] I'm blessed by the peace and quiet spirit inside. I'm not concerned about trying to be more than I am with the other inmates. I'm trying to let them see—not hide or disguise—my lack of knowledge on so many things . . . I don't have a regular prayer time now, but I pray and try to be alert, to be at rest in the presence of God. There is no anxiousness or compulsiveness or resolve to preach or hold prayer sessions or do any "religious actions." I ask God to lead me as God sees fit, and I am so thankful to feel at peace with my life.[1]

After serving three months in prison for the 2009 Plowshares action and another three months for the Oak Ridge action, Father Bix was released on a tether. He returned to the Tacoma CW on February 9, 2012, in great shape physically and spiritually, according to his friends in the Ground Zero Community.[2]

---

1. Father John Dear, SJ, "Fr. Bill Bichsel's Ordeal: Cruel and Inhuman Punishment," *National Catholic Reporter* (June 1, 2011); online: ncronline.org/blogs/road-peace/fr-bill-bichsels-ordeal-cruel-and-inhuman-punishment. Used with permission.

2. Leonard Eiger, e-mail to author, April 7, 2012.

Father Peter Dougherty

Father Peter Dougherty had an old-church Catholic childhood in a small town and then went to Sacred Heart Seminary in Detroit. Ordination, parish service, campus ministry, and two masters degrees followed. Like many of his generation, the Vietnam War and the farm workers' struggle turned him to peace and justice issues, and in 1975 he cofounded the

Abrahamic Community in Lansing. He helped to initiate first the Great Lakes Life Community, then the Lansing Covenant for Peace, and then Michigan Faith and Resistance. Since 1993, he's coordinated the Michigan Peace Team, which offers nonviolent training and fields peace teams in both the US and in foreign countries, especially Palestine.

Father Peter Dougherty, 2010.
Courtesy of Father Peter Dougherty.

Fr. Peter: I was an anxious kid, anxious about getting everything right. I grew up in an alcoholic family and [the parish] school was a safe place, an escape from some of those anxieties at home. I always worked— paper routes, stock boy in a toy store, caddying at a golf club, construction work in the summer. Sometimes during the summers when I was younger, we'd go to our grandparents' place on Lake Cora in Paw Paw, Michigan. Ball games and bonfires by the lake with my cousins. Those . . . those summers were enchanted. But later that ended.

My mother was the pious one, the wholesome, holy one, even in the difficulties of my father drinking. (He never missed work, never missed work.) I went to Sacred Heart Seminary, Detroit, to four years of college; the major was philosophy. It was the old church, you know. Keeping the rules, and the fear about all of that. That was the spirituality, the way to be a good person and a good priest. Guys told me later that I was the "holy one," on my knees a lot in the chapel and that kind of thing. And then, as I say, I grew up. [Chuckles.] I became a human being.

When I went out into the world after ordination, I had to start growing up fast. See, there was all that inner pain. I was highly neurotic out of the woundedness of growing up and maybe half the motivation for becoming a priest was to be "worthwhile." Out of anxiety, I was trying to do it all. That was all part of feeling insecure.

See, I think God uses everything in our lives to help breathe the Spirit into us [so we can] be wholesome and whole and holy. But that realization came later, when I went into psychotherapy. Before that, I was like the kids I see now in the war zones, who survive the violence by developing defense mechanisms. When you're an adult, those skills become self-defeating, and you have to unlearn them. Little did I realize then that there's never an end to growing, that all my life would be a journey of growing and healing and helping the rest of the world do that.

I learned about the United Farm Workers' strike when I was in campus ministry at Eastern Michigan University. A couple of us went out to California and were on the strike line with Cesar Chavez, seeing the hired goons trying to intimidate the strikers.

And the Vietnam War . . . At first, if you'd asked me about Vietnam, I would've said we had to "fight the Communists." I wasn't stupid but I was ignorant, and today that helps me understand other people who are ignorant but not stupid.

Well, I learned fast. Joined a study group, and then went to a four-day workshop to hear Dan Berrigan and other folks. They just blew me away! That was a big part of my never being the same again. All along the way being taught by women about my sexism and having a few dramatic moments because of it being so ingrained. Women help me grow by constantly challenging me.

At Eastern, the call to activism absolutely took over my being, and finally I felt I had to stop talking about it and *do* it. So Milt Taylor and I and others formed the Abrahamic Community. Abraham the patriarch was called out of Ur by God: he didn't know where he was going, didn't know what was over the next sand dune, but he trusted in God.

We are Abrahamic people. We don't know what's over the next sand dune. But you go. In the Abrahamic Community, I no longer had a salary and we were going to live on what comes in. Started taking in the homeless, getting food out of dumpsters and all that.

Ro: What did the diocese think of this?

Fr. Peter: At first, I didn't have permission and didn't fit into the slots, so it was very uncomfortable. Then Ken Povish became the new bishop of Lansing, and formalized my ministry in the Abrahamic

Community, and I was then officially legit. I never went back to normal institutional work or parish work.

We got Great Lakes Life Community going in the '70s, with people from Detroit, Battle Creek, Kalamazoo. My first act of civil resistance was at the military center in Battle Creek. They keep track of where all the hardware of the US military is. We went into the cafeteria, just walked right in, and poured our own blood on the floor and did a skit—a street theater. The employees were stunned. But we weren't arrested.

Oh, so many great things happened! Community was built and we started doing resistance actions at the K. I. Sawyer SAC [Strategic Air Command] base with nuclear cruise missiles on B-52 bombers. Also at Project ELF, the underground communication system for the Trident nuclear missiles, which has since been dismantled. Then the Williams International campaign in the late '70s, near Detroit. They made cruise missile engines and in those days, all cruise missiles were nuclear tipped.

I was only once in federal prison, and the difference was awesome. I remember how thrilled I was to see salads in the prison cafeteria. Once in a county jail, I was supposed to have a vegetarian meal. Ordered by a doctor. It didn't come, it didn't come and didn't come. Finally I said I'd go on a hunger strike and lo and behold, it came! A plop of peanut butter and a vegetable and bread. [Laughs.]

Ro: Did you ever go through a "dark night," a feeling of being alone and forgotten, like Dorothy [Day] did the first time she was in prison?[3]

Fr. Peter: Yeah. You know, there's fear. That was another level of being in a jail. There was one guy who, every time he'd walk by, he'd say, "I'm gonna get you, Pop!" And I wasn't even that old—probably only in my late forties. So I had that fear in my gut. A couple other guys heard him, and said to me, "If he ever lays a hand on you, we'll beat the shit outta him." So I started worrying for *him*!

Then I just knew. There was that experiential knowing. I will never kick him in the groin, slug him in the teeth, smash his head against the wall, because he is my brother. So what am I going to do to protect myself? How do I take back my power as a human being? The next morning, he said it again, and I said, "Hey, I want everybody's attention."

3. Day, *The Long Loneliness*.

"Life is hard in here," I said, "And this is a rotten system. We have to get along together. We need each other, so we have to cooperate and watch out for each other. And if somebody's starting to abuse somebody else, we should expect the rest of us to stop that and yet not hurt the one doing it, either. So we can all survive."

Then I turned to [the guy]: "You just threatened me again. I've told you I'm never going to hurt you. I want you to stop threatening me. Do you understand? Cut it out."

I took back my power by doing that. Later on in the day, when the deputy came by, a couple of the guys said to him, "Hey, you gotta get rid of that guy. Not even Pops can stand him." [Laughs.] So they moved him to a one-man cell.

The longest stint I ever did was eight months, for two actions against nuclear weapons at Wurtsmith Air Force Base. So two in the county jail and then over to the Saginaw halfway house for six months. While I was there, we had our first two meetings of what became the Michigan Peace Team [MPT], what my life is now.

MPT was founded in 1993 and does many nonviolent trainings each year throughout the Midwest. It also sends peace delegations to hotspots in the United States and to Mexico, Palestine, and other trouble spots in the world. MPT folks also help to keep a peaceful presence at US protests, such as those at national political conventions.

Ro: Peter, How do you see protest and resistance changing over the years?

Fr. Peter: Well, after the Cold War ended, a lot of folks believed things would be okay. All the Michigan bases were closed and Williams International phased down from building the cruise missile engines. Anyway, there was a big lull in nuclear weapon resistance. With the first Gulf War, there was a real coming together against war, but then it faded during the Iraq sanctions time. The new Iraq War brought many together but again, even those networks faded. There's still a lot of activism, though. All these old timers in their 50s, 60s, and 70s are still doing it.

The younger folks coming up are a different breed. The anti-globalization stuff attracts a different variety of activists, and they have real questions about methods. Nonviolence isn't looked upon with the same conviction that many had in earlier movements. So there are serious discussions.

Ro: Are you able to reach those young people with your nonviolent training?

Fr. Peter: Some pick up on it, some don't. Whatever the focus of the group, we can give them a nonviolence training. We have a basic eight hours, which we think of as a minimum time for training, and then we design special training for the purpose of the group. The longest training we ever did was eight days, preparing to go to Chiapas, Mexico during those terrible times in the late '90s.

Ro: Peter, what do you say to people who are considering civil disobedience?

Fr. Peter: Well, I think all of us need to be stretched—stretched beyond our comfort zone. Can I do more for peace? The more may not be time-wise more but maybe risking more or making a deeper commitment. Can people with full-time jobs spend two more hours a week doing peacemaking? Can people who are retired build more of their time around peacemaking ? Take the risk. Stretch your boundaries. We all need to enter that discomfort zone.

Very important, too, is to be grounded within yourself. You have to both nurture a spirituality and be nurtured by it. Now by spirituality, I'm not talking about religion. I'm talking about nurturing, out of your inner core, the connections between all people and all things. If you don't have that, you don't have the inner strength for the long haul. You can become cynical, you can become extremely judgmental, you can become depressed and depleted. You have to have something bigger than yourself to carry you through.

Ro: The center of spirituality, then, is a connectedness with all things?

Fr. Peter: Mm hmm. Your practice might be meditation. It might be religious out of a given denomination. It might be Zen Buddhism. Methodist. Jewish. But no matter what it is, you need that dimension, so that you develop a daily spiritual practice. For some people, it's meditating in silence, for others it's very much a part of imagination.

For others, it's reading and being stimulated to reflect. Or prayer—alone or with others. Reading can be key. Not just intellectual reading, but reading to nurture the soul. And you have to be able to do this spiritual practice wherever you are.

Even in prison. We can be teachers in prison, too, teach in many ways. It's great when resisters just say no to things they're ordered to do in prison. Resisters choose our battlefields, in prison or out.

I remember a story about John [Schuchardt], part of the Jonah House community in the early days. He was in jail for resisting and the rule was that you couldn't bring any food or drink to other prisoners at the table when you got yourself a refill. So John brings someone a coffee and gets thrown in solitary. Everybody laughs as he's hauled away.

He comes out. First meal after: "Anybody want a cup of coffee?" So he's thrown in again. They laugh again. It happens again and again, for several days, and always John's getting hauled away. But one day, he brings someone a refill and he's not touched. Nobody laughs and the rule is changed.

Father Bob Bossie, SCJ

Father Bob Bossie is a priest of the Sacred Heart, stationed at the 8th Day Center for Justice in Chicago when I interviewed him in 2006. According to their mission statement, 8th Day is a "coalition of Catholic religious congregations committed to act as a critical alternative voice to oppressive systems and to work actively to change these systems." The group works collaboratively with a wide range of area peace and justice groups, encouraging dialogue and cooperation.

Ro: Bob, are other priests in your Order often arrested on justice and peace issues?

Fr. Bob: In this country, not too many, but internationally they are, especially the Italians. During the Kosovo crisis, one of them there was a human shield between opposing forces on a bridge. The founder of the congregation was a Frenchman who lived during the Industrial Revolution. He was a pretty outspoken critic of what was going on, and although he was a so-called loyal fellow to the Church and the pope, he had his aberrant side, his Left-leaning wisdom. Or I guess a better way to put it would be that he had a love of the people who were suffering.

Ro: Why did you choose that order?

Fr. Bob: In all honesty, it was serendipitous. I was twenty-seven years of age and had served in the Air Force and then started working in the military industry.(An obvious slide, you know.) I had an experience of God that led me to believe I should join a religious order, and so I wrote away to a lot of them. I had no college, so I knew it would be a long grind. At that time, a lot of orders were still focusing on bringing in young boys, but the Sacred Heart Congregation had a commitment to adult vocations and they said, "Come on."

After ordination and some parish work, Bob went to South America with 8th Day staff and realized he needed to work more specifically for peace and justice. His first arrest was for pouring blood on the pillars of the Pentagon with fifty other Chicagoans. Before he left, he had told his Provincial that he wouldn't get arrested.

Ro: What made you change your mind?

Fr. Bob: To be honest, part of it probably was wanting to go along with the in-crowd.

When I came back, though, I started here at 8th Day Center. After another trip to the Pentagon, where I got thirty days or so, we started organizing here in the city and did a lot of resistance activities through what we called the Chicago Life Community. We did regular protests where we risked arrest.

The most visible focus was Morton Salt. In 1983, Morton joined with Thiokol which was a weapons producer. Their headquarters were at 123 North Walker Drive. I got into their first shareholder meeting after the merger, as a stockholder, and challenged them from the floor.

One shareholders meeting was quite amusing. I got up to speak and the CEO lost his temper: "You've been disrupting this corporation long enough!"

I said, "We have?" [Laughs.] Here's this huge weapons company and we're this little group of ten, twenty people. After they made me sit down, [Sister] Dorothy Pagosa started singing a litany: "For Morton-Thiokol, maker of nuclear weapons, we pray to our God."

The rest of us responded, "God have mercy." They threw her out but then someone else started it again, and that went on for about a half hour. They were going crazy, you know. Sometimes they'd arrest us at the meetings, but once, I remember, the judge asked the security officer if we were there legally, and he had to say we were because we were shareholders. "Case dismissed."

For six years—from '83 to '89—we had a protest there every eight days. (We made it every eight days to give an opportunity for different people to fit it into their schedules.) We also had bigger events following our faith tradition, like an Ash Wednesday service, with an altar cloth which had on it the names of victims of their weapons work. We did civil disobedience actions inside the building itself and also at their shareholder meetings.

One year we faked out the guards and snuck in and held an Ash Wednesday service in the cafeteria. They finally got a conviction on that one because we had trespassed. I remember one woman who worked at Thiokol. She was a former nun. She told us one Ash Wednesday when we had our protest outside, that she was on her way to St. Clement's Church where they had a "perfect" Ash Wednesday service. But then she said ours was the *real* Ash Wednesday.

That service in the cafeteria pushed her button, though. She told us we were "disrupting the Morton Thiokol family." And that's where people struggle every day, you know. With their loyalties—to family and to religion and to country. Often they come up to the wall and they don't want to look over. Like the Germans not wanting to look over the wall to the concentration camps. Because of what it would demand of them.

I wonder what my own crunch place—my wall—is. Someone asked me once, and I said, "Oil!" Because I get cold very easily and if I didn't have heat, maybe I'd join the opposition. And of course, it's often very cold in jail, especially in the new ones.

The Chicago Life Community faded when Morton spun off the weapons division to Alliant Tech.[4] I worked with a couple of the Plowshares actions at the missile silos, and after the folks who did the

4. Alliant Techsystems Inc., headquartered in Edina, Minnesota, has been the site of protests against its production of cluster bombs and weapons containing depleted uranium.

Silo Plowshares action got such serious sentences, a lot of folks in the Midwest wanted to do something serious themselves.

So that was the genesis of an action called the Missouri Peace Planting. We took over twelve or thirteen missile silos simultaneously. They'd arrest us and then let us go and some folks just kept reorganizing and coming back. Some folks got a year or more for that and one person got a huge sentence for contempt because she wouldn't name who drove her to the silo.

Ro: Bob, why aren't people filling the jails?

Fr. Bob: Well, first, no one in the peace movement has ever filled the jails. During the civil rights era, there were hundreds of people in jail, but the biggest arrests for peace issues have been at the Nevada test site, and that's just a slap-on-the-hand-and-pass, you know. Then they had a quasi-moratorium on testing, so the wind's out of that sail. And now the missile silos, which were so visible, are gone from the Midwest, so that target's gone.

But I also think it's because people wonder if it's effective, in the good sense of the word. Plus, they give serious sentences for small things. Very serious. There is a brutality in the government's [handling of protesters] right now that maybe compares to the dogs in the civil rights days. Here's Kathy Kelly arrested at the School of the Americas. They threw her down to the ground and beat her when she refused to cooperate, and she weighs about a hundred pounds, for God sakes![5] So it's also partly these intimidation techniques, I think.

Here with the Chicago peace groups, the ones who arrange the big marches and so on, I've recently started targeting for a nonviolent revolution. I'm coming to the point where I don't know what else to say. In a talk at Columbia College, the other day, I told them about the Bolivian peasants who overthrew their government a couple of years ago. Brought down the government about the water issue. And nonviolently. So it's not without precedent.

I'm still committed completely to nonviolence, both as a tactic and as a philosophy, but I regularly deal with people in the Chicago peace movement who aren't [nonviolent] and I feel conflicted. But let me tell you about [this year's protest] at the Chicago Air and Water Show. My brother Paul started the protests there, back in 1992. (He's a religious brother, under private vows for over fifty years.) He says it

5. See Kathy Kelly's interview in Rosalie G. Riegle, *Doing Time for Peace: Resistance, Family, and Community* (Nashville: Vanderbilt University Press, 2013).

doesn't make sense to oppose war if you don't also oppose the means they use to recruit people.

This year, there were more people there who weren't of a non-violent persuasion, including the RCP or Revolutionary Communist Party folks. I know most of them, including a guy named Fred, and he was one of the most nonviolent people there![6]

First some guy came up screaming and Fred talked to him for about fifteen or twenty minutes. The guy got very quiet, and they had a long conversation. I walked over to Fred afterwards and told him, "You have a real nice way about you."

He said, "Bob, you have to find out where you have common ground. Then you find out where you disagree and you talk about that." Later on, a very muscular man knocked the papers out of a woman protester's hands. Fred was talking to the guy, and the guy spit right in his face. But Fred didn't hit him, and later he told me: "I would never fight. I would never hit him."

Now I don't know if he said that out of respect for us—the nonviolent organizers who've been there for years—or because he thought fighting was the wrong thing to do. But here's this man who is committed to a Revolutionary Communist Party philosophy. Nonetheless, something about him has this character of nonviolence. Now, whether it's a strategy or what, I can't speak to that. Should we pigeonhole people? As I said, I'm conflicted.

After Mass last Sunday with some of the activists, everybody was grousing about what was going on. One issue after another. I was holding back, but finally I said it: "What we really need is a nonviolent revolution." And about seven people piped up right away, without thinking about it: "That's right!"

So at the 8th Day Center staff meeting this morning, I brought this confliction out and we talked about it. "Is that where we stand?" Should the peace movement be calling for a nonviolent revolution? Not just stopping torture. Not just getting out of Iraq. But a nonviolent revolution!

Is that naive? I don't know when or if we could do it in this country, but it's not like it's impossible. It hasn't been just Gandhi. There was the Velvet Revolution in Czechoslovakia and others in the Soviet bloc. And Badshah Khan, the nonviolent soldier of Islam.

---

6. The man was Fred Johnson, and he was a supporter of the RCP, not a member. (E-mail to author from rcppubs@hotmail.com, April 6, 2012.)

The Pashtuns were warriors for a living; you didn't mess with the Pashtuns. Well, Badshah Khan turned them into a nonviolent army, for God's sake. Nonviolent revolution might sound preposterous, but history tells us otherwise.[7]

Nonviolent revolutions have shut whole countries down! Look at the tactics of nonviolent resistance—the general strikes and all the other ideas in the books by Gene Sharp.[8] He lists a hundred and ninety-eight ways. Now it's pie in the sky on some levels, but I trust and believe in God that there is some possibility of making the world a better place, and that it isn't just controlled by the powerful.

There *is* a deeper power, and I don't mean something abstract; I mean there is a spark of goodness in people. We're so conditioned to be individualistic in this country that we don't think as a community. But there's no reason to say that something can't help us to start thinking more as community and to tap into that really deep power of love and caring and willingness to sacrifice that's in all of us.

Father Jerry Zawada, OFM

Franciscan priest Father Jerry Zawada has always walked with those on the margins, whether with the peasants of the Philippines, the undocumented in Texas, torture survivors in Milwaukee and Chicago, or the men with whom he shares his many incarcerations as a resister. I met him first in 2004 during the School of Americas [SOA] protest at Fort Benning in Columbus, Georgia. Jerry had already served two prison terms as part of this campaign to close the School. In November of

Father Jerry Zawada at the SOA protest, 2004.

7. See Erica Chenoweth and Maria J. Stephan, *Why Civil Resistance Works* (New York: Columbia University Press, 2011). They quantify that since 1900, nonviolent campaigns around the world have been twice as successful as violent ones.

8. Eugene Sharp, *Waging Nonviolent Struggle: 20th Century Practice and 21st Century Potential* (New York: Porter Sargent, 2005).

2005, he and fellow Franciscan Lou Vitale went again under the Fort Benning fence.

In 2010, he and thirteen others were tried for crossing the line at Creech Air Force Base, home to the "Predators" and "Reapers," apt Air Force names for the deadly drones currently used in Afghanistan and Pakistan. The trial attracted much judicial and media interest and the defendants were finally sentenced only to time served. In 2012, Father Jerry and I joined Catholic Workers, members of CODEPINK, and staff from Nevada Desert Experience to again blockade the base.[9] This time charges were dismissed and some speculate that it's because the Nevada courts don't want the publicity of another trial.

Fr. Jerry: By the time I was ten, I knew I wanted to be a priest. Went to a Franciscan minor seminary in Sturdevant, Wisconsin for high school. I used to refer to it as St. Bonaventure Minor Reformatory. [Laughs.] And guess what the buildings are now? A state prison! I say, "At least now they're honest about it."

I was a quiet, pious kid but was known as a rebel even in high school. The dean at Sturdevant told me, "Don't even think about joining the Franciscan Order. You break the rules just for the sake of breaking them." Well, I broke that rule, too, and I joined them.

I struggled through my seminary days, but I loved St. Francis and loved the maverick way that he went about his spirituality. Dorothy Day and the whole Catholic Worker movement has also been a profound influence on my life. The whole blessed messiness, the blessed chaos. I think that's where God is most present. I prefer to stay on the edge of things, to listen to people on the fringes of society. So one of the best places for me to be is in prison.

Jerry's first assignment was in a poor rural parish in the Philippines. When he returned, he lived in Uptown, which at the time was a rough part of Chicago.

9. CODEPINK is a national "women-initiated grassroots peace and social justice movement working to end US funded wars and occupations, and to challenge militarism" (www.codepinkalert.org/). Nevada Desert Experience of Las Vegas has worked since 1982 "to mobilize people of all faiths to work toward nuclear abolition and nonviolent social change." Online: www.nevadadesertexperience.org.

Fr Jerry: When I was in Uptown—and I say this without any embarrassment—I got into seven long years of clinical depression. The bottom fell out. I . . . I hated God, hated everything. I struggled and struggled to get back.

Finally, in 1983, I heard a story of a Salvadoran school teacher who had been tortured but had escaped. Her face was disfigured from the torturers cutting her with razor blades and . . . I said to myself, "Even if I never get rid of this depression, I don't have the luxury of concentrating on that anymore. I have to *do* something!" Modesta Alicia Rivera. She was my resurrection and I am so grateful to her.

I think now that my depression was a gift because I could begin to walk with torture survivors. Almost every one of them comes to depression because of survival guilt. I feel close to prisoners, too, for the same reason. They have to deal with their guilt as well as with the confinement.

So I had to do something. I went to the Rio Grande Valley and became involved in bringing torture victims into the States. I'd come back in the middle of the night and the pastor never knew that I was using the parish car to transport refugees. I'd stop about a mile or so before the checkpoint, and they'd scurry through the fields, through the underbrush. But they said I had to do meetings and stuff at the parish, instead of working directly with refugees, so I went back to Chicago.

That's where I got arrested the first time. Accidently, actually. I was just walking by a group of people protesting outside the Naval Recruiting Center, down in the Loop, and they scooped up five of us. From then on, it was downhill all the way, as some people would say!

The Pledge of Resistance started and I trained for civil disobedience. "CD," they called it at the time. Mostly the focus was on Central America and the refugees and the sanctuary movement. Keeping people who were fleeing the wars in our apartment—that was part of it all.

Then I was transferred to a parish in Milwaukee. I was reluctant to go. I don't like formal things, have a hard time running Bingos and all that, and don't have patience with meetings. But I was able to get into a really good place and to continue to be involved in social justice things. It was in a poor neighborhood, in the north side of

Milwaukee. A mixture of Black, Hmong, and Hispanic people. And it turned out very well, because I had some freedom and the luxury to connect with the Catholic Worker there, with Casa Maria.

There I learned that I could laugh and connect with the people living on the streets and not feel that I had to change anything. I am not God; I don't change things. I just walk with people. Accompaniment. Acompañamiento in Spanish. That became my sacred word.

Still, I'd keep asking in my heart: "Where is the source of all this misery?" I came to the ordinary answers of greed and power and control, but one thing that stuck out for me as very real is the nuclear threat. How dare we jeopardize the children of the world and the future of our mother earth? So I joined with a group of other people—Kathy Kelly and [the late] Sam Day, and maybe a hundred others—and we met for almost a year to prepare for an action against the nuclear missiles.[10]

We called ourselves the Missouri Peace Planting, '88, and we planted flowers and corn at the nuclear missile silos. Fourteen of us did it first on August 15th. We divided up and went to ten different silos and got in with bolt cutters. We put displays along the fences, showing what we were there for. I had pictures of my nieces and nephews and so on, and in 1995, when we went back to the site, they were still there.

We'd get ban-and-bar letters every day. They'd pick us up and then release us and we'd go to another silo the next day. After the third day, when we burned our ban-and-bar letters on television, we knew there'd be a trial and the judge wouldn't let us go until we promised we wouldn't go to another missile silo.

Father Jerry went back anyway, saying Mass at the nuclear silo, as he had most of the other times. He was eventually sentenced to twenty-five months in federal prison and sent first to the low-security camp at Oxford, Wisconsin.

10. Kathy Kelly co-founded Voices in the Wilderness during the Iraqi sanction days and is now co-coordinator of Voices for Creative Nonviolence and a strong advocate for peace in Afghanistan. Samuel H. Day, Jr. (1926–2001) edited *The Progressive* for years, was a founder of Nukewatch, and a creative Midwest activist who was frequently imprisoned for resistance actions.

Duane Bean and Father Jerry Zawada inside a nuclear silo fence at the Missouri Peace Planting, 1988. Courtesy National Catholic Reporter.

Fr. Jerry: That was the first long one, yeah. I got in trouble at Oxford because I blew the whistle on some of the anomalies in this supposedly model prison. Then I stopped cooperating with a strip search and body cavity search. Now many of the guards would just pretend to do that . . . that full search, but some were sticklers, and one day they called other guards, pushed me against the wall and ripped off my clothes, and they . . . and invaded my body.

It was not . . . I was put in solitary confinement for about ninety days and finally my security level was raised and I was shipped out. They call it "diesel therapy," when they send you from prison to prison around the country. To take you down. You're deprived of almost everything. It's harder to make a phone call, it's harder to take a shower, harder to get anything. Nobody knows where you are. They can hide you for a long time like that. I've known people who've been on diesel therapy for a whole year.

I was in the hole in Terre Haute, Indiana, where Timothy McVeigh was executed; I was in El Reno, Oklahoma for Christmas.

That was a pretty bad place. I ended up in Danbury, Connecticut, where Dan Berrigan and other [resisters] had been. Then the next month I was moved to Sandstone, Minnesota. Carl Kabat was there, and we got to be very, very close friends.

From there I went to a half-way house in Milwaukee to finish my sentence and then was on probation for another year. The first bombing of Iraq took place in January of 1991. I stood in protest and actually got arrested eight times while I was on probation. They didn't find out for a long time, but then I had to do five more months—in Chicago, at MCC, the Metropolitan Correction Center.

After a witness trip to the Middle East, Father Jerry turned to helping torture survivors at Su Casa Catholic Worker in Chicago. He was in Iraq, helping Mother Theresa's sisters with their handicapped children, when the latest Iraq war started. After he became ill, he had to leave. Then in 2001, he crossed the line at the SOA protest and received his first six-month SOA sentence. His second sentence for an SOA action was in 2003. Our interview occurred three weeks after he was released.

Ro: Do the other prisoners see you as a priest?

Fr. Jerry: Some do. It doesn't make a whole lot of difference. I feel it's my privilege to listen to them. People with very severe problems would come to me, sometimes in tears. There's a keen sense of abandonment [in prison]—abandonment by families, abandonment by life. One guy said he wanted to be baptized Catholic, so I baptized him underneath the oak trees. If there was a way I could have stayed in, I would have done that. I . . . I just miss the guys so much.

I'd like to encourage anyone who has the luxury of time that I have—especial religious sisters and priests and bishops—to take some risks along these lines. And to encourage others to take risks. We all have our limitations but we also all have our gifts, and we need to respect that, not only for ourselves but to encourage that in each other. We have to go down to the roots of what's happening in our society, the roots of oppression, the roots of what's causing so much grief in this world, and what's threatening the future. To do that, we may have to let some of the day-to-day parish things go.

Fr. Louis Vitale, OFM, and Fr. Jerry Zawada, OFM, just before crossing the line at SOA, 2005.

Father Louis Vitale, OFM

When I interviewed Father Lou Vitale in 2004, he was a pastor in a downtown San Francisco Church. In his descriptions of young urban activists that day, he could have been talking about Occupy. Since that day in October, he's crossed the line at SOA, been imprisoned for opposing the training of the US military in torture techniques at Fort Huachuca, Arizona, detained in Egypt as peace delegates tried to cross into Gaza in 2009, and tried for civil disobedience at Creech Air Force Base. In 2010, he served his fourth prison term for an SOAW action. This is all part of his position as Action Advocate for Pace e Bene, a Franciscan resource for nonviolent living.

Fr. Lou: I've been a Franciscan for [almost fifty] years. Before that, I was in the Korean War. Actually, I was an interceptor officer in the back seat of air defense fighter planes. Here in the States, in Indiana. We thought we were probably the most dedicated guys in the whole damn Air Force—defending America by protecting Detroit and Chicago. [Chuckles.] We roamed around, ready to shoot down Russian bombers. In fact, once they did send us up to shoot one down, insisting it was clearly identified. Well, we decided we'd better look first, and we saw ladies looking out the windows at us. It was a commercial airplane.

After that I went into the seminary and after ordination in 1963, everything was going on! The Vatican Council, the Church listening to the voices of the poor, the civil rights movement, and then the Farm Worker movement. Cesar Chavez taught me a lot about fasting and civil disobedience. Then I got very involved with draft resistance and Vietnam and we did all kinds of civil disobedience. I kind of expected prison terms during those years, but it never happened.

I think the first time I was arrested was in the early '70s. Las Vegas. We did a sit-in with welfare rights mothers on the Strip. I remember thinking that would be the end of everything in the priesthood. But it wasn't: I ended up a Minister to the Province, and moved to Oakland and got involved in Berkeley.

Dan Berrigan came and got everybody all excited and on Ash Wednesday, probably in 1980, we sat in at the Chancellor's office. I remember a young friar was with us. He's going, "Oh my God! I'll be thrown out of the order."

I said, "Don't worry. I'm the guy who would throw you out." So.

Then we started in on the Nevada test site and Nevada Desert Experience. 1982 was the 800th anniversary of the birth of St. Francis. That Easter, on Good Friday, we got urged by Dan Ellsberg to do civil disobedience. By now, I've probably been arrested 100 or 150 times or something at the Nevada test site. They don't do much, unless you get into a building. We did that once and got three months, but most of the time it works out to only a couple of weeks in tiny county jails.

Later, I spent three months in prison at Nellis Air Force Base in Las Vegas, from an action at the School of the Americas. They were using the same facilities to practice bombing for Iraq, so the camp is in the middle of all the nuclear weapons. In fact, it's there to provide labor for the base. They wouldn't let me near the planes, of course. [Grins.]

Modern technology allows for the narcotizing of the military. You push a button and blow up a city or send out one of those drone bugs to hit a house, but you don't see flesh burning. I remember a pilot in the Vietnam War telling me that he'd dropped bombs everywhere, and "what he was doing didn't really hit him." But one day he was driving a jeep somewhere and it broke down and he had to walk cross country. Well, he ran across the enemy, Vietcong. They got into a hand-to-hand fight and he killed the guy with a knife. "I can still feel the warm blood going down my arm." What turned St. Francis into a saint, I think, was that kind of experience. Because war was always that way in those days. But not now. They say the kids train in the army faster now, because they grow up playing video games.

Ro: Yeah. Doesn't it feel funny not to be able to wear your robe when you're in jail?

Fr. Lou: Oh, I don't wear it all the time. People like me to wear it in demonstrations 'cause the press picks up on it. People ask me how they can get publicity for their actions, get a picture in the paper. I tell them, "Wear a brown robe and handcuffs."[11] The first couple of weeks [of the latest Iraq war,] I probably got arrested a dozen times.

I'm a vegetarian and very active and my health is excellent, but I'm seventy-two now, so I think my biggest asset is being a grandfather figure, offering support and encouragement to younger people. They're so bright and they've got so much commitment and passion. They're going to change the face of America and of the world. Once Dan Berrigan was asked, "Who are your heroes?" And he said, "We don't need heroes, we need communities." So I want to give support to those young communities.

In the eighties, we had these incredible transformations by people power. By getting hundreds of thousands of people in the streets, sometimes called by a Cardinal, like in the Philippines. Or Poland, with the leadership of some of the Church. Nobody, nobody, could have predicted that! No one could have predicted that sudden transformation of power when the Soviets fell in Moscow. And in parts of Latin America, and then in South Africa . . . all these changes.

Some young people say, "Yes, but look what happened. They didn't do this, or they're doing that . . . Mrs. Aquino's still oppressing people" and on and on. But you've got to keep doing it, doing the resistance. You've got to keep doing the organizing.

The young people have enormous imagination, vision, courage, all of that. So not to give up. To work together. Their systems of consensus are much better than anything we had. In the Vietnam era, we were always looking for a leader. Now you've got all sorts of kids making puppets. Learning how to lock themselves into pipes. Fill up

11. A photo of Father Lou's handcuffed hands, "Having a Hand in Protest" by Robert Durell, appeared in the *Los Angeles Times* in 2004. It is reprinted on the front cover of Riegle, *Doing Time for Peace*.

a car with cement and park it in front of the gates to block traffic. They're creative, energetic.

Not weak and not violent, certainly in terms of human beings. But not all of it is stuff that we're comfortable with. We who come out of the faith community, who may be older, kind of like things to be a little more . . . uh, maybe reverent.

Ro: Are you comfortable with a stealth action, a Plowshares, for instance? Where you plan it and do it in secret?

Fr. Lou: Well, we did a de-fencing action at the Nevada test site, cutting down a fence, which I probably wouldn't have done earlier on. You know, when Gandhi started off on the salt march, he didn't tell anybody what he was going to do, he just got up in the morning and started walking. So a certain amount of that goes on. But I also think there's just got to be room for different expressions. On the other hand, I think you can do something that technically doesn't damage any property but insults people and that's more damaging, less nonviolent.

I think you have to look at the quality of what goes on. In the days when this present war started, here in San Francisco, people were talking about disrupting the financial district. The former head of the Pacific Stock Exchange, who was a retired Air Force colonel, had come to some of the first big rallies, and said we had to do something more. So he kind of led us to sitting down on Montgomery Street, in front of the Stock Exchange. He was clear that it had to be absolutely nonviolent and it was. But it *did* stop the people trying to drive to work in the Stock Exchange.

I asked the head of the hotel workers' and janitors' union how he felt about the sit-down. And he says, "Our members don't go to work in the financial district in cars. They're underground [on the BART] or they're on the bus. It was the Jaguars and the BMWs that were stopped in the traffic. And that's OK. [Those people] need to take a little rest from making money to feed the war machine." I *am* cautious about it, though, because I think it gives the impression of violence when you destroy property.

I find so many people with so much enthusiasm and optimism. There's an incredible energy that interlocks all of us together, all over the world, and all that energy is somehow a source of . . . you can call it love, you can call it human goodness, but there's something that draws us to that kind of unity.

Martin Luther King said that the world leans toward justice. I think the human community also leans towards compassion and love. It's deeply built inside of us. We do a lot to cover it up, and it can get choked out of people. But there's so much of it, so much out there. I see it even in the homeless people here. (You get close, because we let them sleep here in the church.) I believe the human community is capable of some dramatic changes, despite political leaders and despite the US culture of money, money, money.

Ro: We're drowning in stuff.

Fr. Lou: Oh, yes! And that conditions us to be dissatisfied. We're conditioned to be dissatisfied with everything, including our resistance movements. We don't do it fast enough, well enough. We didn't have good enough communications, we didn't get enough people. We've got to get over that, to see that in resistance, there's human goodness and life and energy and passion.

Why are people doing these things? Because they really do care. These young people risk their careers. Most of them live pretty grungy, not like me when I was twenty and bought myself a Jaguar Roadster while I was in the military. I mean, it was so stupid. A year later, I entered the Franciscans and was never so happy. Cesar Chavez never lost his optimism, so why should I?

10

War Tax Resistance

From the beginning of what became the United States, people have resisted paying for war. Members of the Society of Friends and others of the traditional peace churches—Amish, Church of the Brethren, Shakers, and Mennonites—not only refused military service but refused levies for war, although that practice wasn't followed consistently after the Civil War.[1] The classic "Civil Disobedience" by Henry David Thoreau was written after he was jailed for refusing to pay a poll tax levied to wage war on Mexico.

Catholic Workers have traditionally been tax refusers, with their voluntary poverty taking earnings below taxable level. They are joined by member of other pacifist groups—War Resisters League (WRL), Fellowship of Reconciliation (FOR) and in 1948 the Peacemakers, a revolutionary and anarchistic pacifist group founded in response to the imposition of mandatory income tax withholding.[2] Members of the New England Committee for Nonviolent Action (NECNVA), under the guidance of Bob and Marjorie Swann, also resisted taxes as part of the complete pacifism of their Voluntown, CT, community.

War tax resistance reached its peak during the Vietnam War, with some 20,000 income tax resisters openly redirecting some or all of their federal taxes. Brad Lyttle was the first coordinator of War Tax Resistance (WTR) when it was launched in 1969. He also was deeply involved with the telephone tax refusal campaign. This tax was "purpose-built" to pay for wars and at the height of the campaign, over a million people

1. Cooney and Michalowski, *Power of the People*, 202.
2. Ibid., 118.

were refusing these generally small sums, according to Brad's memory.[3] After awhile, the IRS simply stopped trying to collect and most phone companies agreed with their customers' requests to remove the refused phone tax from their bills.

By 1972 there were 192 local WTR chapters across the land but in 1975, with the demise of overt warfare, WTR was disbanded. Seven years later the NWTRCC, (National War Tax Resistance Coordinating Committee) was formed in response to in response to rapid growth in military spending.[4] The NWTRCC and WRL websites and NWTRCC members, including Brad Lyttle and Frances Crowe, stand ready to counsel taxpayers in ways to resist war taxes.[5]

This chapter profiles four tax resisters. Juanita Nelson makes her anti-war statement with a life of extreme simplicity. Susan Crane, Karl Meyer, and Randy Kehler recount more complicated ways. All see that not paying for war is a moral imperative.

Juanita Nelson

Juanita and Wally Nelson were cofounders of Peacemakers, along with Ernest and Marion Bromley.[6] Juanita and Wally lived most of their lives together at the Traprock Peace Community in Deerfield, Massachusetts, chopping their own wood and cooking on a wood stove, lighting their home with candles, and growing all their own food. Wally died in 2002. When I interviewed Juanita in 2005, she was eighty-two and had just

Juanita Nelson, 2005.

3. Brad Lyttle interview, Marquette Archives.

4. See online: www.nwtrcc.org/history/WTRhistory.php for a history of war tax resistance that provides deep context for the stories told here.

5. See Chapter 6 of Riegle, *Doing Time for Peace*, for Crowe's war tax resistance strategies and Brad Lyttle's interview in Marquette Archives for his. Other members of NWTRCC can help as well.

6. Cooney and Michalowski, *The Power of the People*, 115.

recently given up chopping her own wood. The candlelit cabin on the hill glowed with warmth, as did she.

Juanita: I met Wally when he was in jail. I was a reporter on the *Cleveland Call and Post* and was sent to interview him. He'd walked out of CPS Camp—Civilian Public Service Camp. You see, he was a conscientious objector, and after he'd been in the camp about a year, he realized that he should never have registered in the first place, and he walked out, along with five other men. I was a very law-abiding citizen at the time.

Ro: At the time. [Laughter.] When did you stop being a law-abiding citizen?

Juanita: Well, I guess shouldn't have said that. I was arrested for the first time back in 1943 when I was a student at Howard in DC. Two friends of mine and I tried to eat at a lunch counter in a drug store. At that time, Washington was probably as segregated as any place in the country. After much clamoring, we were served the hot chocolate we'd ordered and were charged twenty-five cents instead of the usual ten cents. So we put down our dimes and walked into the arms of seven stalwart policemen.

We thought it was going to be a great lark to go to jail and eat with these hardened women criminals, but the Dean of Women at Howard got us out. I've always fasted in jail since, so I can say I've never eaten in jail. [Chuckles.] Anyway, that event led to the formation of the Civil Rights Committee of Howard. We had a sit-in and picket lines and so on, and we changed a small restaurant on the edge of campus in less than a week. The shortest campaign success I've ever had. Later I started working for CORE and that's what I was doing when Wally and I got together in 1948.

Pacifism: I hadn't particularly thought about it before, because at CORE nonviolence was just a strategy, not a life commitment, but Wally's answer to the sixty-four dollar question resonated with me. You know the "What-would-you-do-if somebody-was-going-to-kill-you-or-someone-you-love?" question. As I recall, he said something like, "I'd try to protect myself, but when it comes down to it, I can't decide that my life is worth more than somebody else's." That just made perfect sense. And still does.

When Wally and I got together, we right away became tax refusers. It was the same year Peacemakers was founded. Peacemakers advocated nonviolence as a way of life and two of its major tenets were nonregistration for the draft and nonpayment of war taxes, along with [living in] community, no [usury], and all sorts of things. What did General Alexander Haig say? "Let them march all they want just as long as they pay their taxes!"

We took the tack of not only not paying the taxes but also of not filing or giving any information. At first I was able to claim Wally as my dependent. He did odd jobs where no one took anything out of his paycheck, and I wasn't making very much, either. We'd often be asked to come down to the IRS, but for a long time, they didn't do anything to us. Just a lot of summonses and this, that, and the other. But in 1959, eleven years after I had become a refuser, I was finally arrested.

Wally was away when they came for me. Early, early in the morning. I'd been sleeping in the nude and when the doorbell rang, I put on my robe, of course—my white terry bathrobe—and answered the door. I knew immediately they were federal marshals. (You can tell before they even flap open their wallets and show their credentials.)

So we sat there and talked and no one made a move. Finally, I could see that they were waiting for me to get dressed, and I realized that I really didn't want to go to jail. Why should I get dressed, then? So I didn't. I wouldn't walk so they rolled me into court in a wheelchair.[7] But they held me only a few hours. The magistrate was so kind. Said he didn't want to be the first to jail a woman for tax refusal. That was fine with me 'cause I'm not too interested in going to jail. I just try not to let the prospect deter me from doing what I believe in. [Laughs heartily.]

Ro: Juanita, what sustains you in all these years of living counter-culturally?

Juanita: Well, I wouldn't say that I'm living counter-culturally. I'm doing maybe a few things different from most people, but I'm right in the middle of it, believe me. Right in the middle of what I abhor.

I . . . I have never wanted a whole lot. I was born poor, according to the standards of this country. I've never bought a lot of clothes and I just naturally don't like to shop. I like direct action, and that's why I liked working for CORE.

My mind keeps coming back to the idea that I shouldn't complain about something and still be a part of it. So over the years I'd

7. Juanita describes this incident in "A Matter of Freedom" where she also gives a rationale for both tax resistance and noncooperation with federal agents. This essay originally appeared in *Liberation*, September, 1960, and is available on the NWTRCC website, with the author's permission.

try to incorporate a little bit more, and a little bit more, and a little bit more into my daily life. For instance, the tax refusal. How can I pay for the terrible war, either directly or indirectly?

Ro: So the less you can buy . . .

Juanita: That's my goal now. It's a two-pronged thing. I don't want to support the corporations and the systems that bring these things to me. For instance, there's a utility pole right out there by the cabin, but I'm not hooked up to it. It makes me feel pretty good that I'm not using something that's so close. You know, it's reverse bragging, but . . . The other thing is, as my awareness increases, I realize that I didn't want a lot of the stuff in the first place.

Our great greed comes at the expense of other people on the planet. So I've come to feel that war is not the problem. It's all the things we go to war for, all the oil, all the "stuff!" Of course it's not just us, but we're the top dog. We all have to simplify, simplify, simplify. I'm not saying that what I'm doing is exactly the way everybody has to do it, but we surely have to do something!

Ro: It sounds like you come at it rather naturally, but there's obviously a very deep morality and caring for others at the bottom of this philosophy.

Juanita: No, I care for myself. People always talk about what I'm sacrificing. But the sacrifice would be if I believe something and then didn't try to implement it. That would be a sacrifice, wouldn't it? And I don't have a hard time! We have . . . I have fun.

Some people think it's a great adventure to climb Mount Everest or go around the world in a Viking ship. But isn't it an adventure to try to live what you believe? That's my adventure.

Susan Crane

Susan Crane's life has been full of principled adventure, as well. In her family years, she was a tax resister in Ukiah, California and used her resistance to raise public awareness. Now she lives below the poverty level as a member of the Redwood City Catholic Worker community.

Susan Crane, 2005.

Susan: When I decided to be a tax resister, I didn't earn much money so I didn't owe any tax. I'd send in the forms anyway, saying I wouldn't pay for war-making even if I owed taxes. The IRS responded with a $500 "frivolous fine." Outrageous! They fined me for sending in a statement saying I wouldn't pay money to kill our brothers and sisters. So I guess that was the beginning of my public debate with the IRS tax collectors. Larry Minson, the IRS agent on my case, came to my workplace and talked to me and finally put me down as "non-collectible."

When I started teaching, I was making more money, so I just refused. On each April 15th, some of us had a big gathering in our town, and we'd redistribute the resisted war tax. We gave to the soup kitchen, to the community dining room, to the women's shelter, to different organizations in town. Many people helped with that fund. Maybe it was actually resisted money, or maybe it was money that they donated because their hearts were with us. That was always quite an event, a very good thing.

The IRS would send all sorts of notices, and I'd just throw them away. Then at a certain point they started to garnish my wages. Now it's interesting: in California, if your wages are garnished, you can't get any sort of assistance. No food stamps or anything. Because your gross income is counted even if you don't get it. I was raising my children, and I thought, "I can't do that. I won't be able to pay my rent or get food."

It was a very hard decision because I felt like I was going against my conscience, and shaking hands with the Devil, as it were. But at any rate, I went to the IRS agent and I said, "Okay, let's talk."

Larry Minson said, "I want you to pay $50 a month, and then I'll let you have the rest of your paycheck. I agreed and wrote him a check for $50, and he released my paycheck. This happened in January. In February, I made a big heart—this big [spreads her arms way out to the side]. I talked to my bank ahead of time, and they said they'd accept this great big check. We took a photo of it and it appeared in the newspaper. Then I went down to the IRS office, and I gave that check to Larry Minson.

I decided to make an action out of paying every month, so in March, I got a big piece of pressed board, and I put pictures from the Iraq war on it—the first Iraq war. And I said, "On this day I regret to pay the IRS $50." I took this to the IRS office, along with my pastor and a person who wanted to take pictures of me presenting it to Larry. I could hear them talking through the door. "She's got a photographer with her. Don't open the door!"

They wouldn't accept my check, a fully negotiable check! I thought about that, and then I realized that I shouldn't be paying them anyway! So I said, "Forget it!" I closed my bank account so they couldn't garnish. I'd just get my paycheck, cash it, and use money orders to pay bills. And I guess Larry Minson just kept putting my folder at the bottom of the pile because I never heard from them again.

Karl Meyer

Karl Meyer learned about the Catholic Worker as a very young man and started CW houses in Chicago soon after resisting the Civil Defense take-shelter law with Dorothy Day and Ammon Hennacy. Karl's work on war tax resistance influenced many protesters during the Vietnam War. In 1997 he founded Greenlands CW community in Nashville, Tennessee; in 2012, he celebrated fifty-five years as a Catholic Worker.

Karl Meyer, 2004.

Karl: I haven't paid federal income taxes for forty-four years. Now that we don't have the draft, the only thing that the federal government demands of you is that you pay taxes for militarism and empire. Our great-grandchildren will pay in perpetuity for the yearly increases in weapon spending. So if you don't believe in the oppression and savaging of people in other countries in order to get their oil, you don't pay the taxes. And if they come around and say you either pay or go to jail, you've got to go to jail.

But only a minuscule number of all tax protesters or resisters, whether principled or unprincipled, have gone to jail. It's a very minor risk. There are consequences in your job situation, but the IRS has simply snowed people into believing the worst. So there's a tremendous fear of the Internal Revenue Service. Now I've spent a total of about two years of my adult lifetime in jail but only nine months of that was for tax refusal.

I'd been generally not paying taxes for years, but my serious resistance started in 1960. Eroseanna Robinson, a beautiful Black athlete who was part of the Peacemaker movement, was arrested in Chicago for refusing to file tax returns. She was a complete noncooperator—had to be carried into court on a stretcher—and ended up with a one-year prison sentence for criminal contempt. She didn't cooperate in jail, either, and was fasting in the Cook County Jail. So I organized a round-the-clock vigil in her support.

Like Thoreau said, in a society which imprisons anyone unjustly, the only place where a free man can abide with honor is in jail. If you're going to imprison Eroseanna Robinson in this way, the only place where I can abide with honor is in jail. So I'd picket and leaflet at the IRS office, get arrested, and sentenced to three days. Did it again and again and each time the sentence went up. I served about sixty-five days in jail in this way, until the Bureau of Prisons wrote to the judge and asked them to release Eroseanna Robinson. (That was for the convenience of the Bureau of Prisons 'cause she was just too hard to handle.) When she was released, the court lawyer that had been appointed to represent me got me released, too.

This was the winter and spring of 1960. At that point I figured out what to do so I'd never have to pay federal income taxes again. I began to claim extra allowances on the W-4 form. This W-4 method subsequently became the major method used by tax refusers to prevent the withholding of tax. It made tax refusal accessible to people who worked for wages. So the IRS decided to strike the fear of God in them. Or fear of the IRS. Well, making martyrs never really works because more people just hear about it.

But they tried. Within a period of a couple years, they indicted maybe a dozen people for W-4. I got the most time because I was the inventor or leader of it, and I'd written a lot of tax resistance counseling literature, explaining the IRS regulations and the consequences and also advocating that the tax refusal money be put into alternative funds in order to do good things with it. People were ready for this act of resistance and many people did it.

Here's how [my arrest] actually happened. In 1970, at the height of the Vietnam War, I went into the IRS office in Chicago with some other resisters, shortly before April 15th. We conducted a "Tea Party

Protest." Passed out leaflets and served tea from thermoses to people who were waiting in line.

Then I went into the District Director's office and laid out a poster of the My Lai massacre on his desk, with the *Life Magazine* picture of the bodies of the Vietnamese women and children lying in the trench. I had poked the bees' nest, and he had me investigated and indicted a year later, along with two other W-4 resisters.

I was convicted of claiming extra allowances on a W-4 form. I pleaded guilty, actually, to two counts, and I got two years in prison, for which I served nine months before they released me on parole.

The IRS knows the only thing they can do to me is put me in jail. They can't do that without a trial, and they don't want that kind of public relations. See, once they find you can't be intimidated, and they know they can't collect, you're invulnerable.

You know, Ammon Hennacy was always talking about people who "chickened out," people who refused to stand up under threat. Well, I didn't play chicken on this one. No! No, no!

Ro: Aren't people now getting what's called a frivolous penalty?

Karl: Well, that's for making claims on the tax return that aren't allowable. The IRS found that putting people in jail by enforcing the W-4 regulations on claiming allowances didn't stop people from doing it, and it also costs them money and bad public relations. So they found a type of penalty that was easy to administer, easy to apply, and severe enough to discourage the vast majority of people.

So now their main method of enforcing the W-4 regulations is a $500 civil penalty for claiming allowances to which you're not entitled. Then there's also the $500 penalty for making frivolous claims on a tax return. [*Nota bene:* In 2006, the so-called "frivolous fine" went up from $500 to $5000.]

They can impose [these penalties] without a trial and then you have to go to court to prove that the penalty was improperly imposed, rather than *them* taking you to court. So it's a lot less costly for them and more effective against most people.

One thing people ask me: "Why do you refuse to pay *any* of the federal income tax? Some programs in the federal government are good." Some people say that because 50% goes to the military, they'll refuse 50% of their taxes. First, you don't have any control of where your money goes, anyway: 50% of whatever you pay will go for military costs because of the way income tax revenues are allocated.

There's another argument, too. Say you have $1000 that you want to pay to the federal government for the programs you believe in. Feed the poor, provide housing, shelter, clothing, and so on. Well, $900 of it will go into salary of government bureaucrats. Now everybody needs a job, including government folks. No objection to letting these people make a living, but only about $100 of your $1000 will go to causes and projects that you really believe in.

If you give $1000 to the Catholic Worker for their meal and shelter programs, the volunteers of the Catholic Worker movement will add probably $10,000 worth of volunteer labor. So if you give $1,000 to the Federal Government, you get about $100 worth of services to the poor; if you give $1000 to the Catholic worker, you get about $11,000 worth of personalized services. I think maybe that's what the loaves and fishes miracle was—that people shared.

Randy Kehler

Randy Kehler and Betsy Corner are one of the few pacifist couples who actually lost their property for resisting military taxes. They'd been tax resisters since their marriage in 1976 and continuously active in Massachusetts war tax resistance circles. From 1989 to 1993, the battle between their community and the IRS attracted national attention, and hundreds of supporters from around New England joined Randy and Betsy in their campaign.

Randy Kehler, 2005.

Randy's no stranger to resistance, spending almost two years in federal prison for refusing the draft during the Vietnam War.[8] In the movie, *The Most Dangerous Man in America*, Daniel Ellsberg credits Randy with giving him the courage to publish the Pentagon Papers.

8. Read this story in Chapter 3.

Randy: I was introduced to the idea of tax resistance while working for the War Resisters League in the 1960s. Not letting them use your money to make war if you're not going to let them use your body—it made perfect sense to me. At that point, of course, there was nothing they could take from me 'cause I didn't make any money.

Betsy and I got married in 1976. We have a grown-up daughter, and we've been good partners for each other, a good team because we have similar values. Together we usually made slightly over the minimum income to be taxed, so we jointly refused. We decided not to pay any of our federal taxes because even if we paid a dollar, they'd take fifty percent of that dollar for war. We've done that every year since 1976. Always very publicly, announcing it in a letter to the newspaper and being part of other tax resistance activities.

For years, we'd put the withheld amount in a War Resisters escrow account, so that if they came after us and took money, we would have what we needed. And then in 1987, Brian Willson got run over by the train.[9] He was a dear friend, and we decided that, in view of his commitment, we were no longer going to put the money into escrow because it isn't much of a risk if you keep your money where you can always fall back on it.

Now we give it away. Half to local homeless shelters and food banks and the other half to victims of US war-making in other countries. For years, the money would help build artificial limbs for kids from Nicaragua whose limbs had been blown off by our Contra war. And then to groups that are helping to aid people in Iraq. In recent years, we've actually divided it into thirds, donating a third to groups working to bring about nonviolent methods of conflict resolution, particularly between nations, groups like the Nonviolent Peace Force.

Ro: Did the IRS finally take the money in the WRL escrow account?

Randy: No. In theory, it wasn't our money anymore. Although we could get it back from them at any time, it legally belonged to the fund, so the IRS couldn't take it. The IRS goes after the easiest things first—your bank account, then your employer, then your property. But sometimes they don't go after anybody. It's amazing! So much of it depends on who [they] have in what local office.

---

9. As part of a protest of US weapons shipments to Central America, Willson blocked the train tracks at the Concord, California Naval Weapons Station. The train refused to stop and Willson lost both legs (*Wikipedia*).

Sometime in the '80s, we had our bank account seized, so we stopped using banks and to this day we use only cash and money orders. Then they came after employees, and we'd have to switch employers so they wouldn't garnish our wages. In 1989, they finally came after the house.

People often respond to Betsy and me—knowing only that losing our house was the penalty we suffered for refusing to pay our taxes—with an emphasis on suffered [drags out the word, humorously]. "Oh, you're so brave! I could *never* do that!"

Maybe they don't realize that we didn't walk in out of the blue and say, "Here, come take our house." Over many years, we just put one foot after the next, and it finally led to that. At each step, we'd ask ourselves if we could do it, and we'd decide that we could. We also learned to live with the fear, to the point where now we don't fear the IRS.

It's been a long time . . . They create a hassle for us, sometimes, but we try to turn each hassle into something positive. Like this big demonstration that went on for years, here—day after day, twenty-four hours a day—when they seized the house.

At first they didn't actually take the house physically from us, because there were all sorts of procedural delays, including us going to federal court and trying to argue on the basis of international law that it was the government who was breaking the law and that we were acting to uphold the law by refusing to pay for these crimes.

Motions went back and forth and we spent a lot of time writing briefs and consulting our friendly international law experts, but we didn't even get a hearing. They actually didn't take physical possession of the house until early December of 1991, two years after it all started.

Ro: I remember reading about it in the Midwest and being excited and scared for you. Can you talk about the actual day?

Randy: Sure. They were operating secretly, but we got a tip because the federal marshals had contacted a local locksmith to be at our house early one morning to put new locks on the doors. His daughter found out—just by chance, I think—and got word to us the night before. So we cleared out the house, taking out our papers and books and pictures and stuff that was valuable to us, everything but the old, junky furniture and hand-me-downs.

Our daughter Lillian was twelve at the time, and Betsy left with her. I stayed in the house. We'd had a blizzard the night before. Snow drifts two feet high, and the wind whipping around and the snow in your face. It was probably 6:00 a.m. Still dark.

The marshals banged through the door with guns drawn. Searched the whole house, looking for trap doors and people hiding. They said later, "How do we know that you're not like those right-wing tax resisters, armed and ready to shoot at us, like out West?" And of course, they easily could have known, but I guess they have to take every precaution.

To calm my nerves, I sat down at our old upright piano and just started playing. Not to be dramatic, but I only knew one piece and it was Bach/Gounod's *Ave Maria*. So I'm sitting there playing it, and the marshals are buzzing around the house with their guns and their flak jackets. Finally they handcuffed me and drove me to Springfield and locked me up.

Then they came back and got Betsy, who was with a neighbor across the street, and that was pretty traumatic. But they released her right away. The judge insisted that I promise not to go back to the house because it was government property.

I said I wouldn't cooperate with that, and he gave me a contempt-of-court sentence, which could be renewed every six months indefinitely. So I didn't know how long I was going to be in jail. I was there ten weeks before the IRS decided they were going to hold a second auction of our house.

See, they'd tried to auction it in 1989, and we had this wonderful demonstration with probably five hundred people lining the main street of Greenfield in a more or less silent vigil while this auction took place. We had advertised in a wide community and sent letters to realtors and other folks, saying "Please don't bid on this house and here's why." It also said, if "If you bid on it, we're not leaving it, so you'll have a problem on your hands."

Nobody *did* bid, except us. Our community people bid things like "free massages for overtired IRS workers" and "free labor" and "supplies for Nicaragua." We piled up huge stacks of [donated] canned goods on the street, and we bid the canned goods to go to local homeless shelters and food banks. The minimum bid price that the government was asking was only five thousand dollars. We had maybe $25 or $30 thousand worth of goods and services, but of course they rejected all of it. That was in 1989.

Betsy Corner speaking at a 1991 rally, Greenfield, MA. © Ed Hedemann.

So now it's February 1992 and they decided to hold another auction, this time down in Springfield, farther away from our supporters, and they advertised much more widely, and I think they actually recruited bidders. They got maybe five or six bidders, and the high bid was just above the minimum, a little over $5,000. This young local couple who had one child and another one on the way—he was a part-time Greenfield police officer—he made the bid and they got the house.

Meanwhile our people . . . The moment I was taken out and the new locks were put on, a really elaborate organization of affinity groups took over. They were from all over New England, with a dozen of them from right here. They organized an ongoing occupation of the house. One affinity group per week—week after week after week—would live in the house. And that continued even after this auction.

The new owners were pretty innocent, in some ways. Their attitude was, "Hey, we bought it, and the law is on our side." But the police didn't move in [on the affinity groups] because, first of all, there was sympathy even in the DA's office.

We had claimed all along that they couldn't seize the place, anyway, because the house went with the lease to the land. The land was in a land trust and only the trust could change the lease to somebody else. The police and the DA's office thought it should be resolved in court, so they didn't try to evict us.

Then on April 15, 1992, while most of us were in Greenfield doing our annual tax day vigil, the couple who had bid on the house, along with some of their friends who were really hard-core, did a sort of a commando-type raid on the house. Burst through our doors and . . . There were only three people in the house at that moment and they refused to leave, so the [raiders] essentially held them hostage and moved in and locked the place from the inside. Literally nailed boards across the windows and what-not, and they set up their own occupation of the house. So suddenly all of us were on the outside except for those three.

It was really eerie. The commando folks did everything they could to get our three people out, including blaring loud music at them. They refused to let them use the bathroom, so they had to pee into flowerpots, and they wouldn't give them any food or water. I mean, it was just . . . They yelled and screamed at them, everything they could think of. Finally they got very brutal and our friends left.

Then we were all on the *outside* and we continued a round-the-clock, 24/7 vigil right next to the house, from April of 1992 right straight through September of 1993. Again, the affinity groups, not missing a beat, were coming to vigil week after week after week. Set up tents and a mobile lean-to eventually, because we spent a winter there.

These people had a lawyer who sued everybody imaginable, from Betsy and me to the land trust to the neighbors, for essentially violating their civil rights by refusing to let them live quietly in their home. The court ordered all of us to leave the land, even though the issue of who owned the land still wasn't resolved. About fifty people refused to leave and were jailed for up to ten days. Lots of activity, and we were doing all this stuff in the community to try to educate people about what war taxes were paying for and why we weren't paying and so forth.

The truth is, though, we lost a lot of public support as soon as that couple moved in. They had a child and a new baby. We wanted to face off against the federal government, not their proxies, these naive working-class people.

It was like a strike where they move in scab workers who need the jobs, too. There were class elements, as well, although lot of the people who were with us also came from working-class backgrounds. But certainly as a whole, there was much more of a middle-class, college-educated flavor to the resisters. We tried hard not to make it us versus them, though, and once we proposed a Habitat for Humanity type project: We'd build a couple of houses, one of which would be for them.

At first they were excited about it but they changed their minds. We went ahead and built two houses, anyway. Called the project "Building Our Swords into Plowshares." So now there are two lovely, high-quality, environmentally-advanced homes down in South Greenfield that we tried to the very end to interest them in moving to, but they wouldn't.

Unfortunately, the house became the issue. And this was very discouraging, for Betsy and me particularly, because the issue is where the money goes. It's the wars that are being fought, it's the people who are being killed and wounded, and all the suffering that war causes. But the media honed in on the house. Betsy and I weren't sorry when the vigil finally ended in September, 1993.

Ironically, soon after it ended, the couple decided they didn't want to stay out here anyway. Their whole story is tragic. The woman was in terrible economic straits and her husband was in real bad shape. We started a fund for her and in the years since then, what was intense hostility laced with—on their part—lots of guns being waved around and cars ramming into people and all sorts of stuff in the intervening years—almost everyone who had seemed to hate our guts has managed to develop friendly relations with us. It's been very, very comforting to know that those hostilities have virtually disappeared.

With Betsy's mom, we built this house and now we just lease it from the land trust so we don't own anything that the feds can take. A lovely young couple with small children wanted to join the land trust and they live in the original house, so it has all worked out.

The nicest thing about all of this was the care that our friends gave us during that time. Emotionally and in other ways, too. Doctors and dentists and a nutritionist all gave us free care for years, and we still get free Internet service. So the community has been terrific. Locally and nationally we gained more friends and more community out of this action that you can ever imagine.

Epilogue

Endings and Beginnings

During the Vietnam War, I helped to start the Saginaw Valley Peace Watch in Saginaw, Michigan. I planned vigils, corralled my young daughters to stuff envelopes, recruited students from the college where I taught. Like hundreds of other peace groups in small communities, we held candle-light marches, scheduled speakers, politely asked the draft board to stop drafting so many of our African-American neighbors, and read avidly of the exciting resistance work done in the big cities.

One of my icons from that time of searching and learning was Grace Paley, whose fiction I knew through a growing sense of myself as a feminist. When I interviewed her years later in Vermont, I was thrilled to learn how much our young lives had had in common, despite differ-ences in background, scale, and geography. Grace died of breast cancer a year after we talked and I salute her memory. Rest in peace, heroine of my young mother years!

At the end of her life, Grace took to calling herself "an old Jewish American writer lady."[1] Yes, she was that, but much, much more. Early on she saw the connections between patriarchy and war and ecological disaster, and early on she acted on these connections, particularly in the Greenwich Village Peace Center, with the War Resisters League, at the Women's Encampment at Seneca Falls, New York and in the Women's Action at the Pentagon, where she wrote the Unity Statement.[2] She

1. 1998 interview with Amy Holmes on *Salon*: www1.salon.com/11/depart-ments/litchat1.html. (Note: This page has been removed but was online when I wrote this segment.)

2. The Unity Statement has been reprinted in her collected nonfiction, Grace Paley, *Just As I Thought* (New York: Farrar, Straus & Giroux, 1998).

parented and worked and wrote and planned direct action against war and injustice, all at the same time. Calling herself "a combative feminist and a cooperative anarchist," her short time with me glows with the fire these seeming contradictions imply.

Grace Paley (1922–2007)

"Not in Our Name" Grace Paley, 1984. © Dorothy Marder, Courtesy of Swarthmore College Peace Collection.

Ro: Can we start at the beginning? Do you remember your first action for peace?

Grace: Oh, I was a kid. Like twelve years old. There was the Oxford Pledge.[3] We wore black arm bands. My parents were just normal Jewish Socialists, you know? They'd been imprisoned in Russia, as young people. They'd been great activists, but they didn't like me to be active. "Why here? It's so good here. Don't do it!" So they were upset when they found me suspended for a few days because I'd worn this black arm band.

Ro: And now everyone wears *pink,* including the feminist women in CODEPINK. I raised my daughters on [the album] "Free to be You and Me," so it's a little hard for me to get around the pink, although I admire their doing the gender thing.

Grace: I have that feeling, too. I'd like to talk to [CODEPINK], I'd like to be with them, but I can't get around the computer thing. You know, because we send out our e-mails privately, one of the things we miss

---

3. In the 1920s, a group of Oxford University students in Britain took what came to be known as the Oxford Pledge never to bear arms. Those who signed the US version stated they would refuse to go to war even if their government drafted them.

Epilogue

[today] is sitting around the table and stuffing the envelopes and licking the stamps and getting into arguments at the same time. Talking, and working together, and answering the phone and cleaning up and minding the kids, all at the same time. I think there's a certain loss without this.

Ro: Yes, the women doing it. How did your feminism feed into your work for peace?

Grace: Well, I don't know if it feeds *into* it. I think they're part of the same longing for a peaceful earth, for a world without war and without rage. And it seems that leaving women out of consideration for such a long time was a mistake in *all* the political movements. Now you always had single women jumping off and being powerful women, but the rest of the women were left behind because you can't do anything without a movement.

I . . . I didn't think, really, that I knew I was a feminist because there was no movement. But I began to write stories about women's lives, and it turned out that there *was* a movement and I was in it. We were drops in the second wave.

Ro: You *were* the second wave.

Grace: Yeah. A lot of water. [Laughs.]

Ro: And there was a lot of water, even in the hinterlands, where I was. There was so much hope, then, you know? Do you feel the hope now?

Grace: Well, the hope was created by action. Older people have to keep telling the younger people that. Without action, there's no hope. It doesn't mean we're without hope now, it means we're without enough action.

Actually, before the last election, we had a wonderful group of young people, up here [in Vermont]. I lived in New York, mostly. Did a lot of my work with WRL and the Greenwich Village Peace Center there, but I'd be up here a lot, and up here, people were working together, people about [my daughter] Nora's age, and they were creating something. And they did create it! They did it!

[In the earlier years], there were so many struggles where people didn't understand the connections. Some of the people were not antiwar, they were just anti-nuclear power, and that was it. And the anti-nuclear war people didn't want to talk to the anti-nuclear . . . you know. So it took a lot of time to bring those people together, and it had to be done by people who *wanted* to bring people together.

343

And then the women's movement came along, and all the men in the movement were insulted. I'm talking about our own people, our own movement. That went all the way through, both the nonviolent and the violent part. We had the Women's Pentagon Action [in 1980]. It was just a women's action, and it was really quite terrific because we had agreed that there'd be no speeches, and there were none.

Ro: Which, again, was a very feminist thing.

Grace: Yes, very feminist. It was theater. It was like . . . waves. A wonderful action, but the guys were *so* mad at us! They'd say to me, "You're just taking people away."

And I'd say, "No, we're bringing people in. There'll be more people in WRL once this is over than ever before."

Women's Pentagon Action, 1981. Dorothy Marder, Courtesy of Swarthmore College Peace Collection.

We decided to do this Pentagon thing mostly because we wanted to show what's his name—Reagan—that women were here. And we all decided, without discussion—the people who were young and almost all gay in Connecticut and the people over here in Vermont who were a little older and not gay, I mean very mixed—we all decided that we didn't want to have a single speaker.

There was a very strong influence from the Bread and Puppet Theater. We created it as theater: sadness, rage, defiance, and action.

Defiance was to walk up to the Pentagon, to surround the Pentagon and refuse to leave.

> Four huge female puppets . . . led some 2,000 women in a march past Arlington Cemetery to the Pentagon. There they encircled the building, put gravestones in the lawn, wove yarn across the entrances to symbolically reweave the web of life, and created rituals of mourning and defiance by chanting yelling, and banging on cans. Over 140 women were arrested for blocking the doors at two entrances.[4]

Ro: Can you think of other peace actions that were particularly feminist?

Grace: Well, there was Women's Strike for Peace, but once the war was over, it didn't do much. Up here, I'm closer to WILPF [Women's International League for Peace and Freedom]. They're Raging Grannies, the Central Vermont WILPF.

> Today in Vermont, we go to town meetings. Out of sixty towns, about fifty-seven voted for a resolution to bring the National Guards back here from Iraq. The resolution is too long, I think, and in a town meeting, that's a mistake because people begin to argue about each point, and you're in there all day. What was good about our discussion, though, is that they weren't all on one side. Two military families were there in our meeting, on opposite sides. Very strong views. But at the end, they fell into each other's arms, crying.

Ro: Now that's peacemaking! What other memories do you have about being an anarchist and maybe having it interfere with other parts of your life, with your writing life and your teaching life and your mother life and . . . ?

Grace: You can't look at it that way. If you do, you're dead. Of course, you're pulled in different ways. Like if your kids are sick, you're not going to get to that meeting. It doesn't matter who you are. Unless, of course, you're the only one who can make it nonviolent. [Laughs.]

Ro: But how did you decide what to spend your time on?

Grace: [Pause.] I almost don't know how I did it. When I look at my first three books, I really don't know how I did it. But I know that once I began to write something, that's all I did. Of course, I also

---

4. The Women's Pentagon Action, online: www.wloe.org/WLOE-en/background/wpastatem.html.

worked. We weren't rich. In the beginning we were supers in a rooming house. That was my job, my contribution. Later on I was a typist, and then all of a sudden I was a teacher. So much is luck, you know. But I wouldn't have given up my political interests for anything. And then I had only two kids, and their school was right next door, but suppose I'd had five?

I see that my life is all of a piece. A lot of coherence came from my writing, and my children were just a natural part of my life. It worked the way it should have worked, and it was very good, because my political interests fed into my writing. But I need to say I didn't know a thing about nonviolence when we began the Greenwich Village Peace Center and began working against the Vietnam War. Then we had our first lecture by a big young Black guy, Bayard Rustin. He absolutely turned me around. That was 1961, and that's the way I think and live now.

Ro: Were you afraid when you went to jail?

Grace: No. I thought I'd get two days, like everyone else. But I remember the judge looking at me. "What kind of a woman is this? She should know better!" So he gives me a whole week. I was surprised, but I wasn't afraid. I mean, I figured, "Hey, what's going to happen to me?" I still feel that. This particular prison was right in the middle of Greenwich Village. I passed it every day, so it was funny, in that sense, because finally I'm *in* it, not outside.

We should encourage the [young people] to go be arrested. But sometimes I wouldn't encourage young Black women. It's true that people of color are treated worse in jail than white women. And many of them have jobs they'd lose the minute they were arrested. They say to me, "Well, you're white."

And I'd say, "That's the exact reason I have to do it. The point is, it's too hard for you, so I have to do it." [Pauses for a long minute.]

I'll tell you one hope I have. The time before this latest Iraq War is the first time in history that *every* nation in this new world was opposed to us beginning a war. There've been lots of times when people have been trying to *stop* a war, but there has *never* been a time when everybody was trying to prevent a war from happening. Never! That's a new thing on the Earth. So I tell the kids: "Remember this! In your time, this happened. For the first time, all the nations on the Earth said, 'Don't go to war.' Every one of them." Lesson for the day.

Appendix

For Further Reading

Ackerman, Peter, and Jack Duvall. *A Force More Powerful: A Century of Nonviolent Conflict*. New York: Palgrave, 2000.

Adams, Judith Porter. *Peacework: Oral Histories of Women Peace Activists*. Boston: Twayne, 1991.

Alpert, Rebecca T. *Voices of the Religious Left: A Contemporary Sourcebook*. Philadelphia: Temple University Press, 2000.

Appelbaum, Patricia. *Kingdom to Commune: American Pacifist Culture between World War I and the Vietnam Era*. Chapel Hill: University of North Carolina Press, 2009.

Bennett, Scott H. *Radical Pacifism: The War Resisters League and Gandhian Nonviolence in America, 1915–1963*. Syracuse: Syracuse University Press, 2003.

Berrigan, Daniel. *The Trial of the Catonsville Nine*. Fordham University Press ed. New York: Fordham University Press, 2004.

Boyle, Francis. *Defending Civil Resistance under International Law*. Dobbs Ferry, NY: Transnational, 1987.

Brock, Peter. *Pacifism in the Twentieth Century*. Syracuse, NY: Syracuse University Press, 1999.

Browne, Harry. *Hammered by the Irish: How the Pitstop Ploughshares Disabled a U.S. War Plane—With Ireland's Blessing*. Oakland, CA: Counterpunch, 2008.

Chenoweth, Erica, and Maria J. Stephan. *Why Civil Resistance Works: The Strategic Logic of Nonviolent Conflict*. New York: Columbia University Press, 2011.

Chernus, Ira. *American Nonviolence: The History of An Idea*. Maryknoll, NY: Orbis Books, 2004.

Cooney, Robert, and Helen Michalowski, editors. *The Power of the People: Active Nonviolence in the United States*. Culver City, CA: Peace Press, 1987.

Day, Samuel H., Jr. *Prisoners on Purpose: A Peacemakers' Guide to Jails and Prisons*. Madison, WI: Nukewatch, 1989.

Dear, John. *Put Down Your Sword: Answering the Gospel Call to Creative Nonviolence*. Grand Rapids: Eerdmans, 2008.

DeBenedetti, Charles. *An American Ordeal: The Antiwar Movement of the Vietnam War*. Syracuse, NY: Syracuse University Press, 1990.

Douglass, James W. *The Non-Violent Cross: A Theology of Revolution and Peace*. 1968. Reprinted, Eugene, OR: Wipf & Stock, 2006.

Epstein, Barbara. *Political Protest and Cultural Revolution: Nonviolent Direct Action in the 1970s and 1980s*. Berkeley: University of California Press, 1991.

Foley, Michael S. *Confronting the War Machine: Draft Resistance during the Vietnam War*. Chapel Hill: University of North Carolina Press, 2003.

Frisch, Michael. *A Shared Authority: Essays on the Craft and Meaning of Oral and Public History*. SUNY Series in Oral and Public History. Albany: SUNY Press, 1990.

Kelly, Kathy. *Other Lands Have Dreams: From Bagdad to Pekin Prison*. Oakland, CA: AK Press, 2005.

Kisseloff, Jeff. *Generation on Fire: Voices of Protest from the 1960s*. Lexington: University Press of Kentucky, 2007.

Kosek, Joseph. *Acts of Conscience: Christian Nonviolence and Modern American Democracy*. New York: Columbia University Press, 2009.

Kulansky, Mark. *Nonviolence: The History of a Dangerous Idea*. New York: Random House Modern Library, 2008.

Laffin, Arthur J., editor. *Swords into Plowshares: A Chronology of Plowshares Disarmament Actions, 1980–2003*. Washington, DC: Rose Hill, 2003.

Lynd, Staughton. *Nonviolence in America: A Documentary History*. Rev. ed. Maryknoll, NY: Orbis Books, 1995.

McCarthy, Colman. *All of One Peace: Essays on Nonviolence*. New Brunswick, NJ: Rutgers University Press, 1994.

McCarthy, Ronald M., and Eugene Sharp. *Nonviolent Action: A Research Guide*. New York: Garland, 1997.

McNeal, Patricia. *The American Catholic Peace Movement, 1928–1972*. New York: Arno Press, 1978.

Meconis, Charles. *With Clumsy Grace: The American Catholic Left, 1961–1975*. New York: Seabury, 1979.

Nepstad, Sharon Erickson. *Religion and War Resistance in the Plowshares Movement*. Cambridge: Cambridge University Press, 2007.

———. *Nonviolent Revolutions: Civil Resistance in the Late 20th Century*. New York: Oxford University Press, 2011.

O'Gorman, Angie. *The Universe Bends Toward Justice: A Reader on Christian Nonviolence in the U.S.* Philadelphia: New Society, 1990.

Peters, Shawn Francis. *The Catonsville Nine: A Story of Faith and Resistance in the Vietnam Era*. New York: Oxford University Press, 2012.

Polner, Murray, and Jim O'Grady. *Disarmed and Dangerous: The Radical Lives and Times of Daniel and Philip Berrigan*. New York: Basic Books, 1997.

Schell, Jonathan. *The Unconquerable World: Power, Nonviolence, and the Will of the People*. New York: Holt, 2003.

Sharp, Eugene. *Waging Nonviolent Struggle: 20th Century Practice and 21st Century Potential*. New York: Porter Sargent, 2005.

Solnit, Rebecca. *Hope in the Dark: Untold Histories, Wild Possibilities*. New York: Nation, 2005.

Smith, Christian, editor. *Disruptive Religion: The Force of Faith in Social-Movement Activism*. New York: Routledge, 1996.

Smith-Christopher, Daniel. *The Challenge of Nonviolence in Religious Traditions*. 10th Anniversary ed. Maryknoll, NY: Orbis Books, 2007.

Tracy, James. *Direct Action: Radical Pacifism from the Union Eight to the Chicago Seven*. Chicago: University of Chicago Press, 1996.

Wilcox, Fred, editor. *Uncommon Martyrs: The Berrigans, the Catholic Left, and the Plowshares Movement*. 1st ed. Reading, MA: Addison-Wesley, 1991.

Zinn, Howard. *A People's History of the United States*. New York: HarperCollins, 1980.

———. *The Power of Nonviolence: Writings by Advocates of Peace*. Boston: Beacon, 2002.

Index

NOTE: Within this index, the terms "jail" and "prison" are used interchangeably except in the actual names of facilities. The names of individual narrators and pages referring to their words are in **bold**; pages referring to photographs are in *italics*.

Abrahamic Community (MI), 305–6
Abyssinian Baptist Church, 40
ACLU (American Civil Liberties Union), 74
Afghanistan War, 145, 146, 282, 315, 371n10
AFSC (American Friends Service Committee), 61
Air Force bases. *See individual air force bases*
Albrecht, Scott, 258, **281–85,** *285*
Alderson Federal Prison Camp (WV), 10, 18, 20, 25, 99–100n20
Allen-Doucot, Jackie, 12–13
Allenwood Correctional Institution (PA), 74, 80–81
Alliant Techsystems (MN), 311
American Civil Liberties Union (ACLU), 74
American Friends Service Committee (AFSC), 61
American Socialist Party, 28
Amish, 28, 325
Amnesty International, 268

Amsterdam Catholic Worker (Jeanette Noel Huis), 164, 167
anarchism, 29, 32, 54, 50, 54, 123, 325, 343, 346
    in Amsterdam, 154
    in Glasgow, 145
Andrews Air Force Base (MD), 270, 279
Anger
    as appropriate in resisters, 77, 252
    from army chaplains, 195
    from arresting officers, 170, 211
    in Dorothy Day, 77
    as inappropriate witness, 95
    from judge, 212
    masked by depression, 249
    in political campaigns, 214
    in prisoners, 4, 55, 67, 240
    from prison guards, 216
    in protesters, 85, 209
    in supporters, 86
    in young people in the 1960s, 60

anti-globalization protests, 220, 225, 308

Antioch Area Theater, 38

Apper, Bryan, 258, *258*, **259–62**

Apper, Liza, 258, *258*, **259–62**

Aquino, Corazon, 322

Arlington Cemetery, 346

Aryan Brotherhood, 233

ashes, as symbol of violence, 253, 275, 276–77, 282, 283, 295

Ash Wednesday, 128, 231, 252, 311, 321

Assata (Shakur), 24

Atlantic Life Community (ALC), 133, 263, 291, 293

Ave Maria (Bach/Gounod), 336

Baez, Joan, 66, 99

Baltimore City Jail, 5

Baltimore Four, 61, 90, 91, 99, 101

ban-and-bar letters, 301, 312, 317. *See also under* SOAW (GA)

Bangor Naval Base (WA), 132, 299, 301, 303

Barbara (prisoner), 15

Bath Iron Works (ME), 125, 126

Battle Creek Defense Logistics Services Center (MI), 306

Bean, Duane, *318*

Beck, Julian, 50–52

Belgrade (Yugoslavia), 172

Belknap Indian Reservation, 300

Benedict, Don, 29, 34, *36*, 37, 38, 39, 42, **45–48**

Berrigan, Fr. Daniel, SJ, 111, 121, 128, 133, 271
  on community, 322
  influence of, 60, 74, 96, 120, 255, 278, 305, 321
  and letter from Dorothy Day, 91n16
  property defined by, 60
  in prison, 319
  and *The Trial of the Catonsville Nine*, 71n5

Berrigan House (IA), 111n8

Berrigan, Philip, 133, 165, 167, 246, 267, 275
  and Harrisburg Seven, 95n18
  influenced by draft card burners, 80
  influence of, 60, 96, 111, 112, 137, 176, 205, 218
  and Jonah House, 108–9
  and letter from Dorothy Day, 91n16
  opposition to women-only action, 100, 101
  and Plowshares actions, 109, 111, 122, *126*, 127, 130, 140, 165, 176, 181, 269
  as priest, 108, 122
  in prison, 249, 251
  theology of, 121

Bevilacqua, Joseph, 34, *36*

B-52 bomber, 123, 124, 279, 306

Bible
  as basis for resistance, 109, 139–40, 164, 214, 249
  as forbidden word, 118
  reading of in prison, 4, 16, 94, 221, 231, 233, 239, 261
  reading of during resistance actions, 92
  reading of in El Salvador, 209
  reading of in trials, 93, 142
  See also Jesus Christ; New Testament; Old Testament

Bichsel, Fr. "Bix" (William), SJ, 132–33, *133*, 202, 249, **299–303**

Big Blockade. *See* Faslane 365 action

"Big Boy" atomic bomb, 295

birth families, of resisters
  and change from antagonism to support, 79–80, 221
  lack of communication with, 79–80, 200–201

nonsupport of, 234, 269
siblings in, 63–64
support by, 21, 22, 30, 36, 37, 66, 73, 95, 163, 203, 220, 234
Black Panthers, 24, 105
Blair, Joe, 187
blood, symbolic nature of, 277, 282
in Battle Creek (MI) action, 306
in Cathedral Mass action, 172
in Enola Gay action, 295
in Pentagon actions, 112, 273, 310
in Plowshares actions, 93, 110, 112, 119, 124, 130, 181, 279
in SAC billboard action, 274, 275
in SOAW action, 206, 302
Boertje-Obed, Greg, 4–5
Bolivia, 189, 192, 312
Böll, Heinrich, 180
Boskey, Jill, 99, 100, 103, 104, 106n23
Bossie, Br. Paul, 312
Bossie, Fr. Bob, SCJ, 112, **309–14**
Bourgeois, Roy, 191–94, *194*, 198, 207, 302
in Central America, 188, 189
early life of, 191–92, 196
on fear, 192–93
Ft. Benning protest by, 194–96
prison experiences of, 112, 193–94, 198
and support for women's ordination, 194
Boyden, Fred, 106
Boylan, Kathy, 126, 127, 270, 279, 295
Boyle, Francis, 158
Bradley, C. Arthur, 34, 38n8
Bradley University (IL), 201
Brawley, Stafford (prison carpentry boss), 68

Bread and Puppet Theater (VT), 190, *190*, 211, 345, *345*
Brethren, Church of the, 28, 325
Broege, Carl, 106
Bromley, Ernest, 326
Bromley, Marion, 326
Brooklyn draft board, 102
Brown, Vera, 21
Browne, Harry, 136
Brzezinski, Ziggy (Zbigniew), 276
Buddhism, 126, 129, 153, 166, 267, 301, 308, 340
Building Our Swords Into Plowshares, 340
Bureau of Prisons (BOP), 9, 11, 42n10, 216, 268, 287, 332
Bury the Chains (Hochschild), 161
Busch-Nema, Tina, 213–18
Bush, Fr. Bernard, SJ, 129, 131
Bush, George H. W., 264–65
Bush, George W., 142, 262
Butcher (prisoner), 41

Calley, William, 203.
Câmara, Dom Hélder, 98, 244, 245
Campaign for Nuclear Disarmament (CND), 145, 148n8, 153, 178
Campaign of Civil Disobedience for Disarmament (Germany), 178–82
Camus, Albert, 63
Canada, as haven for draft refusers, 33, 61
Carla (prisoner), 243
Carswell Federal Medical Hospital for Women (TX), 14, 213–14, 215–18
Carswell Peace Crane Project, 218
Carter, Jimmy, 275, 276
Carter, Rosalind, 245
Casa Maria Catholic Worker (WI), 96, 98, 112, 317
Casa Romero (NY), 271

Catholic Church, 309
　and changes after Vatican II,
　　291, 304
　and education, 297–98
　and nuclear weapons, 123,
　　147–48
　and relations with the state,
　　148, 246, 291, 292, 297–98
Catholic Left, 61, 89, 108, 109,
　111
　as opponent of women-only
　　action, 100–101, 106–7
Catholic Peace Fellowship, 60, 99
Catholic Worker, xix, 61, 90, 199,
　256
　analysis in, 2, 272, 282
　archives of, 108
　and civil defense protests,
　　50–58
　community in, 237, 286
　and draft card destruction,
　　72–84
　Euro gathering of, 162, 281
　and the Gospel, 122, 272, 205
　history of, 28–29
　jail as vacation from, 230
　national gatherings of, 162
　personalism in, 90, 113, 116–17
　and resistance, 1, 6, 7, 113–14,
　　208, 239, 279, 286, 315, 334
　romance in, 75, 121, 122–23
　as school, 121, 232, 238
　and Sermon on the Mount, xix
　and tax resistance, 325
　trust in, 237, 278–79
　See also Catholic Worker
　　hospitality; Day, Dorothy;
　　Hennacy, Ammon; and
　　individual Catholic Worker
　　communities
Catholic Worker, The, 10, 50, 79,
　82
Catholic Worker Bookstore, 289n8

Catholic Worker hospitality, 90–91,
　204, 205, 206, 207
　jail and, 6–9, 234–35, 260,
　　273, 334
Catonsville Nine draft board action
　(MD), 61, 84, 99–100n20
　influence of, 85, 99, 120, 126,
　　138, 139
　ritualism in, 101
　trial of actors in, 87, 91, 126
CBS, 52
Center for Constitutional Rights,
　106
Central Park draft card burning,
　99
chaplains, military, 9, 191, 195,
　281
chaplains, prison, 9–11, 261–62,
　268, 303
Charismatic Renewal, 272
Charles (pseud.), 219–27
Chávez, César, 305, 321, 324
Chiapas (Mexico), 308
Chicago Air and Water, 312–13
Chicago City Missionary Society,
　47
Chicago Fifteen, 61
Chicago Life Community, 310, 311
Chicago Naval Recruiting Center,
　316
Chicago Theological Seminary, 36
children in resistance families, 347
　as factor in resistance
　　decisions, 154, 168, 169,
　　330, 337
　and pain of separation, 296
　parental influence on, 64, 285,
　　297
　parenting of (by resister par-
　　ents), 285
　as participants in demonstra-
　　tions and actions, 259, 296
　and photos in actions, 115

support from resistance community for, 214
support of parents' actions by,
176
Chomsky, Noam, 219
Church of the Brethren, 28, 325
Christiansen, Gordon, 76, *78*
Church of Scotland Moderator,
148
City College of New York, 30
City Hall Park (NY), 50–52,
56–57
civil defense protests, 49–58, *51*
"Civil Disobedience" (Thoreau),
325
civil rights. *See* constitutional
rights; freedom of speech
civil rights movement, 66, 73, 182,
269n3, 321
Berrigan, Phil, in, 108
civil disobedience in, 26, 30,
33, 146, 312
and march on Selma, 76
See also King, Rev. Dr. Martin
Luther, Jr.
Civilian Conservation Corps (CCC)
camp (Natural Bridge, VA),
43
Civilian Public Service Camp (CPS),
327
Clancy, Deirdre (Dee), 11, 137,
138–44
Clark, Ramsey, 13, 120, 121
Cleveland Call and Post, 327
Cleveland (OH) draft board, 87
Clinton, Bill, 250
CODEPINK, 315, 343
Cohen-Joppa, Felice, 111
Cohen-Joppa, Jack, 111
Cold War, 49, 182, 307,
Cole, Moana, 123, 124, 125
Coles, Robert, xxii
Cologne Cathedral (Germany),
168, 169, 171–72

Columbia College (IL), 312
Columbus (GA). *See* Ft. Benning
(GA); SOA/WHINSEC (GA)
Columbus Jail (GA), 213
Columbus Ledger-Inquirer, 206
Columbus Stockade, 211
Committee for Nonviolent Action
(CNVA), 82
Commonweal, 84, 95
Communist Party, 38
Community for Creative
Nonviolence (CCNV), 252,
255, 287
community newsletters, 108, 111,
178, 241
Concord Naval Weapons Station
(CA), 335n9
Concord State Hospital (NH), 18
Condon, Mary, 137
Congress of Racial Equality
(CORE), 40n9, 327, 328
Harlem office of, 65–66
conscientious objection (CO), legal
by active duty service
members, 205, 281
in Holland, 162–64
during Vietnam War, 60, 61,
62, 65, 76, 83, 292–93
during World War I, 28
during World War II, 28–29,
30, 33, 39, 327
constitutional rights, xviii, 203,
339. *See also* freedom of
speech
Contra war (Nicaragua), 335
Conwell, Bill, 212
Cook County Jail (IL), 332
Cordaro, Angela, 22, 272
Cordaro, Frank, 7, 8, **15–16**, 111,
137, 258, 268–69, 271,
272–81
photos of, *136, 270, 271, 279*
Cordaro, Tom, 22, 227

Cornell, Tom, 49–50, 61, 73, 78, 82, 82–84
Corner, Betsy, 334–41, *338*
Cotton, Don, 85, 86
Crane, Susan, 24–25, 111, 128–32, *133*, 329, 330–32
Creech Air Force Base (NV), 256, 315, 320
criminal proceedings, contempt charges in, 88, 118, 312, 332, 337
criminal proceedings, following resistance actions
  Albrecht, Scott, **283**
  Apper, Bryan, **261**
  Apper, Liza, **259**
  Bichsel, Fr. Bix, SJ, **301, 302**
  Bossie, Fr. Bob, SCJ, **310, 311, 312**
  Busch-Nema, Tina, **215–16**
  Charles (pseud.), **220–21**
  Cordaro, Frank, **273, 277**
  Cordaro, Tom, **22**
  Dallas, Meredith, **40–41**
  Fewless, Renaye, **235–38**
  Forest, Jim, **92, 93**
  Gardner, David, **231–32**
  Geddes, Maggie, **105–6**
  Heid, John, **253, 255**
  Hughes, Lisa, **210–13**
  Jacobs, Steve, **207–8**
  Jaskolski, Hanna, **170, 171, 172**
  Judy (pseud.), **220–21**
  Kanner, Rebecca, **197–98**, 199
  Kehler, Randy, **66, 337**
  Kelly, Kathy, 316
  Kobasa, Stephen, **295**
  Kuile, Frits ter, **162–64**, 166
  Lovell, Bill, **37**
  Lyttle, Brad, 26n8
  Malina, Judith, **53**
  Marvy, Doug, **86–88**
  Meyer, Karl, 50, 332, **333**
  Miller, David, **73, 74**
  Mollin, Marian, **263, 265**
  Nelson, Juanita, **327**
  Paley, Grace, **346**
  Rosebaugh, Fr. Lorenzo (Larry), OMI, **97, 244**
  Rumpf, Kathleen, **202–3**
  Slatterly, William, **21–22**
  Sprong, Mike, 286, 287–88
  Tallents, Jane, **149–52**
  Vitale, Fr. Lou, OFM, 320, **321**
  Wilson, Jim, **78–80**
  Zawada, Fr. Jerry, OFM, **315, 319**
  in England, 161–62
  in Germany, 172, 177, 179, 181–82
  in Holland, 162–64
  in Ireland, 141–43
  in Scotland, 147, 151–52, 157–60
  See also Plowshares actors, criminal proceedings against
Crowe, Frances, 326
cruise missiles, 167, 177, 182, 306
Cuba, 24
Cullen, Annette (Nettie), 85, 96
Cullen, Michael, 85, 96
Cunnane, Fr. Robert, CSS, 85
Czarnik, Kathy, 100

Dallas, Meredith (Dal), xvii, 29, *36, 38*, 38–44
Dallas, Tony, 38n8, 44
Dallas, Willa, 38, 39, 41, 42, 43, 44
Danbury Federal Correctional Institution (CT) prisoners
  Benedict, Don, **45–46, 47**
  cancer patient, 217
  Dallas, Meredith, **41–42**
  DiGia, Ralph, **31–32**
  Kramer, Rae, 12, 13, **18–19**
  Lovell, Bill, **37**
  Platte, Sr. Ardeth OP, 18

Sage, Doris, **241–43**
Zawada, Fr. Jerry, OFM, **319**
Day, Dorothy, 90, 119
  in alliance with other radicals,
    50–57
  anger of, 77
  and Catholic Church, 54, 77,
    256
  and Catholic Left, 61
  and civil defense protests,
    49–58
  and draft board destruction
    actions, 91
  on the duty of hope, 229
  and friendship, 55–56, 80
  on Hiroshima/Nagasaki, 360n6
  on hope as duty, 229
  as influence on resisters, 77, 94,
    95, 229, 247–48, 266, 315
  letters of, 91n16
  Long Loneliness, The, 256n1
  in prison, 54–56, 256
  and redemptive suffering, 229
  on relationships at the
    Catholic Worker, 75
  and World War II, 28–29
Day, Sam, 317
deadly force area, 124–25, *125*,
  182
Dear, Fr. John, SJ, 133, 303n1
death penalty, 118
Debs, Eugene, 28
Defense Systems and Equipment
  International (DSEI), 282
Dellinger, David, 34, *36*, 47, 80–81
  in community ministry, 35, 38,
    39, 46
  in prison, 33, 42, 43, 45
Deming, Barbara, 26n8
Democratic National Convention
  (DNC) in Los Angeles, 235,
  236, 237
Democratic Party, 73
DeMott, Ellen Grady, 7, 13, 17

depleted uranium, 109, 132, 311
depression (clinical), 5, 44, 223,
  249, 253, 316
Des Moines Catholic Worker (IA),
  16, 275, 286
Detloff, Ariane, 169n2
Detroit (MI), 46–47
Diablo Canyon Nuclear Power
  Plant (CA), 128
Diego Garcia Islands (UK), 146
Dietrich, Jeff, *228*, **228–31**
DiGia, Ralph, **29–34**, *29*
divine love, 35, 102
  of enemies, 120, 205, 281
  in Romans 8 (Paul), 16, 129
divine obedience, 120
Dobbins, Charlie, 104n22
Doing Time for Peace (Riegle), xvii
Dominican religious order, 271.
    See also Gilbert, Sr. Carol,
    OP; Hudson, Sr. Jackie, OP;
    Platte, Sr. Ardeth, OP
Donahue, Larry, 299
Dorothy Day (Riegle), xxin5, 49n1
Dorothy Day Catholic Worker
  (DC), 117, 121–22, 295
Dorothy Day House (London), 282
Dostoevsky, Fydor, 270
Dougherty, Fr. Peter, *304*, **304–9**
Douglass, Jim, 301
Douglass, Shelley, 301
Dow Chemical Company (NY),
  103
Doyle, Maureen, 206
draft card destruction, 72–84
  Cornell, Tom, **82–84**
  Miller, David, **72–76**
  Wilson, Jim, **76–82**
draft file destruction actions,
  85–107
  by Milwaukee Fourteen,
    86–98
  by Women Against Daddy
    Warbucks, 99–107

draft refusal
  during World War I, 28
  during World War II, 29–48
  during Vietnam, 5, 60, 62–65
  See also conscientious objection
    (CO), legal
draft registration, 34, 36, 266
draft registration counseling, 34,
  61, 85
drones, protest against, 256, 315,
  321
Dunlop, Nuin, 138, 140, 141, 143

Easter, 10, 112, 127, 207, 272
Eastern Michigan University, 305
East Timor, 146–47
Ebner, Jerry, 1, **8–9, 11,** 111,
  112–17
ecological movement, 174
Edelman, Marc, 76, 78
Eddie (prisoner), 254
ego, of resisters, 94, 117, 255,
  278, 289
Eighth Day Center for Justice (IL),
  309, 310, 313
Eilerman, Sr. Marge, OSF, 202
Eisenhower, Dwight, 49, 116
El Camino Junior College (CA), 62
Electric Boat shipyard (CT), 253.
  See also Groton/New London
    Submarine Base (CT)
ELF. See Project ELF (Extremely
  Low Frequency)
Elliott, J. Robert, 203
Ellsberg, Dan, 321, 335
El Salvador, 16, 213, 302
  assassinations in, 187, 188,
    192
  mission service in, 208–9, 211,
    246
  torture in, 16, 192–93, 194–96
Elson, Judge, 268
Emmaus House (New York City),
  95

Endo, 145–46
Enola Gay bomber, 294–95, 296
E.P. Dutton (NY), 71
EUCOM (United States European
  Command), 2, 177, 183
Evanston draft board action (IL),
  61

Faircloth, G. Mallon, 190, 200,
  206, 208, 210–12, 215
Fairfield University (CT), 291
faith, of resisters
  as basis for action, 118, 192,
    214, 229, 256–57
  and community, 280, 286, 323
  as divisive in the peace move-
    ment, 120, 153, 166, 212
  in the goodness of resistance
    action, 143, 184–85, 323–24
  importance of, in prison, 3,
    131, 255
  questioning of, 205, 256–57
  renewed by service in war, 191
  renewed by Salvadoran
    peasants, 192, 209
Faith and Resistance Retreats,
  109, 112, 304
Fallon, Karen, 138, 140, 141, 142
Faslane Peace Camp, 146, 148,
  149, 151, 160, 161, 182
Faslane 365 action, 145, 149, 150,
  151, 153, 154–55, 160–61,
  170
Faslane Trident Base, 144, 146,
  152, 153–54, 155
Father John (Trinitarian prison
  chaplain), 10
FBI. See Federal Bureau of
  Investigation (FBI)
"FCI Utopia" (Butcher), 41
fear, in prison, 4, 5, 55, 260, 284,
  306–7
fear, in resisters
  absence of, 52, 52, 347

of arresting officer, 124, 312of
   criticism, 193
of the dark, 102
of disobeying Church teaching,
   304
explored in counseling, 284
of father, 284–85
of the future, 293, 296
of infiltration by spies, 176
of Internal Revenue Service,
   332, 336
of lack of inner strength, 264
of lack of success, 296
in Latin America, 192
nurtured by culture, 52, 59,
   205, 272, 312
of physical harm from lock-on
   protest, 171
of prison, 3, 41, 192, 201,
   214, 232, 255, 312
of professional reprisal, 30,
   45, 218
of rape in prison, 4
Feast of the Holy Innocents, 109,
   267, 282
Feast of the Transfiguration, 114
Federal Bureau of Investigation
   (FBI), 24, 203
   infiltration of peace groups by,
   77, 95
   and role in criminal proceedings, 73, 78, 86, 99–100n20,
   104–6, 196, 302
   surveillance by, 42, 63, 77, 89,
   95, 105
Federal Reserve Bank (Cleveland),
   87
federal youth prisons, 5, 43
Fellowship of Reconciliation (FOR),
   28, 36, 37, 40n9, 61, 325
feminism and the peace movement,
   99, 106, 342–47. *See also*
   Geddes, Maggie; Paley,
   Grace

Fewless, Renaye, 235, 235–38
fire, as symbol of violence, 86, *87*,
   97
Flagg, Brian, 252
Fleming, Peter, 80
FOR (Fellowship of Reconciliation),
   28, 36, 37, 40n9, 61, 325
Ford Foundation, 53
Forest, Ben, 94
Forest, Jim, 85, *90*, 90–96, 97
Four of Us, The, 61
Fox, Tom, 22
Franciscan religious order, 9, 252,
   315, 316, 324
Francis of Assisi, 98, 122, 164,
   315, 321, 322
Frankel-Streit, Bill, 111, 121–25,
   224, 250–52
Frankel-Streit, Sue, 211, 121–12,
   124–25, 251–52
Freedom of Information Act files,
   77, 105
freedom of speech, 26, 27, 65,
   183. *See also* Free Speech
   Zones
Free Speech Zones, 183, 257
"Free to Be You and Me" (Ms.
   Foundation for Women), 343
Fresno Catholic Worker (CA),
   258–62
Fresno County Jail (CA), 256–62
Friend, Tod, 70, 71
Ft. Benning (GA), 187, 188, 189,
   202, 203, 209, 210, 302,
   314, 315
   first action at, 194–96
   See also SOA/WHINSEC (GA);
   and entries beginning with
   SOAW
Ft. Dix Federal Correctional
   Institution (NJ), 250–52
Ft. Huachuca (AZ), 320

Gandhi, Mahatma, 30, 46, 62, 118, 174, 214
and Christianity, 185, 186, 266
and melding of philosophy and practice, 186
as model, 62, 116, 162, 166, 205, 313
on not resisting while imprisoned, 3
philosophy of, 184–86
and secrecy in planning resistance, 323
on witnessing injustice, 170
Gandhian Wave, 206–7
Gardner, David, 231–35, *232*
Gardner, Jerry, 85, *87*
Geddes, Maggie, 61, **99–106**
G-8 Summit, 150
Georgetown University Center for Peace Studies (DC), 269n3
George Washington nuclear submarine, 82
Gerardi, Bishop Juan, 187, 206–7
German Christian Church, 226
German judges, resistance action by, 178–80
German parliament, 179
German peace movement, 168–86
German political culture, 174, 176, 184
Gilbert, Sr. Carol, OP, 10, 18, *270*
Gilbert and Sullivan, 42
Gimblet, Margaret, 158–59
Glasgow (Scotland), 145
Glenstal Abbey (Ireland), 140, 144
God Made Honky Tonk Communists (Miller), 76n6
"God Sees the Truth but Waits" (Tolstoy), 54
Golder, Neil, 18
Good Friday, 112, 128, 321
Gorbachev, Mikhail, 165
Grady (DeMott), Ellen, 7, *13*, 17
Grady, John, 101

Graf, Bob, 85, *87*
Grass, Günter, 180
Great Lakes Life Community (MI), 306
Green, Valentine, 100
Greenfield (MA), 337–40, *338*
Green Haven State Detention Facility, 52
Greenlands Catholic Worker (TN), 331
Greenwald, Lynne, *133*
Greenwich Village Peace Center, 342, 344, 347
Greenwood Prison Camp (IL), 213, 238–41
Griffin, Merv, 84
Griffiss Air Force Base (NY), 111, 123–25, 252
Groppi, Fr. James, 97
Groton/New London Submarine Base (CT), 82–83, 294. *See also* Electric Boat shipyard (CT)
Ground Zero Center for Nonviolent Action (WA), 14, 301, 303
Guadelupe House (WA), 300
Guatemala, 16, 98, 100, 206, 209, 297
Gulf War, 132, 264, 307, 319. *See also* Iraq sanctions
Gumbleton, Bishop Thomas, 108
Gump, Joe, 111, 113, 114

Habitat for Humanity, 340
Hagedorn, John, 85n11
Haig, Alexander, 328
Halliday, Denis, 142
Hamas, 226
Harlem community house (NY), 39, 45, 47
Harlem draft board (NY), 102
Harney, Fr. James, 85, 86, 97
Harris, David, 63

Harris, Marty, 61, 62, **62–65**
Harrisburg Seven, 95
Harry Potter books (Rowling), 216
Harvard University student news-
    paper, 66
Havel, Victor, xxiv
Hawk aircraft, 147
Heid, John, **252–55**, *252*
Hennacy, Ammon, 331, 333
    and civil defense drills, 50–52,
        53, 56, 57
Hennessey, Sr. Dorothy, OSF,
    199–200, 201
Hennessy, Eric, 257
Hennessy, Martha, 18, **256–57**
Hennessy, Tamar, 256
Herngren, Per, 182
Heschel, Rabbi Abraham Joshua,
    199
Higgenbotham, Rev. Jon, 85
hierarchy of resistance actions,
    264, 293–94
Hijden, Susan van der, 161–62
Hinduism, 126, 214
Hippie Soup Kitchen (CA), 228,
    231
Hiroshima/Nagasaki
    and dates of resistance action,
        114, 128, 109, 294
    nuclear bombing of, 132, 145,
        169, 295
    peace walk to, 209, 301
    survivor of, 163
    symbols of, used in resistance
        actions, 129, 131, 154, 156
    See also peace cranes
"History of the World" (Malina),
    52
Hitler, Adolf, 35, 47, 169, 174
Hochschild, Adam, 161
Holland, mandatory military
    service in, 162–64
Holland, parliament of, 165

Holland, peace movement in,
    162–66
Holliday, Martin, 268
Holocaust symbolism, use of, 119,
    124
Holy Ghost Fathers (Congregation
    of the Holy Spirit), 140
Holy Loch US Polaris base (Scot-
    land), 146
Holy Week, 112. *See also* Easter;
    Good Friday
Honduras, 16, 215
Honeywell Project (MN), 263
Hood Canal (WA), 301
Hoone, Geoff, 282
hope, absence of, 184
hope, as duty, 229
hope, in human nature, 257
hope, in 1960s culture, 82, 344
hope, nurture of
    by action, 65, 161, 229, 344
    by historical knowledge, 16,
        246, 347
    by liberation theology, 192
    by quiet time, 194
Hope and Resistance Network, 182
Hosking, Jane, 254–55
Hostage Bold, Hostage Free
    (Weir), 129
House of Detention (NY), 80
House of Peace (MA), 59
Houser, George, 34, 35, *36*, 48
Howard, Caitlin, **20–21**
Howard University Civil Rights
    Committee (DC), 327
Hudson, Sr. Jackie, OP, **14**
Hughes, Lisa, **208–13**, *238*, **238–41**
Huntworth, Ann, 211
Huschauer, Heike, 180, *181*
Hussein, Saddam, 123

Immigration and Naturalization
    Service (INS), 235
Index of forbidden books, 291

Indonesia, 147
Industrial Revolution, 309
In Solitary Witness (Zahn), 229n1
Interfaith Council for Peace and
    Justice (MI), 196
Intermediate Range Nuclear Forces
    Treaty (INF), 165, 178, 182
Internal Revenue Service (IRS),
    326, 328, 330–31, 332–33,
    334, 335–38
International Court. *See* law,
    international
Iraq resistance, 89
Iraq sanctions, 138, 142n4, 307
Iraq Veterans Against the War, 142
Iraq War, 138, 313, 335
    bombing in, 123, 138, 146,
        319, 321
    depleted uranium in, 132
    protests against, 65, 140, 229,
        231, 157, 307, 319, 322,
        330–31, 347
    resistance to, 136, 137, 138,
        281
    service in, 257, 346
Irish Plowshares action. *See* Plow-
    shares actions, individual:
    Pitstop Plowshares
Isaiah 2:4, 108, 113, 120, 133, 277
Israel (Palestine), xviii, 132, 304,
    307, 320

Jacobs, Steve, 11, *138*, 205–8, *207*
Jäggerstätter, Franz, 229
Janicke, Fr. Alfred, 85
Jantschik, Herwig, 175
Jaskolski, Hanna, 168, 169–73,
    173
Jehovah's Witnesses, 63
Jeju Island (S. Korea), 156
Jesuit religious order, 188, 189, 249,
    291, 249, 300, 302. *See also*
    individual Jesuit priests

Jesus Christ
    and freedom, 267
    and Gandhi, 185, 266
    as model, 266, 281
    and nonviolence, 36, 205
    and the poor, 281
    as prophet, 10
    and relations with the state,
        205
    and stewardship, 137
    trust in, 163
    and vocation, 36, 164, 271
    See also Bible
John of the Cross, 193
Johnson, Becky, 191n5
Johnson, Fred, 313
Johnson, Lyndon, 60
John the Baptist, 98
Jonah House (MD), 20, 126, 131,
    245, 253, 275, 309
    archives of, 108n1, 111
    founding of, 108–9
    influence of, 112, 126, 273
    as leader in resistance actions,
        109, 112, 273
    newsletters of, 178
Joplin, Janis, 252
Josephite religious order, 108
Judaism, 56, 233, 300. *See also*
    Kanner, Rebecca; Malina,
    Judith; Mollin, Marian;
    Paley, Grace; Roth, Barry
Judy (pseud.), 219–27

Kabat, Fr. Carl, OMI, 3, 176, 253,
    319
Kairos Community (NY), 295
Kammer, Mickey Dallas, 44
Kane, Rosie, 153
Kanner, Rebecca, 196–202
Kansas City Star, 213
Karpatkin, Marvin, 84
Kavanagh, Brian, 2n2
Kay, Vincent, 265

Keenan, Betsy, 266
Kehler, Lillian Parish, 336
Kehler, Randy, xx, xxii, 61, **65–72,**
  326, 334, **335–41**
Kennedy, Pat, 100, 104, 105
Kent, Bruce, 148
Kelly, Kathy, 14–15, 19–20, 25,
  142, 144, 191n5, 312, 317
Kelly, Mary, 136
Kelly, Fr. Steve, SJ, 7, 9–10, 13,
  111, 133, 245, **245–50,** 251
Kent, Bruce, 148
Kepler, Roy, 66
Kevin (prisoner), 232
Khan, Badshah, 313–14
Kinane, Ed, 191n5, 202
King, Bob, 199
King County Jail (WA), 301
King, Rev. Dr. Martin Luther, Jr.,
  xviii
    assassination of, 300
    influence of, 62, 162, 174, 205,
      300, 324
    and marches against segrega-
      tion, 199, 203
K. I. Sawyer Air Force Base (MI),
  306
Kirchhoefer, Chrissy, 206–7
Kissinger, Henry, 95n18
Kobasa, Clare, 296, 297
Kobasa, Rachel, 297
Kobasa, Stephen, xx, **291–98,** 297
Kolbe Cathedral High School (CT),
  291, 297–98
Korean War, 320–21
Kosovo, 164, 167, 309
Kramer, Rae, 12, 13, 18–19, 191n5
Kronlid, Lotte, 147
Kunstler, William, 80, 87, 88, 93
Kuwait, 123
Kuile, Aiyum ter, 167, 168
Kuile, Frits ter, 162–68, *168, 173*
Kuile, Jia Jia ter, 167–68
Kuile, Onno ter, 168

Laffin, Art, 12, 16, 111, **118–21,**
  165
Laffin, Colleen, 117
LaForge, John, 9
Las Vegas (NV) welfare rights
  protest, 321
La Tuna Federal Correctional
  Institution (TX), 68, 196
law, international, 131
    and documents at Plowshares
      sites, 110
    in resistance trials, 120–21,
      158–60, 177, 336
Lawrence Livermore Laboratories
  (CA), 128, 129, 262
Leavenworth Prison (KS) 11, 22,
  41, 267, 274
LeHavre Jail (France), 25
LeMoyne College (NY), 73
Lewis, Jesse, 237
Lewis, Tom, 127
Lewisburg Federal Penitentiary
  (PA), 5, 32–33, 43, 74, 80
Lexington Federal Prison (KY),
  10,14–15, 20, 196
liberation theology, 137, 192
Life Magazine, 92, 333
Limerick Prison (Ireland), 11
Linner, Rachelle, 264
Lisker, Roy, 76, *78*
Little Flower Catholic Worker (VA),
  121
"Little Man" atomic bomb, 295
Lives of the Saints (Butler), 55
Living Theatre (NY), 50
lobbying, 149, 155, 189, 198
Loch Gare. *See* Faslane Trident
  Nuclear Base
Loch Goil. *See* Trident Three
  Plowshares
Lockheed Martin (CA), 130–31
Lompoc Federal Prison (CA), 5,
  301

London Catholic Worker, 136, 161,
281, 282
Long Loneliness, The (Day), 256n1
Lori, Bishop William E., 298n11
Los Alamos National Laboratory
(NM), 154, 167
Los Angeles to Moscow Peace
Walk, 26
Los Angeles Catholic Worker (CA),
228, 230–31, 235, 238, 259
Los Angeles County Jail for men,
230–31, 232–35, 301–302
Los Angeles County Jail for
women, 235–38
Los Angeles Federal Building, 231,
Los Angeles Rampart Police, 235
Los Angeles Times, 322n11
Lovell, Bill, 29, 34, **35–37**, *36*, 38
Loyola University (IL), 61
Lynsters Farm Catholic Worker
(England), 281, *285*
Lyttle, Brad, 26n8, 325, 326

Mackenzie, David, 156, 158, 159
Madagascar, 146
Magno, Paul, *14*, 289n8
Malina, Judith, 49, 50, **52–56**, *55*,
134
Manhattan draft boards (NY), 102
Marion Prison (IL), 10, 268, 270
Mariona Prison (El Salvador), 16
Mark 12A nuclear bombshell, 109
Marley, Bob, 21, 164
marriage, as casualty of resistance,
46, 75, 82n8
marriage, resistance as strain on,
75, 214, 225, 288–89
married resisters, support for, 122–
23. *See also under* support,
for resisters
Martin Luther King Center (WA),
300
Marvy, Doug, 85, **85–90**, 97
Marxism, 147, 174

Maryknoll religious order, 99–
100n20, 188, 191, 194, 266
"Mass" (Bernstein), 83
Massey, Jimmy, 142
Mater et Magistrata (papal encycli-
cal), 74
Mauch-Friz, Susanne, 180, *181*
Maurin, Peter, xix, 2
Mayer, John, 159
Maytime nuclear lab barge
(Scotland), 156
McAlister, Liz, 108–9, 122, 275,
279
McCarthy, Gerry, 191n6
McCoy, Joni, 10
McLaughlin, John, 159
McReynolds, David, 29, 49, 50,
56–58, 76, *78*
McSorley, Fr. Richard (Dick), SJ,
269
McVey, Timothy, 226, 318
Mercy, Fred, 302
media coverage of resistance
activities, 203, 255, 277,
322n11
building awareness through,
196, 213, 231, 315, 322,
340
in Germany, 171, 177, 179,
180
government control of, 257
in Holland, 163, 164, 166
in Ireland, 140, 142, 143
in Scotland, 165
under-reporting in, 99–100n20,
234, 340
after Vietnam War, 111, 231,
277, 291, 315, 329
See also press releases
Meijenfeldt, Roel von, 163
Meisner, Cardinal Joachim , 169,
171, 172
Melville, Marjorie, 99–100n20
Memorial Day parade, 77

Mennonite Central Committee, 209

Mennonites, 28, 244, 245, 325

mercenaries, 62

Merton, Thomas, 193–94

Methodist church, 10, 129, 308

Metropolitan Correction Center (IL), 319

Metropolitan Correctional Institution (NY), 31, 41, 45

Meyer, Karl, 6, 26, 49, **51–52**, *331*, **331–34**

Miami Jail (FL), 203

Michigan Peace Team, 307

Michigan Youth Congress, 38

Mid-Peninsula Free University (CA), 66

military police (MPs) 124–25

Miller, David, 61, **72–76**, *76*, 80

Milwaukee (WI), 316–17

Milwaukee Fourteen draft board action, 61, 84, 85–98

Milwaukee halfway house, 319

Mindy (prisoner), 240

Minh, Ho Chi, 64

Minson, Larry, 330–31

Minuteman nuclear missiles, 115

Mische, George, 91

Missionaries of Charity (Mother Teresa's sisters), 319

Missouri Peace Planting, 20, 116, 312, 317–18, *318*

Mollin, Marian, 100, 262, **263–66**

Montgomery, Sr. Anne, 60, 132, *133*

Moran, Damien, 138, 140

Morlan, Fr. Larry, **277–71**, *270*

Morton Thiokol Corporation (IL), 310–11

Most Dangerous Man in America, The (Ellsberg), 334

Motley, Constance Baker, 106

Moxley, Ellen, 144, 153, 155, *156*, **156–61**

Moylan, Mary, 99–100n20

Mullaney, Br. Anthony, OSB, 85, 91

Mulligan, Fr. Joe, SJ, 61

Muslim religion, 4, 10, 30

Muste, A. J., 40, 77, *78*

Mutlangen resistance group, 178–184

Mutlangen US Air Base (Germany), 158, 178–80, 182

Mutually Assured Destruction (MAD), 281

Myers, Bishop John R., 270

My Lai massacre, 203, 333

Nachman of Bratslav, Rabbi, 199

napalm, homemade, 85, 86, 92

National Air and Space Museum (DC), 294n9

National Air and Space Museum (TX), 296

National Catholic Reporter, 22

National Council of Churches, 37

National Geographic, 94

National Guard, 2, 346,

National Liberation Front (Vietnam), 89

National Liturgical Conference, 91

National War Tax Resistance Coordinating Committee (NWTRCC), 326, 328n7

Native American spirituality, 10, 126, 239, 300

NATO (North Atlantic Treaty Organization), xvii, 162, 169, 171, 271

Nautilus Submarine Museum (CT), 294, 296

Nazi ideology, 119, 173, 174, 179, 180, 227, 229

Needham, Andrea, 147

Nellis Air Force Base (NV), 321

Nellis Prison Camp (NV), 321

Nelson, Juanita, *326*, **326–29**

Nelson, Wally, 326, 327, 328
neo-Nazi culture, 233, 234
Nevada Desert Experience (NDE),
    315, 321
Nevada Nuclear Test Site, 167,
    312, 321, 323
Newark ashram, 36, 37, 38, 39, 46
New England Committee
    for Nonviolent Action
    (NECNVA), 325
New London (CT). See Groton/
    New London Submarine
    Base (CT)
New Testament, 9–10, 93, 94, 129,
    142, 280. See also Bible;
    Jesus Christ
New York Resistance, 99
New York Times, 84, 253, 277
New York US Attorney's Office,
    29, 30, 105
Newell, Fr. Martin, 161–62
Niantic Women's Prison (CT),
    12–13
Nicaragua, 16, 302, 335, 338
Nix, Brendan, 142
Nixon, Richard M., 266
Nobel Peace Prize, 161, 163
nonviolence, life practice of, 34,
    139, 174, 180, 184, 186,
    214, 239, 327
nonviolence, training in, 175, 180,
    189, 197, 235, 267, 304,
    308, 313, 316, 347
nonviolence, 113
    as identical with God, 130
    and jail solidarity, 198, 235–37
    and large actions, 150–51,
        175, 178–80
    and property destruction, 277,
        323 (see also Plowshares
        actions: property destruction
        in)
    and Plowshares movement,
        113, 124, 130, 147

power of the practice of, 205,
    250, 263, 314n7 (see also
    civil rights movement;
    Gandhi, Mahatma)
as process and/or goal, 82, 226,
    252, 312–13, 327
unexamined ideology of, 226
theory before WWII of, 35
See also under Vietnam War
nonviolent affinity groups, 206,
    209
    aggressiveness in, 139
    definition of, 178, 180
    diversity among, 153
    as providers of support for
        actions, 156, 201, 252, 288–
        89, 338–41
    as vehicles for solving
        disagreements, 114, 123,
        138–39, 178–80
Nonviolent Peace Force, 335
nonviolent revolution, 312–14,
    315, 314n7, 322. See also
    Gandhi, Mahatma
Noonan, Joe, 141
North Atlantic Treaty Organization
    (NATO), xvii, 162, 169,
    171, 271
North Korea, 132
North Suburban Peace Initiative,
    37
Northwood Military Headquarters
    (England), 282
Nuclear Freeze Campaign, 120
Nuclear Heartland, 115n10
Nuclear Non-Proliferation Treaty,
    183
Nuclear Peace: The Story of the
    Trident Three (Mayer), 159
nuclear power, protests against,
    26, 171, 174, 184, 256, 344
Nuclear Resister, 111

nuclear submarines. *See* Polaris
   nuclear submarine; Trident
   nuclear submarine
nuclear waste, 171
nuclear weapons. *See specific
   manufacturing plans,
   installations, missiles, and
   submarines*
Nukewatch (WI), 115n10, 286,
   317n10
Nunca Mas Report (Guatemala).
   See Gerardi, Bishop Juan

Oakland Induction Center (CA),
   66
Oakland Naval Base (CA), 71
Oak Ridge National Security
   Complex (TN), 303
Obama campaign headquarters,
   271
Oblates of Mary Immaculate (OMI)
   religious order, 96, 98, 244,
   245. *See also* Kabat, Fr.
   Carl, OMI; Rosebaugh, Fr.
   Lorenzo (Larry), OMI
Occupy movement, 320
O'Connell, Tom, 303
Offut Air Force Base (NB), 1, 8,
   274, *275*
Ogile, Fred, 85
O'Higgins, Michael, 142
Old Testament, 281, 282. *See also*
   Bible; Isaiah 2:4; Judaism
O'Leary, Br. Basil, CFC, 85, 91,
   96, 97
Omaha Catholic Worker (NB), 112
On Walden Pond (Thoreau), 62
Orange County Jail (CA), 260
O'Reilly, Ciaron, **6–7**, 123, 124,
   125, 135, *136*, **136–37**,
   138–44
Orell, Linda Forest, 100, *102*, 104,
   107
O'Rourke, Bishop Edward, 267

Orthodox Peace Fellowship, 90
Orwell, George, 294
Oxford Pledge, 343
Oxford Prison Camp (WI), 22,
   317–18

Pace e Bene, 320
Pacem in Terris (papal encyclical),
   74
Pacific Life Community, 133, 245
Pacific Stock Exchange (CA), 323
Pagosa, Sr. Dorothy, SSJ–TOSF,
   311
Paine, Thomas, xviii
Pakistan,
   drones used in, 315
   nuclear warheads in, 132
   outsourcing to, 25–26
Paley, Grace, 342, *343*, **343–47**
Paley, Nora, 344
Palmer, Albert, 36
Palmerola Air Force Base
   (Honduras), 16
Pantex Corporation (TX), 245
Panzer, Ulf, 158, 179
Pashtun, 313–14
Pax Christi, 109, 272, 227
Peace Action, 154
peace cranes, 7, 17, 173, 218
peacekeepers at protests, 150–51,
   197
Peacemakers, 325, 326, 327, 332
Pearl Harbor, 36
Pekin Minimum Security Prison
   (IL), 15, 19, 25, 200–201,
   216
Pentagon, 247
   as site for resistance actions,
   109, 112, 255, 263, 267,
   267–68, 273, 310, 342, *345*,
   345–46
   See also blood: in Pentagon
   actions
Pentagon Papers, 334

Peoria diocese (IL), 271. *See also*
Myers, Bishop John R.;
O'Rourke, Bishop Edward
Pershing II missiles, 135, 158, 174,
176, 177, 178
Philippines, revolution in, 315
Platte, Sr. Ardeth, OP, 18, 110n5,
248, 270
Pledge of Resistance, 316
Plowshares actions, 59, 110
descriptions of, xxi, 118, 247
preparation for, 114, 122–23,
129, 165, 246–47, 264
property destruction in, 60,
110, 120, 137, 166, 170,
277, 323
spirituality of, 118, 120, 126,
128, 138
stress before, 123, 138–39, 176
theology of, 113, 122, 128
Plowshares actors, criminal proceed-
ings against, 126, 202, 246
Crane, Susan, **131**
Clancy, Deirdre (Dee), **140–43**
Ebner, Jerry, **116–17**
Frankel-Streit, Bill, **125**
Frankel-Streit, Sue, **124–25**
Kelly, Fr. Steve, SJ, **247, 249–50**
Laffin, Art, **118–19, 120–21**
Morlan, Fr. Larry, **268**
Moxley, Ellen, **157–59**
Roth, Barry, **127**
Sternstein, Wolfgang, **177,**
181–82
Plowshares actions, individual
Aegis Plowshares, 11, *126*,
126–27
Anzus Plowshares, 123–25,
140n3
Disarm Now Trident Plow-
shares, 132–33, *133*, 245,
299, 303
Gods of Metal Plowshares, 270
Griffiss Plowshares, 17

Jubilee Plowshares 2000,
161–62
Jubilee Plowshares West,
128–31
King of Prussia Plowshares
(*see* Plowshares Eight)
NF-5B Plowshares, 165
Pershings to Plowshares, 180–
82, *181*
Pitstop Plowshares, 136–44,
140
Plowshares Eight, 109, 110,
117, 118, 135
Prince of Peace Plowshares,
131
Schwabisch-Gmund, 5, 175–77
Seeds of Hope Plowshares, 147
Shannon Five (*see* Pitstop
Plowshares)
Silence Trident, 286–87
Silo Plowshares, 266, 268, 312
Thames River Plowshares, 119
Transfiguration East
Plowshares, 115
Transfiguration West
Plowshares, 112, 113–17
Trident Nein, 11, 119
Trident Three, 155–59, 157,
159, 161
Trident II Pruning Hooks, 253
Plowshares actors, prison experi-
ences of
Boertje-Obed, Greg, **4–5**
Clancy, Deirdre (Dee), **11**
Crane, Susan, **24–25, 129,**
131, 133
DeMott, Ellen Grady, 7, **13**
Ebner, Jerry, **9, 11, 112**
Frankel-Streit, Bill, **250–52,**
251
Gilbert, Sr. Carol, OP, **10, 18**
Hudson, Sr. Jackie, OP, **14**
Kelly, Fr. Steve, SJ, 7, **9–10,**
13, 247–50, 250

Laffin, Art, **12**, **16**
Morlan, Fr. Larry, **267**,
    268–69, **270**
Moxley, Ellen, **158**
Platte, Sr. Ardeth, OP, 18
Sprong, Mike, **286**, **288–90**
Sternstein, Wolfgang, **2–4**
Poland, revolution in, 322
Polaris nuclear submarine, 82–83
political objector, 62–65
Polner, Murray, 106, n23
Pope Benedict XVI, 229n1
Pope John XXIII, 74
Pope John Paul II, 24, 123, 147
Pope Paul VI, 60
Portland Catholic Worker (OR),
    208, 241
Povish, Bishop Kenneth, 305
Powell, Adam Clayton, 31, 40
Power of the People, The (Cooney
    and Michalowski), 360n2
prayer, 28
    after arrest, 161
    difficulty in, 129, 269
    education in, 129–30
    as integral to a resistance life,
        121, 194, 308
    as preparation for resistance,
        39, 165, 114, *140*, 214
    in prison, 4, 16, 94, 129, 212,
        231, 233, 248, 261, 303
    in resistance actions, 85, 115,
        116, 120, 274, 282, 311
    See also SOAW actions:
        November vigils; rosaries, in
        resistance actions
Predator drones, 315
Preheim, Beth, 287, 288–89, 290
press releases, 91, 95, 105, 127,
    129, 193, 202, 291
    from prisoners, 67, 164, 224,
        290
priesthood and resistance, 8–10,
    122, 279–80. *See also*

Bourgeois, Roy; Sevre-
    Duszynska, Janice; *and
    individual priests*
prison, adjustments after, 52,
    70–72, 81–82, 89, 144,
    194, 214, 225, 234, 284
prison, medical care in, 13–14,
    213–14, 217, 241–43
prison experiences, of individual
    narrators
    Albrecht, Scott, **283–85**
    Allen-Doucot, Jackie, **12–13**
    Apper, Bryan, **259**, 261–62
    Apper, Liza, **259–61**
    Benedict, Don, **45–46**, 47
    Bichsel, Fr. Bix, SJ, **303**
    Bossie, Fr. Bob, SCJ, **311**, **312**
    Bourgeois, Roy, 112, **191–94**,
        198
    Busch-Nema, Tina, **215–18**
    Charles (pseud.), **221–22**
    Cordaro, Frank, **7–9**, **15–16**,
        273–74
    Cordaro, Tom, **22**, 227
    Dallas, Meredith, **41–43**
    Dietrich, Jeff, **230–31**
    DiGia, Ralph, **31–32**
    Dougherty, Fr. Peter, **306–7**,
        309
    Fewless, Renaye, **235–38**
    Forest, Jim, **94**
    Gardner, David, **232–35**
    Golder, Neil, **18**
    Harris, Marty, **5**, **64**
    Harwood, Caitlin, **20–21**
    Heid, John, **252–55**
    Hennessey, Martha **18**
    Hughes, Lisa, **211**, **213**,
        238–41
    Jacobs, Steve, **11**
    Jaskolski, Hanna, **170–71**
    Judy (pseud.), **234**
    Kanner, Rebecca, **200–201**
    Kehler, Randy, **67–70**, **337**

prison experiences, of individual
    narrators (*continued*)
  Kelly, Kathy, **14–15, 19–20, 25**
  Kobasa, Stephen, **295–96**
  Kramer, Rae, 12, 13, **18–19**
  Kuile, Frits ter, **163, 164, 166**
  LaForge, John, **9, 23**
  Lovell, Bill, **37**
  Magno, Paul, **14**
  Malina, Judith, **54–56**, 134
  Marvy, Doug, **88**
  McCoy, Joni, **10**
  Meyer, Karl, **6, 26, 51–52, 332,
    333**
  Miller, David, **74–75**
  Mollin, Marian, **263, 264,
    265–66**
  O'Reilly, Ciaron, **6–7**
  Paley, Grace, **347**
  Richa (Chandler), **5–6**
  Rosebaugh, Fr. Lorenzo (Larry),
    OMI, **97–98, 243–45**
  Rumpf, Kathleen, **13–14, 15,
    17**
  Sage, Doris, **241–43**
  Slatterly, William, **21–23**
  Terrell, Brian, **8, 10**
  Vitale, Fr. Lou, OFM, **9, 321**
  Wilson, Jim, **80–81**
  Zawada, Fr. Jerry, OFM, **317–
    18, 319**
  See also Plowshares actors,
    prison experiences of
prison, medical care in, 13–14,
  213–14, 217, 241–43
Progressive Magazine, The,
  317n10
Project ELF (Extremely Low
  Frequency), 17, 254, 286,
  286, 287, 306
pro-life movement, 148
Promniblockade (Germany), 180
props for resistance actions, 202–
  3, 207. *See also* resistance
  tactics

replicas of weapons, 301
Protestants for the Common Good,
  38, 48
Protester Removal Unit. *See*
  Strathclyde police

Quail, Brian, 145–49
Quakers (Society of Friends), 28,
  158, 214, 325
Quigley, Bill, 212, 215
Quintana, Anne, 295

Raging Grannies, 346
Rakoff, Jed S., xviii
rape, in prison, 4–6, 51–52
Rastafarians. *See* Marley, Bob
Reagan, Ronald, 121, 165, 266,
  267, 345
Reaper drones, 315
Recife (Brazil), 98, 243–45
Redstockings (NY feminist group),
  106
resistance, definitions of, xx, xxi
resistance, dissatisfaction with, 324
resistance and community, 123,
  231, 245, 265, 288–89,
  313, 333–37, 341
resistance community, definition of,
  xx, 293–94
resistance tactics, 220, 322–23
  audio presence, 171–72, 195
  blessing with holy water, 231
  blockades, 178–80, 310–11,
    322 (*see also* Faslane 365
    action)
  disruption of shareholders
    meetings, 310–11
  curating, 291, 294, 295
  de-fencing, 156, 170, 183, 301,
    323
  digging graves, 206, 282
  fasting, 237, 302
  general strike, 313

leafleting, 57, 124, 129, 152,
160, 183, 194–95, 259, 332,
333
lock-ons, 150, 171, 322
human chain, 177
hunger strikes, 43, 306
peace walks, 164, 267
puppetry, 322 (*see also* Bread
and Puppet Theater [VT]).
sit-downs, 322
solidarity, 235–38
solitary witness, 193–94
street theater, 206–7, 306
tire slashing, 166
U-lock for access, 219
vigils, 28, 172, 214, 259, 332,
339–40, 342 (*see also* SOAW
actions: November vigils)
water trepassing, 301
See also blood, symbolic nature
of; props for resistance
actions; tax resistance, to
protest war
Revolutionary Communist Party,
313
Rhine Valley nuclear power
protests, 174–75
Rice, Sr. Megan, SCHJ, 243
Richmond City Jail (VA), 112
Right Livelihood Award, 161
Rikers Island Jail (NY), 51
Rio Grande Valley (TX), 316
Rivera, Modesto Alicia, 316
River Clyde (Scotland), 149
Robinson, Eroseanna, 332
Rockefeller Center (NY), 99, 102,
103, 104, 105, 107
Rock Island Arsenal (IL), 266, 269
Rockwell International (CA), 259
Rocky Flats Nuclear Weapons
Plant (CO), 275
Roder, Ulla, 155, 156, 158, *159*,
161
Roman Catholic Eucharist (Mass)

celebrated at resistance
actions, 169, 317
in prisons, 239, 268, 302
proscribed for priest prisoners,
10, 302
protest at, 168, 171, 172
Romero, Bishop Oscar, 187, 194,
266
sermon broadcast at Ft.
Benning, 188, 193, 195–96
Romero (film), 11
Roosevelt, Franklin Delano, 36
rosaries, in resistance actions, 231,
261, 274
**Rosebaugh, Fr. Lorenzo (Larry),
OMI,** 85, 86, **96–98**, *98*,
194–96, 243–45
Rose Bowl Parade (CA), 231
Rose Hill Books, 289n8Rossman,
Vern, 79–80, 81, 239
ROTC (Reserve Officers Training
Corps), 30
Roth, Barry, 111, **126–28**
Rumpf, Kathleen, 13–14, 15, 17,
202–4, 214, 215, 216
Russell, Bertram, 178
Russian Orthodox Church, 173n13
Rustin, Bayard, 52, 57, 347

SAC (Strategic Air Command), 1,
8, 274, *275*
Sacred Heart Seminary (MI), 304
Sacred Heart religious order,
309–12
Sacred Heart Seminary (MI), 304
Sage, Doris, 241–43
Saginaw Halfway House (MI), 307
Saginaw Valley Peace Watch (MI),
342
Saigon International Airport
(Vietnam), 26
SALT II treaty, 275–76
Salvadoran soldiers at SOA,
194–96

sanctuary movement, 316

Sandine, Max, 66

Sandperl, Ira, 66

Sandstone Prison (MN), 11, 112, 196, 319

San Francisco, protests in, 61, 245, 319, 322–23

San Francisco Federal Building, 245

Santa Rita Jail (CA), 129

satyagraha, 185

Sault, Nicole, 191

Savard, Fr. John, SJ, 245

SCANA (Scottish Clergy Against Nuclear Arms). *See* Scottish Clergy Action

Schaeffer, Rene, 163

Schmorell, Alexander, 173n13

Scholl, Sophie, 173. *See also* White Rose resistance group

School of the Americas. *See* SOA/WHINSEC (GA)

School of the Americas Watch. *See entries beginning with* SOAW

Schuchardt, Carrie, 59

Schuchardt, John, 59, 309

Schwabisch-Gmund US Army Base (Germany), 135, 175, 176

Scott County Jail (IA), 8

Scottish Campaign for Nuclear Disarmament, 135, 145–61

Scottish Center for Nonviolence. *See* Stevens, Helen

Scottish Clergy Action, 153

Scottish National Parliament (SNP), 148, 152, 153, 155, 160

Scranton diocese (PA), 121–22

Seabrook Nuclear Power Plant (NH), 267

Seal Beach Naval Weapons Station (CA), 258

Seattle Preparatory School (WA), 300

Second Vatican Council, 291, 321

Secret Service, 26, 265, 277

Selective Service, 79, 83, 99, 102, 103, 105. *See also entries beginning with* draft

Sevre-Duszynska, Janice, 194

sexism, in prison, 22

sexism in Roman Catholic priest-hood, 107, 305

Shakur, Assata, 24

shank (prison weapon), 4

sites for resistance actions, 109. *See also individual bases, government buildings, and weapons plants*

Shakers, 325

Shannon Airport (Ireland), 136, 137, 138, 140

Sharp, Gene, 249, 313

Sheen, Martin, *189*, 190, 201

Sheridan Federal Prison (OR), 302–3

"shoot to kill" security zone, 124–25, *125*, 182

Sin, Cardinal Jaime, 322

Sisters of Notre Dame (SND) religious order, 213, 214, 215, 216

Slater, Nathan, 215

Slatterly, William, 21–23

slavery, campaign to abolish, 161, 245

"Sleeping Beauty" (Malina), 134

Smithsonian Institution (DC), 29, 120, 294, 295

Smuts, Jan, 197

Snowball Campaign. *See* resistance tactics: de-fencing

Snyder, Mitch, 255

SOA/WHINSEC (GA), 187

base commander of, 196, 206–7

changes at since 9/11, 188

chaplain of, 195

media disinformation of, 189

treatment of resisters by, 195,
196, 197–98, 206–7, 208,
209–10, 211–12, 215
SOAW (GA), xix, 187
ban-and-bar letters, 188, 197–
98, 207, 209, 301
classes on, in prison, 11, 302
media about, 196, 213, 231
support for prisoners of conscience by, 189, 190, 194,
196, 199, 211, 214, 220–21
SOAW actions
accessing entry with U-lock,
219
denying entry, 302
diversity of tactics in, 198,
219–20
Gandhian Wave, 206–7
lobby work in DC, 189, 198
motivation for, 187–88, 192,
199, 204, 208–9, 215, 219,
221, 225
November vigils, 21, 188–89,
196–99, 201, 209–10, 215
photos of November vigil,
*189, 190, 194, 197, 199,
202, 205, 210, 305, 314*
re-enactment of assassinations,
206–7
sign altering, 202–3, *202*
Washington (DC) fast, 302
See also Ft. Benning (GA): first
action at
SOAW individual prisoners of
conscience
Bichsel, Fr. Bix, SJ, **302–3**
Bourgeois, Roy, **191–94**, *194*,
198, 207, 302
Busch-Nema, Tina, 213,
214–18
Charlie (pseud.), 218, **219–27**
Doyle, Maureen, 202
Eilerman, Sr. Marge, OSF, 202
Harwood, Caitlin, **20–21**

Heid, John, **254**
Hughes, Lisa, **208–13**, **238–41**
Huntworth, Ann, 211
Jacobs, Steve, **204–8**
Judy (pseud.) 21, **219–27**
Jones, Christopher, 203
Kanner, Rebecca, **196–202**
Kinane, Ed, 202
Liteky, Charley, 203
Rosebaugh, Fr. Lorenzo
(Larry), OMI, **194–96**
Rumpf, Kathleen, **202–4**
Sage, Dan, 241
Sage, Doris, **241–43**
Sevre-Duszynska, Janice, 194
Skater, Nathan, 215
Slatterly, William, **21–23**
Trotochard, Mary, 202
Ventimiglia, Linda, 194–96
Vitale, Fr. Lou, OFM, 315, *320*
Zawada, Fr. Jerry, OFM, 314–
15, *320*
Socialism, 30, 32, 35, 36, 37, 56,
153, 343. *See also* American
Socialist Party
Solidarity (UAW magazine), 199
Somsel, Anne, 296, 297, *297*
South Bronx draft board (NY), 102
South Congregational Church (IL),
37
South Korea, 156
Spiritual Exercises of St. Ignatius,
129–30
Spragg, Howard, 34, *36*, 37
Springfield (MA), 337, 338
Sprong, Mike, **286–90**, *290*
Stafford Federal Correctional
Institution, 63, 67
St. Ambrose Seminary (IA), 266–67
stand-around actions, exceptions
to, 101, 116. *See also*
Women Against Daddy
Warbucks
St. Anselm College (NH), 73, 76

Starhawk, xviii, 72
St. Bonaventure Minor Seminary
    (WI), 315
St. Clement Church (IL), 311
Steckle, Fr. Greg, 11
Sternstein, Gisela, 173, 174, **186**,
    186
Sternstein, Wolfgang, **2–4**, 135,
    174–86, 186
Stevens, Helen, 156, 157, 158, 160
Stewart, Martha, 18
St. Francis Catholic Worker (MO),
    204, 205, *205*, 206, 207
Stickgold, Marc, 93, 94
St. John of the Cross, 193
St. Leo Church (WA), 300
St. Louis Cardinals, 96
St. Mary's College (MN), 91
Strategic Arms Command. *See* SAC
Strategic Arms Limitation Talks.
    See SALT II
Strathclyde Police (Scotland), 147,
    150, 151
Streit, Bill. *See* Frankel-Streit, Bill
student loans, 208–9
Students for a Democratic Society
    (SDS), 101
Su Casa Catholic Worker (IL), 319
support, for resisters, 109, 117,
    137, 141, 147, 176, 294
    by spouses, 4, 74, 176, 251–52
    during trials, 53, 112
    while in prison, 161, 284, 213,
        237, 288–90
    See also under birth families,
        of resisters; SOAW (GA)
Swann, Bob, 325
Swann, Catherine, 74, 75
Swann, Marjorie, 325
symbols, in actions, 282–83. *See
    also* blood; Plowshares
    actions: symbols in
Syracuse Jail (NY), 17, 202

Syracuse Republican congressional
    representative, 243
Swarthmore Peace Collection (PA),
    61

Tacoma Catholic Worker (WA),
    300, 303
Tallents, Jane, 149–55
Tara (prisoner), 241
tax resistance, to protest war, 66,
    219, 265
    and Corner, Betsy, 324–41
    and Crane, Susan, **330–32**
    demonstrations about,
        329–30, 330–31, 332, 333,
        335, 337–40, *338*
    history of, 28n2, 325–26,
        331–34
    and Kehler, Randy, **324–41**
    and Lyttle, Brad, 325, 326
    and Meyer, Karl, **331–34**
    and Nelson, Juanita, **326–29**
    and Peacemakers, 325, 326,
        327, 332
    use of alternative donated funds
        for, 330, 334, 335
    by withholding telephone tax,
        325–26
Taxman, Dylan, 90–91
Taylor, Matt, 305
Ten Foot Society (Japan), 145
Terrell, Brian, 8
Thomas, Norman, 36
Thoreau, Henry David, 62, 325,
    332
Tiffany, Anne, 191n5
Tina (prisoner), 240
To Wisdom Through Failure
    (Rosebaugh), 243
Tolstoy, Leo, 43, 94, 167
torture, 313
    in Latin America, 16, 188, 244,
        316
    survivors of, 316, 319

training in techniques of, 188,
320
in US prisons, 16
Trappist monastery, 194
Traprock Peace Center (MA), 326
Trident campaign (Scotland), 144,
144–61, 175, 176
Trident nuclear submarines in the
UK, 137, 144–45, 146, 148,
149, 152, 153, 155, 171
in the US, 119, 130, 132, 154n3,
299, 301, 306
Trident Plowshares (Ploughshares),
135n1, 146–47, 149, 151,
153, 154, 155
Trotochard, Mary, 202
Twin City Draft Information Center
(MN), 85
Twentieth Century Fund, 53

UAW (United Auto Workers), 196,
199
Udvar-Hazy Center, National Air
and Space Museum (TX),
296
Uexküll, Jakob von, 161
Ukiah (CA), 329–33
"Ultra-Resistance, The" (Gray),
82n9
UNICOR, 24, 25–26, 217
Union Eight, 29, 35–48
Union Square (NY), 76, 77, *78*
Union Theological Seminary (NY),
29, 38, 39–41, 45
Unitarian Universalist Fellowship,
63, 241
United Auto Workers (UAW), 196,
199
United Farm Workers, 305, 321
UK Lord Advocate, 159
UK Ministry of Defense 147, 157,
282
UK Parliament, 148–49, 152, 160
United Nations (UN), 60

as target of resistance actions,
109
conference on disarmament,
267
sanctions against Iraq by, 138,
142n4, 307
University of Chicago, 292
University of Massachusetts, 265
University of Minnesota, 85, 88
University of Munich, 173n13
University of Wisconsin, 88
Urfer, Bonnie, *286*, 287
Urie, Al, 7
US Air Force. *See individual bases*
US Army, 322. *See also* SOA/
WHINSEC (GA)
US Attorney's office, 29
US Congress, 13, 30, 31, 72, 116,
187, 188, 189, 199, 257
US Declaration of Independence,
64
US Embassy in Brazil, 245
US Embassy in Saigon, 26n8
US flag, 297–98
US Naval Air Systems Command,
136
US Navy, 91, 109, 119, 139, 205.
See also individual bases
US Naval Air Systems Command,
136
US State Department, 121
US Supreme Court, 74, 84
usury, 328

Velvet Revolution, 313
Ventimiglia, Linda, 194–96
Victorville Federal Prison Camp
(CA), 14
Vietnam War, 60–107, 394, 305,
322, 335
nonviolence as practice during,
62, 66, 77, 86, 88, 95
service in, 63–64, 181, 191,
242, 257, 321–22

Vietnam War (*continued*)
women activists during, 77, 84,
262n1 (*see also* Paley, Grace;
Women Against Daddy
Warbucks)
See also Calley, William;
entries beginning with draft;
Vietnam War, resistance to
Vietnam War, resistance to, 257,
262, 300, 305, 321, 347
class elements in, 64, 73, 340
tax refusal as, 325, 331, 333
Vinthagen, Stellan, 180
violence, religiously inspired,
225–26
Vitale, Fr. Lou, OFM, 9, *315, 320,
320–24*
Vix, Karin, 176
Voices for Creative Nonviolence,
317n10
Voices from the Catholic Worker
(Riegle), xxi(n5)
Voices in the Wilderness, 317n10

Walsea, Michael, 37
"War and Prisons" (Schuchardt),
59
War Resisters International, 164,
167
War Resisters League (WRL), 25,
28, 40n9m 52, 53, 61
actions organized by, 52, 53,
72, 295
calendar of, 66
and DiGia, Ralph, 29, 30, 31
and Paley, Grace, 342, 344,
345
in San Francisco, 66
and tax resistance, 325, 326,
335, 342
War Tax Resistance (organization),
325–26
Washington, DC, as segregated city,
327

Waupun State Correctional Institu-
tion (WI), 88, 94, 97
We of Hiroshima (Endo), 145–46
Webster, Barbara, 100, 104
Weinfeld, Edward, 80
Weinglass, Leonard, 113, 364n30
Weir, Benjamin, *Hostage Bold,
Hostage Free*, 129
West Street (Metropolitan Correc-
tional Institution, NY), 31,
41, 45
West Wing (TV show), 201
Western Hemisphere Institute for
Security for Cooperation.
See SOA/WHINSEC (GA)
White House, resistance actions at,
109, 191–92, 274–77
Whiteman Air Force Base (MO),
114
White Rose resistance group,
173n13, 229
Wichlei, Richard J., 34, *36*
Widener, Brent, 196, 206–7
Williams International (MI), 306
Willson, Brian, 335
Wilson, Jim, 61, **76–82**, *78*
Wilson, Jo, 147
Wilson, Nathan, 81
Wilson, Raona, 77, 82n8
Winning, Cardinal Thomas Joseph,
148
Winter, Willa. *See* Dallas, Willa
Women Against Daddy Warbucks,
61, 99–107
Women's Action at the Pentagon,
342, 345, *345*
Women's Encampment at Seneca
Falls (NY), 342
Women's House of Correction
(NH), 18
Women's House of Detention (NY),
54–56, 347
Women's International League for
Peace and Freedom (WILPF),
99, 345

Women's Peace Society, 28
Women's Strike for Peace, 99, 346
Woodson, Helen, 110
World Bank, 219, 221
World Day of Peace, 123, 125
World Trade Center, 309
World War I, 28, 30, 41, 51, 66, 92, 169
World War II, 29, 49, 168, 269n3
    draft reinstatement for, 30
    resistance to, 29–47, 66, 327
    service in, 29, 47, 292
Wounded Knee (SD), 38, 361n27
Wurtsmith Air Force Base (MI), 109, 307
WRL. *See* War Resisters League (WRL)

Yale University graduation, 264–65
Yankton Benedictine Sisters (SD), 288
Yankton Catholic Worker (SD), 287–90
Yankton College (SD), 287
Yankton Federal Prison Camp (SD), 287–88, 289–90

Zahn, Gordon, 229n1
Zambia, 208
Zapatistas, 226
Zawada, Fr. Jerry, OFM, 314–20, *318, 320*
Zelter, Angie, 147, 153, 155, 156, 158, 159, 160, *161*
Zinn, Howard, xviii, 29, 88
Zossima, Fr. (Dostoevsky), 270